SEAFARING LORE & LEGEND

A MISCELLANY OF MARITIME MYTH, SUPERSTITION, FABLE, AND FACT

PETER D. JEANS

International Marine / McGraw-Hill

Camden, Maine • New York • Chicago • San Francisco • Lisbon • London • Madrid • Mexico City
Milan • New Delhi • San Juan • Seoul • Singapore • Sydney • Toronto

The **McGraw·Hill** Companies

1 2 3 4 5 6 7 8 9 10 DOC DOC 0 9 8 7 6 5 4

© 2004 by International Marine
All rights reserved. The name "International Marine" and the International Marine logo are
trademarks of The McGraw-Hill Companies. Printed in the United States of America.

Library of Congress Cataloging-in-Publication Data
Jeans, Peter D.
  Seafaring lore and legend : a maritime miscellany of myth, superstition, fable, and fact /
Peter D. Jeans.
    p.   cm.
  Includes bibliographical references (p.   ) and index.
  ISBN 0-07-143543-3
  1. Seafaring life—Folklore. 2. Ocean—Folklore. I. Title.
  GR910.J43 2004
  398'.27—dc22   2004001080

In affectionate memory of my parents
Evelyn and Clarrie Bishop
and my late sister
Frances Davies

❦ CONTENTS ❦

❈ ACKNOWLEDGMENTS ❈

Compiling a collection of articles that would stand muster as a representative (but not at all exhaustive) survey of lore and legend accumulated throughout the history of seafaring has not been an easy task. I was aware of some of these tales—everyone has heard of Atlantis, Davy Jones's Locker, and the Loch Ness Monster—but there must be others who, like me, were entirely ignorant of the story behind Prince Madoc or of the blood-drenched mutiny on HMS *Hermione*.

Consequently, I am indeed grateful to those of my family and friends who, responding wholeheartedly to my cries of distress, volunteered some dozens more examples that were distinctly pertinent. These helpful people include my wife Judith (who also spent many hours doing Internet searches for me) and the following friends: John and Annette Bunday, David Combe, Lorna DiLollo, Travis and Felicity Lindsey, Rob (alas! now deceased) and Denise Main, "Dusty" Miller, Christine Nagel, Ross Shardlow, and Leo Van Brakel.

In particular I want to acknowledge the support and enthusiasm of my good friend Ross Shardlow, whose familiarity with maritime affairs is extraordinary and whose extensive library was readily and most generously put at my disposal. Ross also cheerfully fielded my countless phone and fax queries regarding esoteric details of things nautical. My thanks go, too, to my brother-in-law Ivor Davies, who spent much time on the Internet searching out information for me; to Chris McLay for his skillful help in matters to do with computers; and to Dr. Bill Andrew, who patiently coached me in matters hydrographic.

I am especially grateful to Denice Mulcahy of the Bindoon Public Library, who with unfailing good humor dealt with my endless queries and requests. Joe Courtney of the Western Australian Bureau of Meteorology and my one-time teaching colleague John Solosy both helped me to a better understanding of weather events at sea.

Thanks, too, to David Hummerston at *The West Australian* newspaper for his cheerful willingness in extracting various items of information from the newspaper's vast library.

To all these folk I offer my heartfelt thanks for their unstinted assistance.

Nevertheless, notwithstanding all this expertise being available to me I am sure that there must be some glaring errors of fact and sad lapses in style to be found in this work; for these I must accept responsibility and apologize handsomely for their unintended appearance.

❊ NOTE TO THE READER ❊

The contents of this book were arranged so as to correspond—however fleetingly—with the timeline associated with the history of seafaring. That is to say, I have begun my survey with an examination (moderately brief in each case) of those myths and legends that deal with the watery world of The Beginning: the Great Flood, for instance, accounts of which are to be found in many different cultures worldwide; the story of Moses and the Red Sea; explanations of the powers and functions of those gods whose task it was to maintain dominion over the world's oceans and rivers; and some of the notable names associated with life at sea such as Castor and Pollux, and Scylla and Charybdis.

Broadly speaking, I have tried to follow this concept throughout the book: starting at the beginning, as it were, and working up toward relatively modern times.

In addition, I have tried to apply the same approach to the contents of each chapter, with—I am sure—varying degrees of success. Chapters 2, 3, and 4 deal with ancient heroes, voyages, events, and places, some of them legendary (the Argonauts, for example), and others historical (the story of Moby Dick, for example, and the search for the Northwest Passage).

Chapters 5, 6, and 7 deal with maritime history and practice pertinent to more or less modern times (the origin of naval salutes, for example; how grog got its curious name); and the reasons behind some of the practices indelibly associated with life at sea: what sort of ships man built and sailed in, for example; the horrors of rounding Cape Horn; and why sailors sang sea chanties, together with the words of some of them.

Chapters 8 and 9 focus on some of the more notable ship types (the clipper ships, for example, and the windjammers), as well as on a handful of some of the more famous commanders (Columbus, of course; James Cook; and John Paul Jones). Chapters 9 through 11 touch upon some of the famous wrecks, mutinies, and wartime engagements of historical times: the wreck and subsequent mutiny of the *Batavia*, for example, and the blood-soaked uproar that destroyed HMS *Hermione*; the ill-fated Spanish Armada; the Battle of Jutland, and that of Copenhagen. This section is rounded off with a brief commentary on some of the disasters that have overtaken ships at sea: the USS *Scorpion*, for example; the sinking of the *Lusitania*; and the practices of the wreckers, those wretched people who deliberately enticed ships and their crews to desperate doom and destruction.

There is a brief account in chapter 12 of how and why, for example, the Panama Canal was brought into being. Chapters 13 through 15 relate how various individuals dealt with being shipwrecked at sea or cast ashore on a deserted shore; Robinson Crusoe is, of course, the best-known story in this category (Crusoe's story was based on the earlier true-life account of Alexander Selkirk). There is a commentary in chapter 14 on piracy and some selected exponents of that art (such as William Kidd and Anne Bonny); and in chapter 15 the reader is offered a brief insight into some of the beliefs still held by modern-day seafarers: mermaids, for example, and the oft-misunderstood story of King Canute.

In chapters 16 through 18 the reader is introduced to a number of still-thriving maritime legends: the altogether perplexing Bermuda Triangle, for instance, and such famous ship mysteries as the *Flying Dutchman* and the *Mary Celeste*. We are brought face to face with various sea monsters, many of which are not easily dismissed as fancies of an erratic mind (Captain M'Quhae's Monster, for example, is one such, although we may be well advised to look askance at what is purported by many to be lurking at the bottom of Loch Ness). This section ends with references to some of the ghosts and phantoms that are to be encountered at sea from time to time by persons of an otherwise sober disposition. The Phantom Pilot of Captain Joshua Slocum, for example, is but one example; another is the veritable fleet of olden-time sailing ships that can, in the right circumstances, be seen battling its storm-tossed way up the Saint Lawrence Seaway.

The final section—chapter 19—deals with some of the many dozens of beliefs and superstitions still stoutly maintained by the modern seafarer: a ship must not set sail on a Friday, for example, if she is not to court inevitable disaster; a pair of eyes painted on the bows of a small vessel represents a good (but not infallible) policy against shipwreck; women and priests are not at all welcome aboard ship (except, occasionally, pregnant women); the feather of a freshly dispatched wren will serve as a reliable guard against death by drowning. . . .

See the sources and notes section at the end of this book. After each entry in each chapter are listed the books I found useful for that particular entry. These books are described in the bibliography. Thus an interested reader can further pursue the topic of any particular entry.

The endnotes for an entry appear after each list of general sources for that entry. Most notes are specific citations to sources, referenced to page numbers and key phrases. Some notes, however, provide ancillary information.

Sources for the epigraphs at the beginning of each entry are generally not found in the bibliography.

All biblical references are to the Authorized King James Version.

Five ship prefixes are used: HMAS: His/Her Majesty's Australian Ship. HMS: His/Her Majesty's Ship. RMS: Royal Mail Steamship. SS: Steamship. USS: United States Ship. British tradition holds that HMAS *Sydney*, for example, may be referred to as "the *Sydney*" or as "HMAS *Sydney*," but never as "the HMAS *Sydney*" and *never* as "*Sydney*," it being long-established (British) nautical custom that "*Sydney*" on its own refers to the captain or commander of that ship, not to the ship itself. (My American publishers squawked but ultimately let me keep this convention.)

I have also followed maritime practice by showing, in a number of cases, the name of a ship's captain immediately following the name of the ship itself; thus *Daphne*, Captain Henderson.

INTRODUCTION

"All the rivers run into the sea; yet the sea is not full."

ECCLESIASTES 1:7

T his book chronicles only a small selection of the vast body of seafaring legend and lore that lies behind many of the traditions that people have followed ever since they first chose to go down to the sea in ships. By "seafaring legend" I mean those traditional tales of the sea often regarded by some as history (but which may or may not be true); and by "seafaring lore" I mean the knowledge people have accumulated as a result of their long and painfully acquired experience of the sea. This book discusses some of these legends—both the better known and the less familiar—that have grown up around this most hazardous of livelihoods and explains a number of the ancient myths that lie behind the beliefs and practices of the modern-day sailor.

Legends as such are but a small part of the extraordinary warp and weft of the seafarer's life. Examples that spring immediately to mind are the *Flying Dutchman* (chapter 16), the *Mary Celeste* (16), Monster Kraken (17), Scylla and Charybdis (1), Mermaids (15), The *Odyssey* (4), The Argonauts (4), Davy Jones's Locker (19), Fabled Atlantis (16), The Bermuda Triangle (16), Jonah and the Whale (17), and a few more—on the face of things, hardly enough to fill a book. Consequently, like Ran, wife of Aegir, the Viking god of the sea, I have cast a somewhat wider net so as to include a broad sampling of nautical customs, beliefs, and superstitions, such as The Albatross, Death by Drowning, Launching a Ship, Our Flat Earth, and a good many others (see chapter 19).

Thus the book addresses many of the characteristics of the seafaring life that make it so utterly different from any other. Legends, superstitions, mysteries, and the like (those that are readily available in English) from a variety of cultures are included, in the belief that seafarers the world over share in common not only a set of unique occupational hazards but also the same underpinnings of many of their beliefs and understandings. My intention has been to illustrate the fact that when it comes to seafaring, we all speak very much the same language.

Some of the more enduring stories of the sea focus on what sailors claim to have encountered in the course of plying their trade across the oceans of the world. These claims include not only the natural phenomena of climate such as the giant seas and freak waves of, for instance, the Southern Ocean, but also the persistent appearance over the ages of Sea Monsters (chapter 17) of astonishing form and size; Mermaids (15), that old standby of maritime experience; and the ghosts and Phantom Pilots (18) that from time immemorial have peopled the imagination of seafarers worldwide. In much the same way, the UFO phenomenon of the twentieth century has yet to be given a rational basis (although there is no lack of people who think otherwise; see, for example, Fabled Atlantis and The Bermuda Triangle in chapter 16).

Sometimes an explanation for the previously inexplicable is eventually found. In one such case, the famous Kraken monster of Norwegian waters, known to seafarers of old and feared by them for hundreds of years for its size and alleged ferocity, was almost certainly *Architeuthis*, a species of giant squid. But for some other apparitions at sea there is still no explanation, other than the accumulated experience and wisdom of the ancient mariner who, asserting that he has seen, for example, a sea serpent in full flight, has seen it, and that's that.

If it were only the gullible and fearfully superstitious who laid claim to a nodding acquaintance with phantoms of the sea, we might more easily pass such encounters off as instances of "too much to drink" or "easily confused," and so on; but when a witness's credibility is beyond reproach, what are we to think then? No less a person than Prince George (the future King George V of England) said he had sighted Vanderdecken's famous vessel, the *Flying Dutchman* (chapter 16). Judgment must, in this case, be withheld; there are, as Hamlet reminds his friend Horatio, "more things in heaven and earth . . . than are dreamt of in your philosophy."

The mariners of yesteryear earnestly believed that monsters and serpents of prodigious size lurked in the gloomy depths of the world's oceans, and they marked their maps and charts thus: "Here Be Monsters." Above this somber warning would appear a creature drawn by an enthusiastic and imaginative artist that might have been more at home in one of the circles of Dante's Inferno or in a painting by Hieronymus Bosch than in any scientific catalog of animals of the world. Even as late as 1588, a Swiss engraving showed a sea serpent consuming an entire ship, including the patently unhappy crew; and the Swedish Archbishop Olaus Magnus bequeathed to posterity a record of a sighting of a giant sea snake that "puts up his head on high like a pillar, and catcheth away men, and he devours them."

There is also surprisingly recent testimony to these awesome creatures:

> *We thus conclude with at least three sea-serpents, one in 1857, one in 1875, and one in 1905, for which we have reasonably satisfactory evidence . . . Most of the witnesses agree on certain outstanding features; it is a long serpentine creature; it has a series of humps; its head is rather like a horse's; its color is dark on the top and light below; it appears during the summer months; and unlike the sea monster it is harmless, for it never actually attacked anybody even under provocation.*

It is not clear whether this refers to the Loch Ness Monster (chapter 17) or some other fearful denizen of the deeps, but one thing is certain from the literature—the consideration shown by these serpents, whether pelagic or lake-bound, in appearing only during the summer months, this being of course the ideal time for sightings by strolling hikers or by seafarers navigating the broad bosom of the ocean. However, it would be unsafe to dismiss out of hand all reported sightings of previously unknown sea monsters, despite the fact that no one has as yet secured a specimen of such a creature; indeed, one of the more sober accounts in this book is from a group of experienced Royal Navy officers, gentlemen not known for imaginative flights of fancy (see Captain M'Quhae's Monster, chapter 17).

Chapter 17, Sea Monsters, includes some of the more famous (or infamous) monsters and sea serpents that have galvanized the imagination of sailors and fishermen and which in the process have delivered healthy circulation figures to a press ever willing to stoke the fevered fires of public horrified fascination.

It would be true to say that no group of workingmen harbors as many superstitions within its collective breast as do sailors; and this, perhaps, is as it should be, for no body of workers endures such dangerous conditions of employment as those mariners who ply the seven seas in pursuit of their daily bread. If your life hangs in the balance day after day as your ship thrashes its way around Cape Horn in the dead of winter—a place more accurately known by seamen as Cape Stiff— or a cyclone in the Pacific or the Indian Ocean is driving you onto a rock-fanged lee shore, you are going to call on every prayer and superstitious belief known to man in the hope of saving your miserable skin.

Never mind that many of these talismans are quite irrational—so is going to sea for a pittance and daily facing the ever-present hazards of storm, shipwreck, disease, or crippling injury. There is nothing rational about such behavior. And if danger doesn't threaten there is always the urge to explain to oneself the immediate world of the birds of the air and the creatures of the deep, the variety of things that bring good luck or bad, and from time to time the events that remain quite inexplicable. Weakness of mind or not, these beliefs and customs have in some way powerfully shaped and informed the mariner's experience of the sea.

Thousands of years ago holes were often cut into a ship's sails so that the evil spirits known to haunt the deeps would not get trapped in the fabric and thus harm the vessel. A sailor never whistled on board ship because that could anger the gods of the sea, although in a dead calm it was permissible to whistle very softly while scratching a backstay in order to bring up a suitable wind. The many British pubs named The Pig and Whistle reflect this superstition, since on land the seafarer could without risk whistle as much as he liked. Also, it was unlucky to use the word "pig" at sea—one said "hog" or "sow" instead—but on land it was perfectly safe to do so.

In earlier times, when a ship was launched she was splashed with human blood as a tribute to the gods of the sea (see Launching a Ship, chapter 19); nowadays we use wine or champagne. Often the vessel was given a female name in token of its becoming a bride to Poseidon or Neptune, this being the reason ships are referred to as "she" or "her." It was also once a tradition not to use a name ending in *-a*, with the *Lusitania* often quoted as the best example of the inevitably bad effects of this practice.

Having been accepted into the sea, no ship would set out on a voyage on a Friday (see Departures, chapter 19), many a seaman being familiar with the old rhyme:

> *On a Friday she was launched,*
> *On a Friday she set sail,*
> *On a Friday met a storm,*
> *And was lost in a gale.*

Cats are welcome on board ship but women aren't. On the other hand, pregnant women are not considered to be unlucky, probably because their condition renders them less of a temptation to mariners. A fisherman becomes nervous if he meets a barefooted woman while going down to his boat; meanwhile he carries his seaboots under his arm rather than over his shoulder and he fervently hopes that no one will wish him "good luck." If it is raining he might take an umbrella with him but on no account will he carry it aboard.

Dolphins are always greeted by seafarers as harbingers of good weather, and—surprisingly, in the light of past and present practice—many seamen believe that no good will come to those who harm whales. Sharks, of course—what Spanish seafarers called the *tiburón*—have never enjoyed a good press with sailors. A dead body on board is always cause for concern; it was once firmly believed that such a sad object would make the vessel slow down, which could be remedied only by immediately committing the body to the deep.

The reason that so many seafarers have tattoos on their bodies (a Polynesian word, recorded as *tattow* by Captain James Cook, chapter 8, in 1769) is that these decorations—especially if they are in the form of crosses, hearts, flowers, and so on—act as good-luck charms which will ward off evil. Tattooing is a remnant of the early practice of garlanding a ship with flowers that were thought to be pleasing to the gods, especially fierce gods of the sea such as Poseidon. The introduction of flags and bunting on board ship probably came about because of the widespread use of flowers at funerals ashore; sailors today are reluctant to have real flowers of any kind on board.

The ancient importance of the gods of the sea is reflected in the ceremony of Crossing the Line (chapter 6), still practiced today on cruise ships; and when a seaman goes ashore he would seek to step onto land right foot first, the left being unlucky in this context (the left, the sinister side—from Latin *sinister*, left—has always symbolized evil or harm; that is why armies step out left foot first, as a dire warning to their adversaries). Our seaman would hope, too, that the first group of people met ashore would be an odd number (the reason for this isn't clear, unless it is that adding his own presence would make the number even, thus avoiding any possibility of duplicating the famously unlucky thirteen. Probably Samuel Pepys had this in mind when in 1675 he devised a system of odd-numbered gun *salutes* [see Naval Salutes, chapter 5] for the living, with even-numbered salutes for the dead).

A sailor would take great care with buckets, too, it being very bad luck indeed to lose one overboard (nothing is more precious to a sailor than a bucket on board a ship that is sinking); seafarers on a ship that was sinking for lack of bailing buckets would no doubt be perilously close to drowning and going down to Davy Jones's Locker (see also Death by Drowning, both chapter 19). On the other hand, a sailor destined to die will do so ("go out") on the ebb tide unless he can stave off this melancholy event with a Wren's Feather (19). As one of many precautions against bad weather he will have placed a Coin Under the Mast (19) of his ship while it was a-building, there would be a Guiding Star (19) carved somewhere on board, and a suitable figurehead at the bow (see Ships' Figureheads, 19). Meanwhile, he might mutter incantations such as

> *Comes the rain before the wind,*
> *Then your topsails you must mind;*
> *Comes the wind before the rain,*
> *Haul your topsails up again.*

During his voyage he might welcome the advent of Saint Elmo's Fire (chapter 19) but be distraught at the appearance of the *Flying Dutchman* (16). Sirens (15) and Mermaids (15) might come his way without undue harm (unless he were ardent enough to want to make their acquaintance under the water), but heaven forfend against the Monster Kraken (chapter 17). He might well pray that there be no Jonah (17) aboard his vessel, but should he hear the sound of Ringing Glass (19) in the ship's mess our doughty dashing mariner would never seek to find a Priest Aboard (19)—that would be more than a body could bear.

But all is not lost.

If our long-suffering Jack Tar, making his way down to his ship for a lengthy and lonely voyage beyond the horizon, should happen to come across a girl bathing nude in the sea, then great is his luck; and the more comely she, the luckier he.

A number of much-storied ships are wrapped in a mystery inside an enigma (Churchill would not have minded the mangled plagiarism, he having been at one time First Lord of the Admiralty), such that over the course of time they have become the stuff of legend. Within these pages are accounts of two well-known ships—the *Mary Celeste* (chapter 16) and SS *Waratah* (11)—each of which in its own way is an icon of maritime mystery.

The importance of myth in human society cannot be overstated. As Gordon points out in his excellent *Encyclopedia of Myths and Legends*, myth helps us to address the eternal mysteries of life represented by those essentially unanswerable questions: Who or what are we? Where did we come from? What are we here for? Where are we going? What must we do? Thus this book includes a number of myths associated with the sea, stories that represent the attempts of early cultures to explain how their world came to be created, by what gods, and the means by which mankind came to inherit the earth and its oceans.

Water in its many forms—spring, creek, river, lake, marsh, inlet, or the vast trackless ocean itself—has since the beginning been of prime importance to human beings.

Each culture's mythology created tales that peopled this watery element with gods and goddesses, spirits and sprites, and all manner of creatures, as a means of trying to come to terms with its power and significance. Today we still break a bottle of wine or champagne over the bow of a ship being committed to the sea for the first time, although we have long forgotten the ancient reason for so doing; and shipbuilders still often fix a figurehead or emblem of some kind to the bow of a new vessel. We do these things because they are what our ancestors did; and when long ago they performed these particular ceremonies it was always for a good and practical reason: to placate the gods of the sea who might otherwise be angry at our intrusion into their personal domain.

The seafarer of old had every reason to be concerned about the state of mind and mood of those deities who controlled the great oceans; he was familiar with the story of Odysseus and the endless calamities and privations visited on him by an outraged Poseidon (see The *Odyssey*, chapter 4), and he certainly did not want to arouse the wrath of that often choleric and cross-grained god of the deeps. Thus when our ancient mariner ventured out onto the heaving main he took every precaution to ensure that none of the sea deities, such as Poseidon, Neptune, Aegir, or Ran his wife, ever had reason to be angry with him; he made the proper libations and sacrifices and thereby (he fervently hoped) warded off the storms and tempests that were an unfortunate but inevitable element in his seafaring life.

The mariner of today has changed but little.

In this selection I have excluded all, except a very few, accounts of legendary islands and mythical places, not to mention a handful of mythical rivers.

King Arthur's Avalon; Circe's Aeaea; Calypso's Ogygia (wherein fair Calypso so effectively enticed foolish Odysseus to interrupt his interminable voyage that he spent seven long years exclusively in her company; see Island of Ogygia, chapter 2); the Magnetic Islands (2) of classical renown; Lyonesse (see Lost Land of Lyonesse, chapter 2), the ancient kingdom slumbering on the seabed somewhere off Land's End—all these and many others were of consuming interest and importance to the seafarer of old.

Antilia was well known to ancient geographers as the fabled island of seven cities, which was to be found somewhere in the Western Ocean (the old name for the Atlantic). It possessed such a salubrious climate and all manner of fruits and other sustenance that voyagers who found themselves cast up on its shores had no wish ever to leave (which accounts, of course, for the fact that its exact location remained forever a mystery, although a marine chart of 1474 did make so bold as to equip it with a specific latitude and longitude).

Other far-off lands of similar attractions—such as Hy Brasil (chapter 2), the Island of Joy, the Island of Fair Women, the Islands of the Blessed—exercised a powerful fascination for sailors and shore-folk alike, because they represented the Utopia that we human creatures perennially long for. They are the far-off lands where things will be different (and immeasurably better), where the sun shines ever-warm on a green, pleasant, and fruitful land, where good health will be restored to the halt and the lame, love to the lorn, riches to the poor, and so on.

These places of perfect idyll were commonly thought of as islands, imagined by our ancestors to be located far out in the dark and mysterious Western Ocean where no ship dared venture (see Our Flat Earth, chapter 19, and the Voyages of Gil Eannes, 3), because islands, being far distant from the otherwise grubby cities and suburbs where normally we live, represent a delightful version of paradise, known to generations of English seamen as Fiddler's Green (chapter 19), where grog and tobacco are to be had in plenty, there is merry music all the while, and the frolicking maids are comely and compliant.

Who could ask for more?

According to some commentators there once were ancient lands that harbored no ills of any kind, where all was light, peace, and plenty. Alas!—they long ago disappeared beneath the tumultuous seas, but persons of an inquisitive disposition are said to have rediscovered the whereabouts of these long-ruined cities—nay, of whole continents indeed. Readers unfamiliar with the various histories of Atlantis (chapter 16), Lemuria (2), and Mu will be enlightened, not to say astonished, to learn that the resurrection and resurfacing of these ancient kingdoms is imminent (and, it must be said, welcomed by certain folk who believe that there is much to learn from these underwater relics of another age).

The literature of the sea is replete with legendary voyages. When the Greek adventurer Pytheas (or Pythias) of Marseilles recounted in marvelous detail his circumnavigation in about 300 B.C. of an island that he called Britannia and described the habits and productions of the people in that interesting land, he was hooted out of court by his contemporaries after he returned home. No one would believe him. How could they? Seafarers of that time were familiar only with the warm waters of the Mediterranean (but see Hanno the Navigator, chapter 3, who in 500 B.C. apparently sailed down the west coast of Africa in an attempt to establish colonies in suitable locations). When Pytheas claimed to have encountered great chunks of floating ice larger than his ship he was branded a charlatan; and his assertions that farther north the sea was entirely frozen over and that the sun never set for weeks on end earned him the ancient equivalent of a monumental raspberry, a Bronx cheer on the grandest scale.

Such is often the fate of the daring.

In a similar vein the late-twelfth-century voyage of Prince Madoc (chapter 3), the Welsh prince, is not at all well received by most scholars, and the navigations of Saint Brendan (3) were apparently so extensive and astonishing that there is still much debate today about their authenticity. The same applies even more so to the accounts of other very early voyagers presented by Charles Boland in *They All Discovered America*. Although there is compelling circumstantial and documentary evidence that the Vikings (among others) did in fact reach the North American coast on a number of occasions some five hundred years before Columbus ventured into American waters, there is still astonishing resistance to this apparently heretical notion (see Vinland USA, chapter 4). It is as if all meaningful maritime exploration began in 1492.

Nevertheless, there is still much to wonder at in more recent times. Thor Heyerdahl's classic *Kon-Tiki* Expedition of 1947 (chapter 3), not to mention Tim Severin's remarkable voyage in 1976 whereby he attempted to recreate the navigations of Saint Brendan (3), deserve our unqualified admiration for both the scholarship that gave birth to these journeys and the seafaring skills that supported them to a successful conclusion.

For somewhat different reasons I have also included an account of John Caldwell (chapter 13), the American merchant seaman who at the end of World War II and possessing not one ounce of experience in handling a sailboat, navigated a small cutter alone across the Pacific in order to rejoin his Australian wife in Sydney. Such a voyage shows what can be achieved when one is armed with little more than tenacity and fierce determination.

The survival story of Poon Lim (chapter 13), who spent 133 days afloat alone and exposed on a raft in the North Atlantic in 1943 before being rescued, is astonishing for his quiet dignity and absence of personal despair (the man is said to have bowed humbly to the Brazilian fishing boat as it came alongside to pick him up).

Also interesting is the story of Herbert Kabat (chapter 13), a U.S. Navy lieutenant whose destroyer was sunk in 1942 by a Japanese submarine in the Western Pacific. Kabat spent many hours in the water fighting off sharks as he tried to attract attention from navy rescue launches, only to see them disappear from sight. The fact that he continued to carry his fight to the sharks is a testament to the courage of certain types of men when they are confronted with imminent death.

Shipwreck has always been a topic of morbid interest among seafarers and landlubbers alike; in this book the fates of HMS *Birkenhead*, RMS *Lusitania*, SS *Waratah*, and the Whaler *Essex* are described (chapter 11). Two famous examples among the many Dutch East India Company vessels that drove onto the fierce West Australian coast in the mid-seventeenth century are the *Batavia* (chapter 9) and the *Gilt Dragon* (11, *Vergulde Draeck*). The *Batavia* is notorious for the mutiny and the wholesale slaughter of passengers that followed the disastrous wrecking of the ship on the Abrolhos Islands, northwest of Geraldton on the central West Australian coast.

The *Gilt Dragon* lost her prodigious cargo of gold and silver when she piled up on the dangerous reefs and rocks along that coast, 118 of her crew perishing in the calamity and another six dozen or so disappearing forever into the arid bush of

Western Australia after fighting their way ashore and scrambling up the terrible cliffs. It is likely that some of them were found and cared for by a local Aboriginal tribe; in any event they have long since been lost to history.

Castaways are represented by the inimitable Robinson Crusoe (chapter 13), the hero of the famous adventure story based on the experiences of the strange but interesting Alexander Selkirk, whose history is recounted in this book because of his immediate connection with what is often claimed to be the first English novel. Another account of castaways concerns the extraordinary story of four Russians who in the mid-eighteenth century survived for six years on the island of Spitsbergen in the Barents Sea, within 10 degrees of the Pole, after their ship had put them ashore to search for a hut believed to be in the area. A fierce storm sent the ship packing, leaving the four men to forge a desperate attempt to stay alive in an utterly hostile environment; that they did so is truly remarkable.

One is painfully aware of just how much has been excluded from this work. The literature of the sea fills whole libraries. There are innumerable accounts of fierce maritime battles throughout the ages, exploratory voyages into unknown or hostile regions, hope and struggle and survival in desperate situations, great and compelling commanders, and the daring and hardy men who were inspired to follow them.

Of the great ocean liners that made so indelible a mark in the periods of transatlantic travel from about 1900 to 1940—such as the *Queen Mary*, the *Mauretania*, and the *Normandie*—only RMS *Queen Mary* and the *Titanic* are discussed (chapter 10). Similarly, only a few of the great maritime conflicts have been given space in these pages: the Spanish Armada, the Battle of Copenhagen, and the Battle of Jutland, together with an account of the sinking of HMAS *Sydney* (all in chapter 10). Barely half a dozen pirates make an appearance (see chapter 14, At Odds with the Law). From accounts of the hundreds—nay, thousands—of mysteries that are an inseparable part of seafaring, the reader is here tempted by only six or seven examples (see chapter 16, Myth and Mystery). To represent the untold number of bold ships and their gallant crews that since the dawn of seafaring have gone to the bottom of the world's oceans, we must be satisfied here with less than half a dozen examples (see chapter 8, The Captain and His Ship).

I can only hope that some of the lore and myths and legends of the sea described within these pages will encourage the reader to seek farther afield, to explore the literature of that most noble and yet ineffably most perilous of livelihoods—the life, art, and times of the seafarer, an unequivocal example of which is the following letter written by a doomed sailor in the middle of the nineteenth century:

> *Dear friends, When you find this, the crew of the ill-fated ship* Horatio, *Captain Jackson, of Norwich, is no more. We have been below for six days. When I am writing this, I have just left the pumps; we are not*

able to keep her up—eight feet of water in the hold, and the sea making a clean breach over her. Our hatches are all stove in, and we are all worn out. I write these few lines, and commit them to the foaming deep, in hopes that they may reach some kind-hearted friend who will be so good as to find out the friends of these poor suffering mortals. I am a native of London, from the orphan school, John Laing, apprentice. We are called aft to prayers, to make our peace with that great God before we commit our living bodies to that foam and surf. Dear friends, you may think me very cool, but thank God, death is welcome. We are so benumbed and fatigued that we care not whether we live or die.

IN THE BEGINNING

W hen people first emerged from the long dark night of their savage and brutal lives as predatory hunters and gradually became more or less contemplative beings, increasingly aware of themselves as but a very small part of what seemed to be a very big picture, doubtless the two questions they asked themselves would have been: *Where did we come from? Why are we here?*

We have been struggling with these fundamental issues ever since.

Ancient civilizations—such as the Greeks, the early inhabitants of Mohendro-Daro in what is now Pakistan, the Maya people on the Yucatán Peninsula of Mexico, the Aztecs of Central America, the Australian Aborigines (the proud inheritors of a continuous culture at least sixty thousand years old), and many others who peopled the "long-ago"—all of them found answers of a sort to explain what otherwise seemed inexplicable.

This chapter deals with some of the myths, stories, and legends that our ancestors gradually accumulated in an effort to make sense of the world about them.

GREAT FLOODS

"In the sixth hundredth year of Noah's life, in the second month,
the seventeenth day of the month, the same day were all the fountains
of the great deep broken up, and the windows of heaven were open.
And the rain was upon the earth forty days and forty nights."
GENESIS 7:11–12

This biblical flood, also called the Deluge, is very important to all seafarers, past and present. It is the great flood that covered the earth as a mark of God's wrath toward man for his sins and general iniquity and a sign of God's regret at having created him in the first place: "And God saw that the wickedness of man was great in the earth, and that every imagination of the thoughts of his heart was only evil continually . . . And the Lord said, I will destroy man whom I have created from the face of the earth; both man, and beast, and the creeping thing, and the fowls of the air."

This biblical account is in fact a fusing of two traditions from which a continuous story emerges; for example, in one version the beasts fit for ritual sacrifice are taken into the ark by sevens and the remainder by twos, and it takes seven days for them all to enter the ark; the other tradition lists all the beasts alike in twos, and seemingly these all embark in one day.

Only the pious Noah and his wife and Noah's three sons (Shem, Ham, and Japheth) and their wives were to be spared, along with a male and female animal of each species, by means of a great ship or ark that God ordered Noah to make. This ark was 300 cubits long, 50 cubits wide, and 30 cubits high, the Hebrew cubit being about 22 inches long—a large vessel even by modern standards. According to legend, Noah's wife was unwilling to enter the ark and she and her husband, or so the story goes, had quite a quarrel about it. Chaucer refers to the quarrel in "The Miller's Tale" in *The Canterbury Tales*:

> *Hastow not herd, quod Nicholas, also*
> *The sorwe of Noe with his felawshipe*
> *Er that he mighte gete his wyf to shipe?*

Seven days later the rain began, lasting for forty days and forty nights in the story that is familiar to many of us (in the parallel tradition the flood doesn't end until after 150 days), a thundering downpour that must have exhausted virtually all of the atmospheric moisture in the heavens at the time. Underground water was caused to flood the earth along with the heavy and continuous rain from above;

this flood "prevailed upon the earth an hundred and fifty days" until all the land was inundated and every living thing had perished—except, of course, Noah and his companions in the ark.

When the rains stop and the ark comes to rest on the summit of Mount Ararat, Noah sends out a raven, then a dove, but they both return repeatedly, showing that there was still no dry land they could alight on. A week later he lets the dove go again, and this time it returns with an olive leaf in its beak, a sign to Noah that "the waters were abated from off the earth." God then instructs Noah to leave the ark, whereupon Noah builds an altar on the newly dry ground and sacrifices animals to show his thankfulness to the creator, who in turn promises that never again would there be such punishment inflicted on mankind ("I do set my bow in the cloud, and it shall be for a token of a covenant between me and the earth"), and as a sign of this a rainbow appears in the heavens (see The Rainbow in this chapter).

Finally Noah and his family and the cargo of livestock are blessed by the creator and given the instruction, in that famous biblical phrase, to "Be fruitful, and multiply, and replenish the earth."

The ark of Noah derives from the Latin *arca*, chest, related to *arcere*, to keep off; hence the ark of Noah that "kept off" the flood. An interesting suggestion for the source of "Noah" is *Nuah*, a moon goddess from Babylonian times, with the subsequent ark being used to ferry men from one world to another, as when Osiris, a principal Egyptian god, ferries the dead to the Otherworld; when Charon ferries his cargo of souls over the River Styx to Hades; and when King Arthur is taken by barge to Avalon.

Similar stories of a universal flood that wipes out an errant mankind are to be found in many other cultures. The best-known of these is perhaps the biblical account, briefly summarized above, this being but a variation of the Sumerian epic of Gilgamesh, a story so old that it predates Homer. In 1853 twelve clay tablets were discovered in the excavated library of the Assyrian king Ashurbanipal. On these tablets, some of which date back to 2000 B.C., were a number of ancient Babylonian stories and myths, the central hero of which was Gilgamesh, legendary king of Erech or Uruk.

Gilgamesh learns that the god Ea has told Utnapishtim, an ancestral being, to build a boat and fill it with his family and relatives, his valuables, and animals both wild and tame; this ark is cube-shaped and measures some 120 cubits along each side (about 220 feet). A storm rages for six days and nights; on the seventh the ark comes to rest on Mount Nisir, whereupon Utnapishtim sends out a dove, which returns, then a swallow, which also returns, followed by a raven, which does not.

Greek myth asserts that Deucalion, one of the sons of Prometheus, and his wife Pyrrha both survive the deluge in an ark and become the ancestors of the renewed human race by means of the novel method of casting stones behind them, which then turn into human beings. Yet another Greek legend, the Ogygian Deluge, has the great flood occurring during the reign of King Ogyges, some two hundred years earlier than the flood that beset Deucalion (see Island of Ogygia, chapter 2).

In the Indian *Rig Veda* (Sanskrit *rig*, rich = praise; *veda*, knowledge)—a series of psalms comprising perhaps the oldest document extant among the sacred scriptures of the world's living religions, dating back to at least 2000 B.C.—the ark of Manu (the ancestor of mankind) is towed to safety by a giant fish that Manu had earlier preserved from death when it was small.

The Norse epic Edda (a word related to the Sanskrit *veda*) relates the death of Ymir, the first being (a giant, in this case). He is killed by the god Odin and his blood swamps the world, destroying all other beings except Bergelmir and his wife, both of whom survive in a boat and who later bring forth a new race.

The Hopi people of Arizona tell how the creator-god Sotuknang destroyed with a flood the inhabitants of a former civilization, the Hopi themselves reaching safety on rafts made from reeds. Maori legend relates how the god Tawaki vented his anger on humanity for their persistent sin by releasing all the waters of heaven on them, only some selected individuals being permitted to reach safety on rafts.

Trow, the mythical ancestor of the Dyak people in North Borneo, finds salvation by crouching in a feed trough until the waters dry out; the Arapaho nation in North America tell of their god Rock being preserved in a vessel made from spiders' webs and fungi; while the ancestors of the Lithuanians were saved by sheltering in a nutshell; and the forebears of the Chane people of Bolivia floated to safety in a clay pot.

Hawaiian legend tells of Nuu who, with his wife, his three sons and their wives, waited out a world-destroying flood by seeking refuge in a huge ship that he had built; when the waters had subsided their vessel came to rest on Mauna Kea, the highest mountain in those islands (the similarities between this legend and that of Noah are striking). Venezuelan lore records the "Time of the Great Water" in rock carvings on very high cliffs, chiseled there by long-gone artists working from their canoes floating on once-high waters.

Scholars have long known of the broad agreement between many flood myths found in many different cultures, especially details concerning the size of the raindrops that fell from the open heavens and the heat of the water released upon the earth. For example, amongst North American Indians the Sacs and the Fox peoples relate that each drop was the size of a wigwam; Saint John describes the hail that rained from the sky as "every stone about the weight of a talent." (A talent was an ancient weight, and also a sum of money, of varying value among the Assyrians, Greeks, Romans, etc., the later Attic people putting it at about 57 pounds troy weight; Gordon, *Encyclopedia of Myths and Legends*, suggests that Saint John's talent was equal to about a hundredweight, some 112 pounds.)

The Zend-Avesta of ancient Persia mentions raindrops the size of a man's head; the Makah tribe of Washington State and the Vugul people of Finland speak of rain that is boiling hot, as does a Jewish account of the Flood myth and that of the Ipurinas of Brazil. In like manner, Syrian legend tells of huge volumes of water being thrown out from the earth followed by torrential rain pouring from above and drowning everyone, as does also the Koran, wherein quantities of hot water burst from an "oven."

Many of these myths share the common belief that man's sinful nature was the cause of the Flood that destroyed all life on the planet, except for those few who were chosen by the creator to replenish the earth with people.

Such a common stock of worldwide beliefs has led various researchers to the notion that the catastrophic deluge that annihilated virtually all living things on earth at some time in the distant past is less myth and more a race memory of an actual event. If it is in fact only myth (so the argument runs) one is left wondering the obvious: how is it that so many disparate and unconnected peoples on the face of the earth persist in relating legends of mass global destruction, legends that all share many points of similarity?

MOSES AND THE RED SEA

"The water of this red see is not redde of his owne kynde,
the colour of it is by reson of the costes and the botom of it
which be redde ground . . . this is the trouthe."
ROGER BARLOW, *A BRIEF SUMME OF GEOGRAPHIE*

The Red Sea is of course the location of the miracle that permitted the children of Israel to escape the wrath of the Pharaoh (its name is a translation of the Latin *Mare rubrum*). One explanation for "red" is that it is a "sea of reeds"; others are that it takes its color from the red coral on its bed or that the water reflects the color of the eastern sky. The more likely reason for its color is that this narrow strip of water, extending from Suez in the north to the Strait of Bab el Mandeb to the southeast, was named from the blue-green algae common to its waters, the algae having also a red pigment that occasionally colors the surface waters.

Moses (Egyptian = "a son") liberated the Hebrews from Egyptian bondage and was their leader for the many years of their desert wanderings to Palestine. During their captivity in Egypt the Israelites increased greatly in number, thereby causing concern among the authorities, who then put the people to forced labor and set out to kill all first-born male children. The child Moses is saved by being placed in a basket made from bulrushes and then hidden among reeds in a stream; ironically, he is rescued, named, and raised by the Pharaoh's own daughter, no less—although the Egyptians are not aware of this—and eventually he finds his way into exile. God reveals himself to Moses as a burning bush and commissions him to deliver the Israelites from Egyptian bondage. These events are thought by most scholars to belong to the period around 1500 B.C.

Moses returns to Egypt and demands repeatedly of the Pharaoh that his people be allowed to journey into the wilderness to worship Yahweh, God. The demand is just as repeatedly refused, whereupon Yahweh afflicts the Egyptians with a series of plagues, culminating in the death of all first-born Egyptians and beasts. Sensibly, the Israelites flee, pursued by the Pharaoh's forces, who overtake the fugitives on the banks of the Red Sea. What happened next has been much debated.

The Israelite host cross the sea safely

> *by means of unusual but natural causes, such as the combination of a very strong wind and a very low tide, so that the Israelites might scramble across to the other side; this was apparently an early tradition ("And Moses stretched out his hand over the sea; and the Lord caused the sea to go back by a strong east wind all that night, and made the sea dry land, and the waters were divided").*

or

> *by a miracle, whereby the sea parts, the Israelites pass across safely, and the sea then reunites of its own accord; this is a later tradition.*

In both scenarios the Egyptian soldiers follow hard on the heels of the Israelites but are swiftly drowned by the rapidly returning waters. The Israelites make their way to a sacred mountain variously called Sinai or Horeb, where they adopt Yahweh as their God and then spend the next forty years trying to reach Palestine from the south (this is the period when they are often sustained in the desert wastes by quail and manna, a wild sweet edible root). Finally they leave the wilderness and successfully enter Palestine by approaching it from the east. Just before they cross the River Jordan, Moses dies.

The parting of the Red Sea has remained as one of the more dramatic of oceanic disturbances in the literature, rivaled perhaps only by the supposed upheaval, then disappearance, of Fabled Atlantis (chapter 16).

THE RAINBOW

"I do set my bow in the cloud, and it shall be for a token of a covenant between me and the earth."

GENESIS 9:13

The biblical account of the Deluge (Great Floods above) relates how the creator made a promise to mankind, telling Noah that he would set a rainbow in the sky as an enduring sign that never again would there occur such a draconian punishment of mankind as the Flood: "And the bow shall be in the cloud."

But not only is the rainbow of significance to Christians, it is also an element in a number of other world myths. In Greek mythology the rainbow goddess is Iris, messenger of the gods and daughter of Thaumas and Electra, both deities of the sea (the colored portion of the human eye takes its name from Iris; the flower of that name does, also). The Norse regard the rainbow as a manifestation of the bridge, known to them as Bifrost, that connects the world of humans with that of the gods; in parts of Africa and India it represents a serpent slaking its thirst in the sea; for the Chinese it is the sky-dragon that joins heaven and earth; and some North American peoples regard the rainbow as a ladder by which they might make contact with the realms of the departed spirits of their dead.

The Bakongo people of central Africa look upon the rainbow as one of the manifestations of the protector god Lubangala, whose function it is to guard their villages and the graves of their ancestors, as well as being protector of the sea. European folklore, with a touch of the whimsical if not the practical, also maintains that if one looks carefully enough one will find a pot of gold at the end of the rainbow.

The sailor's view is perhaps as useful as any:

> *Rainbow to windward, foul fall the day;*
> *Rainbow to leeward, damp runs away.*

MAUI, CREATOR OF NEW ZEALAND

"Was this country [New Zealand] settled by an Industrus people they would very soon be supply'd not only with the necessarys but many of the luxuries of life."
CAPTAIN JAMES COOK, *JOURNAL*, 1770

Maui is one of the great heroes in Polynesian mythology, featured in many tales told by the Maoris of New Zealand and the early Hawaiians and by other Polynesian groups scattered throughout the Pacific (see *Kon-Tiki* Expedition, chapter 3).

He was born prematurely to his mother Taranga, who immediately wrapped him in some of her hair (some accounts say her apron) and abandoned him to the sea, but a jellyfish protected the child with its mantle. Maui's father Tama, the sky, saw the boy in the sea and took him home, placing him on the roof of his house so that the child would be warmed by the fire in the hearth below. From the spirits around him Maui learned a wide variety of skills, hence his reputation as a wily, resourceful, and mischievous figure who takes great delight in tricking others.

His brothers Maui-Pae, Maui-Roto, Maui-Taha, and Maui-Whao were not famous for being intelligent. It was their custom to fish with spears that had no barbs and to try catching eels with pots that had no trapdoors to them, meanwhile always wondering why they were so spectacularly unsuccessful in both pursuits. Maui shows them how to make barbs and trapdoors, and now armed with these useful devices they decide they no longer need him for advice.

Maui had come across an elderly female relative whom his brothers had been instructed to feed regularly, but instead they ate the food themselves. When Maui visits her she is already half dead, so he takes out her lower jaw and fashions a magic fishhook from it. The next day his brothers make plans to go on a fishing trip. Intending to leave Maui behind, they set off in their canoe, but Maui disguises himself as a shrimp and hides in the bottom of the boat with his magic fishhook hidden alongside.

The brothers catch a lot of fish and prepare to return home because their canoe is full, but Maui reveals himself, restored to his proper form, and asks them to let him have a chance at fishing. They are suitably scornful of him, letting him have neither fishhook nor bait. Maui shrugs, pulls out his jawbone hook, bites himself, smears the hook with his blood, and casts the lot into the sea. Using his magical powers he sends his hook to the very bottom of the ocean, where an enormous fish takes the bait. Maui hauls up his monstrous catch and discovers that he has hooked the land that lay at the bottom of the sea. He orders his brothers not to cut it up in any way but they, no doubt chagrined at Maui's skill, slice and hack at it endlessly, causing the land to thrash and flail in the water.

This land is of course Ika-a-Maui, "fish of Maui," long known to Polynesians as the Land of the Long White Cloud, now called New Zealand, its rugged geography and many islands being the result of all that cutting and slashing by Maui's brothers.

OCEANUS

"For all at last return to the sea—to Oceanus, the ocean river,
like the ever-flowing stream of time, the beginning and the end."
RACHEL CARSON, THE SEA AROUND US

Oceanus ("of the swift queen," sometimes Okeanos) was a Greek sea god, lord of the great river Ocean that encircled the flat disk of the earth, the river symbolized by a snake with its tail in its mouth; the sun and moon were believed to rise from the river Ocean and, in turn, sink into it. Oceanus was a gentle and hospitable old fellow who lived apart from the passing parade of the world, his abode being in the farthest west.

Oceanus was a son of Uranos and Gaea and was also the father of all subsequent gods, as well as of all humankind. He was usually represented in art as an old man with a long beard and bull's horns on his head, which was customary with river gods; sometimes the claws of crabs were entwined in his hair, in the manner of sea gods.

Tethys was Oceanus's sister-wife, both Titans. Their daughters were the Oceanids, some three thousand of them, one of whom was Doris, mother of Amphitrite (see below), who in turn was wife to Poseidon (see below), and another of whom was Styx, goddess of the River Styx in Hades. Other sources claim, in addition, about three thousand sons for Oceanus; and as if that weren't enough responsibility he was also sire of all the rivers, fountains, seas, and streams in the world.

According to Homer (the Greek writer who supposedly lived in the ninth century B.C.), the vast flood that constituted Ocean, the later domain of Oceanus, was the beginning of everything; it was the next step beyond the empty primal infinite space called Chaos which preceded the appearance of gods, men, and matter.

Before Chaos there was—nothing.

The ancient Greek concept of the river Ocean encircling the disk that made up earth was no doubt responsible for the belief, held by many people right up until the end of the medieval period (about 1500), that the earth was nothing but a flat disk from which one would fall off—doubtless into terrifying regions of endless perdition and sulphurous hellfire—should one be bold enough to sail beyond the Pillars of Heracles (Roman form Hercules) into the vast unknown of the Western Seas (see Our Flat Earth, chapter 19). This idea of an encircling sea was probably derived from the early Egyptians and Babylonians, whose cosmology envisaged the world as a raft floating more or less serenely on the primeval waters.

KING NEPTUNE

*"Will all Great Neptune's ocean wash this blood
Clean from my hand?"*
WILLIAM SHAKESPEARE, *MACBETH*

In Roman mythology Neptune was the early Italian god of the sea, corresponding to the Greek deity Poseidon (see next section; probably known to the Etruscans as Nethunus), and hence the sea itself, it being very uncommon to refer to the ocean as Poseidon. The representations of both gods are similar, each being depicted as a somewhat older man of stately appearance, usually carrying the trademark trident (useful for stirring up stormy seas and the like), and often sitting astride a dolphin, the hippocampus of Greek mythology (*hippos*, horse, *kampos*, sea monster; hence the Latin *hippopotamus*, Greek *potamos*, river, thus "horse of the river").

Neptune is also often shown with one of his feet resting on part of a ship, so that there could be no doubt concerning who was in charge of the watery realm (see Crossing the Line, chapter 6, for an account of the ceremonial to Neptune that is mandatory when one crosses the Equator for the first time). Roman art often showed Neptune being drawn through or across the sea in a chariot pulled by sea horses, with a triton (the shell trumpet, from the marine gastropod of family Cymatiidae, known for its long conical shell called a triton).

Neptune was the son of Saturn (the Latin name for Cronus, also Kronos, not to be confused with *chronos*, the Greek word for time, hence "chronometer") and Rhea, sister-wife to Saturn. Neptune's wife was Salacia, the goddess of salt water;

Amphitrite was the Greek goddess of the sea and wife of the redoubtable Poseidon.

Neptune also presided over horses and equestrian accomplishments because of his part in bestowing upon mankind this most useful of animals; for this reason he is often shown with a whip in one hand. He was also regarded by the English as the god who watched over their country, a supposition no doubt inspired by the fact of their living in a sea-girt land as well as being wholly dependent on the sea for trade with their not inconsiderable overseas empire. "Neptune's sheep" is another name for the white horses that one encounters at sea—that is, waves breaking into foam.

POSEIDON

*"He commanded and the storm wind rose
And the surges of the sea."*

EDITH HAMILTON, *MYTHOLOGY*

Poseidon ("he who gives drink from wooded mountain") may be a form of *poti-dan*, meaning "drink," "river"; note *potable*, drinkable, from Latin *potare*, to drink. In Greek mythology Poseidon is the god of the sea, the brother of Zeus and next below him in eminence in the pantheon of gods. Poseidon, by nature surly and quarrelsome, is never seen without his trident, a gift from the Cyclopes—gigantic one-eyed beings—in the stylized form of a thunderbolt. This is the three-pronged spear by means of which he could shatter anything he pleased, hence his name "Earthshaker" because of his ability to cause earthquakes.

He was often to be found in his palace of gold at the bottom of the Aegean Sea near the island of Euboea, off the east coast of Greece, with his wife Amphitrite, but he also spent a good deal of his time on Mount Olympus.

In common with all of the gods, married or not, Poseidon carried on endless affairs with whatever goddesses, nymphs, and mortals were to hand; indeed, he once assumed the form of a stallion in order to seduce Demeter, the goddess of mares (Zeus himself was a master of farmyard disguise—and, it must be said, of farmyard behavior as well—having turned himself into a swan in order to father children on Leda, two of whom were Castor and Pollux; see also Saint Elmo's Fire, chapter 19).

One of Poseidon's children by Amphitrite was Triton, the sea god who causes the ocean to roar by blowing through his shell. Poseidon also had children—most of them inheriting his capacity for unbridled rage and violence—by, among others, Gaea, goddess of the earth; Aphrodite, goddess of love; Medusa, the Gorgon whose face was so hideous that all who looked on her were turned to stone, on whom he fathered Pegasus, the winged horse of the Muses; Thoosa, on whom he fathered Polyphemus the Cyclops (see The *Odyssey*, chapter 4, for an account of Odysseus's blinding of Polyphemus and Poseidon's consequent anger directed at the wandering hero); and countless other "wives," divine and earthly.

Poseidon is primarily associated with the sea, especially the Mediterranean and the Black Sea, as well as with rivers and lakes (except for bodies of water not navigated by the Greeks, these being the province of Oceanus, lord of the river Ocean, and Pontus, a god of the deeps), but he is also widely honored for giving mankind the first horse. Indeed, Poseidon was frequently seen rising from the sea in a golden chariot drawn by horses with golden manes and brass hooves and attended by dolphins (also known as tunny-fish), symbols of peace and calm, and sometimes by bulls, symbols of brute power and violence. Horse races and bullfights were dedicated to him, and enormous statues were often erected in his honor in harbors and on promontories facing out to sea.

It was in a contest with the goddess Athene for the patronage of Athens that Poseidon struck a stone with his trident so as to produce the horse; Athene, meanwhile, created the olive tree. The gods deemed her invention to be of greater benefit to mankind, it being a symbol of peace while the horse represented war, and Athene was awarded the victory.

Storm, tempest, and cloud, as well as calm and tranquillity, were at Poseidon's beck and call; when he sent his chariot across the ocean the waves ceased their thunder and the wind was stilled. It was also in his power to grant safe voyages, a boon he withheld from Odysseus for some time.

Neptune (see King Neptune above) is the Roman counterpart of Poseidon; this identification dates from 399 B.C. as a result of a Roman festival of Greek origin (the Lectisternium) held then in order to placate the gods, Poseidon being one of them. See Crossing the Line, chapter 6.

As a punishment for offending Zeus, Poseidon had to join with Apollo (a son of Zeus, sometimes identified with Helios, the sun god) in building the walls of Troy for King Laomedon, but when the king refused to make the agreed payment of two horses (other accounts refer to money), Poseidon sent a sea monster to devour Hesione, the king's beautiful daughter. Happily, she was saved by Heracles, who was passing that way to attend to another of his many labors. Thereafter Poseidon gratified his hatred of the Trojans by siding with the Greeks during the Trojan War.

From time immemorial seafarers have held Poseidon and Neptune in awe and dread for their ability to control all the elements of the ocean.

AMPHITRITE

"Or some enormous whale the god may send
(For many such on Amphitrite attend)."
ALEXANDER POPE, "HOMER'S *ODYSSEY*"

Amphitrite (*amphi*, about, on all sides; *trio*, for *tribo*, rubbing, wearing away [the shore], "the one who encircles," i.e., the sea) was the goddess or queen of the sea, wife of Poseidon and daughter of Nereus (see below), the "Old Man of the Sea" (the Greek version, not the Arabian), and Doris, daughter of Oceanus. Amphitrite was the mother of the Nereids, of Triton, and of many others.

Amphitrite had been carried off by Poseidon when he saw her dancing with the Nereids on the island of Naxos. Another version has it that she fled to Atlas beyond the Pillars of Hercules (see chapter 2) so as to escape Poseidon's attentions but was seen by Poseidon's attendant dolphin, which carried her back to him, whereupon he married her. Homer doesn't refer to her specifically as Poseidon's wife, but rather as a sea goddess who "beats the billows against the rocks, and has the creatures of the deep in her keeping."

The Romans identified Amphitrite with Salacia, the wife of Neptune (see King Neptune above), Poseidon's Roman equivalent. She is often depicted in a chariot of seashells, drawn by various marine animals.

APHRODITE

*"Men have died from time to time and worms
have eaten them, but not for love."*
WILLIAM SHAKESPEARE, *AS YOU LIKE IT*

Aphrodite is included here because of her connection with the sea, and her connection with seafarers—past, present, and inevitably future. She is the Greek goddess of beauty, fertility, and sexual love, so named because she was considered to have sprung from the foam of the sea ("Aphrodite," "foam-born," Greek *aphros*, foam). Another version of the myth is that she was a daughter of Zeus and Dione. Yet again she is said to be a daughter of Uranus, the personification of the heavens; when that worthy's sexual organs were forcibly removed by sickle-wielding Cronus, his youngest son, and flung into the sea, the resultant froth and foam proved to be the begetting agent for Aphrodite. Gaea, earth mother and wife of Uranus, having for some time become very tired of childbearing, desired one of her offspring to deal suitably with her husband; all except Cronus refused.

Venus, the Roman equivalent of Aphrodite, was one of the least important early divinities; originally she was a goddess of spring and protector of vegetation, but the process of her identification with Aphrodite is unclear. Both Aphrodite and Venus were considered unremarkable for fidelity to their marriage vows, they being somewhat lax in this regard. Each is immortalized in statuary, possibly the most famous being Praxiteles's *Aphrodite of Cnidus*, a copy of which survives; and an unknown sculptor's *Aphrodite of Melos* (Venus de Milo), now in the Louvre in Paris, and regarded by some as the finest single work of ancient art extant.

Aphrodite's appearance on Olympus created amorous uproar among all men who looked upon her, and in like manner the charms (not to mention the chaos) that she subsequently bequeathed to mortals have accounted for as much mayhem as they have mania. In this connection see HMS *Bounty* Mutiny, chapter 9.

PORTUNUS

"The king has the prerogative of appointing ports and havens,
or such places only for persons and merchandise to pass into
and out of the realm, as he in his wisdom sees proper."
SIR WILLIAM BLACKSTONE, *COMMENTARIES ON THE LAWS OF ENGLAND*

Portunus was the Roman god of harbors, who with Fortuna, the goddess of good luck, was invoked to ensure safe and prosperous voyages. Because of his importance to seafarers Portunus had a temple at the harbor on the River Tiber, where a festival, the Portunalia, was held on August 17 every year in his honor. It is likely that he was originally the god of house and home; *portus*, the old word for the entrance to such a dwelling, was later transferred to mean harbor, river mouth, haven.

All this is of interest to mariners because of the importance of *port* in nautical nomenclature.

- *port*, the left side of a vessel facing forward, from *port side*, so named because early vessels were steered by an oar or steering board at the stern on the right-hand side of the vessel, thus preventing a ship from docking with that side next to a wharf (hence also "starboard," a corruption of the Old English *steorbord*, steering side; *larboard*, the now superseded word for port or port side, is from the Middle English *ladeborde*, loading side; *ladeborde* is the source of our word "laden")
- *port*, the opening in a warship's side through which a cannon (the "great gun") is fired
- *Portugal*, which takes its name from *Portus Cale* (Latin = warm harbor, from the fact that it was always ice-free; *cale* = warm, hot, hence cauldron, caldera, etc.; *Portus* derives from *Portunus*); the modern name for Portus Cale is Oporto, hence "port wine," the fortified wine originally shipped from Oporto

CASTOR AND POLLUX

"We had also upon our maine yard, an apparition of a little fire by night,
which seamen doe call Castor and Pollux. But we had only one,
which they take an evill signe of more tempest."
RICHARD HAKLUYT, *VOYAGES AND DOCUMENTS*

Castor and Pollux are the two stars in the constellation Gemini (Latin = twins). They were of great interest to early sailors because the twins in human form (sons of Zeus) had distinguished themselves as crew members during Jason's quest for the

Golden Fleece (see The Argonauts, chapter 4). A violent storm beset the expedition, but then a flame played around the head of each twin, and the storm abated at once.

Naturally this impressed the rest of the crew, who thereafter looked upon Castor and Pollux as having the power to protect sailors at sea, and thereafter it became common for mariners to pray to them during bad weather. The phenomenon of the flame was known as Castor and Pollux as well as Saint Elmo's Fire (see chapter 19).

NEREUS

"A trusty god and gentle, who thinks just and kindly thoughts and never lies."
HESIOD, ON NEREUS

Nereus, a sea god in Greek mythology, was known as "The Old Man of the Sea" (not to be confused with the other gentleman of the same name and address in *The Arabian Nights*—see Sindbad the Sailor, chapter 3). The abode of Nereus was the Mediterranean, his special dominion being the Aegean Sea, in the depths of which he occupied a large and comfortable cave.

Nereus was the son of Pontus ("the deep sea") and Gaea ("mother earth"). As was the way with these earliest of creationist deities, fathers, mothers, sons, and daughters usually coupled with each other willy-nilly in order to get things going. The wife of Nereus was Doris, one of the daughters of Oceanus (see above). Their daughters numbered fifty (or a hundred or two hundred, depending on the source of the myth); these were the virginal nymphs of the sea celebrated for their loveliness and known as Nereids after their father. One of the better known of these nymphs was Amphitrite (see above), wife of the redoubtable Poseidon (see above). See The *Odyssey*, chapter 4, for examples of Poseidon's robust nature.

Nereus ranks among those gods who represent the elementary forces of nature; and like many other deities of the sea, he was an accomplished shape-shifter, having the power to change himself at will into any form of animal or other being. It was in this fashion that he tried to evade giving directions to Heracles on how to reach the land of The Hesperides (chapter 2). He also possessed the gift of prophecy. Like Poseidon (and, of course, Neptune), Nereus wore seaweed leaves in his hair and always carried a trident, but seafarers had little cause to fear him, his attitude being one of benevolence and goodwill toward mortals.

HERO AND LEANDER

"A better swimmer you could scarce see ever,
He could, perhaps, have pass'd the Hellespont,
As once (a feat on ourselves we prided)
Leander, Mr Ekenhead, and I did."
GEORGE GORDON, LORD BYRON, "DON JUAN"

This is the famous legend about two lovers, Hero and Leander, who lived one on each side of the Hellespont, the ancient name for the Dardanelles, the strait that separates Asiatic Turkey from European Turkey and connects the Aegean Sea with the Sea of Marmara. "Hellespont" is from the Greek *Helle*, a mythic girl of that name who was drowned there, and *pontos*, sea, hence the Sea of Helle. The strait itself is about 40 miles long and 1½ miles wide.

Leander was a youth who lived in Abydos (also Abydus), a town on the Asian shore, while Hero was a priestess of Aphrodite (see above) in the town of Sestus (Sestos) on the European side of the strait (confusingly, Seyffert places Hero in a tower on Lesbos, an island in the eastern Aegean; perhaps this is a misprint for Sestos). Because she was a priestess Hero was barred from ever marrying. Nevertheless, each night Leander would swim across the Hellespont to be with his lover, guided by a flaming torch held high by Hero on top of a tower (or, according to other sources, guided by the lighthouse at Sestos).

One night there was a particularly violent storm and Hero's beacon was blown out; Leander lost his way, became exhausted, and perished. Hero found his body when eventually it was washed up on the shore; she was so overcome by grief that she flung herself in the sea and drowned, thereby joining her unfortunate lover. Other accounts have Hero recognizing the corpse from the top of the tower, whereupon she flings herself down to her death on the ground below. See Halcyon Days, chapter 15, for a somewhat similar story of lovers reunited in this fashion.

The story was famous even in ancient times, no doubt for the morality of its message—young ladies admitted to the service of Aphrodite should focus only on their task—and has been treated by writers throughout the ages. In 1810 Lord Byron and Lieutenant Ekenhead swam the Hellespont to emulate Leander, covering the distance in 1 hour and 10 minutes.

The Greek word *hero* is itself feminine, derived from Hera, sister-wife to Zeus. The most famous hero of Greek mythology is of course Hercules (Herakles in Greek, a variant of Hera; Herakles means "renowned through Hera," "glory of Hera"). Our English word *hero*, commonly used to denote a male rather than a female, is a back formation from the Latin *heros*, a demigod or distinguished man, the Latin plural (and of course the English) being *heroes*. (See also Pillars of Hercules, chapter 2.)

SCYLLA AND CHARYBDIS

"I then took a strait . . .
'Twixt Scylla and Charybdis."
THE *ODYSSEY*, TRANSLATED BY GEORGE CHAPMAN

The story of Scylla and Charybdis is one of the best known of the myths associated with sea monsters. The phrase "Scylla and Charybdis" has endured through the ages as a metaphor for jumping out of the frying pan, into the fire (two thousand years ago Horace, 65–8 B.C., Roman poet and satirist, used it of writers who, seeking to avoid one fault, fell into another). Scylla is the name of a dangerous rock on the Italian side of the Strait of Messina, a stretch of sometimes turbulent water 2 ½ miles wide separating Italy and Sicily. On the other side of the strait is Charybdis, the whirlpool of legendary fame.

Scylla the sea monster (Latin, from Greek *skulla*, "she who rends") had once been a beautiful nymph much loved by Glaucus, a fisherman who, having eaten a magic herb, became immortal. Unhappily, Glaucus, who had seen Scylla bathing nude, could not win her affections, so he applied to Circe for a love potion, but that good lady instead fell in love with the fisherman and by way of assuring the field for herself she turned Scylla into a hideous creature fitted with a lower body composed of six dreadful dogs, the like of which you would never wish to meet. Each dog's head contained three rows of teeth closely set together, with the entire insalubrious creature anchored to a rock on the Italian coast overlooking the strait. These dogs barked without stop and were incessantly ravenous for the meat and blood of men, an appetite they satisfied (with no apparent diminution in racket) by seizing a sailor from each passing vessel.

Things were not much better across the water. Charybdis (Latin, from Greek *kharubdis*, "sucker down") was the daughter of Poseidon, the god of the sea, and Gaea, the earth personified as a goddess (Gaea not only had intimate relations with virtually every male within hailing distance—including a number of her own offspring—she also managed the useful feat of giving birth to the mountains, the heavens, and other geographical features, as well as human beings, without the intervening benefit of insemination by male or mountain).

Before her later troubles began, Charybdis lived a more or less blameless life beneath a huge fig tree on a rock overlooking the strait. One day Hercules passed through the area, driving before him the cattle that he had stolen from Geryon, a three-headed giant, whereupon Charybdis purloined a number of the beasts and ate them. For her pains Zeus struck her with one of his trademark thunderbolts and hurled her into the sea, where she became a monster living in a cave. It was then her lot to suck in all the surrounding water three times a day, thus swallowing everything that happened to be floating thereon, then spewing it all out again, in the process forming an irresistible whirlpool, a hazard to any ships attempting the passage, Poseidon himself being unable to help mariners in dire peril.

Understandably, then, the Strait of Messina was looked upon by sailors with more than usual trepidation, not to say terror, with Scylla on one hand begirt by her ravening dogs and, on the other, Charybdis threatening the twin mayhems of shipwreck and death by drowning. Odysseus himself in Homer's *Odyssey* barely managed to escape the clutches of this evil place (see The *Odyssey*, chapter 4).

There are a number of variations to this and other ancient Greek myths, the reason being that over the ages these stories so charmed readers with their tales of derring-do and examples of bravery, honesty, steadfastness, true love, and other admirable qualities of human nature, that successive retellings invariably emphasized the shape of one element and changed the details of another, the embellishments reflecting the particular interests and loyalties of the narrator.

MANANNAN, CELTIC SEA GOD

*"The Celts . . . are an old family, of whose beginning there is no memory,
and their end is likely to be still more remote in the future."*
RALPH WALDO EMERSON, *ENGLISH TRAITS*

Manannan (also Mananaan or Manannan Mac Lir = "the strider of the waves") was one of the sons of Ler or Lir, the Celtic god of the sea. Manannan was an important sea deity because of the strong tradition of Ireland's having long ago been invaded from the sea. (In Wales he was known as Manawyddan fab Llyr.)

Manannan was the patron of Irish sailors and merchants and protector of the Isle of Aran and the Isle of Man in the Irish Sea (the latter island takes it name from this deity). To help him carry out his tasks he owned four things of great value to him: a sword that never failed to kill his opponent; a ship called *Wave Sweeper* that propelled itself in whatever direction Manannan wished; a horse, Splendid Mane, that could gallop more swiftly than the wind; and a suit of magic armor that no weapon could pierce. Some accounts credit him with a helmet that conferred invisibility on him; otherwise, whenever he made an appearance it was as a noble and handsome warrior.

James Joyce in *Ulysses* refers to the ocean waves as "the whitemaned sea-horses, champing, bright-windbrindled, the steeds of Manannan." He appears in Welsh mythology as Manawyddan, and is fitted out with a magic cloak (perhaps of fog—see below) and a chariot that, like everything else he owned, possessed magic qualities. Like Poseidon, Manannan could drive his chariot across the ocean as if the watery domain were but a level plain.

Manannan was a famous shape-shifter, which permitted him to appear to anyone in whatever form he chose (Merlin of Arthur's court practiced this art, as did Proteus of Greek myth, and Zeus himself consorted with countless females in a variety of disguises; Circe, the bewitching lady who changed Ulysses's men into swine, "shifted" the shapes of others rather than her own—see The *Odyssey*, chapter 4).

This attribute of Manannan the sea god reflects, of course, the dangerous changeability of the sea. The fog that often shrouds the Isle of Man is taken as a sign of Manannan at work (the coat of arms of this island is in the form of a three-legged *fylfot* or swastika, in which the legs are those of a knight in armor, this being another example of Manannan's shape-shifting; *fylfot* originally referred to the ornament used to *fill* the *foot* of a colored glass window).

2

FABLED LANDS

T he early mariners—principally the Greeks and Romans, who left behind them a long and continuous history of their life and mythology—peopled their watery world in much the same way as they did their land-bound one.

The ocean that lay beyond the Pillars of Hercules (see below), bounded by Oceanus (chapter 1), was presumed to contain wonders unknown to ordinary mortals: the island of Bimini, for example, on which (it was confidently asserted) would be found the fountain of youth. There is an island of this name in the Caribbean; to date, however, it would seem that no one has yet stumbled across, or fallen into, the long-lost fountain.

Beyond what is today known as Gibraltar and lying far out in the Western Ocean (i.e., the earth-circling river of Oceanus) are any number of fabled islands.

Islands have always promised, of course, escape, a passport to freedom, the simple life. On such an island life consists of nothing more onerous than basking in a perfect climate, reaching out a hand from time to time to pluck a coconut or a succulent fruit from a nearby tree, and occasionally strolling along the strand like a dyed-in-the-ethic beachcomber: the Fiddler's Green (see chapter 19) of the modern world.

Alas! there are few enough Utopias in this world.

PILLARS OF HERCULES

"And is that really Gibraltar?"
"Yes, Madam."
"Thank you so much. I understand that when we land
I must on no account miss seeing the Rock."

CARTOON CAPTION, *PUNCH*, JULY 1934

One indeed hopes that the lady did not miss seeing the Rock, as it is a mountain some 1,400 feet high, somewhat bulky, and very precipitous. The Rock of Gibraltar, anciently known as Calpe, a British possession since 1704, is on the southern tip of present-day Spain, and Mount Hacho, anciently known as Abyla, lies directly opposite, about 8 miles away, on the northern coast of Africa in present-day Morocco, where now stands the fortress of Ceuta. These two "rocks"—Gibraltar and Mount Hacho, commonly known as the Rock of Ceuta—are the famous Pillars of Hercules.

Legend tells us that these two rocks or mounts were originally bound together and that Hercules tore them asunder to get to the Western Seas, setting up these rocks or pillars in memory of his journey through Europe and Libya (the name given by the ancients to present-day Africa). This he did while performing his tenth labor, in which he was charged with bringing back to Mycenae the cattle that belonged to Geryon, a monster with powerful wings and three bodies who lived on the island of Erythia, on the farthest borders of the Ocean stream. After many splendid adventures, during which he slew Geryon, Hercules accomplished this task and delivered the oxen to Mycenae.

The twelve labors for which Hercules is famous were imposed on him by the Delphic oracle as a means by which he could expiate the terrible sin of having slaughtered his own family. Hera, sister-wife to Zeus, had made Hercules lose his wits, a vengeance she visited on the poor fellow for his having been sired on a mortal by her own brother-husband, Zeus. In his deranged state of mind Hercules confused his wife and children with the family of his enemy, King Eurystheus, and did away with them.

The entrance to the Mediterranean, known as the Straits of Gibraltar, has always been a site of considerable strategic importance to warring nations. (*Gibraltar* is a corruption of *Gebel-al-Tarik*, the hill of Tarik: Arabic *jebel*, hill, mountain, named after Tarik, leader of the Moors from North Africa who in A.D. 711 invaded and conquered Spain.)

COLOSSUS OF RHODES

"He doth bestride the narrow world
Like a Colossus."

WILLIAM SHAKESPEARE, *JULIUS CAESAR*

Shakespeare's Colossus (Latin, from the Greek *kolossos*, huge, enormous) is a reference to the famous bronze statue of the sun god Helios, which, according to legend, stood at (or astride) the entrance to the harbor at Rhodes, an island in the Aegean Sea not far off the southwestern coast of Turkey. The port of Rhodes (anciently, Rhodos) was commercially and politically important in the third century B.C.

The statue, said to have been about 110 feet high, was built by Chares of Lindus (or Lindos) in about 280 B.C. to commemorate the successful defense of Rhodes against Demetrius Poliorcetes in 304 B.C., Chares cleverly making use of the bronze weaponry, etc., left behind and collected as the spoils of war. It was said to hold aloft a light to act as a beacon to shipping, and was reckoned to be one of the Seven Wonders of the World. It was destroyed by an earthquake in 224 B.C.

Legend has it that the statue stood astride the entrance to the harbor so that sailing ships could pass between its legs, but this seems to be a figment of sixteenth-century imagination, since neither Strabo (63 B.C. to about A.D. 21, Greek geographer and historian) nor Pliny the Elder (A.D. 23–79, Roman naturalist and writer) mention this particular feature.

ULTIMA THULE

"Where the Northern Ocean, in vast whirls,
Boils round the naked melancholy isles
Of furthest Thule."

JAMES THOMSON, "AUTUMN"

Ultima Thule is the ancient Greek and Roman name for an island or region reputed to lie in the most northerly reaches of the world, where corn planted by the inhabitants grew but sparingly and ripened poorly, and the summer nights were long and bright.

The Roman philosopher Seneca (about 4 B.C. to A.D. 65) is reported by Palmer as saying that Thule was at "the end of the earth," a region known as Ultima Thule, which today means the farthest limit possible. Said to be six days' sail north of Britain, it is mentioned in an account by the Greek historian Polybius (about 205–123 B.C.) of a voyage made by Greek explorer Pytheas in about 300 B.C.

Geoffrey Ashe makes the point that Britain itself was so far away, so remote and improbably strange, that when the emperor Claudius (10 B.C. to A.D. 54) ordered his army to prepare for the invasion of that country in A.D. 43, the men promptly staged a mutiny, which of course had to be put down.

Pliny (A.D. 23–79), the Roman encyclopedist and writer, said of Thule, "It is an island in the Northern Ocean discovered by Pytheas after sailing six days from the Orcades"; *Orcades* was the Roman name for the Orkneys, probably from "orc," earlier a sea monster and later the old name for a whale; hence *orca*, the killer whale (see Orcs, Whales, and Leviathan, chapter 17).

Pytheas is not regarded as a very reliable source. Thule cannot be identified from his descriptions, but it is more likely to be Norway than Iceland; Iceland is often said to be the Thule of the north; other suggestions include Norway, Greenland, Denmark, and the Shetland Islands. The reports brought back from this far-off place reflect its strange and even unpleasant nature; the sea, for example, was said to be so thick that oars could not penetrate the surface. Perhaps this was the "stagnant sea" that Pytheas had heard about (and had readily believed), it being reported as a "mixture of earth, air, and water" bounding the earth in the far north.

Ashe makes the intriguing point that when the Greek writer Plutarch (about A.D. 46–120) recorded the Britons' accounts of this remote land (no doubt he gathered them from Roman officials who had visited Britain), he was unconsciously pointing us in the direction of a notion of America.

Sail west from Britain for five days, the Celts said, and you will encounter a land with islands nearby, where the night in summer was less than one hour long (this was very possibly southern Greenland). Journey past that, they added, and there is an expanse of sea some five hundred miles wide where the explorer will meet ice (Davis Strait springs to mind). Go farther, and you will see on the horizon a great continental land mass, where there is a large bay and more islands. Ashe writes that "Plutarch's bay could be the Gulf of Saint Lawrence," the mouth of which, according to Plutarch, lies on about the same latitude as the north end of the Caspian Sea (see Boland 1963 for his opinions concerning the earliest discoverers of the North American continent).

As with many other stories recorded in this collection, Thule reminds us of *Atlantis* (see Fabled Atlantis, chapter 16), that romantic saga beloved by many, a kind of quasi-American continent lurking behind the backdrop of history.

THE HESPERIDES

"Is not love a Hercules
Still climbing trees in the Hesperides?"

WILLIAM SHAKESPEARE, *LOVE'S LABOUR'S LOST*

Hesperides (Latin, from Greek *hesperis*, "western") was the name of the daughters of Atlas who, ably assisted by the serpent Ladon (for which purpose a thoughtful Providence had equipped it with a hundred heads), guarded the golden apples which Hera, the wife (and sister) of Zeus and therefore queen of heaven, had received as a marriage gift from Gaea, the earth goddess; the number of these guardian nymphs is variously given as from three to seven.

The apples were to be found on a tree that grew beyond the seas in a remote part of the western end of the world known as the Garden of the Hesperides; here they were secure against the depredations of thieves. According to Hesiod, the eighth-century B.C. Greek poet, the sisters dwelt on the river Oceanus; he gives them as four in number—Aegle, Arethusa, Erytheia, and Hesperia.

Stealing these golden apples was the eleventh labor of Hercules. Having no idea where the apples are kept, he seeks the advice of Nereus, "the old man of the sea" (not to be confused with the gentleman of the same name in the story of Sindbad the Sailor, chapter 3). Nereus is the father of the Nereids and is also a sea god, his special dominion being the Aegean Sea; he also knows where the apples can be found.

Not only is Nereus omniscient, he is also a master of shape-changing, this being one of the special abilities of gods of the sea; Poseidon possessed the same skills. When Hercules approaches Nereus, the old man turns himself into all sorts of slippery sea creatures in an effort to escape the attentions of his visitor, but Hercules overcomes him and compels him to reveal the whereabouts of the golden apples. It will not be easy, warns Nereus, and he tells Hercules that the trees that bear this desirable fruit are under the care of the Hesperides, who live near their father, Atlas, where Helios (also Helius) daily drives his chariot into Oceanus.

Following an extraordinary series of journeys and adventures (Hercules traverses Libya, Egypt, and Ethiopia, crosses into Asia, passes into the Caucasus, slays giants and other unsavory creatures, makes his way through the land of the Hyperboreans—the happy folk who dwell beyond Boreas, the North Wind—and frees Prometheus from his chains), Hercules then confronts Atlas, who bears the vault of heaven on his shoulders. He offers to shoulder the burden himself if Atlas will get the apples for him. Atlas, for a moment nobody's fool, sees a chance of being relieved forever of his heavy task and he gladly agrees. He hands over his burden, goes off, and in due course returns with the golden apples which, he informs Hercules, he will himself take back to King Eurystheus (he who had set Hercules the twelve labors in the first place), leaving Hercules to hold the world aloft in its accustomed position.

Hercules realizes that his massive strength is, for once, no use at all in getting out of this predicament, so, using his considerable wits, he asks Atlas to take the burden for a moment while he, Hercules, slips a cushion onto his own shoulders to ease the pressure of the heavy load. Sadly for him, Atlas foolishly agrees, whereupon Hercules takes up the apples and hurries back to Eurystheus, leaving Atlas to curse his own stupidity. Alas! Eurystheus, knowing that the golden apples belong to Hera, won't touch them with a barge pole, so Hercules offers them to Athene, goddess of wisdom, but she doesn't want them either and sends them right back to where they came from in the first place—the Hesperides.

One is inclined to commiserate with Hercules.

TARSHISH

"For the king had at sea a navy of Tharshish with the navy of Hiram:
once in three years came the navy of Tharshish,
bringing gold, and silver, ivory, and apes, and peacocks."

1 KINGS 10:22

Tarshish (also Tharshish) was an ancient country said to be located in what is now southern Spain and enjoying a significant sea trade in gold and silver. Tarshish seems to be the Tartessus referred to in an account by the Greek historian Herodotus (about 484–425 B.C.), who told of the voyage of a Greek ship trading to the western Mediterranean and being forced by storms past the Pillars of Hercules (see above). Finally it makes harbor in the Atlantic seaport of Tartessus, usually shown on old maps as Gades vel Tartessus (Gades is an old name for present-day Cadiz).

This journey supposedly took place in about 630 B.C.; for a long time after that this city was trading to the eastern Mediterranean ("Tharshish was thy merchant by reason of the multitude of all kind of riches; with silver, iron, tin, and lead, they traded in thy fairs").

Tartessos (almost certainly a variant of Tarshish/Tartessus) is yet another of those lost kingdoms by the sea that have generated much interest (for a prime example of the type, see Fabled Atlantis, chapter 16). Traders from Phoenicia and other places in the eastern Mediterranean reported Tartessos as being beyond the Pillars of Hercules, the port so rich that ships would return with their anchors cast in silver (a doubtful practice, one would think, as it is not at all unusual to lose one's anchor in a storm or through some other reason). The exotic trade in ivory and apes by way of Tarshish/Tartessus would, of course, have been out of Africa, across the straits.

Tarshish (Tartessus/Tartessos) was, in those days, the uttermost limits of the world; hence one is not surprised that Jonah chose it as the destination to which he could flee in order to escape God's wrath for his, Jonah's, refusal to journey to the city of Nineveh and cry out against its wickedness (see Jonah and the Whale, chapter 17).

TAPROBANE

"Towards the east from the land of Prester John is an isle mickle
[great, sizable] and large and good, the which is called Taprobane."
SIR JOHN MANDEVILLE

One of the most influential books to appear in the fourteenth century was ostensibly written by Sir John Mandeville, who compiled an account of his "travels" throughout Turkey, Armenia, Tartary (an early name for the region roughly corresponding with Mongolia today), Persia, Syria, Arabia, Egypt, Libya, Ethiopia, Amazonia, India, and China, this last on his exhausting itinerary being where he visited Prester John, the fabled Christian emperor of Asia ("prester" is Middle English for "priest," from the Old French *prestre*). Clearly, Prester John, a ruler of great renown, is a latter-day equivalent of Methuselah: not only is he mentioned in twelfth-century documents, in the thirteenth century he is lord over the Tartars, and a hundred years later he reappears as the emperor of Abyssinia.

It is likely that "John Mandeville" was the pen name of a Liège physician, Jean de Bourgogne, or Jehan à la Barbe. The book—in fact a compilation drawn from a number of other travel accounts—first appeared in French about 1356; it is known in English as *The Voyages and Travels of Sir John Mandeville, Knight.*

One of Mandeville's accounts concerns the "anthills of gold-dust," a story that created enormous interest among adventurers anxious not so much to see the ants (they were said to be as large and as ferocious as ill-treated dogs) but rather to view the anthills and, if at all possible, secure a number of them for further study. The anthills, Mandeville reports, were to be found on the island of Taprobane (the name used by the ancient Greeks and Romans for Ceylon, modern Sri Lanka, shown on some old maps as Taprobana and Taprobane). This island, said Mandeville, was large and productive, blessed with a mild climate, and visited by two summers and two winters each year, permitting the inhabitants to harvest two crops instead of the usual one (doubtless this is the narrator's version of the two different monsoons that annually sweep across Ceylon or Sri Lanka).

There are other marvels as well, but the one best calculated to attract the interest of ordinary people is the one concerning the ants. These ants were said to live on a mountain which, apparently, was composed solely of gold; furthermore, the creatures, rather than gather what food supplies ants of that size might require, instead spent their time refining the gold that their industry extracted daily from the mountain. Unhappily, not only were the ants very large indeed, they were also possessed of a vicious and curmudgeonly nature, such that men were loath to go anywhere near them. One day, however, they discovered that the ants commonly retreated below during the worst of the heat of the day, and it was then but a matter of a few moments to drive all the available beasts of burden up the mountainside and load them with as many sacks of gold as each could carry.

Doubtless many a naive adventurer, on hearing of this story, set sail from Europe with hope in his heart and a good many empty sacks in his baggage.

DISTANT OPHIR

"And king Solomon made a navy of ships in Ezion-geber,
which is beside Eloth, on the shore of the Red Sea, in the land of Edom.
And Hiram sent in the navy his servants, shipmen that had knowledge
of the sea, with the servants of Solomon. And they came to Ophir,
and fetched from thence gold, four hundred and twenty talents,
and brought it to King Solomon."

1 KINGS 9:26–28

Ophir is the now-lost realm of biblical fame, recorded in the Old Testament for the fine quality of its gold, which was brought to Solomon by his Tyrian sailors. Ezion-geber, the point of departure for Solomon's ships, lay at the head of the Gulf of Aqaba on the Red Sea, which suggests that the expedition's destination lay somewhere to the south—and the question that has intrigued scholars for generations is: where? The ancient ruins discovered in Zimbabwe have been put forward as a possible site for Ophir, but they don't seem to be old enough. Zanzibar on the east coast of Africa has also been mentioned, but that too is a very doubtful proposition.

Because the voyage of Solomon's gold convoy apparently occupied some three years, more distant lands have been sought as an answer to the question of *where?*, such as the delta of the River Indus (near what is now Karachi in Pakistan), Johore in southern Malaysia, Goa on the west coast of India, Malabar on the southwest coast of India, Malacca (earlier, Malaka) on the west coast of Malaysia, and Sumatra—each of these has been suggested as the possible original Ophir; even Spain, Armenia, Phrygia (now Anatolia, central Turkey), and distant Peru have had their supporters.

It is interesting to note that on the coast of Abyssinia (modern Ethiopia) there is a people who call themselves the Aphar; it does not take much imagination to derive "Ophir" from "Aphar." One atlas of ancient and classical geography suggests that Ophir might have been located in the region of Ceylon (now Sri Lanka).

However, it seems most likely that Ophir is to be found closer to home, so to speak—specifically, it probably once existed in Arabia, perhaps on the west coast bordering the Red Sea or on the south coast facing the Arabian Sea. On the other hand, Charles Boland is quite clear as to its ancient whereabouts: "When King Solomon built his fabulous temple . . . he employed the ships of Tarshish to journey to Ophir (India)."

But wherever this ancient land might have existed in the past, or whether indeed it existed at all, England's onetime poet laureate, John Masefield (1878–1967), captured the timeless romance of a voyage that sets sail down the Red Sea of biblical times in search of gold and other precious commodities in his gloriously resonant poem "Cargoes":

Quinquireme of Nineveh from distant Ophir
Rowing home to haven in sunny Palestine,
With a cargo of ivory,
And apes and peacocks,
Sandalwood, cedarwood, and sweet white wine.

Stately Spanish galleon coming from the Isthmus,
Dipping through the Tropics by the palm-green shores,
With a cargo of diamonds,
Emeralds, amethysts,
Topazes, and cinnamon, and gold moidores.

Dirty British coaster with a salt-caked smoke stack
Butting through the Channel in the mad March days,
With a cargo of Tyne coal,
Road-rail, pig-lead,
Firewood, iron-ware, and cheap tin trays.

MAGNETIC ISLANDS

"Draw out with credulous desire . . .
As the magnetic hardest iron draws."

JOHN MILTON, "PARADISE REGAINED"

The so-called Magnetic Islands were reported by the second-century Greek mathe-matician, astronomer, and geographer Ptolemy. He said certain islands contained such a powerful concentration of lodestone that ships that had been fastened with iron nails were inexorably drawn toward them. What is more, if the lodestone were sufficiently pure, the ship's nails would immediately be extracted from the vessel's timber without so much as a by-your-leave, thus permitting the vessel's now disen-cumbered planks, ribs, and frames to collapse in a heap on the surface of the sea, with the crew presumably clinging to what they might.

There is a reference to the Magnetic Islands in the *Arabian Nights* (a collection of these Indian, Persian, and Arabian stories first appeared in Arabic in about A.D. 850). Sir John Mandeville, the supposed compiler of the book of travels originally written in French, places the Magnetic Islands in Asia. An island in Halifax Bay, Queensland (Eastern Australia), was named Magnetic Island by Captain Cook in 1770 because—or so it seemed to him—his ship's compass was adversely affected by metallic ore in the rocks, but later navigators have been unable to confirm this.

HY BRASIL

"The Islands of Aran . . . are still believed by many of the peasantry
to be the nearest land to the far-famed island of O'Brazil or Hy Brasail,
the blessed paradise of the pagan Irish. It is supposed even to be visible
from the cliffs on particular and rare occasions."

MURRAY'S *HANDBOOK FOR TRAVELLERS IN IRELAND*

Hy Brasil (also known as Brasil, Brazil, Hi Brasil, Hy-Breasail, Hy Brazil, and Isle of Brazil) is another far-off island, this one circular, placed by knowing geographers in various parts of the Atlantic—sometimes attached to the Azores group in the North Atlantic, west of Portugal, where it was known as the Isle de Brazi (shown as such in the Venetian map of Andrea Bianco in 1436), at other times located hundreds of miles due west of Ireland.

The word *Brasil* or *Brazil* is from the Portuguese *braza*, *brassa*, meaning heat, coals (the source of *brazier*, a pan for charcoal); this in turn refers to the red dye obtained from brazilwood (earlier Medieval Latin, *brasilium*), the wood brought from the East for making red dye.

Hy Brasil was the brainchild of Pliny the Elder (A.D. 23–79), Roman naturalist, encyclopedist, and writer. It was said to be a paradise, and explorers searched assiduously for it; so convinced were early geographers of its existence that the island was included in maps and charts for nearly two thousand years. J. Purdy's chart of 1830 confidently advises the mariner that "Brazil Rock" can be found at 51°10' N and 15°50' W, and it appears on A. G. Findlay's maritime chart of currents of 1853; in 1865, however, Findlay had rejected the notion of Brazil Island as well as some other legendary islands.

When the Portuguese navigator Pedro Alvares Cabral (about 1467–1520) discovered a large "island" in the southwest Atlantic on April 22 in the year 1500, he named it Tierra da Vera Cruz but this was later changed to Brasil, no doubt because cartographers thought that he had discovered the elusive island of that name (and, in any event, "Brazil" had long become familiar as a geographical place-name). In 1674 a Scottish sea captain named Nisbet claimed that he had landed on Hy Brasil; it was, he said, inhabited by gigantic black rabbits and a magician in a castle; unfortunately for both science and maritime history, he was unable to produce any evidence of what he had seen.

ISLAND OF OGYGIA

"But not in silence pass Calypso's isles."
GEORGE GORDON, LORD BYRON, "CHILDE HAROLD'S PILGRIMAGE"

Ogygia ("navel of the earth") is the island on which Odysseus (see The *Odyssey*, chapter 4) was washed ashore after his ship had been split in two by the wrath of Zeus, punishing his disobedient crew, who had sought to alleviate their extreme hunger by killing and eating the cattle belonging to Helios on the island of Thrinacia. The vessel sinks and all except Odysseus are drowned.

After drifting for nine days toward the terrible monster Scylla and the equally fearful whirlpool Charybdis, both situated in the Straits of Messina, Odysseus is deposited on the beach of Ogygia and is welcomed by the nymph Calypso, a daughter of Atlas and ruler of the island (see Scylla and Charybdis, chapter 1). Calypso detains Odysseus for seven years, promising him immortality and eternal youth if he will consent to remain with her and be her husband; but although he willingly stays with her he cannot forget his home in Ithaca; neither can he cease yearning for his wife, Penelope—which gives us some idea of either what a ditherer he was or how charming Calypso was.

Finally Athene, goddess of wisdom and the protector of Odysseus, persuades Zeus to take pity on him: Calypso is ordered to release him and provide him with a raft for his further journey. He leaves Ogygia, and encounters yet more difficulties during his long and somewhat tiresome journey back to Ithaca.

ISLAND OF DELOS

"Delos, of a most barren aspect, however flowery in fable, but desolate impact."
HERMAN MELVILLE, *JOURNAL OF A VISIT TO EUROPE AND THE LEVANT*

Delos (also Dhilos) is the smallest island of the Cyclades (Greek *Kikladhes* from *kyklos*, "ring," from the fact that the islands form a ring around Delos), in the Aegean Sea about halfway between southern Greece and the west coast of Turkey. The island was sacred to Apollo, being his legendary birthplace. Delos owes something to maritime legend because of the reputed manner of its own birth

It was said to have been called out of the deep by Poseidon, the Greek god of the sea, thence to remain a floating island until Zeus secured it by chaining it to the seabed as a reward for its providing a home to Leto, whom he loved and who, according to other versions of the legend, had previously been his mistress or his wife, thereby on both counts earning the undying hatred of his present spouse, Hera. Leto was the daughter of the Titans Coeus and Phoebe, she being "dark-robed and ever mild and gentle," in the words of the epic poet Hesiod (? 700 B.C.).

As a result of one or the other of the relationships enjoyed by Zeus and Leto (i.e., nuptial or prenuptial) she found herself with child but was compelled by Hera's implacable hostility to wander from land to land in search of a haven wherein she could safely be delivered of the fruits of this liaison. At last she found refuge on the desolate island of Ortygia (the ancient name for Delos), which until then had been wandering around the Aegean in an apparently quite carefree manner.

When finally she managed to scramble onto its rocky surface (the isle had been pummeled about somewhat by the rude Mediterranean wind, thus affording her no easy access to safety), her request for permission to stay there for the foreseeable future was gladly given. Safe and sound at last, Leto gave birth to Apollo and his twin sister Artemis (Diana).

According to the legend, four huge stone pillars sprouted from the seabed to support the island and anchor it securely; another version asserts that Zeus chained it firmly in place. Whichever ancient constructional method was employed, the island from that day on stayed put.

LEMURIA, LOST CONTINENT

"Madagastar [sic], one of the greatest and richest
Isles of the World, three thousand miles in circuit,
inhabited by Saracens, governed by foure old men."

MARCO POLO

Lemuria is the lost land supposed once to have connected Madagascar with India and Sumatra and the Malay Archipelago in prehistoric times and thought by German biologist and philosopher Ernst Heinrich Haeckel (1834–1919) to be the original habitat of the lemur (from Latin *lemures*, "spirits of the dead," a name suggested by the animal's ghostlike face); thus geologists in the late 1800s gave the name Lemuria to this putative sunken continent. Lemuria is also reckoned by some to have been the original Garden of Eden and the cradle of the human race.

Lemuria, as with nearly all the lost and/or submerged islands and continents in this book, was said to be inhabited by people of a distinctive nature; but where some far-off paradise such as Bensalem or the Island of Joy boasted folk of a happy and settled disposition, blessed by a benevolent climate and free of all sickness and worry, Lemuria was obliged to support a race of people said to be some fifteen feet tall. What is more (according to the Russian theosophist Madame Helena P. Blavatsky, 1831–1891, the cofounder of Theosophy), these brown-skinned people were hermaphrodites, equipped with flat faces and enormous hands and feet, and some of them possessed a third eye in the back of the head. Blavatsky also advised the world that these people had highly developed psychic powers and communicated by telepathy. These folk also owned, she said, two front eyes set so far apart on the front of their faces that they could also see sideways.

Sadly, it is thought that the Lemurians were never very intelligent. Possibly incidental to this fact, there are people who believe that the lost continent of Lemuria is beginning to rise again. Such folk might also wish to keep an eye out for a resurfacing Atlantis (see Fabled Atlantis, chapter 16), the happy land to which, asserts Blavatsky, the Lemurians had earlier migrated.

LOST LAND OF LYONESSE

"Of faery damsels met in forest wide
By knights of Logres, or of Lyones,
Lancelot, or Pelleas, or Pellenore."

JOHN MILTON, "PARADISE REGAINED"

Also known as Logris, Logres, Lugdunensis, Lyonesse is the fabled land said to be found between Land's End and the Scilly Isles in the Atlantic Ocean, southwest of Land's End, Cornwall. It is the reputed birthplace of King Arthur and is also said to be the home of the remnants of his court; the sea flooded the land after his knights had passed to safety there, in order to prevent their being followed. Early legends have it that there was only one survivor of this flooding, Trevilian (or Tre-villon), who apparently had wit and time enough to leap on his horse and dash for safety to Cornwall.

Subsequently, Cornish fishermen (who are well known among themselves for possessing the gift of second sight) have reported seeing the outlines of castle turrets beneath the sea, and they frequently, it is said, converse with Mermaids (chapter 15) and "piskies" (presumably members of the fairy branch of subaquatic beings).

Lyonesse may be a corrupted form of *Leonais* in Brittany or the Scottish *Lothian*, which in Old French was *Loenois*; it is associated with the story of Tristan and Isolde by means of a tenuous connection with King Arthur and his famed Round Table. Lyonesse was by all accounts a rich land that contained 140 churches, but the only remaining traces of this splendor are said to be the Scilly Isles themselves and Saint Michael's Mount, a rocky island connected to the south coast of Cornwall by a causeway that is exposed only at low tide.

3

LEGENDARY VOYAGES

F or thousands of years, ever since mankind first devised a hull and a sail to drive it, people have been going down to the sea and setting off across it, to see what lay beyond the horizon.

So were born the great explorers. Their common goal was to discover and explore unknown territories, usually for the purposes of trade, colonial conquest, or perhaps—as in the case of Thor Heyerdahl (see *Kon-Tiki* Expedition below) or Captain James Cook (see chapter 8)—to test the soundness of some scientific theory. Others set off to see what lay beyond the next mountain range, what peoples inhabited the regions further upriver, what opportunities might be awaiting on the far side of the "great waters."

As Hampden points out in her collection of the important work of Richard Hakluyt (1552–1616), there was much to discover: in 1400 European knowledge of the world scarcely extended beyond the boundaries of Western Europe. Stories of fabled regions like China and Japan and other far distant places soon became the impetus for bold and resourceful explorers to separate fact from fiction. Thus was ushered in a period of intense and widespread discovery, a kind of renaissance of geography.

SINDBAD THE SAILOR

"I used to wish the Arabian Tales were true."

JOHN HENRY, CARDINAL NEWMAN, *HISTORY OF MY RELIGIOUS OPINIONS*

In the set of tales originally known as *Sindbad of the Sea,* Sindbad is the hero of the well-known story of that name—too well known, perhaps, familiarity breeding a carelessness with its spelling: "Sinbad" is more often seen than the correct "Sindbad," due either to a Western preoccupation with the notion of "sin" or to a laziness in matters of orthography. The Sindbad tales appear in *The Arabian Nights* (properly, *The Thousand and One Nights,* and even more accurately, *The Thousand Nights and One Night,* sometimes called simply *The Arabian Nights' Entertainment;* the Sindbad portions occur on nights 536–566).

The whole is a set of 1,001 tales devised supposedly by *Scheherezade* (sometimes Shahrazad) as a nightly entertainment for her husband *Sultan Schariah* (or Shahryar, also Shahriah), of Baghdad, in order to postpone her execution the morning following the consummation of their marriage. Schariah has resolved to avenge himself for the infidelity of his first wife, the sultana, by taking a new wife every night and having her strangled the next morning (or her head chopped off, one of the characteristics of *The Arabian Nights* being that its sources are many and various and are therefore rarely in close agreement with each other in some matters of detail).

Scheherezade, quite naturally, wishes to avoid this unhappy fate, so with much artifice and by enlisting the help of her younger sister Dunyazadiad (or Dunyazad) she amuses him with a tale for each of the ensuing 1,001 nights, making sure that each tale is not finished until the next night or some other night thereafter, at which time she immediately launches into a new tale.

Finally her husband Schariah (she has, not surprisingly, borne him a number of children—three boys—by the end of the final tale) responds to her plea to be allowed to rear his children in a manner that befits his wisdom and fame. Full of admiration for her prodigious skill in whiling away the time so pleasantly, Schariah is moved to revoke his earlier decree, and he declares his love for her. They are reconciled and remain happily so until eventually, in the somber words that seem to catch the very echoes of the original teller of tales, "there came to them the Destroyer of delights, the Sunderer of societies and the Garnerer of graveyards."

The narrator's account of Scheherezade herself at the beginning of *The Arabian Nights* provides the framework for the tales that make up the whole, many of which contain their own stories-within-stories, much like a set of Chinese boxes. Readers will recognize the technique of the frame story as being typical of that master teller of tales Joseph Conrad, for whom the narrator Marlow is as important an element in some of his stories (e.g., *Lord Jim* and *Heart of Darkness*) as Scheherezade is in *The Arabian Nights*.

"Sindbad the Sailor" is only one of the best-remembered tales in this collection; others include "Ali Baba and the Forty Thieves" (a story that later lent itself admirably to the inventive skills of Hollywood) and "Aladdin and His Magic Lamp" (or, "The Story of Aladdin and the Slave of the Lamp").

The Arabian Nights as a whole is a collection of Asian stories that appeared in an Arabic text in the fourteenth or fifteenth century, but they reach much farther back in time to India, whence they found their way into the hands of Persian and Arabian storytellers. The Persian collection, known as *Hazar Afsana*, "A Thousand Tales," was translated into Arabic in about A.D. 850. The earliest stories (including the one about Sindbad) probably date back to the eighth century, with others appearing as late as the sixteenth century.

The stories were first introduced into Europe in a twelve-volume French translation by Antoine Galland (1647–1715). Other translations followed, the first English version being probably that of an anonymous hack writer in the period 1704–17. The most celebrated version is that of Sir Richard Burton (1821–1890); his sixteen-volume edition was published in the Indian city of Benares (now Varanasi) in 1885–88 and became widely known and much admired despite being an unexpurgated text—or indeed perhaps because of that fact.

Arab scholars generally dismiss *The Arabian Nights* as having no relevance to classical Arabic literature, but the tales have achieved an enduring popularity with Europeans, for whom the Orient exudes an endlessly fascinating aura of mystery and romance.

Sindbad was a wealthy citizen of Baghdad, called "The Sailor" because of the seven voyages he had undertaken during his lifetime. We learn of these matters through Sindbad the Porter, who (as Scheherezade tells Schariah) one day finds himself outside the gate of a rich merchant, where he savors the perfume of the beautiful garden within and hears the pleasant sound of music and sweet voices. "Allah," he sings, "teach us thy patience that we may rejoice in thee, no matter what our fate." The master of the house, hearing this paean of praise to the virtues of patience, sends for the porter and sets food and drink in front of him. When the porter has finished his repast the merchant asks to know his name and trade.

"I am Sindbad the Porter," he says, "I carry other people's goods for hire."

"How strange," remarks the merchant, "for my name too is Sindbad—men call me Sindbad the Sailor—and I too have carried burdens on my back and have known many trials in my life; mayhap I can lay before you proof that suffering and hardship in life are a sure path to happiness and prosperity," and forthwith he regales the porter with an account of each of the seven voyages that brought him, Sindbad the Sailor, great wealth and good cheer.

Here follows a brief account of each of the voyages of Sindbad.

Voyage the First

When he is a young man and reckoned rich, Sindbad nevertheless squanders his fortune in the idle pursuits that are common to that age in life; anxious to recoup his losses he buys various trade goods and sets sail for foreign parts where he might sell his cargo for a good profit. His ship anchors off an island in the Indian Ocean and the crew go ashore and prepare a fire so they might eat; but the island is in fact a large whale basking, asleep, on the surface. It awakes and angrily dives to the bottom of the sea, leaving Sindbad and his companions foundering in the water. They are rescued by a passing vessel and Sindbad returns home (see Voyages of Saint Brendan below for a curiously similar story).

Voyage the Second

Tired of life in the city, Sindbad sets sail once more in search of fame and fortune. His ship stops at an island to take on fresh water, Sindbad falls asleep nearby, and alas! the vessel sails away without him. Searching the island, he finds the nest and egg of a roc (Spanish *rocho, ruc,* from Arabic *rukh;* a legendary white bird of enormous size and so strong that it can encircle an elephant in its talons and carry it to its nest, where it may devour it at leisure). Sindbad hides in the nest, and when the roc returns he clamps himself to its leg and the bird flies away to the Valley of Diamonds.

Local merchants line the cliffs (the valley is too steep for them to negotiate), whence they throw pieces of meat to the valley floor below. The diamonds that litter the ground stick to the meat; the birds carry the meat to their cliffside nests and the merchants climb down and steal the diamonds when the birds have gone off again. Sindbad fastens himself to a piece of meat and is lifted by a roc to its nest, whereupon he fills his pockets with the diamonds strewn nearby and, now rescued by the merchants, returns to Baghdad wealthy beyond his dreams.

Voyage the Third

Setting sail yet again, Sindbad and his companions are captured by savage dwarfs and taken off to an island inhabited by a ferocious one-eyed giant, who immediately begins devouring the sailors one by one. In desperation Sindbad heats two pieces of iron and thrusts them into the monster's eye (one is sharply reminded here of

Ulysses and the Cyclops; see The *Odyssey*, chapter 4). The giant, much put out, so to speak, summons his fellow giants, who then eat up most of the remaining men. Happily, Sindbad and two others escape, but a serpent entices them to another island, where the wretched beast attempts to consume Sindbad, who luckily thwarts its wicked intentions by building a wooden fort about his body. A passing ship saves him, and he joins its crew.

Voyage the Fourth

The ship is wrecked and Sindbad and the rest of the crew are cast ashore on an island where they are captured and thrown into prison by cannibals, who feed the sailors well so as to fatten them for table; but Sindbad starves himself in order to remain thin and therefore appear unattractive as victuals.

By various subterfuges Sindbad escapes from the cannibals, and after many travails reaches a kingdom where the use of bridle and stirrup is quite unknown, whereupon he promptly reinvents them, in the process making himself not only rich but also the husband of the king's daughter, the king being well pleased with the stranger. She dies, however, and following local custom Sindbad is promptly immured with her body in the city's catacombs. Not much caring for this, Sindbad makes his way out of the catacomb, meanwhile ransacking the surrounding bodies for their jewels, an act of desecration that permits him to return to Baghdad further enriched.

Voyage the Fifth

Yet again Sindbad sets sail, and yet again his ship suffers calamity, this time from two rocs who (or which), seeking vengeance for the destruction of their almost-hatched egg at the hands of the crew (who feloniously compound their crime by taking the chick aboard and eating it), sink the vessel by bombing it with an enormous boulder. Clinging to wreckage, Sindbad is washed ashore onto an island of plenty, where he comes across an old and apparently infirm gentleman sitting by a stream. Thinking that the fellow would welcome some help, Sindbad takes him on his back, whereupon the old man wraps his arms and legs around his benefactor's neck so tightly that Sindbad is nearly strangled. In this manner Sindbad is tormented by the old man, who cannot be dislodged.

One day Sindbad makes some liquor from nearby grapes and drinks it to forget his woes; then, sensing a possibility, he gives some to the old man, who promptly gets falling-down drunk, whereupon Sindbad seizes a boulder and hurls it against the wretched fellow's head, thereby killing him. He is rescued once more by a passing ship, where he learns that the old man is known as Sheik a-Bahr, the Old Man of the Sea, and further that he, Sindbad, is the first ever to escape his clutches, every other man so captured being ridden until he dropped, quickly strangled by the old man, and then just as quickly eaten.

Voyage the Sixth

On this adventure Sindbad's ship is wrecked on a deserted and barren island. Casting round its shores he finds not only many precious stones but also an underground watercourse. He builds a raft and sails off on this river, fetching up at the city of Serendip (which also happens to be the ancient name for Ceylon, now Sri Lanka). Here he is welcomed by the king, who bestows even greater wealth on him and provides passage back to his own country, together with a present for the Caliph of Baghdad (Harun al-Rashid, also Haroun al-Raschid, about 763–809; already famous as the ruler of that city, he becomes almost a legendary hero in *The Arabian Nights*).

Voyage the Seventh

Harun al-Rashid sends Sindbad back to Serendip with presents and felicitations for the king of that happy country; but, sadly, our much-traveled wanderer, by now a very wealthy man, is captured by a gang of pirates who sell him to a merchant whose livelihood comes from ivory—that is to say, Sindbad becomes an elephant hunter. By now a man of many parts, Sindbad is so successful at this trade that he discovers what all other men have long sought but failed to find: that remote and hitherto unknown country from which no elephant returns; that is, the place where according to legend these animals customarily go to die when their time is at hand.

Sindbad naturally possesses himself of the mountain of ivory that has there accumulated, and as a reward for his pains the merchant gives him his freedom and a handsome cargo of ivory, both of which allow Sindbad to return to Baghdad with a happy heart and a heavy purse. In the fullness of time he meets Sindbad the Porter, to whom he is pleased to impart an account of his many adventures.

What the Porter then does with this valuable knowledge is not known.

GULLIVER'S TRAVELS

"Gull: A simple credulous fellow, easily cheated."
FRANCIS GROSE, *DICTIONARY OF THE VULGAR TONGUE*

Gulliver's Travels by Jonathan Swift (1667–1745) was published in 1726; it is an extraordinary tale of imaginary travel and curious adventure undertaken by the narrator, one Lemuel Gulliver, a ship's surgeon who sees more of the world than he had bargained for.

Swift was one of the sharpest satirists in the English language—see, for example, his brilliant essay "A Modest Proposal"—so it is well to keep in mind that "Gulliver" is suspiciously similar in sound to "gullible." *Gulliver's Travels* is included here because of the story's many references to voyages, far-off islands, and strange peoples across the seas—a reminder, perhaps, of the utopian view that we generally associate with far-off places.

Gulliver's first voyage ends in shipwreck on the island of Lilliput, where the inhabitants are some six inches tall and everything else—buildings, trees, animals, etc.—is in the same proportion: an inch to the foot compared to the ordinary world as we know it. The neighboring country across a nearby narrow channel is called Blefuscu, the inhabitants of which are the same size as those of Lilliput; both countries are perpetually at war with each other, while at the same time engaging in endless internecine feuds among themselves. Eventually Gulliver spies an overturned rowboat—a remnant of his earlier wrecking—floating some distance offshore; he persuades the Lilliputians to tow it ashore with their fleet of ships and later, after repairing it, he makes good his escape.

On his second voyage Gulliver is mistakenly left ashore by his shipmates in the land of Brobdingnag, a country of giants where everything else is in like manner proportionately huge (the mountains, for example, are nearly thirty miles high and are impassable, thus allowing Brobdingnag to remain happily isolated from the rest of the world). These people, however, are cultured and civilized in inverse proportion to the barbaric ignorance of the Lilliputians.

Here Gulliver is well treated; he learns their language and is encouraged to travel around the kingdom, the king providing him with a furnished box as his room in which he accompanies the royal family on their journeys. One day, near the coast, Gulliver's box is seized by an enormous eagle and carried far out to sea; other birds attack the eagle, which thereupon prudently drops the box into the ocean. An English ship (which happens to be nearby) fishes both box and Gulliver aboard, and he is safely returned to his homeland.

Not at all daunted, Gulliver sets out on yet a third voyage, wherein he is captured by pirates and cruelly set adrift in a small boat; eventually he makes his way to a rocky outcrop from which he descries an island floating above his very head. He is rescued—after a good deal of waving and shouting to attract the attention of men who are fishing from the island's edge—and is hauled aboard (or hauled an-island) by means of a chain. This is the floating island of Laputa, capital city of the same name, beneath which lies the land of Balnibarbi, which is under the rule of the island.

Balnibarbi contains an odd collection of scientists, philosophers, and musicians, all engaged in pursuing various scientific and mathematical projects (one scientist, for example, has spent his life devising experiments for the extraction of sunbeams from cucumbers). So absorbed are they in their speculations (all of which prove to be utterly useless and impractical) that in everyday matters of agriculture and animal husbandry they are complete and unqualified fools. This sad deficiency is reflected in the country's unhappy state of economy, where the combined efforts of science have marshaled the citizens within the confining realms of poverty and brought the countryside close to utter ruin.

Gulliver, dismayed by what he sees, journeys by ship to the island of Glubb-dubdrib, where dwell sorcerers and magicians; it is a pleasant and fertile place but it conceals a secret: the citizens are in fact the spirits of the dead. Nevertheless, before Gulliver leaves this strange place he is able, by means of obliging sorcerers, to summon up famous men from the past, whereby he learns of the ways in which the world has sadly long been deceived by historians. He sails on, this time to Luggnagg, the land of the Struldbruggs, a people who possess what Gulliver had once thought eminently desirable: everlasting life; but alas! life for these folk is one of such bitter misery that Luggnag proves to be one of Gulliver's more melancholy adventures.

Gulliver's final voyage is as captain of a ship, but again he encounters travail and trouble with his crew—they raise a mutiny against him and cast him ashore in the land of the Houyhnhnms, the happy abode of horses who, he discovers to his great delight, are amply possessed of reason, civility, wisdom, and eminent good sense (one cannot help being impressed by Swift's ability to conjure up strange names for strange people and places, all of which suggest some meaning; "Houyhnhnm," for example, is a way of sounding a horse's whinny, and indeed is a kind of echo of the word "whinny").

In Gulliver's view the Houyhnhnms are "abounding in all excellencies," which sadly cannot be claimed of the animal-like humans who also live on this island. These are the Yahoos, the superbly wretched, ignorant, unintelligent, and in all other ways unprepossessing servants and beasts of burden for the Houyhnhnms themselves. Indeed, Gulliver is so disgusted by the Yahoos that he becomes estranged from his own kind, so much so that when he finally returns home and is welcomed by his family, he recoils from them in profound disgust. Nevertheless, Gulliver learns to adjust, and he is a better man for his experiences.

Although the tale created an enormous stir of interest and acclaim when it was published, it was reported to Swift that an Irish bishop had denounced the book, saying that it "was full of improbable lies, and for his part he hardly believed a word of it."

HANNO THE NAVIGATOR

"The winds and waves are always on the side of the ablest navigators."
EDWARD GIBBON, *DECLINE AND FALL OF THE ROMAN EMPIRE*

The Phoenician Hanno was a citizen of Carthage (an ancient city-state in northern Africa near modern Tunis, founded in 814–813 B.C.). The dates of his birth and death are obscure, but he is known to have flourished about 500 B.C.

Some two thousand years before the epic voyage of Bartolomeu Dias, who rounded the southern extremity of the African continent in 1488, Hanno sailed out of the Mediterranean and beyond the Pillars of Hercules—an astonishing and extraordinary act of faith and courage at a time when nothing was known about the world beyond the immediate horizon except that it was flat and that it was therefore exceedingly dangerous to venture to the edge. It was also known that the seas were inhabited throughout by the most terrifying monsters (see, for example, Our Flat Earth, chapter 19, and Monster Kraken, chapter 17).

That Hanno and his intrepid crew, in complete ignorance of what really lay ahead, should have chosen to confront these twin perils deserves our unqualified admiration. In about 500 B.C. Hanno, with some sixty galleys filled with settlers, voyaged down the west coast of Africa to explore and set up a colony. The expedition, if it kept the coast in sight (likely, as this was the easiest way to navigate unknown seas, unless of course Hanno was drawing on information gleaned by even earlier explorers—the Phoenicians a century earlier, perhaps; see below), would have passed with the Canary Islands off to starboard, though not necessarily in sight, the nearest of these islands being some 70 miles offshore. He seems to have reached at least as far as present-day Sierra Leone, a voyage of almost 3,000 miles from the entrance to the Mediterranean.

What Hanno did there, and whether or not steps were taken to establish a colony, appears to be lost to history: "How and when Africa swallowed these settlers is hidden by the mists of time." Boland, however, is rather more confident: "Hanno . . . sailed out beyond the Pillars of Hercules and established many African colonies along the western coast."

Hanno wrote an account of this voyage, inscribed on a clay tablet in the Phoenician language; he reported seeing crocodiles, hippopotamuses, and men dressed in animal skins. The tablet was hung in the temple of Bel at Carthage on his return. Oskar Seyffert states that a Greek translation of this account, known as *Hannonis Periplus*, still survives, one of the oldest examples of geographical science available to us.

It is worth keeping in mind that Herodotus (about 484–425 B.C.), the famous Greek historian, tells us—with considerable skepticism—of a circumnavigation of Africa made by Phoenician seamen around 600–595 B.C., a story still much disputed by scholars. According to Herodotus, some Phoenician sailors were ordered by Pharaoh Necos of Egypt to sail south from Egypt, their object eventually to reach the Pillars of Hercules. As we know, such a journey would have entailed sailing down the Red Sea and into the Indian Ocean (which in those times was thought to be part of the Red Sea), thence clockwise west around the southern tip of the continent and north into the Atlantic to the entrance to the Mediterranean—an epic voyage by any measure. They supposedly set off in summer (one shudders at the thought of the fierce heat in the Red Sea at that season; see Traveling POSH, chapter 6), lived ashore during the winters to grow food, and arrived at the entrance to the Mediterranean in the third year of their voyage.

Herodotus claims that the account these men gave of their journey contained an unacceptable geographical error: "On their return, they declared—I for my part do not believe them, but perhaps others may—that in sailing round Libya [as the African continent was called by the ancients] they had the sun upon their right hand." Herodotus knew a great deal about the geography of Europe, having himself traveled much of the Mediterranean, and he frequently questioned other travelers about their experiences; but what he seemed not to understand was that the Phoenicians were saying that they had in fact sailed *south of the Equator.* Only someone who had actually been there could possibly have made this report about the sun being on the right hand when facing west; no dweller in the Mediterranean could otherwise have had this experience. Nobody had ever ventured that far south before.

The voyage must have been a terrifying experience, to say the least. When they had set out from Egypt the midday sun would have had a southerly aspect; then as they traveled south it would increasingly have approached the overhead position, until south of the Tropic of Capricorn it would have appeared to be slipping farther northward. To make matters even worse, their prime source of navigation—the Pole Star—would gradually have vanished altogether. Add to this the fact that they had no idea where or when the coast would finally (if at all) tend to the west and, they hoped, northward, then you have the makings of an extraordinary accomplishment, one that far outweighs the achievements of the explorers who set out across the ocean two thousand years later armed with navigational instruments and a magnetic compass.

If Herodotus's account of this voyage that was set in train by Necos is true, then in Edward Burman's words it "must rank with the greatest voyages in the history of mankind—far superior in its audacity and courage to that of Columbus." (See also Christopher Columbus, chapter 8, and Prince Madoc, below.)

Prince Madoc of Wales

"Madoc will be read, when Homer and Virgil are forgotten."
Richard Porson, *Epigram: On Latin Gerunds*

Madoc (also Madog), a Welsh prince, son of Owain Gwynned (1137–1169), was claimed by some to be the discoverer of America. Madoc is said to have left Wales because of family quarreling, sailing west in 1170 across the North Atlantic with 120 people on board two ships from Aber-Cerrig-Gwynion near Rhos-on-Sea, finally landing at what is now Mobile Bay in Alabama. Finding matters much to his liking in this new land, Madoc settled his original companions along the Mississippi and (so the story goes) went back to Wales, loaded ten ships with willing settlers, and returned to his colony. These settlers gradually moved into the northern reaches of the Mississippi as far as the Dakotas, where they apparently thrived and presumably managed an accommodation with the Indian tribes of the region, probably the Pawnee and the Sioux (something rarely achieved by other settlers during the following seven hundred years).

In time the descendants of these settlers supposedly became the legendary Welsh-speaking Mandan Indians, about whom much has been said and written but alas! precious little proved. It is claimed that the Mandan people built boats in the style of the coracle, which of course is a Celtic craft, and when later settlers from other areas saw these, the myth was given added impetus. The Mandans as a recognizable group have been extinct since the nineteenth century because of assimilation with others and diseases introduced by white soldiers and settlers. There are fortifications north of Mobile Bay which enthusiasts claim are built in the style of castles in pre-Norman Wales, but many commentators assert that in fact no authentic trace of a Welsh-speaking tribe of Indians can be found.

Boland includes an extract from Hakluyt's earlier book of 1582 (some sixteen years before his famous *The Principal Navigations* appeared; see Hakluyt in the bibliography), in which Hakluyt is retelling a tale told to him by Gutton Owen, a Welsh bard, who in turn allegedly found the story of Prince Madoc's voyage in the Abbey of Conway in North Wales. Part of Owen's account follows.

> *Madoc . . . left the land in contentions betwixt his brethren and prepared certain ships with men and munitions and sought adventures by seas, sailing west and leaving the coast of Ireland so farre north, that he came to a land unknown, where he saw many strange things.*
>
> *This land must needs be some parts of the Country, of which the Spanyards affirm themselves to be the first Finders since Hanno's Time [see Hanno the Navigator above], whereupon it is manifest that the country was by Britons discovered long before Columbus led any Spanyards thither.*
>
> *Of the voyage and return of this Madoc, there be many fables framed . . . but sure it is, there he was. And after he had returned home . . . he prepared a number of ships and got with him such Men and Women . . . and . . . took his journey thitherwards again.*
>
> *This Madoc arriving in that western country . . . in the year 1170 . . . I am of the opinion that the land whereunto he came was some part of the West Indies.*

The so-called West Indies (known today as the Antilles) took this name from Columbus's excited declaration that he had found a route to the Orient as a result of his first voyage across the Atlantic in 1492 (see Christopher Columbus, chapter 8). Hakluyt would have known the true location of the West Indies, since the Spanish had been voyaging there regularly for nearly a hundred years before Hakluyt wrote his great work.

Boland is in no doubt about the veracity of the bard Gutton Owen. He says that because Welsh custom "caused reports of all events considered important to be preserved in the abbeys of the land . . . it may be stated that the story of Madoc is founded in truth." "We can, I believe," Boland adds, "rely on Gutton Owen as being an honest man, not given to falsifying. His reputation seems to have been of the best, for he was commissioned by Henry VII to search that monarch's family tree, presumably because Henry needed some background to justify his ascent to the throne of England." He goes on to speak of Hakluyt as "the eminent Hakluyt, scrivener of voyagers of exploration and deeds of derring-do."

But what Boland seems to have overlooked was the powerful need of the House of Tudor to establish an English presence in the Americas so that it could assert a prior claim over the Spanish (the Tudors reigned from 1485 to 1603, beginning with Henry VII and ending with Elizabeth I). Owen's account of Prince Madoc's colony in the new land to the west looked promising to the monarchs. What better way for the Tudors to press a claim than by supporting a Welsh connection with the Americas in the form of the Madoc story? As Burman says, "Tudor propaganda was effective . . . the story was printed along with those of real voyages in the first edition [1582] of Hakluyt's collection of travel narratives."

Thus, ninety years after the first voyage of Columbus and seventy-three years after Henry's death, Madoc has acquired the status of fact. Kemp tells us that the Madoc story was widely believed in Wales, nurtured by reports from this new land to the west that hunters and explorers had often encountered Indians who spoke Welsh. Its apotheosis was established in 1669 when the Reverend Morgan Jones returned to Wales from a missionary tour through North Carolina. Jones related that when he and his friends were about to be killed by Indians, he had told his companions in Welsh to prepare themselves for an early demise, whereupon—yes!—the Indians (much astonished) recognized the language of their forefathers, joyfully greeted Jones and company as cousins, and gladly set them free.

Subsequent searches for American Indians who spoke Welsh have proved entirely fruitless (indeed, until very recent times the Welsh themselves had seemingly lost their own language).

VOYAGES OF SAINT BRENDAN

"And we came to the isle of a saint who had
sailed with Saint Brendan of yore,
He had lived ever since on the Isle and his
winters were fifteen score."

ALFRED, LORD TENNYSON, "VOYAGE OF MAELDUNE"

Brendan was also known as Brendan the Bold, Brandan, and Brandon; Mercatante suggests that the name might mean "stinking hair, dweller by the beacon." (The story of Maeldune, or Maelduin, has much in common with Brendan's; see quotation above.) Brendan was an Irish saint of the second order; the date and place of his birth vary according to the chronicler, but it seems that he came into the world sometime between A.D. 480 and 490. Equally vaguely, he is said to have died somewhere between 570 and 583.

Whatever the dates that bracket his life, Brendan (or our memory of him) possessed legendary accomplishments. There is general agreement that he sailed to the Western Isles off Scotland, and he possibly visited Wales, Brittany, the Orkney Isles, the Shetland Isles, and the east coast of England, journeys that earned him the nickname "the Navigator"; and as the abbot responsible for organizing a number of Irish monasteries Brendan was certainly familiar with the west coast of Ireland. It is, however, the account of his seven-year voyage to the Land Promised to the Saints, sometimes known as the Isle of Saint Brendan, far across the Western Ocean (the early name for the North Atlantic) that has secured his place in clerical and maritime legend.

The classic text of Brendan's voyage (or, rather, Voyage, it being held in such high regard by many clerics, scholars, and mariners) first appeared in Latin, titled *Navigatio Sancti Brendani Abbatis* (The Voyage of Saint Brendan the Abbot). Its date of composition cannot be ascertained exactly, since it is clear that the account is the result of an accretion of much oral history and folklore, but its gestation seems to span the period 800–1000. Ashe states categorically that the *Navigatio* was "composed between 900 and 920." In the words of Mercatante, this story "is filled with adventures, many based on earlier Irish pagan sagas."

Legend has it that on the night of Brendan's birth a great light shone over the area and during his baptism at Ardfert three castrated rams leapt from a nearby well known as Tobar-na-Molt (the significance of this incident is rather obscure). Brendan was educated by Saint Erc and ordained at Tralee, and he subsequently became one of the Twelve Apostles of Ireland. These apostles, having examined a remarkable flower said to have come from Hy Brasil, the Isle of Paradise (chapter 2), chose Brendan to go in search of that very same island.

The *Navigatio* recounts how Brendan is visited by an Irish priest who tells him of a voyage across the Western Ocean that he has himself made, to the Land Promised to the Saints, it proving to be the earthly paradise of Christian belief. Brendan thereupon gathers seventeen companions and sets sail across the Atlantic in search of this vale of perfection, peace, and plenty. In the words of Boland, "The first voyage of Brendan the Bold began in A.D. 545, and lasted for seven long and exhausting years."

For a long time he and his companions wander the Atlantic, discovering islands and living on them for extended periods. Along the way they have a number of astonishing adventures, the best known of which is probably the one when the wanderers land on what appears to be a small island and light a fire to cook some food; but the island proves to be a whale that, taking umbrage at the indignity of its nap being disturbed by a conflagration on its back—not to mention the discomfort suffered therefrom—rouses itself, and the adventurers narrowly avoid a wetting if not worse.

(By way of showing that this incident need not necessarily be dismissed as fable, Boland reminds us that a very similar thing happened to four Kerry fishermen who in the 1920s found an apparently dead whale. While two of their number rowed off to get help to tow the beast ashore, the other two lit a fire on the whale's back because of the biting wind; whereupon the outraged animal—until this moment fast asleep rather than dead—behaved in a disgraceful fashion by immediately diving and thus ignoring the plight, not to say the imminent peril, of the two fishermen, who happily were rescued shortly thereafter by their companions.)

Eventually Brendan and his crew stumble upon a large mass of land (later called Saint Brendan's Island, shown thus on maritime charts as late as the eighteenth century; Christopher Columbus himself in the late fifteenth century regarded the isle as maritime fact), where an angel advises them that they are in fact standing on the very borders of paradise, which happy land will one day be made available to all Christians as a refuge from persecution. In the meantime, declares the angel, they must return whence they came. They do so, and their adventures subsequently become the stuff of legend.

As Ashe makes clear, even though the *Navigatio* is not an actual record of any real voyage, its apparent fiction contains so much practical detail regarding ship handling, climate, direction, distance, and records of natural phenomena that many experienced mariners and others were convinced of its authenticity.

The *Navigatio* has prompted various scholars to wonder if this curiously plausible account of a supposed pre-Columbian and pre-Vinland voyage (or a series of such voyages; see, for example, Vinland USA, chapter 4) suggests that perhaps the land mass that we now call America was discovered long before the arrival of those whom more recent history has so honored.

VOYAGES OF GIL EANNES

"[The] Portuguese . . . were the original civilisers of Africa.
They had the bad luck . . . to get only the coast."
CECIL RHODES

Beneath the huge red sandstone cliffs of Cape Bojador on the northwest coast of Africa, at about 26 degrees North, just south of the Canary Islands, the Atlantic Ocean erupts in an almost constant fury, the seas crashing into the clefts and gullies of the cliffs and exploding into huge columns of compressed water; it is a place where the water looks like molten metal because of the schools of sardines turning and flashing in the turbulent sea. Fearsome waterspouts savage the shallow sand-laden sea, and dust storms howl off the cliff tops in the constant northeasterlies. To seamen of old this place was the gateway to hell, and beyond it lay the Sea of Darkness, inhabited by terrible sea monsters and the spirits of dead sailors (see Our Flat Earth, chapter 19). It was, clearly, the end of the world, a fitting emblem of the Dark Ages.

The maelstrom within the reefs along that coast provoked such terrifying legends that for nearly two thousand years, between 400 B.C. and the fifteenth century, the pace of exploration southward along the west coast of Africa had come almost to a stop (but see Hanno the Navigator above). The Pillars of Hercules (the Straits of Gibraltar, at the western limit of the Mediterranean) represented the limit of confident navigation. Beyond this point lay the Western Ocean, into which seafarers ventured only with the greatest reluctance, knowing full well their fate should they go too far—they would perish in a sea that boiled vigorously in the noonday sun or be consumed by the prodigious monsters known to lurk therein (see, for example, Monster Kraken, chapter 17); or, in attempting to avoid these unhappy misadventures at Cape Bojador by sailing far out to sea, would risk falling off the precipitous edge of the world into the very pit of Hell. What was more, the hills along that coast were said to be composed of a powerful lodestone that would inevitably draw out the metal fastenings of a ship, thus spelling doom for the sailors. Clearly, there was a limit to what a man should be asked to bear.

Then in 1434 Prince Henry of Portugal (1394–1460; known to history as Henry the Navigator), who had no time for such superstitious nonsense, persuaded one of his captains, Gil Eannes (or Gileannes), to sail beyond the Canary Islands and discover what lay south of Bojador. The dreadful fury of this region which had terrorized seamen for so long was caused, Henry firmly believed, by nothing more sinister than rough seas pounding against the cliffs (he did not know at the time that these effects were actually produced by a northerly swell colliding with an offshore northeasterly wind). As Henry's chronicler, Gomes Eannes de Zurara, wrote in 1453, "Although he sent out not only ordinary men but such as were of foremost name in the profession of arms, yet there was not one who dared to pass Cape Bojador."

When they approached the cape the crew were in a fever of fear and rebellion, but Gil Eannes calmed them with reason and common sense, then set course farther out to sea, where lay the end of the world, and everyone on board prepared to plunge over the edge. The outcome must have surprised all of them, for they soon cleared the sinister Bojador barrier and broke out into calm waters, with nary a monster in sight (neither, indeed, did they make acquaintance with the hitherto dreaded pit of Hell).

Their collective fears now behind them, they steered south and east, back toward the coast of Africa, and were rewarded with the sight of new and unexplored territory stretching far out to the horizon and beyond.

It had taken European traders and explorers a thousand years to inch their way southward from the Pillars of Hercules (see chapter 2). Gil Eannes's bold dash into the dreaded Sea of Darkness had now opened a door to a new wave of discovery, and the remaining long stretch of West African coastline was charted within the following seventy years. By early 1488 Bartolomeu Dias had reached the cape at the southern tip of Africa and named it Cabo Tormentoso ("Stormy Cape," later renamed by King John II of Portugal as Cabo da Boa Esperança, "Cape of Good Hope," as a better inducement for future trade). Ten years later Vasco da Gama, following those who earlier had blazed the trail, rounded the Cape of Good Hope and sailed across the Indian Ocean to Calicut in India.

Thus began the world's first great overseas trading empire.

POLYNESIAN SEAFARERS

"God's best—at least God's sweetest works—Polynesians."
ROBERT LOUIS STEVENSON, LETTER TO CHARLES BAXTER

If you throw a stone into a pond, the pattern of ripples that is set up will be disturbed by any rocks that break the surface. If you also had a chart or photograph of all these ripples and a knowledge of mathematics, it would be possible to calculate the positions of all the rocks. Now substitute an ocean for the pond and islands for the rocks, and you can apply the same mathematical principles to pinpoint the location of an island 100 miles away. About three thousand years ago the ability to read the messages of the waves in this way allowed a race of master navigators to sail to, and colonize, almost every habitable island across the Pacific.

The Polynesians had no maps or sea charts to guide them, neither did they have compasses, sextants, or telescopes; there was not even a written language by which they could pass on the lessons of hard-won experience. Yet over a period of some thousand years they populated a huge triangular area covering more than 7 million square miles of ocean, from Easter Island in the east to Hawaii in the north and New Zealand in the south.

They achieved this incredible feat simply by means of intelligent observation. These seafarers had noticed that when waves hit an island some of them were reflected back in the direction from which they had come, while others were deflected, continuing on to the other side of the island but in an altered form. By continued observation these people built up a vast store of knowledge about wave behavior so detailed that they could accurately judge, from the pattern of an island's reflected and deflected waves, its location 100 miles away.

When European sailors first encountered the strange interlocking web of bamboo sticks known as a *mattang,* they thought it was a primitive type of map; but in fact these constructions were devices for teaching island boys the principles of wave motion. The *mattang* was so built that it demonstrated all the basic patterns that waves can assume; with its help a young navigator could learn and understand the implications of the many different wave formations that he might encounter.

Clearly, it was both an intricate art and an intimate one; the Polynesian sailor had to be so close to the waves that he could feel their motions through touch. He would go to the bow of his canoe, crouch down in the hull, and literally feel, with all of his body, every motion of the craft. Within minutes he would be able to determine the positions of the nearest island, any intervening reefs, and other islands nearby. A *mattang* intended for local use would show individual islands and groups, with particular islands being indicated by shells or pieces of coral fastened to the web of sticks.

Using these methods the Polynesians were able to explore most of the Pacific, yet where these people came from originally is a mystery, although Thor Heyerdahl strongly suggested that they owe their beginnings to successive migrations from the west coast of South America (see The *Kon-Tiki* Expedition, next). Some three thousand years ago they passed through Fiji, settled in Tonga in Melanesia, and then moved on to Samoa. On an island that was far enough away from a mainland to be immune to disease the population would explode, so a group would sail off again; in this way the Marquesas were settled perhaps two thousand years ago.

From the Marquesas they made spectacular voyages to Easter Island, Hawaii, and New Zealand, covering these vast distances in huge dugout canoes lashed together in pairs with a deckhouse built on a platform between the two hulls. The interesting thing about these enormous migrations is that the Polynesians, spread out as they were across the world's largest ocean, still retained a sense of being a single people with a more or less common language, so that today it is possible for a Maori from New Zealand to make himself understood to another Polynesian in Hawaii.

THE *KON-TIKI* EXPEDITION

"Kon-Tiki was high priest and sun-king of
the Incas' legendary 'white men' who . . . were massacred,
but Kon-Tiki himself and his closest companions escaped and . . .
disappeared overseas to the westward."

THOR HEYERDAHL, *THE "KON-TIKI" EXPEDITION*

In 1947 the Norwegian anthropologist Thor Heyerdahl and five male companions built a balsa raft and sailed 3,800 miles across the South Pacific to support their theory that the ancestors of the Polynesians could well have journeyed westward from

South America to the Pacific islands known collectively as Polynesia. The raft, launched at Callao on the coast of Peru, was 45 feet long and 18 feet wide. After nearly four months of drifting in the Humboldt Current and the South Equatorial Current the *Kon-Tiki*—named after the Inca sun god—fetched up on Raroia Reef in the Tuamotu Archipelago, east of Tahiti.

Until that moment, Heyerdahl and his migration theory had been casually but widely dismissed. But after their wet but highly successful arrival on the coral reef at Raroia, the voyage—which achieved instant fame worldwide and is still spoken of with some awe—divided anthropologists into two camps: those passionately opposed to the likelihood, because of its impracticality of a Peruvian ancestry for the Polynesian peoples; and those intensely excited by the possibilities of a migration of that very nature.

The official position is probably best represented by the following statement:

> *The vast weight of archaeological as well as racial, linguistic and ethnological evidence continues to support the long-standing hypothesis of the settlement of Oceania by a succession of migrants from the southeast Asia region, with at most very minor contacts eastward to America.*

This "succession of migrants from the southeast Asia region" would certainly account for two of the three groups into which Oceania has been divided: Melanesia, the island groups of dark-skinned and frizzy-haired peoples in the South Pacific, such as New Guinea, Bougainville, the Solomons, and so on (Greek *melas*, black, *nesos*, island, a reference to the black appearance of these islands when seen from seaward); and Micronesia, referring to the small Pacific island groups lying north of the Equator and east of the Philippines and comprising the Mariana, Marshall, Caroline, and Gilbert groups (Greek *mikros*, small).

The third group, Polynesia, refers to the Pacific island groups east of Melanesia and Micronesia, a vast area reaching from Hawaii north of the Equator to New Zealand in the south, and from Samoa in the western Pacific to Easter Island thousands of miles to the east, and embracing groups such as Fiji, Samoa, French Polynesia (the Society Islands—which includes Tahiti—the Tuamotus, the Marquesas, and some smaller groups), the Cook Islands, Tonga, the Line Islands, and others.

The interesting thing about these widely scattered people is the fact that, as Heyerdahl points out, "even if the Polynesians live scattered over an area of sea four times as large as the whole of Europe, nevertheless they have not managed to develop different languages in the different islands." These isolated Polynesians, dispersed across the immensity of the Pacific, all speak dialects of a common language.

How could a race that had no writing still manage to share the same fundamental tongue? Heyerdahl persuasively argues that this came about because of their common background of ancestor-worship, which they transmitted down the generations by means of a highly developed oral tradition. Across this vast oceanic nation anthropologists had discovered that men could recite the names of their dead chiefs right back to Tiki, the white chief-god who was son of the sun (in Peruvian history, Atahualpa, the last Inca king of Peru, was executed by the gold-mad Spaniard Francisco Pizarro in 1533; Atahualpa also claimed to be the son of the sun, and his people certainly believed that he was). To record and remember their ancestors Polynesians used a complicated system of knots on strings, just as the Inca Indians did in Peru.

Another name for the sun god Tiki is Viracocha (also Virakocha), ancient ancestor of the Incas; he was also the rain god who lived in Lake Titicaca, a large lake high in the Andes between southern Peru and western Bolivia, famous for the enormous ruins on some of its islands and along its margins. Viracocha made the earth, sky, stars, and mankind; but mankind displeased him, so he destroyed them with a flood.

The Incas who ruled in South America from the twelfth century onward spoke of "Viracocha" when referring to this god, but in earlier times he was known as Kon- (Sun) Tiki or Illa- (Fire) Tiki. Tiki was the high priest and sun god of the legendary "bearded white men" who had built the ruins on Lake Titicaca before being driven west into the Pacific by Cari, chief of a warlike people from the Coquimbo Valley. The curious thing, as Heyerdahl had already discovered, is that the Polynesian people themselves kept alive the legend of Tiki and his white companions as the founders of their race, complete with references to Tiki's "homeland far to the east"—that is to say, these Polynesians were quite familiar with ancient names of places around Lake Titicaca in the faraway Andes of South America.

These white men of Inca legend had long beards, and it is an astonishing fact that European explorers of the Pacific discovered that many islands contained two kinds of people: the first had a white or fair skin, hair that ranged from red to blonde, blue-gray eyes, and a prominent thin nose, with many of the men bearded; the others were the Polynesians themselves, descendants of Indians from the Pacific northwest, with golden brown skin, raven hair, a beardless face, and the flat fleshy nose characteristic of their race.

The legend of the origins of these "long-eared white-men" is intriguing. Boland explains his theory of how a monk—white, and bearded—left North Salem in New Hampshire in about A.D. 1010, sailed with his Viking Christians down the East Coast, entered Mexico at what is now Veracruz, and made his way to the city of Tula, where in time he found himself venerated as a version of Quetzalcóatl, an ancient god. He is later forced by circumstances to leave Tula, whereupon he finds himself among the Maya at Chichén Itzá on the Yucatán Peninsula, where he is revered as the god Kukulcán. Eventually he has to leave, possibly because of his aversion to human sacrifice, and then he appears among the Inca people, who look upon this bearded white man as a reincarnation of their god Viracocha (or Kon-Tiki Vira-cocha, to distinguish him from an earlier Viracocha). Again, the monk leaves—we don't know why—and sails west; Boland suggests that he departs from the coast of Ecuador.

It's a neat theory—perhaps too neat, since it accounts nicely for the legend encountered by Heyerdahl among the Polynesians—but Boland is confident: "I think the identification of the Abbot of North Salem as Quetzalcoatl, Kukulcan, and Kon-Tiki is safe." He cites evidence from local legends as depicting the "god" as old, white, and bearded (beards among Indians in South America are very unusual, hence the notice that is taken of a man who has one); he wears a long robe and carries a small cross around his neck. Boland's is an intriguing notion.

Whatever the case, throughout his absorbing account Heyerdahl presents us with more and more suggestive evidence of a migration from the east in long bygone times. Shortly after the *Kon-Tiki* was brought up against the reef of Polynesian Raroia, Heyerdahl and his men were visited on the beach by the local chief and his people. What happened next is worth recounting here:

> *The chief's first request was to see the boat which had brought us ashore on the reef alive. We waded out towards the* Kon-Tiki *with a string of natives after us. When we drew near, the natives suddenly stopped and uttered loud exclamations, all talking at once. We could now see the logs of the* Kon-Tiki *plainly, and one of the natives burst out:*
>
> *"That's not a boat, it's a* pae-pae!*"*
>
> *"Pae-pae!" they all repeated in chorus.*
>
> *They splashed out across the reef at a gallop and clambered up onto the* Kon-Tiki . . .
>
> Pae-pae *is the Polynesian word for "raft" and "platform" . . . The chief told us that such* pae-paes *no longer existed, but that the oldest men in the village could relate old traditions of* pae-paes.

Shortly afterward, when Heyerdahl explains to a large gathering the *Kon-Tiki*'s transpacific role in attempting to reconcile the legend of the Peruvian sun god Tiki with that of the Polynesian sun god Tiki by means of a *pae-pae* like the ones used in ancient times, the assembled natives become very excited indeed. It is clear that for them, here was confirmation of their oldest beliefs: their ancestors had come from the east.

There is no doubt that Heyerdahl's voyage has inspired considerable rethinking concerning the meaning and origins of many aspects of Polynesian legend. A common ornament available in New Zealand is the *tiki*, a wooden or greenstone image of the creator of mankind or of an ancestor. One cannot help wondering how the Polynesian people chanced upon a concept that was central to the beliefs of the Inca people in faraway Peru almost a thousand years ago.

The feat of completely crossing the South Pacific by raft has been attempted twice—once successfully—by the same man, German-born American citizen William Willis; his 1954 voyage from Callao in Peru on a balsa raft ended in American Samoa, and his 1963 voyage on a steel raft, again from Callao, ended safely on a beach in Queensland, eastern Australia. Both voyages proved yet again that he and Heyerdahl had achieved in modern times what the ancestors of the twelfth-century Inca empire might well have done long ago.

Heyerdahl built his raft in Callao as a faithful copy of Peruvian Indian vessels, using balsa logs for the hull and bamboo lengths for the cabin and decking, the whole lashed together with hemp rope; no nails or other metal fastenings of any kind were used anywhere. For reasons of safety they carried a radio, and a movie camera recorded various highlights of the trip.

4

SEA QUESTS OF OLD

Marine literature is replete with accounts of seagoing odysseys, of groups of men and women sailing off beyond the farthest horizon in search of new lands to settle, new opportunities to grasp. Many of the earliest migrations happened in this fashion.

The Ancient Greeks established settlements around the Mediterranean and along the coast of the Black Sea long before the coming of Christ; the early Phoenicians sailed out from the Levant (the eastern shore of the Mediterranean, centered on present-day Lebanon) and established huge and wealthy trading empires along the northern margins of Africa (for example, see Hanno the Navigator, chapter 3).

The western Pacific Ocean was populated by migratory groups setting out from eastern and southern Asia, and—if Thor Heyerdahl's theory is correct—by bands of astonishingly skillful seamen voyaging across this vast ocean from the west coast of South America (see The *Kon-Tiki* Expedition, chapter 3).

Because the act of going to sea draws upon enormous reserves of skill, courage, and practical ability, ancient chroniclers used this maritime setting as a means of illustrating many of the desirable and undesirable characteristics that make up human nature.

The following entries show some of these qualities.

THE ARGOSY

"Your argosies with portly sail . . .
Do overpeer the petty traffickers."
WILLIAM SHAKESPEARE, *THE MERCHANT OF VENICE*

An argosy was a large merchant ship in medieval times (known as an Aragousey shippe), especially one with a rich and varied cargo (also a trading venture, which is what Salerio was referring to when he mentioned Antonio's cargo ships—see quote above).

Commonly it was a carrack, a three-masted vessel that traded around northern and southern Europe between the fourteenth and seventeenth centuries. It was a handy type of ship because it was square-rigged on the foremast and mainmast and lateen-rigged on the mizzen, which represented a compromise between the rigs of the north and the south. The carrack was the forerunner of the three-masted square-riggers that saw yeoman service in the navies of the world and that were typified in the magnificent wool and grain carriers and tea clippers (see The Clipper Ships, chapter 8) during the nineteenth century and into the twentieth century.

The carrack was fitted with a high forward castle topped with a palisaded platform from which archers could attack an enemy vessel; this was the origin of the forecastle or fo'c'sle where seamen on naval and merchant ships slung their hammocks or, in more modern times, slept in wooden bunks. The stern of a carrack was also a massive high-built affair, but by degrees both the forecastle and the stern poop were reduced, until by the seventeenth century this type was superseded by the much more efficient galleon (the "low-charged" ship designed by Sir John Hawkins, regarded as the father of the Elizabethan navy), which because of its lowered foreward profile was able to sail much closer to the wind.

The word *argosy* is thought by some to derive from *Argo*, the name of Jason's famous ship (see The Argonauts, below), but it very probably is a corruption of Ragusa, the Italian name (*Ragusea nave*, Ragusean vessel; in sixteenth-century English known as Arragouse, Aragosa, etc.) for the ancient port in the eastern Mediterranean (actually the Adriatic Sea), known today as Dubrovnik, on the Dalmatian coast of Croatia. The region was colonized by Italians in the seventh century and for the next thousand years the growing city-port was a center of enormous mercantile power, with trading links extending as far as the Americas and Asia. (There is also a town in Sicily called Ragusa, but it has no maritime connections.)

THE ARGONAUTS

"Where the boxing contest took place between
the King Amycus and the argonaut Pollux."
GEORGE GROTE, *HISTORY OF GREECE*

This is the story of one of the first great maritime journeys or quests; traditionally, it took place at least a generation before the Trojan War, the legend being so ancient that even Homer, who reputedly lived in the ninth century B.C., speaks of it as widely known. The legend is probably best known through Apollonius Rhodius (Apollonius of Rhodes, born about 295 B.C.) in his work *Argonautica* and in more modern times through *Life and Death of Jason* by the English writer William Morris (1834–1896).

This quest is led by a hero who was said to have lived even earlier than Odysseus (see The *Odyssey* below). It was carried out by the Argonauts, who were brought together by the Greek hero Jason, the son of Aeson, king of Iolcos. Aeson's throne had been usurped by his half brother Pelias, and Jason was then immediately sent by his mother into exile, where he was raised by the wise centaur Chiron.

When Jason returned to claim the throne, Pelias said he could have it in exchange for the Golden Fleece, which was a fleece of pure gold shorn from a winged ram; it hung from a tree in a sacred grove in Aea and was carefully guarded by a dragon that never slept. Pelias swore that on receipt of the fleece of gold he would surrender his throne, privately believing that no one could make the attempt and return alive.

Jason set about preparing for the journey. His ship *Argo* (Greek for "swift" or "bright"), arranged to accommodate forty oarsmen, or fifty, according to the account one consults, was built by the shipwright Argus, helped by Athene, the warrior goddess. According to legend, the *Argo* enjoys the distinction of being the first seagoing ship ever constructed. Among the Argonauts were Heracles (or Hercules); Orpheus, the musician whose task it was to set the rhythm for the men at the oars; the twins Castor and Pollux; and others, together with their leader Jason.

When all was ready the *Argo* was launched and the heroes set sail. Their first port of call is the island of Lemnos, inhabited only by women, where they stay for a considerable period, taking time off from their quest to marry the women and beget children. Finally leaving Lemnos, they make their way to the island of Cyzicus beyond the Hellespont. Here they are hospitably received by the young king Cyzicus. The Argonauts are given a splendid banquet, their supplies are replenished, and in due course they are sent on their way again. Their next port of call is further to the east to the coast of Mysia, where they are welcomed by the inhabitants and made much of.

Here a disaster occurs. Heracles had brought with him a beautiful young man called Hylas, with whom he had fallen in love. By a spring Hylas meets some Nymphs who, drawn by his beauty, lure him into the water, where of course he is drowned. Heracles is worried by the young man's disappearance; he and Polyphemus set off into the forest to search for him. The Argonauts meanwhile hoist sail and abandon the two men.

The *Argo* reaches the land of the Bebryces, which is ruled by King Amycus, the giant son of Poseidon (see chapter 1). Amycus is very fond of boxing and forces passing travelers to spar with him; invariably, the luckless stranger is killed. Amycus challenges the Argonauts to put one of their number up against him; Pollux accepts, and Amycus—much to his momentary astonishment—is killed forthwith.

The Argonauts' next landfall is on the coast of Thrace (the western region of modern Turkey), where Phineus, the blind seer and king of Thrace, warns them of the dangers of the Cyanean Rocks, also called the Symplegades, the two "Clashing Rocks" that float at the entrance to the Unfriendly Sea (known today as the Black Sea, so-called because of its dangerous and unpredictable weather and its lack of sheltering ports). Phineus advises Jason to send a dove ahead of his vessel; should it succeed in passing safely through the strait the Argonauts will be able to follow. The *Argo* nears the Symplegades and a dove is released; when it is almost through the strait the rocks close up on it and sheer off its tail feathers. The men bend to their oars and with the help of Athene their ship gets through, but barely, as the rocks damage the stern slightly, causing the vessel to lose her steering oar.

Passing Thrace, where the Amazons (see The Amazon River, chapter 12) dwell, the *Argo* is brought finally to the mouth of the River Phasis in the land of the Colchians, ruled by King Aeetes. Jason explains his mission to the king, who grants him permission to take the Golden Fleece on condition that Jason should, by himself, yoke to a brass plow two huge bulls fitted with brass hoofs and breathing gouts of fire from their nostrils, then plow the field of Ares (the Greek god of war, traditionally the father of the Amazons) and sow the furrows with the teeth of Ares's dragon at Thebes. Jason then has to overcome the armed soldiers who will spring from this curious crop-sowing. Understandably, Jason is downcast at the enormity of the task.

The king's daughter Medea is inspired by Aphrodite (see chapter 1), the Greek goddess of love, to conceive an immediate passion for Jason. When he promises to to conceive an immediate passion for Jason. When he promises t carry out the tasks that Aeetes has set him, Medea gives him a magic ointment that, when spread over his body, will protect him from being harmed by fire or iron.

Jason yokes the two bulls, plows the field, and sows the dragon's teeth. When the armed soldiers leap up, Jason throws a rock in their midst, whereupon the distracted soldiers begin to fight and slay each other, leaving our hero free to finish them off himself. Aeetes goes back on his word; he refuses to give up the Golden Fleece and instead tries to destroy the *Argo* and her crew. Medea immediately puts the sleepless dragon to sleep with a spell, Jason secures the fleece from the sacred grove, and they both make their escape with the Argonauts, Medea taking with her Apsyrtus, her young brother.

Aeetes immediately gives chase, but Medea has anticipated this. She cuts Apsyrtus into pieces and scatters them, forcing her father Aeetes to stop and gather his son's limbs for proper burial. The Argonauts enter the River Istros (now the Danube) and follow it until it empties into the Adriatic (at the time of this story it was believed that the Istros or Danube connected the Black Sea with the Adriatic Sea). However, Zeus—much angered by the slaughter of Apsyrtus—sends a storm and the *Argo* is blown far off course. Now follows another long and arduous voyage to the island of Aeaea, where the sorceress Circe purifies Jason and his men.

The ship sets forth once again. Passing the island where dwell the Sirens (see chapter 15), Orpheus on board the *Argo* sings so sweetly that his shipmates are able to resist the blandishments of the two temptresses; the *Argo* then passes safely by Scylla and Charybdis (see chapter 1), losing but one man (see also The *Odyssey,* below, for Odysseus's encounters with Circe and the Sirens). Finally the *Argo* arrives at the land of the Phaeacians, where Jason marries Medea.

They are within sight of the Peloponnesus, the southern peninsula of Greece, when a violent storm drives the ship onto the coast of Libya (the ancient name for Africa). Triton, god of the entire sea, helps them and they are able to continue their voyage to Crete.

Finally the heroes return to Iolcos, where the aged Pelias has put to death Aeson, together with Aeson's son. Medea gathers together the daughters of Pelias and in their presence cuts up an old he-goat and boils it in her magic cauldron, a culinary procedure that restores the goat to life as a young buck. In like manner, Medea says to the daughters, can she restore Pelias to his wonted youthful vigor. Much impressed, the girls kill their father, swiftly dice him into pieces of a suitable size, and toss them into Medea's cauldron. Alas! She then deserts them, having achieved her desired revenge.

The Golden Fleece is now restored to Iolcos, and Jason assumes the throne. After some ten years Jason grows weary of Medea (and perhaps also somewhat wary, considering her skill in the magic arts); he discards her and marries one of the daughters of Creon, the king of Corinth. Medea takes umbrage at this and sends the new bride a poisoned wedding present that speedily brings about that good lady's demise. Not content with this, Medea then murders her two children by Jason and escapes to Athens in a chariot drawn by winged dragons.

Jason, according to one account, then returns to Iolcos and assumes the throne. He meets his end when resting one day beneath his old ship, the *Argo*; without warning, the stern, damaged years before when negotiating the Symplegades, abruptly falls on his head and kills him. There is a poetic irony here, of course, since Jason dies by means of the very vessel that has brought him fame and fortune.

The travails and wanderings of the legendary Argonauts have lent themselves to marine biology; there is a cephalopod mollusk called the Argonaut or Paper Sailor, also known as the Paper Nautilus. It was long supposed by Aristotle and others that this animal navigated the seas by floating on the surface, shell opening uppermost, with its arms held out in the manner of sails so as to catch the breeze; but this is a story as truly fabulous as that of the kingfisher in the story about the origin of the expression Halcyon Days (see chapter 15).

THE *ODYSSEY*

"The surge and thunder of the Odyssey.*"*

ANDREW LANG, THE *ODYSSEY*

The *Odyssey* is perhaps the greatest of all maritime legends, so much so that even today any long and perilous journey or quest is often called an odyssey (see also The Argonauts, above).

The *Odyssey* is the famous epic poem attributed to the ninth-century B.C. Greek poet Homer, in which he tells the story of the many wanderings of the Greek hero Odysseus ("angry"; Latin Ulixes, anglicized to Ulysses) as he makes his way home to Ithaca after the victory of the Greeks in the Trojan War (which was very likely in the thirteenth or twelfth century B.C.).

This return journey takes Odysseus ten years, during all of which time his wife Penelope ("with a web over her face" or "the striped duck") and his son Telemachus ("decisive battle") have been waiting in stoic patience—indeed, their loyalty and faithfulness have already been sorely tried, Odysseus having spent ten years at the Trojan War itself before deciding to return to his own hearth and home.

He does in fact finally find his own front door, but only after ten years of harrowing and often fearful adventures. He is, for instance, detained for seven years by Calypso on her Island of Ogygia (see chapter 2), where she induces him to be her lover and by whom she has two children before permitting him to return to Ithaca; not to mention the ordeal visited upon him by Circe, the enchantress who dwelt on the island of Aeaea, this lady—by unfairly utilizing her considerable charms— takes advantage of Odysseus's blind but honest oafishness, seduces the poor fellow, and bears a son by him.

Homer's *Odyssey* is a remarkable and often moving account of derring-do; it is also a parable of endeavor and fortitude. The epic is divided into twenty-four books, taking us from the fall of Troy and the victorious Greek fleet setting out for home to the blood-curdling homecoming of Odysseus when he confronts and slays all the idle, arrogant lay-about suitors who have incessantly besieged Penelope, demanding that she accept that her husband is dead and that she forthwith choose one of them as her new husband.

The sacking of Troy saw unrestrained slaughter on a grand scale, both of Greeks and Trojans, but the Greeks won the day; and so pleased were they with what they had achieved that when finally they set sail for home they had quite forgotten to what agency they owed their victory. Poseidon and Athene looked down from Olympus with fierce anger as the Greeks, all unheeding, congratulated themselves on their prowess but neglected to give proper thanks to the gods, thereby condemning themselves to terrible punishment as they made their way home.

"Give the Greeks a bitter homecoming," Athene begs Poseidon. "Stir up your waters with wild whirlwinds when they sail. Let dead men choke the bays and line the shores and reefs." Poseidon agrees, and the Greeks suffer fearfully, but none for as long as Odysseus; he is made to wander for ten long and weary years, yearning endlessly for Penelope and the small son he has left behind.

Soon after Odysseus and his men leave Troy, his ships are beset by a fierce storm and driven to the Thracian city Ismarus, home of the Cicones; Odysseus sacks the city and kills all in it except Maron, a priest of Apollo. Out of gratitude Maron gives him twelve jars of strong sweet wine, a gift that later proves to be of great use in the land of the Cyclopes.

Odysseus and his fleet then sail for Cape Malea on the southeast tip of the Peloponnesus, but a violent wind from the north hurls itself upon them and for nine days they are carried south until they fetch up on the coast of North Africa, in the land of the Lotophagi, the lotus-eaters, to eat the fruit of which is to lose all memory. Here his men soon abandon their desire to return to Ithaca and Odysseus has to drag them by main force back to their ships.

The voyage now enters the western seas, a region then little known to the ancient Greeks. The band of men come to the country of the Cyclopes, one of whom is Polyphemus, the gigantic son of Poseidon and the nymph Thoosa; the Cyclopes are known as the "round-eyed ones" because of their single eye in the middle of the forehead. Odysseus disembarks with twelve men and, carrying some wine in goatskins as a gift to people they might meet, they enter a cave where they find cheese, milk, and other foodstuffs. Polyphemus, a shepherd and occupant of the cave (and also a ravenous eater of raw flesh), returns at that moment, seizes the wanderers, and makes them his prisoners; when he is hungry he sets upon Odysseus's men and devours them in pairs.

In despair Odysseus gives some of the wine to Polyphemus, who thereupon becomes drunk and a little more amiable, promising to eat the hero last of all. When asked his name Odysseus tells the giant that it is "Nobody"; Polyphemus then falls asleep. Odysseus and his surviving companions sharpen an enormous stake in the fire, then drive it into Polyphemus's only eye. There follows much uproar, and in the morning the Cyclops is at the exit, checking his sheep as they file out to go to pasture; but Odysseus and his men have concealed themselves by gripping the underbellies of the rams, thus evading the giant's hands. Polyphemus calls to his fellow Cyclopes for help; when they ask him who the attacker is, he replies "Nobody," whereupon they shake their heads and wander off. By this action Odysseus has further aroused the implacable hatred of Poseidon, the father of Polyphemus, and his anger pursues the Greek warrior for a long time yet.

Odysseus and what men are now left to him make sail, and soon they come to the island of Aeolus, the Warden of the Winds, who receives them with much hospitality. On their departure Odysseus is given a leather bag containing all the winds of the world except the one that will take his ship straight back to their home on the island of Ithaca, off the west coast of Greece. But while Odysseus sleeps the crew open the bag, believing it to be full of gold. Alas! the winds escape, a hurricane ensues, and the ship is driven back to the island of Aeolus, who understandably enough has had his fill of these visitors; he orders them off, regarding them as enemies of the gods.

Odysseus heads north and reaches the country of the Laestrygonians, who unknown to our hero are cannibals of enormous size whose gastronomic fancy it is to devour foreigners. Odysseus anchors in the harbor and sends some men to explore the area. They encounter the daughter of the king; she takes them to meet her father, whereupon he immediately consumes one of them on the spot. The Greeks rush back to the harbor, followed by the aroused and hungry Laestrygonians, who hurl boulders at the luckless Greeks, thereby destroying eleven ships and killing all the men in them. Only Odysseus's vessel escapes the slaughter.

He sets sail yet again, to the island of Aeaea, the home of Circe, a sorceress, and Odysseus sends some of his men to investigate. True to her nature, she turns them into swine, but Odysseus, with the help of Hermes, threatens her with death unless she returns his men to their former state. She complies readily, having already fallen in love with this bold fellow, and she induces him to spend a whole year with her on the island. He does so (thereby bringing into question the strength of his desire to return to the heroically patient Penelope at Ithaca); but his men tire of their paradise and, under their urging, Odysseus sets off once more.

He sails far to the west to Oceanus (see chapter 1), the ancient river that flows around the earth. Following Circe's instructions, Odysseus approaches the entrance to the lower world, the realm of Hades on the farther bank of Oceanus, so as to consult the shade of Teiresias (Latin, Tiresias), the famous blind soothsayer of Thebes. Teiresias tells Odysseus that eventually he will return to Ithaca; that he must punish his wife's suitors; that he must set off inland with an oar over his shoulder and stop only when people ask what it is he is carrying, thus revealing that they know nothing of ships or the sea; that he must then make a sacrifice to Poseidon to make amends for his earlier pride; and finally, that he will die in happy old age, far from the sea.

But, warns Teiresias, Odysseus's speedy return is conditional upon his men's offering no violence to the cattle belonging to Helios; failing this, Odysseus will wander for a long time yet, subject to the continuing malice of Poseidon until, deprived of all his comrades, he will eventually arrive at Ithaca, but on a foreign vessel.

Odysseus returns to Circe and with his remaining men at last sets sail for home. Passing the island of the Sirens he avoids the entrapment posed by the irresistible singing of the two sweet-voiced creatures resident on the island. (Circe has advised Odysseus to stop up the ears of his men with wax and then to get them to bind him to the mast; seafarers who failed to take these precautions invariably approached too close to the rocky coast, were wrecked, and in short order suffered a speedy devouring by the singing duo.) When the Sirens see that they have failed to entice Odysseus ashore, they throw themselves into the sea and promptly drown.

The next obstacle that Odysseus has to face is Scylla and Charybdis (see chapter 1), the dreadful monster and whirlpool, respectively, that guard the Strait of Messina dividing Italy from Sicily. Despite the best efforts of the dog-girt Scylla and the fearful whirlpool of Charybdis, Odysseus and his ship pass safely through and eventually reach the island of Thrinacia (now thought to be Sicily), where his men compel him to land so that they might rest. But contrary winds detain them for a month, their food runs out, and finally, disregarding the solemn oath that they had earlier sworn to Odysseus, the starving seamen kill and eat the finest of the white cattle belonging to Helios.

The outraged owner complains bitterly to Zeus, who waits until Odysseus sets sail once more, then hurls a fearful storm on the band of men and with a terrible flash of lightning sunders the ship end to end. The ship goes down, together with all the crew—all except Odysseus, who is saved because he refused to partake in the sacrilegious feast. He clings to wreckage from the ship, is carried by the waves back to the terrors of Scylla and Charybdis, which he barely escapes, and for nine days drifts aimlessly until he is washed up onto the island of Ogygia, the abode of the nymph Calypso.

Here he stays for seven years—the period varies according to the source—seduced by the promises (and, one imagines, the not inconsiderable charms) of Calypso, who offers him immortality and eternal youth if he will stay and be her husband. He yields to the one but not the other, enjoying the pleasures of her company but forever yearning to be at his own hearth with his own true wife (although, given his seven-year sojourn with Calypso, one must wonder at the strength of his yearning). Finally Athene, the protector of our hero, has Zeus send Hermes to order Calypso to release him.

This he does; and Calypso complies. She reluctantly gives Odysseus enough wood to make a raft, on which he sets out toward the east, and eighteen days later comes in sight of the island of Scheria, where dwell the Phaeacians. Unfortunately, the still angry Poseidon catches sight of him and forthwith smashes the raft to pieces.

But not everyone is against Odysseus. Ino Leucothea, a marine divinity of the Mediterranean, rescues Odysseus from danger by throwing him her veil, and he staggers ashore on Scheria, where he is met by Nausicaa, the beautiful daughter of King Alcinous of the Phaeacians. Here he is entertained most hospitably, a banquet is given in his honor, and Alcinous offers him the hand of Nausicaa; regretfully he declines the offer, proclaiming that his one aim is to return to his home, hearth, and heart's love. A ship is put at his disposal, and Phaeacian sailors take him to Ithaca where, having fallen asleep, he is put down on a remote spot, together with the gifts from Alcinous.

After an absence of twenty years Odysseus has changed beyond recognition (however, his old dog Argus recognizes his master immediately, leaps up in joy, and then inexplicably falls dead at his master's feet).

With the help of Athene, Odysseus disguises himself as a beggar, making himself known only to Eumaeus, his faithful old swineherd, and to his son Telemachus, now a man, who tells his father of the trouble posed by the 108 suitors who had moved into the palace and besieged Penelope. She has informed these importunate men that she will make a decision when she has finished weaving a shroud for her father-in-law, which she works on by day and then unravels by night. But her subterfuge is betrayed by one of her attendants, and she is forced to complete the garment.

Desperate for news of Odysseus and still hopeful that he might yet be alive, Penelope arranges a competition among the suitors, each of whom has to use the bow of Odysseus to shoot an arrow through a line of rings formed by a row of axe handles; she promises to marry the winner. Odysseus meets with Penelope but does not reveal his identity; he approves of her competition, which he attends, still disguised as a beggar. None can bend and string the bow.

To a volley of scorn from the suitors, Odysseus takes up the bow, strings it in an instant, and sends an arrow through the rings. Then, with the help of Telemachus and Eumaeus, he begins the slaughter of the suitors. The servant girls who had consorted with the suitors are forthwith hanged. Odysseus then reveals himself to Penelope, proving his identity by describing their nuptial chamber, which was known only to those two; then he goes into the countryside and makes the appropriate sacrifice as recommended by Teiresias.

Later additions to the legend have him marrying the neighboring queen Callidice, fathering a son by her, then returning to Penelope when Callidice dies, there to discover that Penelope has in turn borne him another son. Telegonus, the son of Circe and Odysseus, finds himself on Ithaca, where he plunders a herd of cattle; Odysseus comes to help the shepherds and is killed by Telegonus.

VINLAND USA

"Next morning Leif said to his men: 'Now we have two
occupations to attend to, and day about; namely, to gather grapes
or cut vines, and to fell wood in the forest to load our vessel.'
And this advice was followed . . . Towards spring they
made ready and sailed away; and Leif gave the country
a name from its productions, and called it Vinland."

SNORRE STURLASON, *THE VOYAGE OF LEIF THE SON OF ERIC THE RED*

Leif Ericsson (also Eiriksson, Ericson, son of Eirik the Red) flourished around A.D. 1000—his dates of birth and death are obscure. He was a Scandinavian seafarer and discoverer of Vinland (Wineland), variously claimed by later historians and archaeologists to be Nova Scotia, Rhode Island, the mouth of the Hudson River in New York, Virginia, Florida, and many other locations along the North American East Coast. There is little doubt that the Norsemen—or Vikings as they are often called—visited the shores of North America and possibly lived there for a time; what is in dispute is exactly where they landed.

Ericsson was by all reports a well-set-up young man: tall, strong, handsome in the manner of Norsemen, given to thoughtful contemplation of matters, and temperate in all things. (In most things, anyway. While still a young man living with his father Eirik in Greenland during Eirik's exile from Iceland, Leif took a vessel to Norway with trade goods. The ship touched at the Hebrides, as was customary, and Leif called on a girl who was the daughter of a local noble. When he left her, however, she was pregnant, a situation he remedied to his satisfaction by paying her off with Greenland trade items and departing the Hebrides forthwith.)

After a visit to the Norwegian court of Olaf Tryggvason in 999, Ericsson's mind turned to exploration. In 985 one Bjarni Herjolfsson, during a return voyage from Norway to Greenland, set far off course by a terrible storm, had sighted and coasted the eastern shores of North America (probably Labrador) and a bleak and remote island (very likely Baffin Island) farther north before sailing east to rejoin his father at the Greenland settlement. The account of the voyage was well known to Leif, and fifteen years later, in 1000, he determined to find this mysterious land. He consulted with Herjolfsson for sailing instructions and then set off.

Plotting a course due west, Ericsson eventually sighted and inspected Herjolfsson's forbidding island of glaciers (Ericcsson named it Helluland, "Flatland"; it was probably Baffin Island). He then steered south and sighted a splendid wooded shore that Herjolfsson had earlier seen, which Ericsson then named Markland for its forests. (From the description in the Norse sagas, this region seems to correspond with a 30-mile stretch along the coast of Labrador, near Cape Porcupine; Boland reports that "Leif was now in Nova Scotia.")

Two days' journey later they discovered and landed on an island (this was probably Belle Island, about 15 miles north of Newfoundland), then they sailed west again through the channels, got themselves beached in some shallows, finally towed their ship off, then decided to live ashore during the coming winter. They set up living quarters, existing on salmon and other food staples, and explored what seemed to these Greenlanders to be a veritable paradise.

According to the Norse sagas, principally the Flatey Book (Flateyjarbok, or Flat Island Book, compiled during the fourteenth century), they had found what appeared to be self-sown wheat, mösur wood, and, most surprising of all, grapes. These were tentatively identified in the twentieth century as Lyme grass, the white birch—later made famous by the canoes of the American Indians and the French *voyageurs*—and the wild red currant or mountain cranberry, respectively.

It is the grapes that have proved to be the puzzle for modern historians. During a search for one of their group (a German named Tyrkir or Tyrker, a friend of Leif's father) the men found him in a state of excitement. He had, he said, found grapes and grapevines; according to old Norse accounts, Tyrkir then showed them vines laden with fruit. Because of this Ericsson named the region Vinland. When spring came the men loaded their ship with timber and grapes and sailed away, back to Greenland, thereby bequeathing to posterity almost a thousand years of controversy.

Where exactly was Vinland, this land of grapes? There was no doubting that the Norsemen had visited the North American continent—the sagas are too detailed to be dismissed readily—but Newfoundland is not a place where grapes easily grow. On the other hand, everything else fits a specific area near the northern tip of this island, a place called L'Anse aux Meadows, "cove of the meadows," not far from Sacred Bay. (This claim was supported in 1987 by the Norwegian archaeologist Helge Instad. Mowat also places Ericsson's Vinland in Newfoundland, but his site is much farther to the southeast, in Tickle Cove Bay, at the southern extremity of Trinity Bay. Boland, however, places Ericsson's landing place at the Jones River, near

Rocky Nook Point, not far from Plymouth in Cape Cod Bay, Massachusetts, roughly a thousand miles southwest of the Newfoundland site.)

What's more, at L'Anse aux Meadows and nowhere else in North America are found remnants of what appear to be Norse dwellings. The only items missing from this site are the grapes and the vines, which are specifically mentioned in the sagas and referred to as such by the German-born Tyrkir. But Newfoundland is too far north for them to grow. On the other hand, perhaps the Norsemen were using "grape" loosely for "berry"; northern Newfoundland does support squashberries, gooseberries, and cranberries, all of which will produce wine.

Perhaps the answer to this riddle of the grapes lies in the nature of the Ericssons, father and son. Greenland is one of the bleakest places one may hope to visit, yet Eirik the Red managed to attract settlers there by a simple expedient known to real estate vendors the world over: he gilded his vast frigid and somewhat less-than-Elysian ice-capped island with the name "green." Who could resist it? And it is not unreasonable to imagine Eirik's son Leif doing the same with his proposed settlement in Vinland, easily accomplished by reporting that he and his men had feasted on "grapes."

The Vinland controversy shows no sign of fading away. In 1957 a map—said to have been compiled in the 1440s and purporting to show Viking exploration along the northeast coast of North America—was discovered, and because it clearly predated anything that Columbus might have drawn, a sensation soon erupted. An anonymous donor gave it to Yale University in 1965, but nine years later Yale announced that this Vinland Map was a fake: the ink used to draw it contained titanium dioxide, which apparently was not used in ink manufacture until 1920. Mowat's book was published the same year Yale acquired the map; his remarks indicate that he accepted it as authentic.

The impact that this document made between 1957 and 1974 was significant. *Webster's Guide to American History* (published some three years before Yale declared the map to be spurious) reproduces a section of the map with a rather solemn caption telling the world that it was "probably drawn by a church scholar during an extended church council held in Basel from 1431 to 1449." Unhappily for the unbelievers, it seems that this is true: the map was apparently produced early in the fifteenth century because, it is now claimed, other books published in that period also had titanium dioxide in their ink. Thus Mowat may be vindicated.

THE NORTHWEST PASSAGE

*"Whereas the Earl of Sandwich has signified to us his Majesty's
pleasure, that an attempt should be made to find out a
Northern passage by sea from the Pacific to the Atlantic Ocean."*

"SECRET INSTRUCTIONS FOR CAPTAIN JAMES COOK"

So read the instructions that sent James Cook off on his third and last voyage of exploration, which ended with his death in the Sandwich Islands (now Hawaii) in 1779 (see section on Cook, chapter 8). The possibility of a sea passage leading from the northwestern portion of the North Atlantic, across or through North America and thence into the North Pacific, had long been a dream of European merchants and traders who wanted to tap into the fabled wealth of the Far East. Over a period of nearly four hundred years scores of expeditions sailed bravely into the north polar regions, and inevitably they struggled back—or at least the survivors did—full of horror stories of the unbelievably cold and bleak desolation that awaited the intruder.

This search for the Northwest Passage begins with John Cabot (about 1450–1498), a Venetian navigator who, having taken a trading ship to Mecca, had been astounded at the variety of spices, silks, and jewels available there. When he discovered that these goods had come overland by caravan from Asia, Cabot reasoned that if he could reach Cathay (China) and Cipangu (Japan) by crossing the Western Ocean (the Atlantic), he would be able to establish a profitable trade directly between Europe and the Far East.

Another incentive for searching for a means of trading directly with Asia was the fact that by the late fourteenth century the Turks had conquered the eastern Mediterranean and secured control of the ancient overland caravan routes. Additionally, in 1493 Pope Alexander VI, in an astonishing display of religious control over the planet's real estate, had proclaimed a line through the world—the historic Line of Demarcation—roughly corresponding to 50 degrees West longitude running through modern Brazil and apportioned all new discoveries west of it to Spain and to the east of it to Portugal. This was challenged by Spain and Portugal in 1494, resulting in the Tordesillas Line, which was intended to settle territorial conflicts arising from Christopher Columbus's first voyage in 1492 (see chapter 8). Thus when the sea routes to the Orient by way of the Cape of Good Hope and the Strait of Magellan were opened, they immediately came under Spanish and Portuguese control.

Cabot would certainly have been aware of these restrictions placed in the way of those wishing to participate in the highly lucrative trade with the East, especially the trade in spices, necessary for the preservation of many foodstuffs in Europe. Why not, then, search for another route directly to the west? The best way to go about this, Cabot reasoned, would be to enlist royal support. But as happened to Columbus, Cabot could find no backers, so he went to England. There the merchants of Bristol agreed to support his proposal for the expedition, with the proviso that Cabot first had to visit Hy Brasil and the Isle of the Seven Cities (mythical lands of legendary wealth and beauty); but when news was received that Columbus had already supposedly reached the Indies, the merchants agreed that Cabot might well go direct to Asia.

He set out from Bristol in May 1497 in the *Mathew*, with a crew of eighteen men. He sighted and in the name of King Henry VII of England took possession of Newfoundland, convinced—as Columbus had been in 1492 when, much farther south, he found himself wandering among the islands of the Caribbean—that the gaunt face of this large island was but an outrider of fabled Cathay, the kingdom of the Great Khan. Because his small ship was running short on provisions, Cabot had to return to England, his only treasure-in-hand for King Henry being the news that his men had caught extraordinary quantities of cod while sailing over what the world now knows as the Grand Banks, a cod fishery lying in a shallow patch of ocean south and east of Newfoundland. Cabot's reward from the king was £10.

Undaunted and fired with enthusiasm for returning to what he firmly believed was the coast of Cathay, Cabot secured the king's support for another expedition, whereupon with five ships and three hundred men he sailed from Bristol in May 1498—and promptly disappeared.

His son Sebastian (1476–1557) later set up a company of Merchant Adventurers in Bristol, which in 1554 and 1555 outfitted two expeditions, this time specifically in search of the Northwest Passage, from the first of which only one ship returned (albeit empty-handed), nothing being heard of the other vessel. In 1535 Jacques Cartier (about 1491–1557) discovered the Saint Lawrence River and, thinking it might traverse the continent, he attempted to sail up it but was defeated by rapids.

By the mid-sixteenth century it was clear to geographers that a vast continent straddled the route across the Atlantic to the Far East. The English, and later the Dutch, tried to establish a Northeast Passage by sailing north into the Barents Sea and thence east into the Kara Sea bordering the Russian north coast, but ice conditions proved so adverse that until more modern times no explorer ever managed to penetrate farther than the western portion of the Kara Sea.

In 1804 President Thomas Jefferson (1743–1826) set in motion the Lewis and Clark Expedition, the most famous expedition of exploration in American history. One of its principal objects was to explore the land acquired from the French in 1803—the huge Louisiana Territory that extended from the Mississippi River in the southeast to the Rocky Mountains in the northwest, more than doubling the size of the United States. Another of its aims was to determine whether or not there was a feasible means of water access across the continent to the west coast: the long-sought Northwest Passage, which many believed was possible.

But the topography of hope was rudely shattered by the geography of reality. Although Lewis and Clark brought back a great deal of extraordinary information about the lands and the peoples far to the west, the Rocky Mountains made it abundantly clear that no feasible water route from the Atlantic to the Pacific, and beyond it the Orient, lay in this region.

English interest in a Northwest Passage continued with Martin Frobisher (1535–1594), one of the ablest of the great Elizabethan seamen. Frobisher commanded three voyages, in 1576, 1577, and 1578, to what we know as Baffin Island. He was followed by, among others, John Davis (or Davys; 1550–1605) who during three voyages in 1585, 1586, and 1587 discovered Davis Strait between Greenland and Baffin Island, which later proved to be the first leg of the route through to the Pacific.

Between 1607 and 1611 Henry Hudson discovered Hudson Strait and Hudson Bay, but neither of these offered access through the continent to the Pacific. William Baffin in a number of voyages between 1612 and 1616 penetrated as far as Baffin Bay, off the northeast coast of Baffin Island and at the northern reaches of Davis Strait.

Over the next two hundred years there were a number of important expeditions that, although they did not of themselves discover the sought-for passage, nevertheless added greatly to the sum of knowledge about the northern polar regions. Sir John Franklin (1786–1847) and his two ships disappeared after having been sighted in Baffin Bay, but during the forty expeditions sent in search of Franklin and his men, the route to the Pacific was finally established and mapped, particularly by Robert McClure (1807–1873), who in 1850 discovered the existence of what finally proved to be the Northwest Passage.

Beginning with Roald Amundsen's successful expedition in 1903, a number of other explorers traversed the passage between the North Atlantic and the Pacific. Probably the most dramatic was that of Commander William Anderson, who in 1958 took the nuclear submarine USS *Nautilus* through the passage from the Pacific to the Atlantic, using charts no doubt based on observations made by James Cook during his own search for the elusive sea route. The four-hundred-year-old dream of a northern commercial route between these two oceans was realized when the oil tanker *Manhattan* took a cargo of crude oil from Alaska to the U.S. East Coast in 1969, although during the voyage the vessel was severely damaged by ice.

THE GREAT SOUTH LAND

"The discovery of a Southern Continent is the object I have in view."
COOK'S LOG

The early Greeks, such as Homer in the ninth century B.C., believed that the world was a disk bounded by an enormous river called Ocean, which flowed endlessly around the earth. Other ancient peoples in the East believed that the world they lived on was a plate or disk held aloft by four elephants standing on a turtle (see Our Flat Earth, chapter 19).

Some three hundred years after Homer, the Greek philosopher and mathematician Pythagoras (about 582–500 B.C.) described the earth as a sphere, a radical departure from the flat earth belief (a notion revived during the Middle Ages). Pythagoras insisted that in order to keep the sphere "balanced" there would have to be a continent in the Southern Hemisphere of about the same mass as that in the Northern Hemisphere.

In about A.D. 44 Pomponius Mela, a Latin geographer, warned that it would not be possible to search for this southern continent because of the zone of unbearable heat that lay between the two hemispheres, an idea readily accepted by many because of the common experience of mariners, who reported that the farther south they sailed the hotter it became (see, for example, Voyages of Gil Eannes, chapter 3).

At about this time it was accepted that the earth was spherical. Eratosthenes (about 276–195 B.C.), the Greek mathematician and astronomer in Alexandria, the Egyptian capital at that time, had already calculated the circumference of the earth (he was within 50 miles, or 80 kilometers, of the true figure, which is about 25,000 miles, or 40,000 kilometers). Not long after the beginning of the Christian era a system of latitude and longitude had been developed by the Greeks, which then led to the notion of *klimata* or zones of different climate based on latitude.

In the second century the Greek mathematician and astronomer Claudius Ptolemaeus, better known as Ptolemy (A.D. 127–151), who like Eratosthenes four hundred years earlier was living and working in Alexandria, revived the notion that a supercontinent had to exist in the Southern Hemisphere in order to balance the planetary sphere and maintain stability. This Terra Australis Incognita—"unknown south land"—had its northern shores, he said, at 15 degrees South latitude.

When western Europe fell to the invading barbarians from the east (the Goths, Vandals, and Huns) at the end of the fifth century, the learning of the ancient world was largely wiped out, to be replaced by the Church's received wisdom that Jerusalem lay at the center of a flat and circular earth, which in turn was the hub or central point of the universe. This view prevailed for nearly a thousand years until it was dispelled, at last, by the Polish astronomer Nicolaus Copernicus (1473–1543). Many church scholars argued that since the Bible did not make any reference to a southern continent, it therefore did not exist; and even if it did it would be uninhabited because the descendants of Adam and Eve could not have reached it.

Marco Polo (about 1254–1324), the Venetian traveler in Asia, claimed that some of the islands to the south of India were extremely rich in gold and other valuable commodities. Many of those who read the book of his experiences took this as a reference to Terra Australis Incognita, so when during the fifteenth and sixteenth centuries—the classical period of exploration—seafarers persisted in bringing back reports that they had sailed around the world, there was renewed interest in Ptolemy's assertions about this exciting new continent, which was shown in maps of the period as a huge land mass centered on the South Pole, reaching north as far as 60 degrees South latitude and, in the region we know as the Pacific, extending to the Equator.

By the early 1500s the Portuguese were venturing down the west coast of Africa, and when Bartolemeu Dias rounded the southern tip of Africa in 1488 and when Ferdinand Magellan forced his way through the tangle of inhospitable channels at the southern extremity of South America in 1520, it was now possible to examine the truth of Ptolemy's geography.

The contact that early Dutch explorers made with the Australian coastline led many to believe that the "South Land" had at last been discovered. In 1606 Willem Jansz in the *Duyfken* charted the western edge of Cape York Peninsula, in the north-eastern part of the continent; ten years later, in 1616, Dirk Hartog in the *Eendracht* touched on the northwest section of Western Australia and named it T'Landt van d'Eendracht. In 1619 Frederik de Houtman sighted a more southerly section of the west coast and named it d'Edels Landt after Jacob d'Edel, a merchant traveling with him. Houtman also named the Houtman Abrolhos, a particularly dangerous archipelago of low-lying rocks and reefs lying off the midwestern coast.

In 1621 the captain of the *Leeuwin* named the southwest corner of the continent T'Landt van de Leeuwin, a name commemorated today in Cape Leeuwin (the name of the Dutch captain is not known; apparently he had disregarded his sailing instructions and as a consequence the Dutch East India Company removed his name from his report). Jan Carstenz in 1623, commanding two ships on the northern coast of the continent, charted the Gulf of Carpentaria, naming it after Pieter de Carpentier, the Dutch governor-general at Batavia, while Arnhem Land was discovered and named after the *Arnhem*, one of Carstenz's ships.

During the rest of the century there were many other instances of Dutch contact with sections of what appeared to be a large land mass often referred to as the "South Land"; not surprisingly, the Dutch East India Company named it Hollandia Nova (New Holland). It remained for a later navigator in the latter half of the eighteenth century, Captain James Cook (see chapter 8), to clear up the question of Terra Australis Incognita and determine whether or not New Holland was part of Pythagoras's supercontinent.

During his first voyage (1768–1771) Cook showed that New Zealand was made up of two main islands that were unconnected with any supposed southern land mass; on his second voyage (1772–1775) he circumnavigated what we know as Antarctica and in so doing proved conclusively that the Great South Land did not exist. His third voyage (1776–1779), which was aimed at determining whether or not a Northwest Passage could be found connecting the North Pacific with the North Atlantic, also finally confirmed that apart from Australia, no other super-continental land mass was to be found in southern waters.

In the words of Cook himself, "The intention of the voyage has in every respect been fully answered, the Southern Hemisphere sufficiently explored and the final end put to the searching after a Southern Continent."

MOBY DICK

"Fish," he said, "I love you and respect you very much.
But I will kill you dead before this day ends."

ERNEST HEMINGWAY, THE OLD MAN AND THE SEA

"Is Moby Dick the whale or the man?" asked the humorist Harold W. Ross, and well he might, as Captain Ahab of the *Pequod* is perhaps as famous as the whale itself. But it is, of course, the name of the huge and legendary white whale that is the fo-cal point of Captain Ahab's mad and obsessive hatred in the novel *Moby-Dick* by Herman Melville (1819–1891), first published in Britain in 1851 as *The Whale* and in America later the same year as *Moby-Dick, or, The Whale.*

Captain Ahab, the King Lear of whaling, searches for the white whale so that he may wreak his vengeance on it, the beast having bitten off the captain's leg on an ear-lier whaling voyage ("And then it was, that suddenly sweeping his sickle-shaped lower jaw beneath him, Moby Dick had reaped away Ahab's leg, as a mower a blade of grass in the field"). This whale, in the eyes of Ahab, represents all the evil in the world, and he sees it as his task to seek out the beast and destroy it. In the end, however, Ahab and his ship and all the crew except the narrator Ishmael are in-stead themselves destroyed by Moby Dick (the wrecking of the *Pequod* is based on the true story of the *Essex*, a whaling ship that was repeatedly rammed and then sunk in the Pacific Ocean in 1820 by an enraged bull sperm whale; see The Whaler *Essex*, chapter 11; see also Philbrick in the bibliography for a detailed and thor-oughly researched account of this incident).

This classic story of the American whale fishery is told by the narrator Ishmael, who signs aboard the doomed whaler *Pequod* because he is restless and disen-chanted with life on land. The novel opens with the famous line, "Call me Ish-mael," the narrator's name being an allusion to the biblical Ishmael, the outcast son of Abraham and Hagar (from the Hebrew Yishmael, "God is hearing"); Ishmael is the prototype of the outlaw, the wanderer in the wilderness, which is what Melville's narrator becomes. The whale Moby Dick is regarded by various critics as the embodiment of evil, where the urge to destroy lurks always at the center of creation; and others see the beast as the symbolic victim of modern man's need to dominate nature.

Listen to Captain Ahab himself:

All ye mast-headers have before now heard me give orders about a
white whale. Look ye! d'ye see this Spanish ounce of gold? . . . it is a
sixteen-dollar piece, men . . . Whosoever of ye raises me a white-headed
whale with a wrinkled brow and a crooked jaw; whosoever of ye
raises me that white-headed whale, with three holes punctured in his
starboard fluke—look ye, whosoever of ye raises me that same white
whale, he shall have this gold ounce, my boys!

And the stage is set for Captain Ahab's meeting with the legendary white whale.
Robertson introduces his account of whales and whaling with an interesting comment:

"If you're writing a book about whaling," I was advised by an experienced
Whaling Inspector, "don't tell the exact *truth. If you do, nobody ashore*
will believe you, and nobody in the whaling world will recognize you as
a whaleman; for no whaleman author ever *has told the exact truth*
since Herman Melville set the standard of whaling mendacity."

Life on board a whaling ship was one of endless tedium occasionally broken
by the excitement of the chase (and not infrequently by the death or injury of one
or more of the men), the fixing of the harpoon, and the subsequent lancing and
flensing and trying-out, when the whale's blubber was boiled for its oil, which was
stored below in barrels. A cruise often lasted three years, and it was not unknown for
a whaling ship to return to its home port with not one barrel of oil in its hold.

In between times, while the whaler crisscrossed the seas in pursuit of its quarry
the men off watch slept or smoked or carved whale teeth or bone into a variety of
odds and ends. ("We are regularly cruising with not enough to do to keep a man
off a growl," wrote William Davis in his journal for January 23, 1874.) And if they
weren't doing any of these things they were usually yarning—"gamming," in the ver-
nacular of whaling men, exchanging legendary tales (some true, some not quite)
about whales and whalers they'd known.

Many of these yarns concerned whales that had been struck and then had broken free, such as when in 1802 Captain Peter Ruddock fixed his whale then lost it,
only to regain it thirteen years later when his men killed the whale they were chas-
ing, to discover Ruddock's old rusting harpoon embedded in the beast's side. A
whale taken by the *Milton* was unusual in that it whistled shrilly when it spouted;
the reason for this was that the blade of a harpoon from the whaler *Central America* had been lodged in its blowhole some fifteen years earlier, in such a fashion that
it somewhat resembled the workings of a steam whistle.

At some time in the early 1870s a right whale (so named because it was the
"right whale" to go after, a slow swimmer with very thick blubber and much *baleen*
[whalebone]) was caught in the North Pacific by the *Cornelius Howland*. During
flensing (stripping the flesh) a harpoon iron from the *Ansell Gibbs* was discovered

buried in the animal. But for the past ten years the *Gibbs* had been whaling only in the North Atlantic, which meant that this whale had either gone round the Horn or discovered the Northwest Passage. But right whales, for whatever reason, had never been known to cross the Equator (which in this case it would have had to do twice), so presumably the leviathan captured by the *Howland* had entered the North Pacific by way of the long-sought Northwest Passage.

The most popular legends were those of whales known for their fighting qualities. For example, in the early 1800s the black sperm whale known as New Zealand Tom (he was named for the feeding grounds that he favored) was famous for the dozens of whaling boats that he had destroyed (when he was finally taken by the *Adonis* he managed to turn nine pursuing boats into matchwood before dying). His aggressive nature is probably explained by the several harpoon blades found in his hide during flensing. There was also Timor Jack, who frequented the Timor Sea and during his career accounted for many whaleboats before finally succumbing to the keen and cruel lance.

But among all the stories that whalers exchanged during their many idle hours while cruising or drinking and yarning in the seedy bars that infest the seaports of the world, one name stood out above all others: Mocha Dick, a bull sperm whale known both for the enormous white scar across his gigantic head and his ferocity in attacking whaling ships and the boats that chased him.

This whale took his name from the first reported attack that he made against a whaleboat in 1810 near Mocha Island, about 360 miles south of Valparaíso on the Pacific coast of South America. So renowned was Mocha Dick for his ability to escape capture and at the same time destroy almost everything sent after him, that no doubt many attacks laid to his account were in fact made by other whales; but the stories about him didn't suffer in the telling, to the extent that for the next fifty years he became "the white whale," still attacking whaleboats, whaling ships, and the men in them.

After some hundred or so battles in which thirty men had died and many dozens of whaleboats had been destroyed, blind in one eye and carrying nineteen irons in his scarred hide, it is generally agreed that Mocha Dick met his end at the hands of a Swedish whaler in 1859; and though he passed, finally, from the wide oceans, his reputation ensured that one day the story of his exploits would become one of the pillars of the world's great literature. It remained only for Herman Melville—already experienced in the whale fishery as one of the crew of the *Acushnet*, out of Fairhaven, Massachusetts—to produce his masterpiece about Moby Dick.

5

MARITIME HISTORY

Seafaring, like farming and fishing, is one of man's oldest professions (one apologizes to seamen everywhere for the workaday comparison offered here, but the analogy had to be made); and, like any long-established and noble profession, seafaring boasts a history that defies comparison.

Every branch of the profession of arms—army, navy, air force—creates its own history, the force of which derives from the fact that men and women have stood shoulder to shoulder in sharing the task of repelling their country's enemies. Facing death alone is no light task; it is made a little easier, perhaps, when your comrades are with you.

National navies, as instruments of political policy, date back to ancient Persia, Greece, and Rome; some other early navies, necessarily organized on a much smaller scale, include the longships of the Vikings, harassing the coasts of Britain and Western Europe during the Middle Ages. But it was the age of discovery during the Renaissance period—the fifteenth and sixteenth centuries—that more urgently brought into focus the kind of navy we are familiar with today. Examples follow of how navies the world over write their own histories.

THE BRITISH ROYAL NAVY

"It is upon the Navy that, under the good Providence of God,
the wealth, prosperity and the peace of these Islands and
of the Empire do mainly depend."

ARTICLES OF WAR

The word *navy* is from the Latin *navis*, ship; originally it applied to the entire shipping of a nation, including warships, merchant vessels, and fishing craft. The Royal Navy dates from the time of the Restoration in 1660, when Charles II (1630–1685) regained his throne and the Admiralty Office was established. The navy as such had existed under the reigns of Edward IV (1442–1483), Henry VII (1457–1509), his son Henry VIII (1491–1547), and others, but it is only from the time of Charles II that we have a continuous history of a navy closely supported by, and identified with, the monarch.

During the reign of Charles II, Samuel Pepys (1633–1703; he was the writer of the famous diary) established the Admiralty as an effective administrative organization. He was instrumental in introducing the Articles of War, navy establishments for war and for peace, and—perhaps of greatest importance—in laying down the requirement that experience rather than influence would be the basis for promotion.

A hundred years later, Lord Anson (see chapter 8), who circumnavigated the world in 1740–1744, added to Pepys's excellent administrative achievements. Anson regularized naval discipline, resisted political influence, and attempted to reform the dockyards, which were sinks of appalling venality and corruption. He also introduced uniform clothing for officers (1748), supervised the introduction of copper sheathing for hulls (1761), and expressed interest in Harrison's chronometer (1761). He also showed great enthusiasm for the gunnery experiments carried out by Benjamin Robins between 1743 and 1750.

When war broke out between Britain and her American colonies in 1775, the Royal Navy had become weakened by political and financial neglect, and it was unable to maintain its accustomed supremacy at sea (for example, see John Paul Jones, chapter 8). In turn the French Revolution and the subsequent Revolutionary and Napoleonic wars of 1793–1815 destroyed the discipline of the French navy, leaving Horatio Nelson (see Lord Nelson, chapter 8) to introduce into naval warfare the concept of ruthless and total destruction that so characterized the British navy of that particular period. The peace of 1815 ushered in an era when the British Merchant Service found itself in almost total control of the world's trade routes, which had earlier been opened up by the Royal Navy.

The age of steam, which finally ended the epoch of the sailing ship in the late nineteenth century (see, for example, The Age of Sail and The Clipper Ships, both chapter 8, and The Suez Canal and The Panama Canal, both chapter 12), introduced a powerful awareness of the importance of a nationally organized, modernized, and properly maintained navy. The Naval Defense Act of 1889 completed the transition from sail to steam and laid down a settled building policy for a modern navy ready to take its place among the nations of the twentieth century; see, for example, HMS *Dreadnought*, chapter 10.

Naval Salutes

"I sent a lieutenant ashore to acquaint the governor of our arrival,
and to make an excuse for our not saluting."
Captain James Cook, Third Voyage

For a long time the only form of personal salute in the British navy was by doffing the headgear; naval ratings always removed their hats when approaching or being approached by any officer, and junior officers removed theirs to all senior officers. Queen Victoria put an end to this practice because she did not like seeing her fighting men in uniform standing about bareheaded; in today's navy, however, hats are still removed under certain circumstances. In the U.S. Navy, headgear is always worn outdoors and removed indoors, with a few minor exceptions.

The origin of the present form of the hand salute is lost to us. It may date from the days when an inferior always uncovered his head in the presence of his superior, the hand movement being explained as the first part of the motion needed to remove the headdress. The salute may also be a holdover from the days of armor; when two warriors raised their visors to each other with opened hands they were exchanging tokens of trust, as each was laying himself open to attack from the other. Another theory suggests that the hand salute is a modification of the Asian custom of shading the eyes when in the presence of an exalted personage.

All naval ratings and officers must salute whenever they enter ship by way of the gangway, and whenever they set foot on the quarterdeck. This custom may well derive from the fact that ships used to carry a shrine in the after part of the vessel, the salute being a mark of obeisance to the religious object kept in the shrine. On the other hand, it may simply be that the salute is a mark of respect to the sovereign whose authority is represented by the ship's colors, which are displayed at the stern.

Until 1923 all hand salutes in the British navy were given with the left hand, but this was switched to the right hand because a left-hand salute was considered a gross insult by personnel from India and Africa, who at that time swelled the ranks of the British armed forces (in a number of ethnic groups—especially in the Middle East—the left hand is used in the latrine).

Warships traditionally saluted each other by lowering their topsails or letting fly their t'gallant sheets; releasing a sail was a way of signifying that the ship's presence was innocent because it would lose headway with a started sheet or loosed sail and should therefore not be regarded as a threat. It was also obligatory for merchantmen to salute a warship; Masefield recorded that he once saw a schooner lower its topsail to a cruiser, but this particular custom has long since died out (see William Kidd, chapter 14, for an instance of what could happen if in earlier times you omitted to show proper respect to one of HM's warships).

When sail was eventually displaced by steam a new means of saluting by an unarmed vessel had to be devised. The custom that evolved required that the ensign (national flag) be dipped—that is, lowered halfway and not rehoisted until the ship being greeted had acknowledged the salute. It is a maritime convention that merchant ships, and sometimes private yachts, today dip their ensigns to warships of all nations on the high seas; furthermore, the ensign is kept at the dip until the warship has rehoisted hers. Yachts and other vessels customarily fly the flag of the country in whose national waters they are sailing; it should be flown on the starboard side of the crosstrees or, if these are not fitted, from high in the rigging.

Gun salutes were always fired bows-on to the ship being saluted, because a broadside of shotted (loaded) guns (regarded as necessary in order to make a satisfactory noise, which apparently appeals to the naval sense of propriety) could be construed as a hostile act if fired toward the other ship; a vessel firing bows-on could not possibly hit the ship being saluted, even if shotted guns were discharged.

Originally, warships saluting each other would fire off their guns at a prodigious rate, as naval officers were then far more prodigal about filling the sky with the thunderclap of cannon than prudent with the powder that wrought it. In 1675 the British Admiralty introduced rules that limited the number of guns to be fired by warships intent on saluting each other, this having the happy effect of regularizing an international custom as well as conserving expensive gunpowder.

The secretary of the Admiralty at that time, Samuel Pepys, worked out a scale in which the most junior admiral (there were three grades of admiral: red, the most senior; white; and blue the most junior) received three guns, with an increase of two guns for each step up in rank to the admiral of the fleet, who would receive nineteen guns. The monarch was awarded twenty-one guns, which custom is still observed today, with a twenty-one-gun salute also being awarded visiting presidents or royalty. The odd number of guns came about because it had long been a custom to fire an even number at naval funerals.

PLIMSOLL LINE

"Waves of intoxication, lapping against the Plimsoll Line of articulation."
ANTHONY POWELL, *A DANCE TO THE MUSIC OF TIME*

The Plimsoll Line or Plimsoll Mark is the series of marks painted onto the side of a merchant ship to indicate the greatest depth to which the vessel may be safely loaded under various conditions. They take their name from Samuel Plimsoll (1824–1898), MP, a coal merchant, British politician, and social reformer, who after a great deal of effort on his part and determined resistance from shipowners on their part, introduced his regulations into Parliament, which ratified them in 1876, thus earning Plimsoll the nickname "the sailors' friend," which indeed he was.

Plimsoll's efforts for reform were directed especially at "coffin ships," unseaworthy, overloaded vessels often heavily insured by their unscrupulous owners, who thereby risked the lives of the crews that manned them. Plimsoll entered Parliament in 1868, and having failed to pass a bill dealing with this criminal overloading of ships, in 1872 he published a book entitled *Our Seamen*, which made a great impression throughout the country.

A royal commission was appointed to investigate the matter and in 1875 a government bill was introduced, which Plimsoll, though regarding it as inadequate, agreed to accept. However, Prime Minister Disraeli announced that the bill would be dropped, whereupon Plimsoll abused the members of the House and shook his fist in the Speaker's face. Nevertheless, popular feeling throughout the country forced the Government to pass a bill, which in the following year was amended into the Merchant Shipping Act (1876), which gave stringent powers of inspection to the Board of Trade.

Plimsoll later became president of the Sailors' and Firemen's Union and was instrumental in raising further agitation about the horrors of cattle ships.

LLOYD'S OF LONDON

"Insurance: An ingenious modern game of chance in which the player is permitted to enjoy the comfortable conviction that he is beating the man who keeps the table."
AMBROSE BIERCE, *THE DEVIL'S DICTIONARY*

Lloyd's of London is the well-known international insurance market in London; it is also the world center of maritime intelligence—the daily movements of merchant ships, marine casualties, and the like. Its history of marine underwriting dates from 1688, when Edward Lloyd's Coffee House (situated first in Tower

Street, then in Lombard Street, later in Pope's Head Alley, whence finally it was relocated in 1773 to rooms in the upper part of the Royal Exchange) became the gathering place for businessmen and marine insurance underwriters. Insurance was accepted at Lloyd's by individual underwriters representing different firms, not by Lloyd's itself; the coffeehouse simply provided the premises and information-gathering facilities, great convenience for shippers looking for insurers willing to underwrite a merchant venture.

Lloyd's gradually became the center for this type of insurance which, given Britain's extensive sea trade with the rest of the world, conferred on it a considerable degree of importance. In 1696 Lloyd himself issued a printed news sheet called *Lloyd's News*, which in 1734 was replaced by the well-known and still current *Lloyd's List*, a daily paper specializing in shipping news (Lloyd himself died in 1726). It is second only to the *London Gazette* as London's oldest newspaper.

Lloyd's *Register of Shipping* is an annual publication containing the particulars of all known seagoing vessels, compiled by an independent society of shipowners. This society surveys ships and reports on their condition, *A1* being the old and famous classification indicating very seaworthy. The letter *A* refers to hulls that meet Lloyd's requirements concerning materials and method of construction, while the numeral *1* refers to a vessel's ground tackle; if her anchors, cables, and such meet Lloyd's standards they are given the classification *1*. Thus, to be *A1* was to be first rate (see First Rate, chapter 7), the very best. The more modern system uses the notation *100 A1*, but the older classification is still widely used and has since the eighteenth century gone into colloquial usage to designate anything that is of the best quality.

Whenever an important announcement is to be made at Lloyd's the Lutine Bell is rung, this being the bell from HMS *Lutine*, which sank in a gale off the Dutch coast in 1799 with the loss of everyone on board except one person, who died shortly after being rescued. A great deal of coin and bullion was lost in the wreck; during salvage operations in 1858 the ship's bell and rudder were recovered, along with some of the bullion. The bell was presented to Lloyd's, who had insured the ship and her cargo, and the rudder was made into a chair and desk for Lloyd's chairman and secretary.

The Lutine Bell is rung once whenever a total wreck is reported and twice for an overdue ship. It was also rung in 1963 for the death of President John F. Kennedy and in 1965 for the death of Sir Winston Churchill. (See also Plimsoll Line, above.)

P&O Shipping Line

"Four hoarse blasts of a ship's whistle still raise the hair on my neck."
John Steinbeck, *Travels with Charley*

The letters P&O stand for Peninsular and Oriental (Steam Navigation Company), which, with Cunard, is one of the most famous shipping lines in the world. It has been long associated in the public mind with travel to exotic places, and for this reason alone it is strongly embedded in the warp and weft of the fabric of maritime lore.

The company grew out of a London shipping agency business started by Brodie Wilcox and Arthur Anderson after the Napoleonic War (1803–1815). In 1826 they added the City of Dublin Steam Packet Company to their agency and with it began a steamship service to Portugal. A packet boat was a fast vessel dedicated to carrying mail between ports on a regular basis; it also carried passengers and goods. Its name dates from the sixteenth century, when government letters, dispatches, etc., were collectively called "the Packet."

The City of Dublin Steam Packet Company prospered, and in 1837 it was awarded a contract from the British government to carry the mails from England to the Iberian Peninsula (Spain and Portugal, named from the early Iberian people who lived there; hence the River Ebro of today, from the ancient River Iberus). By 1840 the shipping line had been renamed the Peninsular Steam Navigation Company; and in the same year, when it gained the mail contract for Egypt and India, the word "Oriental" appeared in its name, the service being inaugurated by the paddle steamer SS *Oriental.*

In 1842 P&O—the name by which the company had become known and which later became arguably the most famous name in world shipping—began a regular service between Suez, the Egyptian seaport at the southern end of what is now The Suez Canal (see chapter 12), and Calcutta, on the northern portion of the east coast of India. Travelers from Europe could now disembark at Port Said, on the Mediterranean coast of Egypt, journey overland to Suez, on the northernmost reach of the Red Sea, and thence take a sea passage to India. Ten years later, in 1852, P&O added the Suez–Bombay run to its schedule, and in the same year it secured the mail contract to Australia. By now P&O ships were already sailing to Singapore, as well as to ports in China, thus establishing the line as a major force in the Indian Ocean and the West Pacific. When the Suez Canal opened in 1869 it was now possible for travelers to make an unbroken journey to India, Australia, or the Orient in a style of comfort considered state of the art for those times.

The Red Sea–Indian Ocean route gave rise to the notion that *posh*, said to mean "*p*ort *o*ut *s*tarboard *h*ome," originated from the belief that passengers could, for a premium, secure a cabin on the port side (left side) of the ship when steaming across the Indian Ocean from Suez to India, thereby placing themselves on the supposedly cooler side of the vessel and away from the glare of the sun off the sea (and the reverse, of course). This persistent myth—for myth it certainly is—is dealt under Traveling POSH in the next chapter.

In 1914 P&O amalgamated with the British India Line and then absorbed the New Zealand Shipping Company and other lines. After World War I, despite having lost some 1.5 million tons of shipping to German attacks, P&O had emerged as a large and significant world shipping fleet. A few people may remember some of the post–World War I P&O passenger ships, all with names that began with the prefix *Strath,* and all painted in the colors that became immediately and famously recognizable as P&O—white hulls and yellow masts and funnels—such as the *Strathaird* (1931), the *Strathnaver* (1931), and the *Stratheden* (1937).

During World War II the line lost over a million tons of shipping, more than half of its holdings. Between 1950 and 1960, tankers were added to their fleet of cargo ships, while their passenger vessels were reduced in number and replaced by fewer but larger and faster ships such as the *Canberra,* named after the national capital of Australia.

The colorful P&O lithograph posters of exotic cruises became well known in those heady postwar days when the adventure of sea travel to foreign parts had at last become available to ordinary folk. The famous P&O house flag still flies on its shipping round the world: a rectangle divided by its two diagonals into four triangles, the top one white, the lower yellow, the right one (the fly) red, and the left one (the hoist, the side nearest the flagpole) blue.

BEAUFORT WIND SCALE

"She says, 'Did you hear the wind, did it keep you awake last night?'
I says, 'No.' And then she says, 'Wait until your sons go to sea,
you won't sleep the same,' and it was true."
MRS. GRACE HOLLAND, *THE BRITISH SEAFARER*

The Beaufort Wind Scale, an empirical means of determining wind force at sea, was devised by Rear Admiral Sir Francis Beaufort (1774–1857) during his tenure as hydrographer of the Royal Navy. The scale depends on observing the effects of wind on waves, with respect to wave length (see Ocean Waves, chapter 7), wave height, spray created, breaking crests (white horses), foam streaks, wind-borne foam, visibility, and so on.

It is a reasonably accurate system of gauging wind force within 2 or 3 knots at the lower end of the scale and within 6 to 10 knots at the higher end—at which point one is preoccupied with a howling hurricane anyway, and the question of wind speed becomes academic. (See also Trade Winds and Of Knots and Logs, both chapter 7.)

BEAUFORT NUMBER	WIND SPEED IN KNOTS	WIND DESCRIPTION	HEIGHT OF SEA IN FEET	DEEP SEA DESCRIPTION
0	<1	Calm	—	Flat calm, surface mirrorlike
1	1–3	Light airs	¼	Small wavelets like fish scales, no crests
2	4–6	Light breeze	½	Small wavelets, more pronounced, glassy crests do not break
3	7–10	Gentle breeze	2	Large wavelets, crests begin to break, foam is glassy
4	11–16	Moderate breeze	3 ½	Small waves, breeze becoming longer, white horses more frequent
5	17–21	Fresh breeze	6	Moderate waves, and longer, many breaking crests and white horses, chance of some spray
6	22–27	Strong breeze	9 ½	Large waves beginning to form, white crests more extensive, some spray probable
7	28–33	Near gale	13 ½	Sea heaps up, white foam is blown in streaks
8	34–40	Gale	18	Moderately high waves of greater length, crests form spindrift, foam is blown in well-marked streaks
9	41–47	Strong gale	23	High waves, dense streaks of foam, crests begin to roll over, spray may affect visibility
10	48–55	Storm	29	Very high waves with long overhanging crests, sea surface becomes white with large patches of foam, visibility affected
11	56–63	Violent storm	37	Exceptionally high waves, sea completely covered with foam
12	64+	Hurricane	—	Air is filled with spray, visibility very seriously affected

The following wind scale for use on land, based on Newby, may be used with confidence by those who prefer not to go to sea for their excitement.

WIND FORCE	WIND DESCRIPTION	HUMAN ACTIVITY	BIRD ACTIVITY	INVERTEBRATE ACTIVITY
7	Moderate gale	Walking becomes difficult	Small perching birds grounded	Butterflies grounded
8	Fresh gale	General progress impeded	Swifts, ducks, swallows, and few raptors flying	Only dragonflies still airborne
9	Strong gale	Children blown over	Only swifts remain airborne	All insects grounded
10	Whole gale	Adults blown over	All birds grounded	

6

NAUTICAL CUSTOM

O f all humanity's many pursuits and occupations, there is none so interwoven with the warp and weft of belief, superstition, and time-out-of-mind practice than seafaring.

This is the very fabric of the lore and legend of the sea. Scratching the backstay during a calm while whistling very softly may well entice a useful breeze to blow; whistling aloud, however, could very likely annoy Saint Anthony (patron saint of wind), and thereby bring on a blow from exactly the wrong quarter. In any case, whistling aboard ship could be confused with the bosun's call, the shrill pipe that he uses for conveying orders. Thus whistling is discouraged on board ship (as are women, interestingly enough; see also chapter 19 for many more examples of established seafaring superstitions).

Along with other curious practices, crossing the Equator has been celebrated since ancient times as an occasion for initiating first-timers into the brotherhood of the sea. Following are a number of other old and interesting and well-established customs much observed by seafarers.

THE *BUCENTAUR*

"It looks, at a distance, like a great town half floated by a deluge."
JOSEPH ADDISON, ON VENICE

Bucentaur (from the Italian *buzino d'oro*, golden bark or ship) was the name given to the state barge or galley of Venice in which, on every Ascension Day, the doge or leader (commonly an elected duke) renewed the republic's wedding vows with the Adriatic Sea by having himself rowed out, with a great deal of pomp and ceremony, to the lagoon, into which he then cast a golden ring.

This event, known as the Sposalizio (from *sposare*, to marry), was always an intensely public affair. The Venetian lagoon would be crowded with ships of every description, over the sides of which hung rich and varied tapestries; waves of music and the echoes of booming cannon filled the air, the bells of all the churches in the city pealed throughout the day, and the men and women who crowded the ships and gondolas and barges continuously expressed their joy in song. And all the while, the great golden 100-foot *Bucentaur* moved slowly and solemnly out into the lagoon, pulled by her forty oars rising and falling in unison. When the state barge was in position, the men would rest on their oars and the doge would rise from his seat in the stern and address the ocean thus: "We espouse thee, O Sea, in token of our true and perpetual dominion over thee"; then he would slowly remove a gold wedding ring from his finger and fling it into the water.

This ceremony commemorated the victory of the Doge Pietro Orseolo II over the Dalmatian pirates. On Ascension Day (the fortieth day after Easter, commemorating the ascension of Christ) in A.D. 1000, the Venetians launched an expedition against the hordes of pirates who infested the Dalmatian coast on the eastern shores of the Adriatic Sea. The raid was so successful that each year thereafter the chief notable of Venice would perform a public ceremony in which the sea was blessed both as a thanksgiving for the victory vouchsafed to the republic and as a means of propitiating and calming the unpredictable waters (see Launching a Ship, chapter 19, for a ceremony with a similar background; see also Earrings for Cutthroats, chapter 14, for an analogous practice involving gold rings).

By the thirteenth century these rites had taken on the trappings of a wedding ceremony, it being an article of faith that a husband had a natural and God-given right of dominion over a wife and all her possessions; hence the vow made by the doge at the height of the ceremony. Venice had by this time become a powerful maritime empire whose greatness was wholly dependent on the sea; if this pledge were not renewed every year, it was believed by many, the sea would regard herself as jilted and thereafter deny the city the benefit of her very considerable dowry.

In fact, the enormous wealth, prestige, and power of Venice depended on her ability to control and maintain a maritime empire that stretched the length and breadth of the Mediterranean, the Black Sea, and the eastern reaches of the Atlantic. Her trading ventures (one will recall Antonio's remark in *The Merchant of Venice*: "My ventures are not in one bottom trusted") ranged from Crete to Egypt, Britain, and Flanders (in the medieval period a sovereign country comprising portions of modern Belgium, northern France, and southwest Netherlands). Venice traded in slaves from the Slav countries, silks from Byzantium (the predecessor of Constantinople, now Istanbul), spices from Alexandria, timber and pitch from Dalmatia, iron and woolen cloth from the Alps region—all to be reexported to western Europe at a very handsome profit.

The wealth and power of the city-state of Venice, which in the fifth century began as an untidy agglomeration of villages in the swamps of the northern Adriatic, lasted for more than a thousand years. During this period of prosperity the basilica of San Marco was built, as was the huge market alongside the Grand Canal.

The last *Bucentaur* was built in 1729, but in 1798 Bonaparte's French forces invaded the Italian states and broke up this splendid ship for its golden tapestries and artifacts. Some of its remains are kept in the Museo Civico Correr in Venice, remnants of a once proud and important link with the sea.

CROSSING THE LINE

*"Afternoon. Crossed the Equator. In the distance it looked like a
blue ribbon stretched across the ocean. Several passengers kodak'd it."*
MARK TWAIN, *FOLLOWING THE EQUATOR*

Crossing the line is the ancient custom of initiating into certain arcane mysteries of the sea those passengers or crew who have never before crossed the Equator. At a suitable time during the day on which the ship has moved from one hemisphere to the other, all those who have not previously crossed the line are assembled and then inspected, addressed, and dealt with by King Neptune (see chapter 1) and his court. In the days of sailing ships this group of nautical worthies went to a lot of trouble to be as fearsome in appearance and as raucous in voice and manner as possible, having at some time in the past been similarly dealt with—and roughly, too—at their own initiation.

King Neptune (commonly selected from one of the less inhibited members of the crew) makes a suitably boisterous appearance on the forecastle, cunningly disguised as the old sea god, bristling with barnacles, festooned with masses of seaweed, a golden crown perched on his dripping locks and a trident in his horny hand. His wife, Queen Amphitrite (properly, the wife of Poseidon, see also chapter 1), appears at his side, hardly less fearsome in appearance than her husband, she being another of the hardcase sailors from the foredeck.

Making up the rest of the king's court are a barber, the more evil-looking the better; a surgeon, chosen solely for his villainous nature; and a bevy of nymphs and bears, the former being representative, after a fashion, of those winsome creatures once commonly found in the oceanic environment, and the latter—the bears— awarded a guest appearance no doubt because of their reputation for creating and sustaining mayhem when so required.

The king and his motley crew stalk around the ship for some time, then the king holds court next to a large canvas bath filled with seawater, and the fun begins. Veterans of previous crossings are acknowledged and given an award of some sort, then the novices are paraded before King Neptune, made to account for their miserable selves, attended to by the barber and the surgeon in a somewhat cavalier fashion, then one by one they are tipped backward into the waiting bath of water, where the nymphs and bears make certain that each initiate experiences a thorough wetting. For their pains the novices are then each issued a certificate that ensures their exemption from similar dealings should they ever be so bold as to cross the line again.

The description of this age-old ceremony that Rogers gives us bears repeating:

> *The crew are mustered in the waist [aft of the mainmast] and the captain is on the poop [aftermost deck] when a cry comes from somewhere forward:*
>
> *"Ship ahoy! Ship ahoy!"*
>
> *"Who hails us?" demands the skipper in a foghorn bellow.*
>
> *" 'Tis Father Neptune," says one of the men.*
>
> *"Bring him on board, then," orders the skipper.*
>
> *Now there is seen coming aft a strange company led by Old Neptune himself. He wears a beard and wig made of yellow rope-yarn, and one tattooed hand grasps the shaft of a boat-hook, which serves him for a trident. Over his body is draped part of an old sail held at the waist by a leather belt, into which is thrust Neptune's razor, a huge comic-opera weapon made of hoop-iron and wood. In his wake come, first, Amphitrite, his wife, a masculine-looking female, and then his henchmen, carrying a large tub, which will be filled with water. Before the gathered men Neptune halts and delivers himself somewhat like this:*
>
> *"You have greenhorns on board this ship who have never been shaved*

*and baptized by Neptune; so let them stand forth." Then each victim
in turn is seated on an upturned bucket while the ancient buffoonery
is gone through. First he is asked his name, and while his lips open to
frame the words a dirty swab covered with soapsuds and grease is
slapped into his mouth and liberally applied to his face. Then comes
the shaving with the comic-opera razor, after which the tyro is tipped
backwards into the tub of sea-water, from which he emerges a tyro
no longer. He has crossed the Line, and now may call himself a deep-
water sailor.*

Rogers points out that things were much rowdier in earlier days, as when Captain Frederick Marryat (1792–1848) was at sea. In those times it was more of an
ordeal for novices rather than just a bit of fooling around; roughhousing was the
order of the day and woe betide any unpopular members of the crew—invariably
they had the worst of it.

The origin of all this ceremonial tomfoolery attached to crossing the Equator
lies in the sailor's felt need to make offerings so as to propitiate the gods of the sea,
such as Neptune (Poseidon for the Greeks). Pagan seafarers rounding a prominent
headland or landmark would make a sacrifice to the appropriate deity, probably in
the form of an animal; and at such geographical features it was common to find a
temple set up to that particular god. Another kind of ordeal is mentioned in an
account of passing through the Straits of Gibraltar in 1675:

*Ape's Hill is a rock of great height, and extreme steep; on the top of it
lives a Marabout wizard or Enchanter; and what vessel soever of the
Turks goes by, gives him a gun [fires it] as she goes to beg a fortunate
voyage. Here everyone that hath not yet been in the Straits pays his
dollar or must be ducked at the yardarm.*

When paganism was gradually supplanted by Christianity the saints replaced the
old heathen deities. In the early sixteenth century the French instituted, instead of an
ordeal, an accolade called Les Chevaliers de la Mer (Knights of the Sea), when novices
rounding certain headlands were awarded a knighthood of this order.

At a later date, crossing one of the two Tropics called forth the same sort of ceremonial as crossing the Equator does today. Kemp tells us that King Neptune's visits to ships are first recorded in Aubin's *Dictionnaire nautique* (1702), and that
Woodes Rogers in his book *A Cruising Voyage round the World* (1712) gives an account of festivities featuring King Neptune that attended a crossing of the Tropic of
Cancer. According to another account, it was the custom in French ships in the
1600s for Neptune, in the person of the second mate, to initiate all novices on
board into the mysteries of crossing the line by the simple expedient of belaboring
each of them with a wooden sword and then tipping a bucket of seawater over
their heads.

To Flog a Dead Horse

"They say my horse is dead and gone,
And they say so, and they hope so.
They say my horse is dead and gone,
Oh, poor old man!

I'll hoist him to the main yardarm,
And they say so, and they hope so.
I'll hoist him to the main yardarm,
Oh, poor old man!"

"Dead Horse Chanty"

There are many hundreds of everyday expressions that have come down to us from the days of sail, some examples of which are *to come adrift, beachcomber, to lose one's bearings, to blow over, between the devil and the deep blue sea, first rate,* and so on. But of all the metaphors that have passed from the language of the old-time sailor into the daily coinage of the twentieth century, *to flog a dead horse* is one of the most unusual, not because of its meaning, but because of the fact that seamen and horses are a most unlikely combination.

"Dead horse" was the seaman's term for the first month he spent at sea after signing on for a voyage. When a sailor joined a merchant ship he received a month's wages in advance; invariably he spent it before the vessel left port and consequently he worked his first month afloat without the prospect of being paid for it. That is to say, of course he knew he'd been paid for that period but he had nothing to show for it—his wages had gone to purchasing grog, tobacco, and the company of women; like it or not, he had to perform those services for which he had earlier accepted his wages. This was a clever device on the part of the shipowner, because when a seaman signed the ship's articles he was legally bound to that vessel for that voyage. Should he change his mind it would be too late; the law would hunt him down and punish him. Besides, there was nowhere for a seaman to hide; his dress, his manners, and his way of speech marked him immediately as a sailor, and he would be instantly recognizable as such to everyone.

For that first month it seemed to the seaman that he was working for nothing, and so he called this period "the dead horse"; having already been paid, he was duty bound to deliver his labor for that period, but he would resist working harder than he ought to. This was the meaning of the phrase: for that first month the horse (the seaman himself) was, as with an exhausted farm horse, "dead"; it was pointless belaboring him into additional activity beyond what had already been contracted for.

At the end of the "dead horse" month the crew would make a canvas or bag-and-straw effigy of a horse and parade it around the ship (if there were passengers on board they would be encouraged to make a donation of money). Then, with a lot of noisy hoo-ha the horse would be hoisted aloft on the main yardarm and set on fire, the "Dead Horse Chanty" was sung by all the crew, and it was then cut down from the heights and dropped into the sea. It is worth noting that this chanty was the only one ever sung for pleasure rather than as an accompaniment to work.

The expression today means to persist in a useless argument or effort, to try to revive interest in a topic that has long since been settled.

THE GETTING OF GROG

"Deceased had been accustomed to drink a vile mixture procured at spirit stores known as grog, and compounded of drippings from wine, spirit, and beer casks."
THE STANDARD (ENGLISH NEWSPAPER), FEBRUARY 1884

Nowadays grog is alcohol of any kind, but originally it was the seafaring term for rum that had been diluted with water. Brandy used to be the seaman's daily ration of spirits (they also drank prodigious quantities of small beer because their casked water went foul very quickly). However, in 1687 brandy was replaced by neat rum as a result of Britain's defeat of Jamaica, which led to the Royal Navy's acquisition of cheap rum. The daily ration was one pint of rum (slightly over half a liter) for men and half a pint for boys, issued in two halves, one at noon and the other at 6:00 P.M.

In 1740 Admiral Edward Vernon (1684–1757), at the time commander-in-chief of the British Fleet in the West Indies Station, became alarmed at the drunkenness prevalent in the Fleet and ordered that the daily pint of rum be diluted with a quart of water. He thereupon advised the Admiralty of what he proposed to do, as follows:

> *Observing that recent frequent desertions have principally arisen from men stupefying themselves with Spirituous Liquors, I have, after consulting my captains and surgeons, ventured to attack that formidable Dragon, Drunkenness, by giving the general order enclosed.*

This order read:

> *To Captains of the Squadron! Whereas the Pernicious Custom of the Seamen drinking their Allowance of Rum in Drams, and often at once, is attended by many fatal Effects to their Morals as well as their Health, the daily allowance of half a pint a man is to be mixed with a quart of water, to be mixed in one Scuttled Butt kept for that purpose, and to be done upon Deck, and in the presence of the Lieutenant of the Watch, who is to see that the men are not defrauded of their allowance of Rum; it is to be served in two servings, one in the morning and the other in the afternoon. The men that are good Husbands may from the*

savings of their Salt Provisions and Bread purchase Sugar and Limes to
make the water more palatable to them. Dated 21 August 1740 on
board HMS Burford *in Port Royal Harbour.*

The admiral was already known as "Old Grogram" (usually shortened to "Old Grog") because his seagoing cloak was made of a coarse material called grogram (from the French *grosgrain*, "rough texture"). His introduction of the watered-down rum was immediately unpopular and the drink was speedily given the name *grog*. The tradition of the daily issue of spirits was kept alive in the Royal Navy until July 1, 1970, when the grog ration throughout the navy was officially terminated.

Traveling POSH

"Passengers traveling by the P&O . . . would, at some cost,
book their return passage with the arrangement
'Port Outward Starboard Homeward,' thus ensuring
cabins on the cooler side of the ship . . .
Passages were booked 'POSH' accordingly."

Ebenezer Cobham Brewer

Thus the life, if not the birth, of a colorful maritime myth, this one being, like poverty and the common cold, almost ineradicable.

In British English the word *posh* (now perhaps somewhat old-fashioned) means smart, stylish, first rate, high class, well-off, as in *a posh hotel, posh clothes, a posh accent*. Many commentators claim that it is a leftover from the heyday of the British Empire, when travel from Britain to India, Australia, and the Far East was by P&O steamship through the Suez Canal (see P&O Shipping Line, chapter 5).

The outward passage down the Red Sea and across the Indian Ocean north of the Equator was, even at the best of times, unbearably hot. It is said that passengers booking their return journey from Britain to the colonies would try to secure a cabin for the outward-bound journey on the port side of the vessel—that is, on the left-hand or northern side. This was done (it is claimed) because the ship, in approaching the Equator from the north and west, had the sun always on the right-hand or starboard side; the idea was that a cabin on the port side was (supposedly) a little cooler. In a similar fashion, the voyage home to England would be booked for the starboard side. The myth confidently asserts that P&O booking clerks would endorse the passenger's ticket "POSH," which was supposedly their acronym for "*P*ort *O*ut, *S*tarboard *H*ome." Furthermore, because of the demand for these better-located cabins the steamship company would charge a premium on the fare. Consequently, the acronym POSH became associated with those travelers who could afford the higher fare, and they themselves became known as "posh"—that is, well-off, belonging to the moneyed class.

Alas! there is one major obstacle to this theory: despite the fact of its widespread acceptance, there is no evidence to support it. In *A Hundred Year History of the P&O* (1937) Boyd Cable calls the story behind *posh* "a tale"; and in 1962 the P&O librarian reported that he could find no evidence that the initials POSH were ever stamped on the company's tickets or documents of any kind. Not only does the company not have a single record of a POSH booking, there was in fact no differentiation in price according to side of the ship (one wonders, too, if there would have been any worthwhile difference in cabin temperatures on either side of the vessel while in the Red Sea and the Indian Ocean in summer).

One other point seems to have been overlooked by the myth-makers. A P&O booking clerk could be expected to know which cabin numbers were on which side of the ship. It wouldn't be necessary to endorse a ticket with POSH or anything else: the booking clerk would simply give the traveler the appropriately numbered ticket according to that traveler's preferred side. This is not to say that in the days of steamship travel travelers themselves never asked for a port-out-starboard-home cabin, but it is certain that their tickets were never so stamped.

The truth behind the word *posh* is far more prosaic. The term is obsolete Romany (gypsy) slang meaning both *dandy* (elaborate, well-dressed) and *money*. In 1839 (some years before the P&O company was operating) *posh* meant a farthing, a halfpenny—a very small amount; anyone who had some money (a lot of posh) was a *dandy*, a *swell*, what Americans would later call *swank*. Such a person gradually came to be known as *posh*, and later the word was also applied to the comfort and convenience that money could buy.

7

LIFE AT SEA

I n earlier times, especially in the sailing navies, the seaman was treated as little better than a beast of burden, whose only function was to do as he was told and do it promptly; failure to comply would commonly earn him a rope's end across his back, or in more serious cases a flogging that could—and sometimes did—cause his death.

Added to the miseries of usually stern commanders and brutal officers (see, for example, HMS *Hermione* Mutiny, chapter 9) were the frequently rotten and even putrid food, sold to the shipowner by onshore contractors whose chief concern was profit, and of course bad weather. The curious fact is that, even though seafaring was often a wretched life, the seaman who signed off one ship in port—it might well have been a hell ship, like many that plied the Cape Horn (see below) route—just as often signed on to some other vessel.

The mariner of old knew no trade other than a precarious life at sea, which had become his often unhappy lot.

OCEAN WAVES

"We'll rant and we'll roar, all o'er the wild ocean,
We'll rant and we'll roar, all o'er the wild seas."

"SPANISH LADIES"

One of our common life experiences is watching waves and very often swimming or cavorting in them; there are few people today who are unfamiliar with at least an impression of the ocean, and the life-threatening severe storm is perhaps one of our wilder terrors. The mechanics of wave formation are outlined here, and the experiences of some seafarers who have encountered waves very much larger than normal—colloquially known as giant or freak waves—are described.

Waves are caused by the wind blowing across the surface of the ocean (except that the so-called tidal wave, properly a "bore," and the tsunami, come from different causes—see below). If there were no wind, there would be no waves. Friction between the surface water and the wind causes the water particles to oscillate up and down, creating waves that move forward in the direction in which the wind is blowing. An analogous movement occurs when two children hold a jump rope loosely stretched between them, with one child lifting and dropping her end rhythmically until a wave or ripple is created in the rope that moves along its entire length until its energy is absorbed by the child at the other end.

In a similar fashion the wind-blown sea surface moves up and down, with the water particles describing a rotary motion, moving forward at the crest and backward in the trough, and the waveform thus created traveling forward while the surface of the water itself simply rises and falls, in the same way that while the particles of the jump rope do not actually move toward the child at the other end, the ripple so caused does.

The top of a wave is called its crest and the valley between two waves is the trough; the height of a wave is the vertical distance from its trough to its crest, while the length of a wave is the distance between one crest and the one that follows (wave length has nothing to do with the linear or sideways measurement of any particular wave). Wave velocity is the speed at which a waveform moves along the sea surface; the water itself advances at only about 1 percent of the wave velocity: this is called surface drift. The maximum velocity observed in waves is about 25 knots. Wave period is the time interval between two successive crests measured at a fixed point.

All wind-generated waves move moderately slowly, but the tsunami (from the Japanese *tsu*, harbor, and *nami*, wave), which is a surface waveform caused by vertical displacement of the seabed along earthquake fault lines, can have a velocity in deep water of up to 420 knots and a length of up to 500 miles. Tsunamis do not usually attain any great height; in the open ocean they have been observed as a ripple a foot or two high moving very swiftly across the sea surface, with a period generally ranging between 10 and 60 minutes. When a tsunami enters coastal waters the sea level falls for some minutes as if a very low tide were occurring, followed by a very rapid increase in height far beyond any high-tide level; severe damage and heavy loss of life can then occur in inhabited areas. A tsunami may form a tidal bore when it enters the mouth of a large river, often traveling many miles upstream as a solitary wave.

So-called "tidal waves" owe nothing to the action of wind or tide but instead are caused by earthquakes and submarine landslides (the tsunami is one type), and by volcanic eruptions. They typically cause enormous damage on low-lying coasts. When Krakatoa exploded in the Sunda Strait in 1883, the sea waves produced were about 50 feet high; more than 36,000 people perished as their coastal villages and settlements among the neighboring islands were overwhelmed by these massive waves. The long wave produced by the primary explosion reached Cape Horn (see below), a distance of nearly 8,000 miles, and it may have been detected in the English Channel 11,000 miles from the source.

The waterborne shock waves produced by submarine earthquakes can be severe; a vessel struck by one may tumble violently, leading the sailors to believe that they have struck a rock. Because of this, early charts often showed "rocks" where later surveys showed extreme depths of water.

Internal waves can also occur within the ocean itself. They are usually found at the boundary separating a layer of light water (relatively warm and of low salinity) from a layer of heavier water (colder and of higher salinity). The height of such a wave may be as much as 50 feet, but its velocity rarely is above 2 knots. Internal waves cannot be detected at the sea surface.

The face of an advancing wave is always steeper than its back, and if there is a moderate breeze blowing, a small vertical wall forms on the crest. If wind pressure is sufficient, this wall collapses and falls forward, thus becoming a moving mass of water which in a storm or severe gale may sweep across the deck of a vessel and damage her superstructure. Large ships in the vicinity of the Cape of Good Hope and Cape Horn have been known to be completely overwhelmed by the combination of a high and steep breaking wave and the deep trough that intervenes between two such waves.

The relationship between the length of a wave and its height is normally about 13:1; in winds above 10 to 12 knots the ratio may quickly become 7:1. Wave height is commonly determined by the force of the wind, its duration in the one direction, and its fetch (the distance over which it blows unimpeded; some of the huge waves that reach England have come from Cape Horn, a fetch of more than 6,000 miles). This explains why giant or freak waves are more usually encountered only in the Southern Ocean, where the resident westerlies and storm fronts are uninterrupted by any significant land mass.

Waves 55 feet high come with a wind of 60 knots blowing for 24 hours over a fetch of 500 miles or more in the open ocean; waves higher than this are caused by hurricane-force winds of 64 knots or more blowing for a greater time and over a greater distance than the life of the hurricane itself. On the other hand, peaks of coinciding wave crests may reach 80 feet in height.

Raban quotes from Rachel Carson's classic *The Sea Around Us* the following:

> *In February 1933 the USS* Ramapo, *while proceeding from Manila to San Diego, encountered seven days of stormy weather. The storm was part of a weather disturbance that extended all the way from Kamchatka to New York and permitted the winds an unbroken fetch of thousands of miles. During the height of the storm the* Ramapo *maintained a course running down the wind and with the sea. On 6 February the gale reached its fiercest intensity. Winds of 68 knots came in gusts and squalls, and the seas reached mountainous height. While standing watch on the bridge during the early hours of that day, one of the officers of the* Ramapo *saw, in the moonlight, a great sea rising astern to a level above an iron strap on the crow's nest of the mainmast. The* Ramapo *was on even keel and her stern was in the trough of the sea. These circumstances made possible an exact line of sight from the bridge to the crest of the wave, and simple mathematical calculations based on the dimensions of the ship gave the height of the wave. It was 112 feet.*

When a storm abates somewhat the waves lose height, but their length from crest to crest remains the same, and commonly they travel for a very considerable distance across the ocean as a long and slowly reducing swell. Morton reports that a sailor on a windjammer in the nineteenth century observed that the "Cape Horners" (a name for the waves of that region) that his ship was experiencing had a length of 2 miles, which is a very long wave indeed. Another storm will raise a sea on this swell, so that the surface of the sea is a combination of swells from decayed storms and waves generated by current or very recent weather disturbances.

There is much controversy among seafarers about the height of very large waves. Waves 35 feet high with a length of only 100 yards have been measured off the west coast of Ireland, whereas in the English Channel and the North Sea a 20-foot wave would be considered exceptional. Morton reports Sir Francis Chichester in *Along the Clipper Way* speaking of giant waves up to 120 feet high, certainly a freak wave if ever there was one. Moitessier quotes from *The Cape Horn Breed* by Captain W. H. S. Jones:

In the high southern latitudes, where the seas can be 50 feet high and 2000 feet long, they roll forward in endless procession, with occasionally one sea of abnormal size towering above the others, its approach visible from a considerable distance.

Coles regards with much suspicion the wave heights often reported by seafarers, believing from long experience that "the real height is probably only about half the apparent height." Nevertheless, Colin Stewart does not question a reputedly reliable report of a 112-foot monster in the Pacific, although such a wave would require a 100-knot wind blowing for at least 30 hours over a fetch of some 1,000 miles—a very unusual but not impossible combination of events.

The wave system that we observe on the sea surface is in fact a combination of many wave trains traveling in the same direction at speeds that are constant but slightly different from each other, each with its own height and period. These wave trains continually get into and out of step with each other, so that from time to time some of these trains coincide to produce a series of waves higher than usual, to be followed by relatively quieter water.

Every so often a large number of these wave components fall into step with each other, and an exceptionally large wave is often the result. Coastal fishermen are only too familiar with the King Wave, which can without any warning suddenly rear up out of a normal sea, smother the angler with roaring foam, and drag him back into the water. This sort of wave is the result of coinciding patterns of wave trains.

Laurence Draper indicates that one wave in twenty-three is over twice the height of the average wave, one in 1,175 is over three times the average height, whereas only one in 300,000 is four times higher than the average. While very large waves can cause serious damage, it is also likely that troughs that coincide may be just as serious a challenge to a vessel, since a ship has no way of counteracting the sudden "hole" that confronts her. Coming off the crest of a large wave and suddenly diving into a deeper than usual trough may allow an oncoming or a following sea to overwhelm a ship completely. This is probably what happened to the SS *Waratah* off the coast of East Africa in 1909. Draper tells of a large vessel stopped so suddenly by a large wave that her whole bow section was bent 20 feet downward, with her main beams immediately becoming white hot because of the friction at the point of bending.

A wave meeting a current traveling at only a quarter of its speed will be stopped completely, its energy then translated into height and an extraordinary wall of water that suddenly appears. When a wave meets shallow water its speed is reduced and the distance between successive waves is shortened; the wave then becomes higher and it may well break. Experienced seamen prefer to be out at sea where wave activity is likely to be much less dangerous than in coastal waters. Moitessier reports that while being pursued by squalls of hurricane force in about 45 degrees South latitude he saw huge waves breaking continuously for some hundreds of yards without disintegrating into a collapsed crest and the roller that carried it, an indication of the stupendous energy that waveforms can generate.

TRADE WINDS

"A constant trade-wind will securely blow,
And gently lay us on the spicy shore."

JOHN DRYDEN, *ANNUS MIRABILIS*

It is a curious fact that the two oceanic elements of most importance to the seafarer—wind and current—are designated using opposite referents: a wind is named for the direction *from which* it is blowing (a westerly breeze is a light wind from the west), but a current is named for the direction *to which* it flows (a westerly current flows to the west). There seems to be no good reason for this, but the practice is not likely to be changed. In any case, the convention has to be kept in mind when considering wind systems.

The trade winds are much celebrated in the literature of the sea. These are the winds that blow more or less constantly and steadily in one direction in the Northern and Southern Hemispheres, on all the open oceans to a distance of about 30 degrees north and south of the Equator. They blow from the northeast in the Northern Hemisphere and from the southeast in the Southern. Where they meet they tend to neutralize each other, creating regions of calm on either side of the Equator; these regions are known as the doldrums (see below). It was the reliability of these winds that made possible the establishment of trade routes across both the Atlantic and Pacific Oceans, hence their name: trade winds or simply "the trades."

If all the earth's surface had the same temperature, the atmospheric pressure at sea level would be equal everywhere and there would be no wind, because what makes air flow from one place to another is a difference in temperature, which in turn is responsible for differences in atmospheric pressure. Warmed air becomes unstable and cooler air flows to replace it; air also naturally flows from an area of high pressure to one of lower pressure.

Between the latitudes of 20 and 40 degrees north and south of the Equator there are belts of relatively high pressure over the oceans; on each side of these belts the pressure is relatively low (particularly over the Equator). If the earth were stationary, wind would blow along the lines of longitude from the high-pressure belts to the low-pressure belts, and the displaced air would return high in the atmosphere in the opposite direction. However, the earth is not stationary; because it rotates on its axis in an easterly direction any mass of air moving toward a low-pressure center is deflected to the right in the Northern Hemisphere (from the point of view of an observer facing the Equator); this is known as the northeast trade wind. In the Southern Hemisphere these directions are reversed; the flow of air toward the Equator is deflected to the observer's left to become the southeast trade wind.

The doldrums around the Equator, which vary between 200 and 300 miles in width, are infamous among seafarers for their calms, light variable winds, heavy rains, and thunderstorms (the name probably derives from a combination of *dolorous*, sad, and *tantrum*, bad temper). They were of particular significance to the crews of sailing ships because the men were often reduced to a state of severe depression and querulousness from having to lie becalmed, often for weeks on end, in torrid heat and windless conditions, searching for the fitful gusts that occasionally reached out from passing rain squalls.

Lying between the trade winds and the westerlies of higher latitudes are the variables, also known as the horse latitudes, regions in which light, variable, and very baffling winds are encountered about 30 degrees north and south of the Equator. One explanation of the name is: sailing ships carrying horses across the Atlantic to the Spanish colonies in the New World were frequently becalmed in these seas, and the crews often had to throw the horses overboard because the vessels could not carry enough water for both crew and animals while drifting for weeks and making little headway.

There are other versions of the naming of the horse latitudes. One is that the name is adapted from the Spanish Golfo de las Yeguas ("Gulf of Mares") because of the fickle and quite unpredictable nature of the winds in the area (mares themselves being, presumably, also fickle and unpredictable). Another is that it was so named because of the contrast it offered with the stretch of ocean farther to the west, known as the Golfo de las Damas ("Gulf of Ladies"), reflecting the smoother and more favorable winds to be found in this area between the Canaries and the West Indies—a reflection, no doubt, of Spanish womanhood of the period.

Still another explanation is that in the earlier days of sail, ships out of the English Channel took about two months to get clear of these particular latitudes, by which time the crew had worked off their advance pay, known as the dead horse. The crew commonly celebrated this event by parading a straw horse around the deck, flogging it with a rope's end, and then throwing it overboard (see To Flog a Dead Horse, chapter 6). The mutiny on the *Bounty* (see chapter 9) took place in the horse latitudes of the South Pacific.

The monsoon, a seasonal wind commonly encountered in the Indian Ocean and the Western Pacific, is essentially a modification of the well-established trade winds (the word is from the Malay *musim* and the Arabic *mawsim*, a time, a season). These winds are caused by the unequal heating and cooling rates of land and water; in particular they owe their origin to the summer heating and winter cooling of a large land mass, such as the whole of Asia and Australia, with the contiguous oceans being important factors in the subsequent exchange of energy.

There are three main monsoons: the southwest, the northeast, and the northwest. The southwest monsoon occurs between May and September over the northern part of the Indian Ocean and the western regions of the North Pacific. From October to April, in the same areas, this wind is replaced by the northeast monsoon. From November to March the northwest monsoon blows across the equatorial reaches of the Indian Ocean, the Arafura Sea, and the western portion of the Pacific Ocean. It is this monsoon that brings the fabled "Wet" to Northern Australia, south of the Equator, and it is in fact the southern aspect of the northeast monsoon from north of the Equator, having been deflected by the earth's rotation while approaching and then crossing the Equator.

The most famous prevailing winds (or infamous, if you happen to be a watchkeeper on a small sailboat that is trying to double Cape Horn; see below) are the westerlies, a wind system that encircles the earth south of approximately 40 degrees South. Because there is no substantial land mass to deflect them (apart from the southernmost portion of South America), these winds—known as the Roaring Forties in the 40- to 50-degree belt of latitude and the Shrieking Sixties beyond that—can engender very bad storms and raise exceptionally large seas (see Ocean Waves, above). Similar westerlies prevail in the North Atlantic and the North Pacific, but they are not usually as fierce as those in the Southern Ocean.

Other seasonal winds of interest to the seafarer are tropical revolving storms, which go by different names according to where they occur. They get their name from the facts that they are spawned in the tropics, the winds so generated are caused to spiral around and into a center of low pressure (a depression), and the wind speeds can reach 125 miles an hour or more—an extremely powerful force for destruction. In the Northern Hemisphere tropical storms revolve in a counterclockwise direction (as viewed from above), whereas in the Southern Hemisphere the direction of rotation is clockwise. They commonly occur in the western portions of open oceans (but not in the South Atlantic), between latitudes 10 and 20 degrees on either side of the Equator, and their breeding period is during the late summer and early autumn for each hemisphere; in the Arabian Sea they generally appear at each change of the monsoon.

Such storms in the western Northern Pacific are called typhoons (from the Arabic *tufan*, hurricane, combined with the Chinese *tai fung*, great wind, the spelling being assimilated to Typhon, "father of the winds," from the Greek *tuphon*, whirlwind). In the western South Pacific, the southern Indian Ocean, the Arabian Sea, and the Bay of Bengal, they are known as cyclones (from the Greek *kuklos*, circle). The same storm in the Caribbean is a hurricane (from the Spanish *huracán* and the Taino *hurakán*, the god of the sea).

There are some technical differences between these storms, such as their rate and direction of advance, but the results they can produce and the havoc they can wreak are to all intents and purposes the same: shrieking winds of unbelievable force and mountainous seas of unbridled ferocity, unremittingly focused on the total destruction of human beings and all their works. (See, for example, John Caldwell, chapter 13; see also Joseph Conrad's story "Typhoon" and Hank Searls's novel *Overboard*, which is perhaps the best description ever penned of a storm at sea.)

THE SARGASSO SEA

"In this area of forty thousand square miles or so,
all the floating, drifting weed peculiar to the North Atlantic,
gathers in vast fields until the strongest gale that ever blew
is powerless to disperse it or to raise a wave or drive a vessel
through the closely packed masses of sea growth."

FRANK T. BULLEN, *BEYOND*

This quotation refers to the dreaded Sargasso Sea of ill repute, much feared by seafarers of old because of its supposed ability to hold ships fast in the vast net of accumulated weed floating at the surface. The Sargasso Sea is a relatively motionless region of ocean water in the central North Atlantic strewn with extensive patches of floating seaweed of the genus *Sargassum*. This vast "plain" is bounded approximately by 25 and 35 degrees North and 40 and 70 degrees West; it is roughly elliptical, lying east of the Bahama Islands on the inner curve of a powerful current system that circulates in a clockwise direction, the Gulf Stream forming part of the western rim. Rainfall here is low, evaporation is high, winds are light, and the water is remarkably clear. Bullen's figure of 40,000 square miles is perhaps somewhat cautious; a more recent source reports this as a plain of algae some 2 million square miles in area.

Columbus named this field of weed the Mar de Sargazo ("Sea of Seaweed"), from the Portuguese *sargaço*, gulfweed, perhaps derived from *sarga*, a kind of grape, from the grapelike fruit often found on these algae; the Spanish word for this phenomenon is *sargazo*. The crew accompanying Columbus on his voyage of 1492 to what he fondly hoped would prove to be the fabled empires of Cathay and Cipangu feared that the weed that appeared on every hand would hold them fast, but in fact their ships parted the clumps easily and sailed on without impediment. Nevertheless, it was long and earnestly believed by later sailors that their vessels would be stuck in the mass of floating weed until starvation overtook them. Actually, the weed is not dense enough to do this; a wind of any strength sends a ship through without difficulty.

Sargassum natans, or gulfweed, is a brown algae bearing small but prominent berrylike bladders. This ocean weed, drifting with wind and current, supports specialized animals, some of which are found nowhere else. Although this floating weed was first reported by Columbus, it is possible that the Carthaginians (the Phoenicians who settled on the coast of North Africa; see Hanno the Navigator, chapter 3) reached the Sargasso Sea as early as 530 B.C. The widely believed story of ships becoming helplessly embedded forever in the weed was disproved in 1910 by the *Michael Sars* expedition of Sir John Murray, who showed that the Sargasso Sea was covered in random patches of weed rather than an unending blanket. Also it has been found that the region is the spawning ground of the common eel, the elvers that use the Gulf Stream to carry their good elver selves to the rivers of Europe.

THE SEVEN SEAS

"I love to sail forbidden seas, and land on barbarous coasts."
HERMAN MELVILLE, *MOBY-DICK*

"The Seven Seas" is one of those phrases much loved by writers of nautical romance who, familiar with the jargon if not the reality of seafaring, imagine that cruising the likes of the Spanish Main or the South China Sea is an endless idyll of trade winds comparable only to a pleasant picnic in the broad and pleasant fields of Elysium (see On the Spanish Main, below). Such it might be, on occasion; but far more often going to sea is a serious business, blessed once in a while perhaps with the "wheel's kick and the wind's song and the white sail's shaking," as celebrated in Masefield's "Sea Fever," but far more likely to be blighted by a rude and tempestuous storm and an unseemly sea . . . not to mention the hideous discomforts of seasickness.

Nevertheless, it would be a cruel injury to deny the romantics their romance. And, in any case, there are seven seas across which one may wander—always with due care, of course (as encouragement, see Pirates, chapter 14). But with some 300 million cubic miles of water covering almost three quarters of the earth's surface it comes as no surprise to learn that there are many more "seas" than simply seven.

Why originally seven, then? The Turkish hydrographer Piri Reis in the sixteenth century drew up a list naming the seven as the South China Sea, Bay of Bengal, Arabian Sea, Persian Gulf, Red Sea, Mediterranean Sea, and Atlantic Ocean, but as these were the known waters of the Muslim world at that time, the list was very logical.

Why not just one? The answer lies partly in the alliteration of the words *seven seas* (Kipling recognized this when in 1896 he named a new book of his poetry *The Seven Seas*), and it lies also in the mystical nature of 7, composed of the numbers 3 and 4, both of which were regarded by the ancients as lucky numbers.

The Babylonians and the Egyptians believed in seven sacred planets, and in Hebrew the verb *to swear*—to affirm—means literally "to come under the influence of seven things," as in the oath between Abraham and Abimelech at Beersheba, which involved seven ewe lambs. The Arabs swore their oaths by seven stones smeared with blood, and we are reminded in Proverbs 9:1 that "Wisdom hath built her house, she hath hewn out her seven pillars" (whence the title of T. E. Lawrence's masterpiece *Seven Pillars of Wisdom*).

The Japanese swore by the *Shichi-fukujin*, the "Seven Gods of Luck" (the Chinese made do with five, which is also a mystic number); the Hebrews postulated seven days in creation (hence our seven-day week), and the early Christians set great store by the seven virtues, while at the same time issuing dire warnings against engaging in any of the seven deadly sins (it is a curious fact of human nature that if you can't name the seven virtues you probably don't possess them, whereas the same rule does not at all apply to the seven deadly sins).

Some readers may be browsing through this book while on a sabbatical—a break or leave of absence following six years of work—and, one hopes, they may feel that they are in seventh heaven while doing so. There are, of course (or there were, in earlier times), the seven hills of Rome, the seven joys of Mary, the seven liberal arts, the seven wonders of the ancient world, and (for those who alas! are not on a sabbatical and whose spirits are therefore somewhat jaded) there is perhaps recourse to the dance of the seven veils. Should one (unhappily) succumb to the many temptations in this world, the hell of Islam is divided into seven compartments. Egypt suffered a seven-day plague of bloody waters, and Pharaoh's dreams were interpreted by Joseph as predicting seven years of plenty followed by seven years of famine.

Somewhat later, Jesus fed the multitude with seven loaves; our early heroes got around in seven-league boots, and our later idols often suffered the seven-year itch; Sindbad the Sailor embarked on seven voyages (see chapter 3), while Snow White undertook the care and feeding of seven dwarfs.

Thus there is ample precedent for pinning the name "Seven Seas" on all the navigable salt waters of the world. The ancients gave this name to the Mediterranean, the Red Sea, the China Sea, the West African Sea, the East African Sea, the Indian Ocean, and the Persian Gulf. Today we think of the oceans as the seven seas: the North Pacific, the South Pacific, the North Atlantic, the South Atlantic, the Indian Ocean, the Arctic Ocean, and the Antarctic Ocean (the last is also commonly known as the Southern Ocean).

There still remain the Red Sea, the Black Sea, the Baltic Sea, the Caribbean Sea, the Caspian Sea, the North Sea, the Norwegian Sea, the Barents Sea, the Beaufort Sea, the Sea of Otkhotsk, the Arabian Sea, the Bering Sea, the East Siberian Sea, the

Kara Sea, the Sea of Japan, the Yellow Sea, the East China Sea (and, of course, the South China Sea), the Irish Sea, the Aegean Sea, the Adriatic Sea, the Chukchi Sea, the Greenland Sea, the Timor Sea, the Arafura Sea, the Coral Sea, the Solomon Sea, the Andaman Sea, and—not to get mired down in seas—there is the Sargasso Sea (see above). This is not to mention the great many gulfs, straits, bays, and channels that one may voyage through or across besides.

For those who plan to sail around the world and want to know what is under the keel, the deepest part of the Pacific measures nearly 7 miles down, the average depth of the whole Atlantic is just over 2 miles, while the Indian Ocean bottoms out at an average of 2½ miles. One cannot recommend taking a dip in either the Arctic or Antarctic Oceans, as such a swim would be inimical to good health. Nevertheless, as noted by Alan Villiers, there is still a lot of water available in which one may disport oneself:

> There are fifteen times more water in the sea than the entire volume of all the exposed land. Sea covers seventy per cent of the globe—139 million square miles of it. The sea at its deepest—in the Marianas Trench of the Pacific Ocean—is more than a mile deeper than the highest mountain.

CAPE HORN

"I would prefer it [Strait of Magellan] twenty times over to the going round Cape Horn."
ADMIRAL JOHN BYRON

Probably the most famous place-name in the history of seafaring and in the literature of the sea, past and present, is Cape Horn. Legendary Cape Horn is a headland on Horn Island, which lies off the southernmost tip of Tierra del Fuego ("Land of Fire," a reference to the habit of the local Indians—the Tierra del Fuegians—always carrying fire with them in their movements around their hostile environment); Tierra del Fuego is a group of islands separated from the South American mainland by the Strait of Magellan.

Here, enormous swells roll eastward with a fetch of thousands of miles, driven by the fierce westerly winds and storms of the Southern Ocean. It is a cold and forbidding place even in the summer season of November–January, often beset by fog, rain, snow, and changeable winds. In the winter season it could be a dreadful place for passagemaking in either direction, as was well known by the Cape Horners, the name given to the men and the ships that used this route to get from the American East Coast to the West Coast from the 1850s onward, when the Californian goldfield fever was in full swing and, later, when the guano, nitrate, and grain trades were developed in the Pacific.

The Horn took its name from the Dutch town Hoorn, the home of the chief backers of the expedition which was the first to reach the Pacific from the Atlantic by rounding the South American continent (in January 1616). Sir Francis Drake, during his famous circumnavigation of 1577–1580, had noted in his journal that "the Atlantic Ocean and the South Sea meet in a large and free scope."

The Strait of Magellan had been claimed under a monopoly imposed by the Dutch East India Company, the famous VOC (Vereenigde Oostindische Compagnie), founded in 1602. The VOC also controlled the Cape of Good Hope route, thus reserving to itself all trade opportunities with the newly discovered regions in the Indian Ocean and western Pacific Ocean.

Isaac Le Maire, a director of the VOC, resigned out of frustration with its restrictions on trading to the Far East, being determined to set up on his own account. Le Maire had also considered the possibility of a Northwest Passage (see chapter 4), but he chanced to read Drake's remarks about the meeting of the Atlantic Ocean and the South Sea in Hakluyt's *The Principal Navigations* (1598–1600) and decided to investigate the possibility of such a route. In 1615 he founded the Australia Company (from *auster*, the old Latin name for the south wind; hence Terra Australis Incognita, the Unknown South Land, see chapter 4, that was thought to extend without a break to the South Pole itself) and sent two ships, the *Hoorn* and the *Eendracht* ("Unity"), under his son Jakob and Willem Schouten (Schouten had been a ship's captain in the VOC) to see if a new route could be opened up to the Pacific.

The *Hoorn* was lost by fire at Port Desire (Puerto Deseado, at 47°45' South latitude, on the east coast of southern Argentina) before the expedition reached the Strait of Le Maire, as they named it. The expedition, now the *Eendracht*, named the island to the southeast of the Strait of Le Maire Staaten Island, after the States General, the Dutch parliament (hence also Staten Island, which faces New York Harbor). Four days later, southwest of Staten Island, the *Eendracht* sighted the southernmost island of the continental land mass, whereupon Schouten and Le Maire designated it Kaap Hoorn after the Dutch town of that name, rounding it at 8:00 P.M. on January 29, 1616. It has been known as Cape Horn ever since.

Ironically, when the *Eendracht* crossed the Pacific and after many adventures reached Batavia on October 29, 1616, the Dutch governor of the VOC, Jan Pieterszoon Coen, refused to believe that Le Maire and Schouten had discovered a new route from Europe into the Pacific, declared the ship's log a forgery, confiscated all their papers, impounded the *Eendracht*, and gave the crew the choice of working for the VOC or being sent back to Holland. Le Maire and Schouten, as the principals, were sent home; Le Maire died during the voyage, and we hear no more of Schouten.

But Cape Horn itself remains, to haunt the men, such as Richard Henry Dana, who had to sail around it:

At four P.M. (it was then quite dark) all hands were called, and sent aloft in a violent squall of hail and rain to take in sail. We had now all got on our "Cape Horn rig" . . . we were obliged to work with bare hands . . . Our ship was now all cased with ice . . . the running rigging so stiff that we could hardly bend it . . . and the sails nearly as stiff as sheet iron.

Dana originally published his account anonymously as a protest against the dearth of books that "present the life of a common sailor at sea as it really is"; he wrote his classic as "a voice from the forecastle."

Here is another voice from the forecastle, that of William Willis, who went to sea in 1908 at the age of fifteen on board the *Henriette*, a German four-masted bark out of Hamburg. The following quotation gives some idea why these vessels and the "common sailors" who manned them were known as "iron ships and iron men."

A little after daybreak the gale began to ease up and by early afternoon we had all the canvas on her again. It was a job for all hands and took hours . . . we were making westing now—westing south of Cape Horn . . . A little after four bells on the twelve to four watch, the mizzen and main royals were blown out of the bolt ropes . . . the mizzen-topgallant sail split and beat itself into shreds . . . we had our usual breakfast of a bluish grey cereal . . . A line of white appeared in the night coming towards us—the sea driven into a foaming wall by the gale. The moaning had become a howl and was about to engulf us . . . The gale, the sea and the ship became one frenzied mass . . . The world had become chaos . . . this was a hurricane howling out of the Antarctic . . . Sleet and hail were pelting us like bullets . . . the sailmaker said in his even voice, "I was on an iron bark, the Ottilie, *and we were off the Horn, just like now . . . six men were in their bunks, the whole watch below, when a sea came over and took the house and every man in it.*

THE CAPE HORNERS

"And now the storm-blast came, and he
Was tyrannous and strong;
He struck with his o'ertaking wings
And chased us south along."
SAMUEL TAYLOR COLERIDGE, "THE RIME OF THE ANCIENT MARINER"

Cape Horner was the name given originally to the American full-rigged ships that plied the route between the American East and West Coasts in the nineteenth century by way of Cape Horn. This era was sometimes called the age of "iron ships and iron men" because of the wretched weather conditions in the Southern Ocean and the breathtakingly brutal treatment that was often meted out to the crews by hard-driving "bucko" mates and hard-nosed captains.

After gold was discovered in California in 1847, there was an increasing demand in the goldfields for supplies of all kinds, so a regular service between New York and San Francisco was instituted by The Clipper Ships (see chapter 8), a type that developed from the Baltimore clippers, which had become well known in the War of 1812 and later as slavers and privateers (the Baltimore clipper was in fact a schooner). Few of the clippers survived the terrible combination of the harsh conditions of the Cape Horn route and the unrelenting drive for record speeds imposed on them by uncaring ship's officers and greedy owners.

The building of the railway across the Isthmus of Panama in 1857 ended the reign of the Cape Horner "hell-ship," but other trade routes developed in its place, especially the cargo route from Europe or Africa west around the Horn to the Pacific coast of South America. The return voyages carried cargoes of grain (especially wheat), nitrates, guano, and hides to the American East Coast and to Europe in the three-masted barks of Britain, France, Germany, Spain, and Finland and, during the decades up to 1930, in the giant five-masted ship-rigged vessels of the German "Flying P" line, such as the *Pamir*. (See Richard Henry Dana's *Two Years Before the Mast* and Eric Newby's *The Last Grain Race* for authentic accounts of life aboard The Windjammers—see chapter 8.) When the Panama Canal was opened in 1914, the wind ships finally had to give way to steam; some of those that survived have been converted into sail-training ships.

Cape Horner is also the name for the gigantic waves often met with in this region; see Ocean Waves, above.

ON THE SPANISH MAIN

"My father dear he is not here; he seeks the Spanish Main."
RICHARD BARHAM, *THE INGOLDSBY LEGENDS*

Spanish Main is a term much beloved by writers of romantic stories about the sea—about pirates, buccaneers, and sea chanties during the sixteenth, seventeenth, and eighteenth centuries, when the Spanish ruled the New World. Properly speaking, the Spanish Main comprises the north coast of South America from the mouth of the Orinoco River to the Isthmus of Panama, what the Spaniards called Tierra Firme, meaning the mainland bordering the Caribbean Sea, that is, the Spanish Mainland, where an extraordinarily cruel and rapacious Spanish hegemony was installed following the seminal voyage of discovery by Christopher Columbus in 1492 (see chapter 8).

In short order, however, the term "Spanish Main" came to include the entire Caribbean basin—the islands within the Caribbean and the Gulf of Mexico, from Trinidad in the south to Cuba and the Straits of Florida in the north, and all the seas thereof. Thus, as Kemp points out, the meaning of the term underwent a complete change; whereas in the sixteenth and early seventeenth centuries "Spanish Main" referred to the mainland of northern South America, by the late seventeenth century and thereafter it referred to the seas of that region, rather than to the bordering coasts.

The Caribbean was discovered by Columbus in his search for a passage to the lands of the Far East: specifically, Cathay (China) and Cipangu (Japan). Its name—Mar Caribe—stemmed from its association with the fierce Carib Indians who inhabited the Lesser Antilles, the group of islands in the eastern Caribbean that include Grenada, Martinique, Guadeloupe, Saint Kitts, and others.

Spanish control of the Caribbean after its discovery was practically undisputed during the first century of development. Adventurers from Spain (Hernan Cortés, Francisco Pizarro, Pedro de Alvarado, and other conquistadors bent on plunder) searched for quick fortunes, and the discovery of gold and silver around the Caribbean resulted in a steady and massive flow of treasure from the new lands back to Spain.

In 1523, for example, Cortés dispatched three caravels to Spain with a first installment of treasure that he had extracted—with force, cruelty, and tyranny—from the Aztecs in Mexico. After a long and slow voyage, the three ships were barely 30 miles off Cape Saint Vincent, on the southwest tip of the Iberian Peninsula, when they were intercepted by French corsairs, the pirates of the Mediterranean and the eastern Atlantic. After a brief fight the Frenchmen boarded two of the caravels (the third had fled as soon as the pirates were sighted) and greedily inspected their holds.

What they found was astounding. A quantity of pearls taken from the Aztecs weighed 680 pounds, bagged gold dust accounted for some 500 pounds, there were three huge cases of gold ingots, not to mention many more chests of silver and assorted jewels—clearly, far more than a king's ransom. No wonder the Spanish king was aghast at the effrontery of the French thieves who had purloined this incredible treasure.

Nevertheless, Spain did very nicely out of her vast empire in the New World. During the sixteenth century alone—the first year of her conquest—she carried back to her coffers some 750,000 pounds of gold, which was more than a third of all the gold produced by the rest of the world for that period. And this was only the gold in the form of artifacts that had been melted down by the conquistadors impatient with objets d'art and far more focused on gold itself. When they discovered apparently limitless amounts of gold and silver ore in places such as Potosí in the Andean plateau and Guanajuato in Mexico, there seemed to be no limit to the wealth available to the bold and the brave (if also necessarily the brutal and oppressively cruel).

But increasingly, as the Spanish ravaged the Indian peoples of the Antilles, Mexico, Colombia, and Peru for the untold riches of their cultures and lands, so too were they beset by freebooting brigands and buccaneers such as John Hawkins, Francis Drake, Henry Morgan, and countless others who hated the Spanish with as much passion as they in turn loved gold. Whether gentlemen or scoundrels, they fell upon the Spanish Main with unfettered ferocity as they disputed the monopoly over the New World granted to Spain by papal edict in 1493, immediately after Columbus's ill-fated discovery of the region.

The importance of the Caribbean as a route for convoys of Spanish treasure ships soon led to raids by a veritable fleet of pirates, privateers, freebooters, and buccaneers. Fortified cities on the Spanish Main and the surrounding islands were raided by English, French, and Dutch sea robbers and at various times by warships of these nations. The Lesser Antilles, having been passed over by the Spanish because of their lack of treasure, then became objects of international conflict, especially between Britain and France.

During the seventeenth century the Lesser Antilles were settled by British, French, Dutch, and Danish colonists, and in 1655 Jamaica was wrested from Spain by Britain. Spain suffered considerably from the capture or sinking of many treasure-laden ships (see Lord Anson, chapter 8, for an example of what a Spanish treasure ship might yield to a bold and determined attack). France ousted Spain from the western part of Hispaniola in 1697 and set about developing it as a colony, but the Negro slaves revolted successfully during the French Revolution, and Haiti became independent in 1804.

It wasn't long before the impulse to independence began to affect other Spanish possessions, and they soon sought to break away from Spain's control. New nations then appeared on the borders of what had become known as the Spanish Lake. By 1850 the independent nations of Mexico, Guatemala, Honduras, Nicaragua, Costa Rica, Colombia, Cuba, Venezuela, the Dominican Republic, and Haiti were established in the Caribbean. It then remained for Spain to lose Puerto Rico to the United States and for Colombia to lose Panama to independence around the turn of the twentieth century.

When in 1697 England, France, and Holland finally made peace with Spain under the terms of the Treaty of Ryswick, it remained only for these four powers to cooperate in hunting down and destroying buccaneers in the Caribbean and the Gulf of Mexico as common pirates who could no longer claim protection under the flag of any of these nations. Those who were caught faced an almost certain fate on the gallows (see, for example, William Kidd, chapter 14).

Prize Money

"The Court of Admiralty has, in time of war,
the authority of a prize-court."

Sir William Blackston, *Commentaries on the Laws of England*

Prize here is not related to prize as in reward; rather, it is from the French *prendre*, to take, and *prise*, a taking, as in *to prise open*. Prize money was the money that resulted from the sale of captured ships and any cargoes they might be carrying; and a prize court was a British court of law set up in time of war to examine the validity of any claims made against such captures at sea by the Royal Navy. This court operated on the general principle "prize or no prize"; and any vessel lawfully captured and accepted by the court as such was then said to be "condemned in prize," that is, judged as lawfully taken.

Before 1692 the prize money (known then as "bounty moneys") that followed the condemning of ships and goods was commonly distributed between the crown and the admiralty (the so-called droits or legal rights of the crown and the droits of admiralty, respectively); after that date the crown waived a portion of its rights and contributed that portion to the seamen involved in a capture, as a means of encouraging more men to take up naval service. Then in 1708 Queen Anne allocated all droits of the crown to naval captors, with prize money to be shared out in eighths: three to the captain, one to the commander-in-chief (usually the admiral of that station), one to the officers, one to the warrant officers, and the remaining two to the crew. (It was not until the end of World War II that the British government abandoned the institution of prize money.)

Some prize money amounts were enormous, even by the standards of those days. When the Spanish treasure ship *Hermione* was captured in 1762 by two Royal Navy frigates and condemned in prize for £519,705, each of the two captains received £65,000, every lieutenant £13,000, and every seaman in the two ships £485—even in the case of seamen, this was a very substantial amount of money two hundred years ago. The capture of the Spanish ship *Nuestra Señora de Covadonga* by Lord Anson (see chapter 8) in 1743 yielded more than £500,000 in prize money, his share in that being very considerable.

Any captain who was the favorite of some admiral often prospered because the admiral saw to it that his protégé was dispatched on cruises likely to yield suitable prize moneys, to both captain and admiral alike. Such a captain was Hugh Pigot, serving on the West Indies Station in the 1790s under Admiral Sir Hyde Parker. (Pigot was also the cause of the bloodiest mutiny in the history of the British navy; see HMS *Hermione* Mutiny, chapter 9.) Parker was the admiral whose signal to withdraw during the Battle of Copenhagen could not be seen by Nelson because he had clapped his telescope to his blind eye.

FIRST RATE

"Pyrrhus certainly considered her as a first-rate military power."
SIR GEORGE CORNWALL LEWIS, *EARLY ROMAN HISTORY*

The rating of ships was introduced into the Royal Navy during the reign of Charles I (1600–1649), whereby ships of the line (vessels that could take their place in the line of battle) were divided into six classes, first rate to sixth rate, according to the number of men they carried, which thus determined the number of guns that could be manned in battle. Ships of the line of battle were so called because it was their traditional tactic to go into battle in the formation known as line astern, that is, one behind the other, with the first rates leading.

During the First Dutch War (1652–1654) the line of battle consisted of first rates (about 100 guns) down to fourth rates (about 30 guns). In the Second Dutch War (1664–1667) the English put three three-decker first rates into the battle, with 100 guns, 80 guns, and 70 guns, respectively; the two-decker second rates carried between 52 and 66 guns. Somewhat later the line of battle consisted of first-, second-, and third-rate ships, with the remaining rates being only occasionally used as ships of the line. Fifth- and sixth-rate ships (there were very few fourth-rates) were commonly known as frigates.

In 1677 Samuel Pepys (1633–1703), when he was first secretary to the admiralty, drew up a manning quota for each ship according to its rating, which by this time was determined according to the number of guns carried onboard. The following table of rates is based on figures taken from Christopher Lloyd.

RATE	GUNS	MEN
First	100+	800+
Second	82	530
Third	74	460
Fourth	54	280
Fifth	30	130
Sixth	20–28	65

The figures given by Masefield and Blackburn differ a little from those of Lloyd, but this is not significant; ships within a given rate commonly showed a range of guns and men (for example, a first rate might have more than a hundred guns and almost a thousand men to sail and fight her). These line-of-battle ships, especially the three-decker first rates, were ponderous monsters to look at but when under a full press of sail they were daunting and vastly impressive ("line of battle" is the source of both "battleship" and "liner").

Despite the enormous number of men carried on the larger ships, and in spite of the fearsome sea battles waged between the navies of Britain, France, Spain, Holland, and Portugal from the medieval period to the advent of the ironclads in the mid-nineteenth century, less than 10 percent of all deaths were due to battle action. Half of all casualties on board were the result of disease, most commonly Scurvy (see below), as well as the fevers that were endemic to areas such as the West Indies (for example, yellow fever). Accidents carried off a third of the remainder (parting rigging, breaking spars, falling from aloft, drowning—virtually no seaman could swim—a gun bursting or coming loose in a gale, and so on). Shipwreck, foundering, explosions—always a deadly possibility with tons of gunpowder kept on board—and fire accounted for the rest. One way or another, it was a hard and uncertain life.

Although today we use the expressions to refer to something that is the best of its kind ("first rate"), very poor ("third rate"), and so on, these distinctions did not apply to warships, which were rated simply according to their ability to throw a certain weight of metal in a single broadside of gunfire.

Seamen were also rated; the traditional test was whether a man could "hand, reef, and steer"—that is, whether he was skillful in handling and reefing sails and steering the ship. The common ratings in the days of the wooden navy were landsman, ordinary seaman, and able seaman, then up to the petty officers (bosun, mate, and so on). Captains had the authority to rate and disrate without reference to the admiralty.

OF KNOTS AND LOGS

*"We were going twelve knots an hour,
and running away from them."*

FREDERICK MARRYAT, *PETER SIMPLE*

The knot is the nautical measure of speed, one knot being one nautical mile per hour; no seafarer would ever use the expression "at a rate of knots" or "at a speed of x knots" since "knot" (from the Anglo Saxon *cnotta*, ball) already expresses the notion of rate. Having said this, it is puzzling that Frederick Marryat, who for some time was a captain in the Royal Navy and who later became a successful novelist, should have used just such an expression (see quote above). As a measure of speed one says so many knots, never knots per hour, as in "HMS *Dreadnought* achieved 21 knots on her sea trials."

Theoretically, a nautical mile is one minute of arc measured along a line of latitude, the standard being 48 degrees North latitude with the apex of the arc being at the center of the earth. In practice a nautical mile is 6,080 feet long, or 2,025 yards, reckoned to be one sixtieth of a degree of latitude (at 48° North). The English statute mile is 5,280 feet, or 1,760 yards. The so-called geographical mile is the same as the nautical mile.

The knot as an indicator of speed has come down to us from the old chip log, sometimes called the Dutch log, which for hundreds of years was used by sailing ships to measure their rate of progress through the sea. The original log or chip was a flat piece of wood about the size and shape of a large slice of pie, with a bridle of three lines attached to its three "corners," the whole being spliced to a long line which was commonly wound onto a hand-held reel. The circular segment of the wedge-shaped log was fitted with a piece of lead to make the wooden chip float upright and thus offer resistance to being towed through the water. One line of the bridle had a peg that fitted into a hole on the chip; when the log was to be hauled in, the log line was given a smart jerk to draw the peg out and the chip could then be pulled easily through the water and thence on board.

Experience had revealed to seamen the total length of line that could be heaved overboard and retrieved by hand, according to the best likely speeds of their ship. The hourglass (commonly called a sandglass) best suited for timing this operation was the 28-second glass; a glass that gave a longer duration—a 30-second glass, say—would be a little more accurate, but so much more log line would run over the stern in this extra time that it would be a burden to haul on board again.

The relationship between 28 seconds and one hour was then applied to the relationship between the required divisions on the log line and a nautical mile of 6,080 feet. Thus we have

$$\frac{28}{3,600} = \frac{x}{6,080}$$

In this equation the unknown *x* works out to be 47.25. The log line thus had knots tied into it at intervals of 47 feet 3 inches (47.25 feet).

Three seamen (A, B, and C) were generally needed to measure the ship's speed through the water: (A) to take the nip, (B) to turn the sandglass, and (C) to hold the reel. When the log or chip was heaved over the stern (A) would let the log line run out through his fingers until he felt the "start knot," so placed that the chip was far enough astern to be clear of turbulence from the wake of the ship; he would then shout "Turn!" and (B) would promptly turn the sandglass over. When the sand had just run out (B) would shout "Nip!" and (A), who had meanwhile been counting the knots as they ran through his fingers, would sharply brake the log line and estimate the fraction of the last knot that had passed. (C) would then wind the whole thing inboard.

The result could be something like 6 knots, say, or if greater accuracy was required (such as when navigating a dangerous shoal or passage) it might be 6 knots and 5 fathoms; and so on. The speed would then be entered into the logbook, which obviously takes its name from the procedure just described.

Many of the tea and wool clipper ships of the late nineteenth century sometimes logged bursts of 15 knots or more, while some achieved 19 knots and, on occasion, even higher speeds. Most everyday sailing yachts do between 4 and 8 knots, depending on their waterline length, while those that compete in the America's Cup often achieve double figures.

SCURVY

"Whatsoever man . . . be scurvy or scabbed."

LEVITICUS 21:18–20

Scurvy is a deficiency disease caused by lack of vitamin C (which was not isolated and measured until 1928); it was once thought to be the result of an exclusive diet of salt meat but in fact the cause was what was not eaten, that is, fresh fruits and vegetables (see Lord Anson, chapter 8, for a description of the ravages of scurvy on a ship's crew during a long voyage without access to fruits and vegetables). The word is from the Anglo Saxon *scurf*, scaly, scabby, influenced by the French *scorbut*, scurvy, and perhaps also by the Russian *scrobot*, to scratch.

For some time it was thought that scurvy was caused by wet conditions onboard ship; thus a number of humane captains, such as James Cook (1728–1779), insisted that their men keep their quarters clean and dry; others, such as George Vancouver (1757–1798), lit fires between decks so that the men's quarters would dry out and drafts would cause fresh air to circulate (nevertheless, some crews complained that the resulting smoke itself caused the disease). Curiously, considering the importance it has in modern times, stress was thought by some to be a predisposing factor in contracting scurvy, along with laziness, weakness (one might legitimately wonder which came first in this particular case: the disease or the weakness), inactivity, fear, anxiety, discontent, and similar conditions of the mind. Shortage of good drinking water was often cited as a cause; but although Anson was able to give his men fresh rainwater during his crossing of the Pacific, the incidence of scurvy did not thereby abate one whit.

The disease was well known in the countries of northern Europe during the long winters, when greens containing vitamin C were unavailable, and it was frequently encountered in ships that sailed the long circumnavigation routes, particularly in the sixteenth to eighteenth centuries. Cook was one of the first Royal Navy captains to introduce measures onboard ship to counter the threat of scurvy, but twenty years earlier Dr. James Lind—alarmed at Anson's losses (of the 1,995 men he took with him, 1,051 died of scurvy) and intrigued by the fact that in the Austrian army in Hungary in the 1720s scurvy had carried off thousands of common soldiers but had affected none of the officers (who had a different diet)—had shown that citrus juices, particularly the juice of lemons, oranges, and to a lesser extent limes, were an excellent preventive of, and cure for, this wretched disease.

No one nationality was affected more than another; Vasco da Gama's Portuguese and Magellan's Spanish suffered as much as the French and the Dutch and those seafarers from the northern countries, the English and the Russians; all that was needed was a long time at sea (guaranteed by the distances sailed by the early explorers) and the absence of fresh fruit and/or vegetables in the seamen's diet. The following description of the effects of scurvy is taken from a letter written in 1579 by Thomas Stevens, in Goa on the west coast of India, to his father in England.

> And by reason of the long navigation, and want of food and water,
> they fall into sundry diseases, their gummes waxe great, and swell, and
> they are faine to cut them away, their legges swell, and all the body
> becommeth sore, and so benummed, that they can not stirre hand nor
> foot, and so they die for weaknesse, others fall into fluxes and agues,
> and die thereby.

During his epoch-making voyage of 1497–1498 down the west coast of Africa, east around the Cape of Good Hope, and then north and east across the Indian Ocean to India, Vasco da Gama (about 1469–1524) watched his men suffer the horrors of scurvy:

> Their gums turned livid, puffy and rotten, then oozed black blood
> and crept over their teeth. Their legs turned weak and gangrenous.
> The worst afflicted had too little strength even to fight off the ships'
> rats that gnawed at the soles of their feet.

Many of the early navigators were aware of the antiscorbutic properties of lime and lemon juice, but the problem that confronted all sea commanders was finding quantities of fresh fruit at suitable intervals during the voyage. Fresh food of any kind does not keep well, and with the Pacific occupying a third of the entire globe it is possible to sail for months before sighting land where fruit might be expected to grow. Coconuts were useful as a treatment, quite apart from being entirely welcome as a new article of diet for crews living month in and month out on salted meat and ship's biscuit.

In 1854 the British Government made it compulsory for all vessels registered in Britain to carry lime juice on board (hence the American nickname "limejuicers" for British ships and "limeys" for British seamen). Although lemon juice was known to be more effective, lime juice was substituted because limes were more readily available and therefore cheaper. Despite the advances of medical knowledge through the earlier work of Dr. Lind and the famous naval surgeon Dr. Thomas Trotter, the persistent use of lime juice rather than lemon juice led to the recurrence of scurvy in many sailing ships of the nineteenth century.

Not until the beginning of the twentieth century was it discovered that limes were considerably less effective than lemons in treating scurvy, and that black currants were far superior to both. One might note here that as long ago as 551 Saint Brendan, the legendary Irish voyager, is said to have taken with him on his voyages a quantity of blue sea holly as a safeguard against scurvy (see Voyages of Saint Brendan, chapter 3).

Anson's voyage of circumnavigation (1740–1744) proved beyond doubt that scurvy was not the result of eating salt meat to the exclusion of other foods. When he crossed the Pacific in the *Centurion* his crew lived on the livestock that had been taken onboard in Mexico, and the men also fed on a wide variety of the abundant fish that were caught during the voyage; nevertheless, they died of scurvy at the rate of a dozen each day.

Many treatments were tried or suggested by different explorers. The consumption of vegetables, when available, produced so dramatic an improvement in sufferers that the cure was seen as obvious, but these foods were rarely available when needed. What was known as scurvy grass was sought whenever a ship made a landfall; infusions made from the tips of pine or fir leaves were prepared; beer brewed from spruce trees was known to be valuable, sometimes with wine—even pine, cedar, and probably others were also tried; fermented wort and sugar was thought useful; pickled cabbage had its adherents; cider was (like wine) popular as a treatment, though none of these alcoholic "medicines" contained ascorbic acid (vitamin C); prickly pear juice, coconut milk, vinegar, tea, cranberry juice, wild celery, various herbs, palm cabbage, marmalade made from carrots, mustard seed, spices of all kinds (including gunpowder when the food was especially bland)—all were tried by many and sworn to by some.

The answer of course was raw fruits or vegetables, as fresh as possible (Morton tells us of a seaman put ashore to die of scurvy; instead he cured himself by chewing at the green sward, which happily proved to be that species known as scurvy grass).

Captain Cook is often put forward as the savior of seafarers in the matter of scurvy, but in fact it was more his firmness in insisting that his men eat the sauerkraut that was carried aboard than his insights into the causes (and therefore the cure) of this terrible disease. Nearly two hundred years before Cook's time, Captain James Lancaster knew of the antiscorbutic properties of citrus juice; but the world had to wait for Dr. Lind's *Treatise of the Scurvy* a hundred and fifty years later, in 1753, before official apathy could bring itself to accept the blindingly obvious.

DEEP-SEA DIVING

*"There is no dilemma compared with that of
the deep-sea diver who hears the message from
the ship above, 'Come up at once. We are sinking.' "*

ROBERT COOPER

There are two kinds of diving: unassisted and assisted. Unassisted diving, or what we today call skin diving, is as old as man. Wherever there were communities by the sea or located near some other large body of water such as a lake or a river, there were men (or, in Japan, women) who had learned how to dive to gather oysters, crabs, sponges, and the like. The later need to recover cargo lost overboard or to dismantle dangerous wreckage, as well as the economic necessity of harvesting the seabed for food, quite naturally led man to experiment with devices that would allow him to spend longer periods underwater.

In assisted diving, the present-day snorkel is merely a refinement of a device that goes back to our very earliest lakeside settlements—a long hollow reed that a hunter could breathe through after he had slipped beneath the water to stalk prey such as duck and other water birds. This early aid to diving underwent many improvements over the hundreds of years that followed.

Thus assisted diving is nearly as old as skin diving. Aristotle in about 300 B.C. mentioned divers being provided with an apparatus to draw air from the surface of the water. He didn't describe the method, but it was probably some sort of metal or leather tube. Elsewhere he wrote of a metal vessel let down to the diver, who then used the air retained in it. This is obviously a very early application of the principle of the diving bell, a development of the mid-fifteenth century that allowed a diver to spend long periods underwater.

The diving bell works on the simple principle of lowering a bell-shaped container into the water, with its open bottom facing downward. The air inside is compressed in proportion to the depth of descent. If air is pumped from the surface into the bell-shaped housing so as to equal the pressure of water at that depth, the container will be exactly full of air. A diver can then work on the bottom for some time, using the air contained in the bell.

The first mention of a diving helmet, as distinct from a simple air-breathing tube or snorkel, occurs in a work by Vegetius published in 1553, in which there is an illustration of a diver wearing a leather helmet, with straps securing it to his chest and a long leather pipe extending to the surface where its open end is supported in the air by an inflated bladder. There is no evidence of a vision panel in the helmet, and Vegetius doesn't indicate how the diver's exhaled air was disposed of, but the device certainly gave considerable impetus to further experimentation. In 1679 Giovanni Borelli invented a diving apparatus that included a large bellows to force air down to the diver's leather helmet, thus allowing the diver to descend to greater depths because his air supply was delivered under pressure.

This very improvement in itself led to increased cases of the "bends," known as caisson disease but more properly called decompression sickness. This is the condition that occurs when nitrogen, which is naturally present in air, is released too rapidly from the blood, where it has been kept in solution under pressure during the dive. When the diver makes a rapid ascent the nitrogen is suddenly released into the circulatory system and the body tissues in the form of bubbles. These bubbles prevent oxygen from reaching the brain, in which case brain damage can result. If the oxygen deprivation is prolonged, then death usually follows. One of the characteristics of decompression sickness is the agonizing crippling of the body joints, hence the colloquial name "the bends," which accurately describes the contortions that the victim undergoes when he is suffering the extreme pain of this disease.

Assisted diving received its greatest boost when the German inventor Augustus Siebe introduced his "open" diving dress in 1819. In essence, Siebe's suit consisted of a metal helmet and breastplate attached to a watertight jacket. A constant stream of fresh air was pumped to the diver from the surface via a flexible metal pipe. The air was allowed to escape from the lower edge of the jacket, but water was prevented from entering the suit by the pressure of the air from the surface. This suit was by far the most successful diving gear yet invented, but it had one fatal drawback: if the diver stumbled and fell, his dress soon filled with water and he drowned unless he could very quickly be brought to the surface.

Siebe worked to overcome the dangers of his open suit and after a number of experiments he introduced his "closed" diving suit in 1830 (for an early example of Siebe's suit in use, see HMS *Royal George*, chapter 11). The diver was now fully enclosed in a watertight suit, and an air outlet was incorporated in the helmet. If the diver did stumble and fall over it no longer mattered; his whole suit remained watertight, and lead-weighted boots helped him to recover his balance. The Siebe dress enabled work to be carried out at considerable depths, often as much as 200 feet; in its essentials this is the diving suit still used today in salvage work and underwater construction, such as docks and piers.

For some time after Siebe had introduced his diving suit in the early 1800s, other men had been experimenting with an apparatus that would allow true freedom of movement under the water, what today we call free diving. Until then, the diver had necessarily been tethered to the surface by both his air-supply line and his safety line. In 1825 W. H. James, an Englishman, designed an independent breathing unit with a supply of compressed air contained in an iron reservoir strapped around the diver's waist. For some reason, despite its practical appeal, this device was never tested. A few years later an American by the name of Condert actually used a similar system, but the results were inconclusive because, unhappily, his air tank failed while he was on a dive and he drowned.

In 1865 two Frenchmen, Benoit Rouquayrol and Auguste Denayrouze, built what they called an aerophore, a compressed-air apparatus fixed to the diver's back which allowed him to spend a short period underwater. This device incorporated the world's first diving mask and demand valve, two inventions which, along with the portable air cylinder, marked man's most important first step in his search for freedom of movement in the undersea world.

For the next forty years various designs and modifications to the air-cylinder concept were tried until in 1924 two Frenchmen, Yves Le Prieur of the French navy and his compatriot Vincent Fernez, devised a system that consisted of a chest-mounted cylinder of compressed air at a pressure of 150 atmospheres and a special mouthpiece coupled with a mask that covered the entire face. The mask was linked with the demand valve that had been invented earlier, in 1865. This device worked extremely well despite its cumbersome nature.

World War II accelerated the development of oxygen-breathing apparatus for use by what came to be known as navy frogmen. Initially the experts were the Italians, who demonstrated the possibilities of this new type of underwater warfare by penetrating the British naval base at Alexandria in 1941 and severely damaging the battleships *Queen Elizabeth* and *Valiant* with delayed-action limpet mines.

In 1943 Jacques Cousteau (later to become the world's most famous explorer and filmmaker of the world beneath the sea) and Emile Gagnan, a French engineer, developed a fully automatic compressed-air breathing device. It was simple in design, robust in structure, and safe to use, and it proved to be the final passport for man's entry into the ocean. Thus the stage was set for the emergence and widespread use of what we now call the aqualung or SCUBA, the acronym for Self-Contained Underwater Breathing Apparatus.

This first aqualung consisted of three cylinders filled with air at a pressure of 150 atmospheres, connected to an air regulator. Two tubes joined the regulator to the mouthpiece, where air was delivered to the diver's lungs at local water pressure. Eyes and nose were covered with a watertight rubber mask with a glass front, and rubber foot fins or flippers completed the dress of the free diver. The aqualung had now completely freed the diver from the constraints of the world above the surface of the water. To Cousteau, more than to any other man, is due the vast development and popularity of the sport of free diving in the postwar years.

Sea Chanties

*"But perhaps the most venerable custom of all
is that of singing chanties as an accompaniment to labour."*

Stanley Rogers

A chanty, sometimes *shanty*, was a labor song (i.e., a chant; hence its name, from the French *chanter*, to sing) sung by the seamen on watch on a merchant ship to lighten their labor as they hoisted yards and sails, weighed anchor, worked the pumps, and so on. It was also a device much used by French Canadian lumbermen who sang in unison as they hauled their logs down to the river.

The chanty became popular some hundreds of years ago, when for reasons of profit merchant ships were grossly undermanned; the rhythmic tune and simple wording of a song made it easier for seamen to coordinate their efforts in pulling and hauling. The advent of steam—where much of the hard labor of weighing anchor, swaying up a heavy yard, and so on, was done by powered machinery—saw the gradual demise of the chanty from its familiar context; sea chanties are known to us today only through the music hall, party songfests, and so on. Chanties are rarely sung on warships, mainly because there is machinery available for performing the heavy tasks, and of course there are many men available for any particular job.

The chanty was generally made up of short verses, often sung by one of the men in the watch, the chantyman, interspersed with a rollicking chorus in which all the men joined. Many of these chanties have become famous in their own right as tunes, such as "Shenandoah," "Rolling Home," "Bound For the Rio Grande," and the haunting "Spanish Ladies." Although the words of chanties might vary from ship to ship, the tune rarely changed; and if the words of a chanty ran out before the hauling task was completed a good chantyman would be able to improvise so as to keep the group effort going.

Two broad categories of sea chanties have evolved over the years: the working chanty, the kind used to accompany the pulling of ropes such as in hauling yards and sails aloft and for laboring at the capstan when weighing anchor; and the forecastle chanty, usually in the form of a ballad sung during off-watch leisure time.

The working chanties can themselves be divided into two groups: the halyard chanty and the capstan chanty. The halyard chanty (from "haul yard") has certain points or nodes in its tune that encourage a collective pull by the men hauling the sail or yard aloft (in the larger vessels some yards were so heavy that a winch had to be used to position them properly). At each nodal point the men would heave down together in a concentrated effort, with either all of them singing the chanty or, as was very common (especially for a capstan chanty), one man—the chantyman, often perched on the barrel of the capstan itself—would sing the words so as to keep the men working evenly. One of the best-known halyard chanties is "Blow the Man Down," also a favorite when toiling at the capstan bars, as in this version:

> *Strolling the highway one night on the spree,*
> Hey-ho, blow the man down,
> *I met a flash packet, the wind blowing free,*
> Give us some time to blow the man down.

Of the port that she hailed from I cannot say much,
Hey-ho, blow the man down,
But by her appearance I took her for Dutch,
Give us some time to blow the man down.

Her flag was three colors, her masthead was low,
Hey-ho, blow the man down,
She was round in the counter and bluff in the bow,
Give us some time to blow the man down.

I fired my bow chaser; the signal she knew,
Hey-ho, blow the man down,
She backed her main topsail and for me hove to,
Give us some time to blow the man down.

Another kind of halyard or pulling chanty is the short drag, used when a few strong hauls will do the job, as in setting a skysail, hardening in a sheet, and so on. "Haul Away O" is probably the best known of the short-drag chanties, one version of which follows.

Louis was the King of France afore the Revolution,
Away, haul away, boys, haul away O!
Louis was the King of France afore the Revolution,
Away, haul away, boys, haul away O!

But Louis got his head cut off, which spoiled his constitution,
Away, haul away, boys, haul away O!
But Louis got his head cut off, which spoiled his constitution,
Away, haul away, boys, haul away O!

The capstan chanty, on the other hand, is so constructed that it allows for a continuous and rhythmical movement around the capstan barrel, this being needed because of the great effort that sometimes had to be applied in order to break out the anchor flukes from the holding ground and, finally, win it home. Such a chanty was also sung when the vessel had to be warped into her berth. Perhaps the most familiar of the capstan chanties are "Yo Heave Ho," "Rio Grande," and the beautiful "Shenandoah":

Shenandoah, I love your daughter,
Away you rolling river;
Shenandaoh, so long I've sought her,
Away, we're bound away, 'cross the wide Missouri.

Shenandoah, I've come to take her,
Away you rolling river;
Shenandoah, my bride I'll make her,
Away, we're bound away, 'cross the wide Missouri.

Shenandoah, my boat is ready,
Away you rolling river;
Sheets are braced all taut and steady,
Away, we're bound away, 'cross the wide Missouri.

Shenandoah, give us your blessing,
Away you rolling river;
We must sail, for time is pressing,
Away, we're bound away, 'cross the wide Missouri.

Before steam finally ousted the clipper ship and the so-called windjammers (the big square-riggers that replaced clipper ships as the workhorses of the sea; see chapter 8 for both types), it was not uncommon for residents of waterside Sydney in the 1880s and 1890s to be treated to a round of chanty singing the like of which will never be heard again. With a whole fleet of clippers gathered at their anchorage, waiting for the wool to come in from the outstations, the crews would often spend an evening filling the still night air with some old and much-loved chanty:

The men of one ship would start a chanty. Soon it would be taken up on another ship, then another and another. Presently the harbor echoed with the harmonies of a dozen crews. Occasionally one crew would sing a verse, the entire fleet joining in the chorus, another crew taking the next verse, and the chanty thus proceeding through the fleet.

8

THE CAPTAIN
AND HIS SHIP

I n no other human endeavor has the notion of "captain" been as important and significant as in seafaring. Seamen were prepared to put up with very difficult living conditions ("hard lying," as they called it) if they had a captain who both knew his job as ship handler and navigator on the one hand and on the other hand knew how to lead and discipline men without forfeiting their respect (see Captain James Cook, below).

Readers of maritime literature will be familiar with the likes of Bully Hayes, the hard-driving South Pacific trader in human cargo, and Hugh Pigot, who in 1797 precipitated the worst mutiny ever to occur in the British navy (see HMS *Hermione* Mutiny, chapter 9). Richard Henry Dana in his famous book *Two*

Years Before the Mast gives us a stark impression of the ferocious brutality of one particular captain in the 1830s.

Before the discussion of specific captains, this chapter briefly examines the kinds of ships common in the Age of Sail, when wind-powered vessels attained the heights of efficiency and beauty.

SHIP TYPES

"What thing of sea or land . . .
Comes this way sailing,
Like a stately ship
Of Tarsus, bound for th' isles
Of Javan or Gadire,
With all her bravery on, and tackle trim,
Sails filled, and streamers waving,
Courted by all the winds that hold them play."

JOHN MILTON, "SAMSON AGONISTES"

Ship is from the Anglo-Saxon *scip* (pronounced *ship*), connected with other Teutonic words such as Dutch *schip*, German *schiff*, Old Norse *skip*. A ship today is generally regarded as any large oceangoing vessel; in the days of sail any vessel propelled by wind was called—loosely—a ship. The seaman, however, understood the term *ship* to mean a specific kind of vessel—strictly, one with a bowsprit and at least three masts, with each mast made up of three sections: a lower mast, a topmast above that, and a topgallant mast surmounting both. Furthermore, in order to be called a ship the vessel had to be square-rigged on all masts (that is, ship-rigged).

Four- and five-masted ships were also built in the late nineteenth century, but by that time it was unusual to see a full ship-rigged vessel. The more common rig incorporated fore-and-aft rig on one or more of the aftermasts, with square sails on the remainder. Such a combination required a smaller crew and was therefore cheaper to maintain. The three-masted ship was common in the eighteenth century, and a number of four-masted ships appeared in the nineteenth century. At the beginning of the twentieth century the only five-masted ship-rigged vessel ever built took to the sea: the mighty *Preussen*, of German registration.

Sailing vessels came to be classified according to the number of masts they carried and the way each mast was rigged (square-rigged, fore-and-aft rigged, or a combination of both). Seamen in the late eighteenth century and the nineteenth century used the following terms.

- *Brig:* Two masts, square-rigged on the foremast, with the crossjack (a square sail) and spanker (fore-and-aft sail) both set on the mainmast (the aftermost mast).

- *Brigantine:* Exactly like a brig, except that it never carried a crossjack on the mainmast.
- *Hermaphrodite brig:* Two masts, square-rigged on the foremast and fore-and-aft rigged on the mainmast.
- *Bark* (also *Barque*): Three masts, square-rigged on the foremast and mainmast and fore-and-aft rigged on the aftermost mast (the mizzen). Four- and five-masted barks (fore-and-aft rigged on the aftermost mast only, square-rigged on the remaining masts) became very common in the late nineteenth and early twentieth centuries as an economy measure in the struggle against steam.
- *Barkentine* (also *Barquentine*): Three masts, square-rigged on the foremast and fore-and-aft rigged on the mainmast and mizzen (the two aftermost masts). This rig was much more efficient sailing to windward than the other types and required fewer crew; thus four-, five-, and six-masted barkentines became common.
- *Jackass bark:* Three masts, a bark with the addition of a fore-and-aft sail on the lower mainmast. A four-masted jackass bark was square-rigged on the two foremost masts and fore-and-aft rigged on the two aftermost masts.
- *Ship:* Three masts, each mast in three sections, square-rigged on all, with a bowsprit. Four-masted ships were also built, but only one five-masted ship was ever launched (the *Preussen*).
- *Schooner:* (From the Dutch *schooner*, found in other seafaring tongues, and probably deriving from the old Scottish verb *scon*, to skip over water like a flat stone, as in the game of ducks and drakes.) The basic type has two masts, fore-and-aft rigged on both, with the foremast shorter than the mainmast or (a modern development) both masts of equal height. The schooner originally carried square topsails on the fore topmast, but the jib-headed topsail soon replaced the square sail. A few topsail schooners can still be found in various parts of the world. Schooners with three or more masts had equal-height masts; a number were built with three, four, five, and six masts. The biggest schooner ever built was the massive seven-masted *Thomas W. Lawson*; launched in the 1890s, she carried only sixteen crew and was fitted with steam winches; she was lost in a storm in 1907, with only one survivor. A double-topsail schooner carried square sails on two masts (generally the foremast and mainmast): the term *topsail schooner* is applied to the schooner that carries a square sail on the foremast only.

Modern sailboat rigs include:

- *Schooner:* Generally only two or three masts, fore-and-aft rigged on all, occasionally with square topsails.

- ◆ *Ketch* (originally *Catch*): Two masts, fore-and-aft rigged, with the foremast (the main) taller than the mizzen and the mizzen stepped forward of the rudder post.
- ◆ *Yawl:* Exactly like a ketch, except that the mizzen is stepped aft of the rudder post.
- ◆ *Sloop:* One mast only, fore-and-aft rigged with a mainsail and only one headsail.
- ◆ *Cutter:* Like the sloop, except that it flies two headsails and the mast is usually stepped a little farther aft to accommodate them. Often rigged with a bowsprit to take the foremost headsail.

These five main rigs are further delineated by the shape of their driving sails: bermuda (also called jib-headed, marconi, or leg-o'-mutton), the triangular sail characterized by the jib or headsail; and gaff, a four-sided sail with its uppermost side held aloft by a spar to which the sail is attached. This spar is in turn hoisted on the mast and controlled by its own running rigging.

Thus a ketch may be gaff-rigged or bermuda-rigged on one or both masts. The gaff rig has definite advantages in off-the-wind sailing, whereas the bermuda rig cannot be surpassed for close-hauled sailing (sailing on the wind). Yacht races such as the Sydney–Hobart and the America's Cup are contested by bermuda rigs; cruising sailors have shown a more or less equal preference for the marconi rig and the gaff rig.

The Age of Sail

"No man will be a sailor who has contrivance enough to get himself into a gaol;
for being in a ship is being in a gaol, with the chance of being drowned."
Samuel Johnson, in Boswell's *Life*

We do not know when man first began to build boats or use the wind as motive power, but the oldest unmistakable pictures of sailing craft come from Egypt, where the Nile was ideal for the emergence of primitive shipping. Papyrus, the pithy reed from which early paper was made (and from which paper takes its name), widely available throughout the Nile Valley, provided the material for the earliest rafts used on this vast waterway. Because the wind in Egypt blows from the north practically year-round, it was only natural that people should soon hit on the idea of somehow using it for wind-driven voyages southward up the long reaches of the river.

The earliest known representation of a sailing craft is on an Egyptian vase from about 3200 B.C. The hull is constructed of papyrus reeds bound together in long bundles, with both ends drawn to a point and turned up for some distance. The sail is made of strips of matting woven from reeds and sewn together to the required size. In 1970 Thor Heyerdahl and some companions sailed from Morocco to Barbados in the West Indies in *Ra II*, a large seagoing vessel constructed entirely of papyrus reeds; the object of the expedition was to demonstrate that the ancient Egyptians had the means for undertaking oceanic voyages (see also The *Kon-Tiki* Expedition, chapter 3).

Good boatbuilding timber of a suitable length has never grown in Egypt; thus the earliest wooden craft were constructed of short planks lashed and dowelled together edge to edge. Cedar was imported from Lebanon as early as 3000 B.C. for building larger, more sturdy vessels.

Organized seafaring is, of course, far older than the Egyptian vase paintings. Evidence of seagoing vessels has been found in the Mesolithic campsites of 8000 B.C. on a number of islands in the Aegean Sea, in the eastern Mediterranean. The remarkable Minoan maritime civilization appeared during the early Bronze Age in about 3000 B.C. and flourished for some fifteen hundred years until it was wiped out by an invasion of primitive Greeks around 1500 B.C., leaving behind scattered fragments of large seagoing vessels of advanced construction (see Fabled Atlantis, chapter 16).

Since ancient times oceangoing ships have always been built of wood. More primitive materials such as reed, skin, and bark were used only for local sailing in relatively protected waters (see Voyages of Saint Brendan, chapter 3, for an account of a remarkable journey in a leather boat).

Two methods of building in wood evolved: carvel and clinker. The carvel technique was developed in the eastern Mediterranean countries where, for example, the Egyptians and Phoenicians built seagoing vessels by fixing the planks edge to edge with each other and then nailing, lashing, or dowelling them to the boat frame (see Hanno the Navigator, chapter 3, for an example of an extended oceanic voyage by the Phoenicians). *Carvel* is from the Dutch *karviel*, referring to the kind of nail used in this building method; it is not at all related to the European ship type caravel, which comes from the Latin word *carabus*, meaning coracle, an early craft made from the skins of animals. This method of carvel planking came into general use throughout the Mediterranean, and during the Middle Ages it spread along the coast of western Europe, reaching the Baltic in the fifteenth century. It then became the dominant method of shipbuilding in the Northern Hemisphere, and after the middle of the sixteenth century all large vessels were built in this manner.

The second method, the clinker technique, originated in northern Europe during the Viking Age in the ninth century when large clinker-built vessels made regular voyages to Iceland and Greenland. In this method of construction, each plank overlaps the one below it and is then riveted or dowelled to the frames inside the hull, rather similar to the construction of a clapboard or weatherboard house. Another term for this technique is lapstrake; *strake* is an old shipwright's word for plank. The word *clinker* is a variant of *clinch*, *clench*, from the Anglo Saxon *beclencan*, to make cling to, to hold fast.

Experimental ships were built of iron during the first half of the nineteenth century. When the steam engine was introduced as a means of propulsion, iron became the most commonly used shipbuilding material. The first working steam-powered vessel was the French paddle steamer *Pyroscaphe*, built in 1783 and successfully tested by steaming fifteen minutes against the current of the River Saône, near Lyons. Nevertheless, sail was still being used commercially well into the twentieth century, even on square-rigged ships constructed wholly of iron or steel. Coal-fired steamships proved in the long run to be far more economical, however, especially when the opening of the Suez Canal in 1869 and the Panama Canal in 1914 allowed shipping companies to reduce their operating costs. By the 1930s most of the remaining square-riggers had disappeared from the oceans of the world. The three-masted steel bark *Penang*, probably the last example of the age of working sail, was still in commercial use in 1941.

Perhaps the most beautiful of all the ships that ever sailed the seas were The Clipper Ships (see below) of the mid-nineteenth century. These three-masted, square-rigged vessels engaged in the tea trade between China and England in the latter half of the 1800s and, toward the end of that century and into the early part of the next, in the wool-clip trade from Australia. These ships were modeled on the very fast and successful Baltimore clippers of the late eighteenth and the early nineteenth centuries, built mostly in Maryland and Virginia.

The word *clipper* originally denoted the idea of speed rather than a ship type, because these very fast craft could "clip" the time usually taken on passage by the regular packet ships, which were fast vessels appointed by the crown in the sixteenth century to carry government letters and dispatches on a regular basis between two ports. Names of clipper ships such as *Sea Witch*, *Flying Cloud*, *Ariel*, *Taiping*, and *Cutty Sark* live on in the legends of the sea, but today only the *Cutty Sark* survives from that golden age of sail, preserved as a museum in drydock at Greenwich, London.

The age of commercial sail is long since over, but a number of seafaring nations maintain a wide variety of sailing vessels for the purpose of training young people in the art of ship-handling and seamanship. The sailing ship, perhaps humanity's most beautiful creation, still has much to teach us in teamwork, discipline, and personal discovery.

The sea, Joseph Conrad once said, is the great testing and proving experience, or as Kenneth Grahame put it in a lighter vein,

> *Believe me, my young friend [said the Water Rat to Mole], there is nothing—absolutely nothing—half so much worth doing as simply messing about in boats.*

THE CLIPPER SHIPS

"The graceful, yacht-like clipper, perhaps the most beautiful
and life-like thing ever fashioned by the hand of man."

A CLIPPER SHIP OFFICER

Clipper ships, widely regarded by seafaring men of the mid-1800s as the "most beautiful wooden sailing vessels the world had ever seen," were a type of very fast square-rigged sailing ship introduced by American builders in the 1840s. The so-called Baltimore clipper, which saw much service in the War of 1812, was in fact a schooner, and a fast one at that.

A clipper was instantly recognizable by her long, low, and moderately narrow hull, a sharply raked knife-edge stem (what Kemp calls "the true mark of the clipper"), somewhat hollow bows, and an overhanging stern. Square-rigged on three masts and commonly wearing three jibs (flying, outer, inner) and a foretopmast staysail, with a spanker on the mizzenmast and stuns'ls (studding sails) rigged to the outer limits of the yards, some clippers were capable of 20 knots or more. A clipper under a full press of sail was an astonishing sight, the beauty of which was recognized by even the most hard-nosed captain: " 'She was a perfect beauty to every nautical man,' one clipper captain said of his vessel."

When gold was discovered in California in 1848 and in eastern Australia in 1850 and the China–England tea trade was thrown open to foreign interests, the development of fast cargo-carriers was given an impetus that resulted in the appearance of beautiful American clippers like *Flying Cloud, Lightning,* and *Champion of the Seas* and British examples like *Taeping, Ariel,* and *Thermopylae,* together with the famous and much-admired *Cutty Sark.*

The tea trade with China was very profitable for Britain, and a number of clippers were purpose-built, very strongly constructed so that chests of tea could be hammered and wedged into the hold in an effort to utilize every inch of available space. Every year these vessels would assemble in the Chinese tea ports (the main one was Foochow), load their cargo of leaf, and race home to London, where the first cargo onto the dock could command high prices, the captain commonly being paid a premium for his skill in winning the "tea race."

The most famous of these races was staged in May 1866, when the *Fiery Cross, Ariel, Taeping, Serica,* and *Taitsing* all left Foochow within three days of each other. Three months and one week later, having voyaged some 15,000 miles through the South China Sea, then by way of Sunda Strait to the Indian Ocean, west around the Cape of Good Hope, and finally north into the South Atlantic and on to the North Atlantic, *Taeping* and *Ariel* docked in London within half an hour of each other, the *Serica* made fast in the next two hours, and the *Fiery Cross* and *Taitsing* came alongside two days later—collectively perhaps the greatest feat of navigation and seamanship the world has ever seen, achieved as it was under the trying conditions of racing against time through regions of fearful heat and terrible storm, all the while driven under as full a press of sail as each master dared fly.

The opening of the Suez Canal in 1869 and the impetus it gave to steam propulsion hastened the death of the tea clippers on the China trade. For a while they engaged in the wool trade between Australia and England, with old rivals *Cutty Sark* and *Thermopylae* often competing against each other to get their cargoes of wool to the London exchange first. Both vessels managed the astonishing time of eighty days for the passage.

Perhaps the greatest days of the *Cutty Sark*'s career began in 1885 (she was launched in 1869, five days after the opening of the Suez Canal), when her owner, Jock Willis, often referred to as Captain John, Old Jock, or Old White Hat (from the fact that he habitually wore a pale top hat), appointed Richard Woodget (or Woodgett) as her master. Woodget stayed with *Cutty Sark* for nearly ten years, setting records on the wool trade between England and Australia and in the process becoming a legend himself as a man who knew how to get the best—and the most—out of the beautiful vessel under his command.

Jock Willis had named her from Robert Burns's poem "Tam O'Shanter," which tells of a young Scottish farmer Tam O'Shanter who on horseback late one Halloween night came across three witches dancing in a clearing, one of the three the young and beautiful witch Nannie, dressed only in a short shift or chemise. When Nannie caught sight of Tam she flew into a rage and chased him. Tam in terrible fright sent his horse Meg flying through the forest, with Nannie in hot pursuit. Meg was fast, but not fast enough to prevent Nannie from grasping her tail and alas! pulling it off. Tam and horse—minus her tail—then bolted madly for freedom.

In 1885 she won the wool race in 73 days from Sydney, having defeated her old nemesis *Thermopylae*. In 1889, off the Australian east coast, the Sydney-bound *Cutty Sark* was overtaken by the mail steamer *Britannia*, said to be the fastest ship in the world. Undeterred, Woodget waited for wind, and when it arrived he piled on every stitch possible and passed the *Britannia* at 17 knots, to the great astonishment of the *Britannia*'s master and everyone else on board. When *Britannia* dropped anchor in Sydney half an hour behind the *Cutty Sark*, all on board the steamer cheered the clipper wildly for her magnificent performance.

In 1895 the *Cutty Sark* was sold to a Portuguese firm and for twenty-seven years she sailed under a foreign flag as *Ferreira*, rerigged as a barkentine, but so well known was this masterpiece of shipbuilding that her Portuguese crews referred to her as *Pequena Camisola*—"Little Chemise," a reference to her Scots name *Cutty Sark*, which means short shift or shirt.

When Jock Willis built his *Cutty Sark* (she was intended to be a direct rival to the already famous *Thermopylae*) he had a figurehead image of Nannie mounted immediately beneath her bowsprit (the word is from the Low German *bogspret*, a spar at the bow) to signify her swiftness and desire for revenge. It then became customary for each crew of the *Cutty Sark* to make sure that Meg's tail was represented by a short length of frayed rope fixed in Nannie's hand, as a symbol of the ship's speed and ability to overtake any other vessel (see Ships' Figureheads, chapter 19).

In 1922 Captain Wilfred Dowman bought the *Cutty Sark* and restored her original clipper rig; after his death she was used as a training ship. Eventually this grand old ship was berthed in a specially constructed dock on the Thames at Greenwich, near the National Maritime Museum, and after more restoration work she was opened to the public in 1957, where she remains today, much admired as the only survivor of the famous British tea clippers.

THE WINDJAMMERS

"Another windjammer day has begun."
ADRIAN SELIGMAN, *THE VOYAGE OF THE "CAP PILAR"*

Windjammer was the contemptuous epithet given by crews on engine-powered ships to the huge square-riggers that were struggling to compete with steam across the trade routes of the world. These sailing ships, smirked the deckhand and stoker, were nothing but great clumsy contraptions that had to scuttle sideways into the wind in order to go forward, with their yards and sails braced hard back against the shrouds and backstays so that the vessel could be jammed at an angle into the wind, unlike the steamer, which simply pointed her nose to wherever she wanted to go.

But the steamer, ugly as she was, won the day by sheer force of economics, and the windjammers—those enormous square-riggers that once plowed the seven seas with cargoes of wheat, wool, hides, guano, timber, coal, nitrates, and anything else the world wanted—died a lonely death, lamented only by those who loved the silent beauty of a tall windship under a full press of sail as she ran down her easting or slanted across the Pacific under the steady trade winds or flogged her storm-tossed way around Cape Horn.

Windjammer was never a nautical term, although it was probably used by seamen from time to time; more often they would refer to a vessel by its type: as a bark, for example (three or four masts, or more), barkentine, ship-rigged, and so on. The most common general name for these vessels was square-rigger, which refers to the fact that the main driving sails are square, laced to yards that lie athwartships and square to the mast. It is an ancient rig that originated with the single square sail set on a short mast to take advantage of a following wind (the longboat of the Vikings is a good example).

In about A.D. 1000 it was discovered that it was possible to sail such a vessel to windward by hauling the yard around so it made an angle to the fore-and-aft line of the vessel. This discovery led to a much greater versatility in the rig, and as hulls grew in size it was not long before the single mast was replaced by two or more masts, with more than one square sail set from each mast.

As hull length was increased so masts became taller; a topmast was added to the existing lower mast and then a topgallant mast was added to the topmast, with the square sails taking their name from the mast section from which they were hung (*topgallant* is from *top-garland*, referring to the rope or wooden collar attached to the top of the original pole mast, used for supporting the standing rigging; when the third mast section appeared it took its name from this old top garland). The lower mast thus flew the "lower" sail (known as the course), above which were the topsails (tops'ls), and then the topgallant sails (t'gallants).

By the sixteenth century the most common European vessel had two or three masts and carried three square sails (course, topsail, topgallant) on each mast, with each sail named by the mast and mast section from which it was flown: forecourse, foretopsail, foretopgallant, and so on. Commonly there was a spritsail carried below the bowsprit and a lateen on the mizzenmast, right aft. Staysails—the triangular sail familiar to us today as the jib—appeared on the stays between masts in the mid-seventeenth century, and the jib replaced the spritsail not long afterward.

This configuration—square sails on all masts—became known as *ship rig,* although technically to qualify as a "ship" a vessel needed to have its masts in three sections (lower mast, topmast, and topgallant), with a bowsprit at the bow. This rig remained more or less standard until the end of the eighteenth century.

Burgeoning world trade during the nineteenth century and the rapid development of larger hulls to carry it necessitated new sail plans. What emerged was a combination of square rig and fore-and-aft rig, such as in the bark and barkentine for three-masted ships and the brig and brigantine for two-masted ships. This combination proved to be as efficient under sail as the ship-rigged vessels and had the great advantage of requiring a smaller crew because of the replacement of square sails by fore-and-aft sails on the mizzenmast. A further innovation during the nineteenth century was the introduction of the clipper ship, though this was more a development of hull form than rig.

The final development of the square rig came in the early twentieth century, using the one great trade route still open to sailing vessels: the Cape Horn route for the Chilean nitrate trade, plied by the great Cape Horners. The steamer had killed the sailing ship on all other routes, but she could not compete in the Southern Ocean for two reasons: there were no coaling stations along the route, and when steamship propellers raced in the air in the troughs of the huge seas the engines often suffered serious damage. Until the Panama Canal was opened in 1914, this trade remained in the hands of the big sailing ships: the windjammers, the fully developed square-riggers.

Much of this nitrate trade was carried in the big three-masted barks of Britain, France, Germany, Spain, and Finland, but world demand for nitrates encouraged the building of four- and five-masted ship-rigged and bark-rigged vessels. A five-masted full-rigged ship in fine weather could set as many as six square sails on each mast (plus four or more studding sails, known as stuns'ls), together with four jibs, eight staysails, and a spanker (a fore-and-aft sail on the mizzen).

A number of these big square-rigged ships, which for power combined with beauty could not be beaten, were built in Germany for Reederei F. Laeisz for its famous Flying P Line (ships such as *Passat, Pamir, Pera, Peking, Potosi, Padua, Pommern,* and the five-masted full-rigged giant *Preussen,* known around the world as the "Queen of the Seas"; in 1910 she met her end on the rocks off Dover). The "Flying" in Flying P Line came from the speed of its ships. The origin of the "P" is less obvious: the first ship the firm had built, the *Sophie,* was named after the daughter-in-law of the firm's founder; Sophie's nickname was Pudel (German for "poodle"), because of her thick curly hair. The *Sophie* became the *Pudel,* and all vessels subsequently owned by this firm were given P names.

The largest sailing ship ever built was the *France* (launched in 1911 at 5,806 gross tons). She was a five-masted bark, square-rigged on four identical masts and fore-and-aft rigged on the jigger mast or mizzen, the aftermost mast; all the masts were taller than a five-story building. Under sail only, her best day's run was 420 nautical miles, averaging an astonishing 17.5 knots, which must have been a supremely thrilling experience for those on board, with her more than 64,000 square feet of canvas developing thousands of horsepower of energy as she thundered headlong across the seas. In 1922 the *France* was wrecked on a coral reef near New Caledonia, some 700 miles off the northeast coast of Australia, having lasted longer than many other square-riggers, which during World War I were sunk by submarines, raiders, or mines.

Some of the famous windjammers of those wonderful seventy years of square sail from about 1870 to 1940 included the *Archibald Russell,* the *Arethusa,* the *Borrowdale,* the *Blackbraes,* the *Cedarbank,* the *Cromdale,* the *Danmark,* the *Fingal,* the *Grace Harwar,* the *Herzogin Cecilie,* the *Lynton,* the *Monongahela,* the *Moshulu,* the *Otago* (the Australian bark that was Joseph Conrad's first command), the *Padua,* the *Parma,* the *Peking,* the *Potosi,* the *William Law . . .*

Nostalgically remembering his 1938 voyage on *Moshulu,* Eric Newby wrote:

> *At the wheel a Swede and a Dane were fighting to hold her as she ran 13 and 14 knots in the gusts. I knew then that I would never see sailing like this again. When such ships as this went it would be the finish. The windbelts of the world would be deserted and the great West Wind and the Trades would never blow on steel rigging and flax canvas again.*

CHRISTOPHER COLUMBUS

"When he started out he didn't know where he was going,
when he got there he didn't know where he was,
and when he got back he didn't know where he had been."

ANONYMOUS, ON COLUMBUS

Probably more has been written, debated, and disputed about Christopher Columbus (Cristoforo Colombo, Italian; Cristóbal Colón, Spanish; 1451–1506) than any
other seafarer. Nevertheless, the cruel witticism above aside, and disregarding for the
moment whether he was in fact the first European to discover America (see, for example, Hanno the Navigator, chapter 3, and Vinland USA, chapter 4), it is certain
that the four voyages made by Columbus (1492, 1493, 1498, and 1502) led directly
not only to the colonization of the United States (commemorated in some fifty or so
U.S. place-names such as Columbia, Columbiana, Columbiaville, and, of course,
Columbus) but also to a long period of Spanish hegemony, greed, and cruelty that
brought ruin and misery to entire nations of native people throughout the Caribbean
and South America (see, for example, On the Spanish Main, chapter 7).

Columbus was born Cristoforo Colombo in Genoa in 1451. When he went
to Spain to seek royal support for his "Enterprise of the Indies" (a supposed direct
westerly route to the region once known as the East Indies, now Indonesia, the
Philippines, and surrounding islands, as well as Japan and China—fabled Cipangu
and Cathay, respectively), he became known as Cristóbal Colón.

After he married in 1479 and settled with his wife in Funchal in the Madeiras
(she died when their son, Diego, was five years old), Columbus set about learning
Portuguese, Castilian, and Latin, read and annotated books of travel such as Marco
Polo's, and in every way prepared himself for what he regarded as his sacred mission:
finding a direct route to the Orient (note Boland's confident assertion: "Columbus
sailed . . . west to America because he knew it was there"). He was already a thoroughly experienced seaman, having made voyages throughout the Mediterranean, to
Iceland, Lagos, and England, and as master of a Portuguese vessel to the Gold Coast.

Columbus could well have pursued a life as a professional mariner, but instead
he relocated to Lisbon and spent the next ten years vainly trying to sell his dream
to John II of Portugal, Henry VII of England, and Charles VIII of France. (John
Cabot underwent a curiously similar experience not ten years earlier when trying
to enlist support for his planned search for The Northwest Passage; see chapter 4.)
Finally, Ferdinand and Isabella, king and queen of Spain, having already refused him
twice, relented, granting him in 1492 all he asked for.

Which was a lot. He wanted three vessels fully crewed, provisioned, and stocked
with trade goods; in the event of his success he demanded ennoblement, jurisdiction
as admiral, viceroyalty over all new lands that he discovered, and a ten percent

commission on all resulting trade. The Spanish monarchs granted all this, as well as guaranteeing future power, status, and profits for himself and his descendants.

Columbus made his preparations. His plan was to go down to the Canary Islands, pick up the southeasterly trade winds, and then sail west along 28 degrees North latitude, which would, as the geographers of the time agreed, lead him straight to Japan or to that country's outlying islands. His ships were the caravels *Pinta* and *Niña*, each a little less than 60 feet in length, and the somewhat larger *nao* (ship) *Santa María*, his flagship, about 95 feet.

Columbus and his small fleet left Palos in southwest Spain on August 3, 1492, and sailed off into glorious history, but not before enduring the setbacks common to great enterprises. Before they reached the Canaries the *Pinta* lost her rudder and sprang a leak; after making repairs and sailing into the unknown Atlantic there was a false landfall, then no wind, followed by an incipient mutiny by the increasingly unhappy crew, averted only by Columbus's promise to turn back after three days if no land had been sighted.

Late at night the next day the miracle happened: a light was seen ahead and the expedition's first landfall was entered into the ship's log.

Early the next morning Columbus went ashore and named his discovery San Salvador—"Saint Saviour"—today Watlings Island, on the eastern edge of the Bahamas group. He and his men were welcomed by the Arawak natives, whom Columbus immediately called Indians, convinced that he had at last discovered his Indies of the Orient. (Alas! unknown to him then and not known in Europe for another twenty years, was the fact that the real Indies lay another 9,000 miles farther west, with a huge land mass inconveniently blocking direct access.) The Orient, he reasoned, could not be far off.

A few days later, while in search of his longed-for Cipangu, Columbus encountered a large island his Arawak pilot called Cuba; Columbus heard this as "Cipangu" but thought it so little resembled Marco Polo's description of that country that he decided it must instead be a promontory of China. He explored the northern coast of Cuba and named Cape Alpha and Cape Omega from his confident belief that they represented the eastern terminus of the Eurasian continent. Hispaniola (originally La Isla Española, the island today shared by Haiti and the Dominican Republic) was discovered and named. On Christmas Eve the *Santa María* ran hard and fast onto a coral reef nearby; Columbus—now called, somewhat prematurely, "the Admiral" by his admiring men—built a fort there from the remains of his disintegrating ship and named the fort Navidad, "Christmas."

Leaving some men as guards, on January 4, 1493, Columbus set out from Navidad in the *Niña* for the north coast of Hispaniola; he was joined by the *Pinta* and on January 16 both ships laid a course for home, arriving—after considerable weather difficulties—at Palos, eight months after his departure from that port. Ferdinand and Isabella received him with honor, confirmed him in his privileges and admired his "Indians," caged parrots, and gold artifacts from Hispaniola.

The Spanish monarchs then immediately supported a second voyage that was to further explore the Indies, initiate trade from there, and provide for Spanish colonies there. The fleet of seventeen vessels sailed from Cádiz on September 25, 1493, and on Sunday, November 3, in what is now called the Lesser Antilles, they anchored off a high-topped island that Columbus named Dominica (a variation of *Domingo*, Spanish for "Sunday"). Near the island of Santa Maria de Guadeloupe he encountered the Caribes ("heroes," "brave ones"), the fierce man-eating people much feared by the Arawak. The English *cannibal* is from the Spanish plural *canebales*, a variation of the earlier Spanish word *caribes*.

A steady succession of islands fell to Columbus's zeal for naming—now the Leeward Islands, the Virgin Islands, Puerto Rico (originally the name of the town founded in 1508 by Juan Ponce de León, a companion of Columbus on this second voyage). Then he returned to Navidad in Hispaniola.

However, no one came out to greet him because no one was there. They were all dead, having in succession fought over gold and women and then with each other, finally being killed to a man by a local tribe. Columbus relocated to Isabela on the north coast, where hundreds of his men promptly fell ill. Matters weren't improved when an exploring party brought back such large nuggets of gold that others who had been assigned to fishing and crop planting promptly threw down their tools and demanded the same opportunity for acquiring such wealth. Columbus sent twelve ships home with twenty-five captured "Indians," the gold nuggets, and a consignment of what he called Oriental spices.

During the next five months Columbus cruised throughout the region. South of Cuba—which he still believed was a promontory of China—he discovered Jamaica (an Arawak name, Xaymaca, "island of springs"); he named it Santiago for the landing he made there on Saint James's Day, but the native name has survived. Then he returned to Isabela, where matters had come to a sorry pass. Virtually all the Spaniards were roaming the interior and terrorizing the natives in their single-minded lust for gold; some men seized the supply ships that had only recently arrived, turned them around, and sailed for Spain with their treasure. For their part, the tribes, by now resentful of the greed and cruelty of these men from over the sea, tried to resist, but Caribbean spears proved sadly ineffective against Spanish gunpowder.

The result was disaster. Many of the natives were killed, others tortured or otherwise brutally dealt with, and hundreds were sent back to Spain as slaves, Columbus himself shipping off five hundred on his own account.

On March 10, 1496, the admiral set out for home in the *Niña*, accompanied by another caravel; three months later, on June 8, they anchored off Cádiz, sufficiently on the point of starvation that the cargo of slaves was now being eagerly assessed as a source of food. His reception from the royals was cool. It was obvious to them that the Indies Enterprise embraced a number of flaws, and it took Columbus two more troublesome years to get up a third voyage.

Finally he departed with three vessels on May 30, 1498, intending to search for his Eurasian continent south of the Lesser Antilles, the islands at the eastern reaches of the Caribbean. He sailed along 10 degrees North latitude and on July 31 sighted and named Trinidad, presumably from its three hills or peaks but perhaps also from the fact that it was Trinity Sunday. A few days later he went ashore on the Paria Peninsula in what is now Venezuela ("little Venice," from an Indian village built on piles driven into the water, discovered by Spaniards in 1499).

Columbus then began beating back through the Caribbean to Hispaniola, where on his arrival on August 31 he discovered not only that Isabela had been replaced by Santo Domingo as the capital but that affairs in the colony had deteriorated: rebellion was in the air, the Indians were dying from forced labor, and the Spanish royals were thoroughly disenchanted with the way Columbus was handling things. Ferdinand and Isabella were especially discontented with what they saw as an inadequate flow of gold into Spanish coffers from the "Indies."

To rectify matters they sent Francisco de Bobadilla as viceroy, who when he arrived in Santo Domingo promptly clapped the astonished admiral in irons and shipped him back to Cádiz, where he was permitted to languish in prison for six long weeks. Columbus was then invited to court, where he expected to be promptly reinstated as governor when the obvious misunderstandings had been cleared up.

Not a bit of it. He was immediately replaced as governor of the Indies by another man, Nicolás de Ovando, meanwhile being allowed to prepare a fourth voyage, the object of which was to find a passage from the Atlantic Ocean through to the Indian Ocean (clearly, no one even suspected that some other large ocean was lying in the way). Columbus left Cádiz with four caravels on May 11, 1502, and just three weeks later reached Santo Domingo, where he asked the new governor, Ovando, for permission to shelter in the harbor from a hurricane that was brewing. Ovando refused, somewhat churlishly, and by way of showing his contempt for the "admiral" he thereupon sent out thirty treasure ships, homeward bound.

The hurricane struck. Only one of Ovando's vessels reached Spain, while all but three of the rest were destroyed; one might imagine a brief smile of satisfaction creasing the admiral's weather-beaten face. Columbus then sailed west across the Caribbean until he struck the mainland at what is now Honduras (named by Spanish seafarers in 1524 from *hondura*, depth, the sea being very deep between Honduras, Yucatán, and Cuba). From here he coasted south and east and entered the Chiriquí Lagoon just north of the Golfo de los Mosquitos, thinking it might be a way through to the ocean that local Indians had told him was not far away.

For two desperate months the fleet beat back and forth along the coast of today's Panama, spending Christmas off what is now Colón (the northern entrance to the Panama Canal). He tried to establish a trading factory but was driven out by Indians, leaving behind a caravel that had collapsed with rot. Columbus then sailed east, lost another ship to worms, turned north at Cabo Tiburón ("Cape of Sharks"), and tried to beat toward Hispaniola.

But sea, wind, and his leaking ships were against him. With every man pumping and bailing for dear life, the two remaining caravels staggered north across the Caribbean, barely reaching Jamaica, with their decks almost awash. Columbus ran the two ships aground and he and his long-suffering men remained there for a whole year, living on the hospitality of the local natives. When even these amiable folk became heartily sick of their uninvited guests, Columbus stirred them into greater efforts by means of a fortuitous total eclipse of the moon: if they would give him food he would give them back the moon. He sent to Hispaniola for help, and Ovando obliged with a caravel—nine months later.

Finally Columbus reached Santo Domingo, chartered a ship, and returned to Spain on November 7, 1504. For the eighteen months of life that now remained to him he nursed a powerful resentment toward the Spanish monarchs for the ill usage he felt had been his lot at their hands. When he died he was intensely frustrated at not having found his way to the courts of Oriental rulers, and he sorrowed for his failure both as an administrator and as an apostle of Christianity among the heathen. Despite his utter failure to govern Spaniards, Columbus managed to deliver to the Spanish throne the key to the immeasurable riches of empire: the New World.

It would have been of little comfort to Columbus at the time, but history has come to regard him not only as the effective discoverer of a vast new continent but also as one of the great navigators in maritime history. Some fifty years after Columbus's death, the Spanish chronicler Francisco López de Gómera wrote that Columbus's first voyage was the "greatest event since the creation of the world." On the other hand, Burman sees the man's achievements in a rather different light: "Since the 1492 voyage did little more than confirm previous hypotheses . . . it would be better to consider it as marking the climax of the discovery of the external world."

Perhaps the truth lies somewhere between these two assessments. As Ralph Waldo Emerson said in *Representative Men*, "Every ship that comes to America got its chart from Columbus."

LORD ANSON

"The navy's here!"

ATTRIBUTED TO JOHNNY PARKER

Johnny Parker, British naval lieutenant, called out this greeting to the 299 British prisoners held below when he was boarding the German tanker *Altmark*. Made famous because of the dramatic nature of the rescue when the British destroyer *Cossack* intercepted the *Altmark* in Norwegian waters on February 16, 1940, and released the British prisoners who were on board, this remark is often quoted to symbolize the professionalism of Britain's navy. The basis of the efficiency and competency of this navy was established by Lord George Anson (1697–1762) who, with Sir John Hawkins (1532–1595), can lay claim to being one of the principal founders of the modern British navy.

Anson joined the navy as a young man, saw service in the Baltic, made a number of cruises in American and African waters, as well as in the West Indies, and was appointed post captain in 1740, when England found herself at war with France and Spain. He was given a squadron of six ships to cruise the Pacific, where he might cause difficulties for the Spanish and, it was hoped, capture one of the treasure ships that each year sailed from Acapulco, Mexico, across the Pacific to Manila in the Philippines.

The story of Anson's subsequent circumnavigation (1740–1744) is a harrowing account of storm and scurvy, the latter causing such debilitation in the squadron that Anson was obliged to destroy the *Gloucester* so as to use her crew on his own vessel, the *Centurion*, on which only thirty of his men were unaffected by this wretched but easily avoided disease. An indication of how serious a problem disease could prove to be on a long voyage is the fact that Anson lost only four men in action with the enemy but more than 1,300 to scurvy and other ailments (see Scurvy, chapter 7).

Despite these considerable setbacks Anson was able to capture a Spanish treasure ship near the Philippines; this was the *Nuestra Señora de Covadonga*, the loss of which must have occasioned much anguish among the Spanish authorities because the treasure on board proved to be worth more than £500,000—many millions of dollars in today's terms. Anson's share of the prize money—which was generously supplemented when he captured some thirteen French ships in the Atlantic in 1747—set him up as a very wealthy man.

By now an admiral, Anson was soon made a peer and first lord of the admiralty, in which position he was able to bring about some much-needed reforms in the dockyards, where waste, inefficiency, and corruption had long reigned. He also reorganized the marine regiments into a corps of marines (an administrative stroke of genius that has been emulated in many of the world's navies). Anson introduced the notion of a regular uniform for officers, updated the Articles of War, established the rating of naval vessels (see First Rate, chapter 7), and in many other ways so improved the professional standing of the British navy that it continues to enjoy a reputation today as one of the preeminently professional navies of the world.

CAPTAIN JAMES COOK

"He was . . . the greatest sailing ship seaman there ever was."
ALAN VILLIERS

The story of Captain James Cook (1728–1779) has been told many times, but, like all great and compelling narratives, Cook's is ageless. In his lifetime he was highly regarded as a seaman, commander, navigator, and explorer; and since his unfortunate death in the Sandwich Islands (present-day Hawaii) some two hundred years ago, his achievements have led to his being recognized as perhaps the greatest navigator and explorer that England has ever produced. And this, in an age of great men.

To anticipate, one must not forget the claims of divine providence: if a lump of coral had not wedged itself fast in the hole that the Great Barrier Reef had punched into the hull of the *Endeavour* on the night of June 11–12, 1770, not only would the ship itself and the men on her have very likely been lost to history, but so too the English-speaking colony of Australia, established only eighteen years later, might have instead been speaking French, if not indeed Dutch.

Cook is best remembered for the three voyages of exploration that dispelled many of the mysteries of the Pacific: 1768–71, 1772–75, and 1776–79.

He was born into a Yorkshire farming family and taught reading, writing, and arithmetic at an early age, but was otherwise self-educated. In 1746, at age eighteen, he was apprenticed to the Walker family's coal-carrying trade. He applied his natural aptitude for mathematics and his active and inquisitive mind to learn the skills of a seaman and navigator, and in 1752 he was made mate of a Walker ship. Three years later, seeking wider scope for his ambition, he entered the British navy as able seaman (later known as an AB, short for *able*, not as is commonly thought the initials of *able-bodied*).

The navy recognized in Cook the qualities they wanted. Within a short period he became a bo'sun (boatswain, the warrant officer in charge of the ship's gear and stores, but not the ship's boats), and by 1757 he was a master, responsible for navigation and pilotage. As master of the *Pembroke* he surveyed the Saint Lawrence River so accurately that he was appointed master on the flagship, enabling him to survey the coasts of Nova Scotia and Newfoundland.

After the Seven Years War Cook was given his own command, the *Grenville*, in which he spent five more years on survey work in Newfoundland waters. His work attracted the attention of the Royal Society, which was planning to send a party to Tahiti to make observations on the transit of the planet Venus across the face of the sun. Cook was chosen to be the commander of an expedition that would observe the transit and also search for Terra Australis Incognita, The Great South Land (see chapter 4) that geographers for centuries had believed existed in the far south of the globe. To this end he was to explore the coast of New Zealand (discovered by Abel Tasman in 1642 and named by him Nieuw Zeeland, from the province Zeeland in the Netherlands) to determine whether or not it was part of this supposed southern land mass.

By now a lieutenant, Cook persuaded the admiralty to fit out a Whitby collier, this being the type of vessel he thought most suitable for the work ahead. Renamed HMS *Endeavour*, and with the botanist Joseph Banks on board, she sailed from Plymouth on August 26, 1768. When the *Endeavour* dropped anchor at Tahiti, not one man had shown any signs of the dreaded scurvy, a mark of Cook's careful attention to the health of his men. The transit of Venus was duly observed in Tahiti on June 3, and the following month the *Endeavour* set sail for the high latitudes of the Southern Ocean.

Tahiti had been a halcyon time for Cook and his men; the Polynesians had proved to be extremely friendly (see, for example, HMS *Bounty* Mutiny, chapter 9) if at the same time being the most persistent and adept thieves that Cook had ever set eyes on, a characteristic of theirs that eventually helped precipitate Cook's death. He circumnavigated New Zealand, thereby proving that it did not in fact belong to the long-conjectured southern continent. Cook then took possession of New Zealand in the name of George III, disregarding the fact that the Polynesian Maoris were in visible and very vocal possession of the land they had been living in since the fourteenth century.

Cook decided to return to England by way of the east coast of Australia, known at the time as New Holland. He then turned north, making a running survey of the coast all the while; after anchoring in Botany Bay, where he encountered hostile Aborigines, he sailed ever northward until, as already mentioned, the *Endeavour* was holed on the Great Barrier Reef.

Eventually, after a most trying time that brought forth Cook's superb practical skills as seaman, the vessel was nursed to the mainland thirty miles away and carefully worked into the mouth of what is now the Endeavour River on the Queensland coast, where she was beached and repaired. From here Cook continued to Cape York, the northernmost tip of eastern Australia, and then followed in the footsteps, so to speak, of the Portuguese explorer Luis Vaez de Torres, who in 1606 had discovered the difficult passage between New Guinea and the Australian mainland (Torres Strait).

Finally, sailing home by way of the Cape of Good Hope, Cook anchored in English waters on July 13, 1771. Typically, Cook was modest about his accomplishments, giving most of the credit for the expedition's achievements to Banks, who was knighted as a result.

But the southern continent, if it did exist, had not been discovered, and the British government was determined that if it was, it should be claimed for the British crown before the French or the Spanish could. Thus a second expedition was planned and on July 13, 1772 (a year after his return home from the first, but this time without Banks), Cook in HMS *Resolution* and Tobias Furneaux in HMS *Adventure* left Plymouth in search of the Great South Land by way of Madeira and Cape Town.

Sailing south, the two vessels encountered heavy seas, pack ice, icebergs, and almost unendurable cold. On January 17, 1773, both ships crossed the Antarctic Circle and sailed to 67°15' South latitude, farther than any other vessel had yet ventured. Here they were confronted by the vast ice walls of Antarctica; here, too, the ships became separated during a gale, and it was mid-May before they were reunited in Queen Charlotte Sound in the South Island of New Zealand, an anchorage much beloved by Cook from his first voyage.

George III had asked that livestock be set ashore in territories newly discovered. Cook thereupon released some sheep, goats, and pigs onto the South Island. The sheep died from eating poisonous plants and the goats died from being eaten by the Maoris, but Farmer George's pigs survived and thrived, and their descendants are today commonly called Captain Cookers.

Cook then explored the eastern and southern reaches of the Pacific in search of the rapidly fading Terra Australis Incognita. Finding nothing but empty ocean, he retired to Tahiti for a rest in better surroundings (which to his men meant keeping company with the delightful women of that region, whose morals—or conspicuous lack of them—caused the stern Cook to purse his lips in dour Yorkshire fashion). While sailing back to New Zealand the ships again became separated; Cook took the *Resolution* down to 71°19' South latitude, then swung north to Easter Island, that lonely outpost in the southeast Pacific. (See The *Kon-Tiki* Expedition, chapter 3, for Thor Heyerdahl's theory of how the Polynesians populated these Pacific islands.)

The *Resolution* returned to Queen Charlotte Sound, but still finding no sign of the *Adventure*, Cook sailed east and reached Tierra del Fuego in time to celebrate Christmas 1773. Furneaux meanwhile had returned to England by sailing four hundred miles south of Cape Horn, which must have been a bitterly cold and wet voyage. Cook made a final sweep of the Southern Ocean and, convinced that any habitable Great South Land did not exist, and with his ship sound and the crew still in good health, he returned to the central Pacific to make accurate charts of a number of island groups.

After a month's recuperation at Tahiti, Cook sailed west toward Australia, then turned south, discovering and naming New Caledonia and Norfolk Island before making for Queen Charlotte Sound once again for a refit. In early November 1774 he set off for home, rounding the Horn, then heading for the Cape of Good Hope and into the Atlantic. The *Resolution* reached Portsmouth on July 29, 1775, almost a year after Furneaux in the *Adventure*.

In recognition of what he had achieved, Cook was made post captain (i.e., promoted to command a rated ship—see First Rate, chapter 7), made a fellow of the Royal Society, and given a captaincy at the Royal Hospital for Seamen at Greenwich. He then devoted his time to his hospital duties and to preparing an account of the second voyage, but he was restless: if the South Seas had proved not big enough for him, what can be said of a hospital in Greenwich?

At that time there was renewed interest in the notion of the Northwest Passage, a route that might link the North Atlantic with the North Pacific by way of a sea route up the East Coast of North America into Arctic waters, then south into the Pacific by way of the Bering Sea (see The Northwest Passage, chapter 4). Cook offered to help organize an expedition to search for this supposed northern passage, and he was then given command of it.

He left Plymouth in the *Resolution* on July 12, 1776. HMS *Discovery*, a Whitby collier under Captain Charles Clerke, who had sailed with Cook on his previous voyages, followed soon after. The dockyard had done a miserable job of refitting the *Resolution*; her caulking sprang loose when the hull worked in even a moderate sea, and the rigging was poor-quality stuff. Cook had his leaking ship repaired at the Cape of Good Hope, and when the *Discovery* arrived they set off east, touching at Tasmania (not realizing it was an island) before making to Queen Charlotte Sound in New Zealand.

From here Cook sailed to the Friendly Islands (now Tonga), then to Tahiti, where some livestock was put ashore, to the great astonishment of the islanders, who of course had never seen a horse in their lives. In the North Pacific, on January 18, 1778, Cook discovered an island group he called the Sandwich Islands, after John Montagu, fourth earl of Sandwich and first lord of the admiralty (the very same man whose habit of eating slices of beef between two slabs of bread while gambling led to the naming of the sandwich). These islands are now called Hawaii.

Better that Cook had never set eyes on them.

Early in March the two ships raised the Oregon coast of North America, then sailed north until they reached Nootka Sound on the west coast of present-day Vancouver Island; here Cook made repairs to the *Resolution*'s ever-failing rigging.

Farther north they encountered indigenous hunters (now properly called Inuit, "the people"), passed into the Aleutian Islands, and pushed north into the Bering Sea in search of a sea passage, but they were stopped by thick fog and pack ice and Cook, concerned about the deteriorating condition of his ship, made all sail back to Hawaii for repairs.

Here they were well received, Cook being proclaimed the reincarnation of the merry and somewhat earthy god Lono or Rono (perhaps not a true reflection of the sobersided Yorkshireman known to us; on the other hand, the American missionaries who forty years later descended on the Hawaiian Islands had nothing good to say about either Cook or the islanders, calling him "vain, rebellious, contemptible" and the island people "stupid, polluted").

Nevertheless, the burden of providing so much food and so many gifts to so exalted a god proved almost too much for the islanders, so much so that when the ships finally departed on February 4, 1779, both sides were heartily relieved; for Cook's part, the incessant thieving, especially of iron objects, had been a serious concern. Alas! two days later the foremast of the *Resolution* was split in a gale and Cook had to return to Hawaii to make repairs.

The scene was now set for trouble. The natives were sullen and resentful, while Cook and his people became seriously alarmed at the level of thieving that was again taking place. When a cutter from the *Discovery* was stolen, Cook followed his usual practice and went ashore to take a chief hostage for the ship's boat. Meanwhile a rumor had spread among the Hawaiians that the British had killed one of their chiefs, so by the time Cook got ashore most of the island men had their weapons at hand in order to resist the arrest of their chief.

There was a melee, and a battle broke out. Cook and his shore party were attacked, Cook was felled and repeatedly stabbed, although his marines managed to put up a desperate defense. Meanwhile, the officers and crew on board both ships anchored out in Kealakekua Bay watched the disaster in horror. It was over as quickly as it had begun.

The upshot was, of course, a terrible blow for both sides: the Hawaiians had lost a true friend in Cook, who had always treated the islanders with decency and dignity; and the world had lost perhaps the greatest sea commander and explorer of any era. (Long after, it was learned that the stolen cutter had been broken up by a minor chief for the sake of its metal fastenings—all in all, a paltry gain for the price of a great man's life.)

Clerke, although by now dying of consumption, was a sailor in the Cook tradition. He took command of the expedition and set out to finish exploring the Pacific, but he later died, and it was left to Lieutenant Gore to bring both ships back to England, where they eventually arrived toward the end of 1780. Before Gore left Petropavlovsk on the Pacific coast of Siberia—having again been driven back by the Arctic pack ice—he had arranged to have mail sent overland to England, containing copies of Cook's log and, of course, the news of his death. For six months relays of dog teams and horsemen carried the mail bags across Siberia and Russia, until finally a mail packet took the news across the channel to England.

When Gore and his expedition arrived six months after the mails, his ships were battered and bleached almost beyond recognition—their sails threadbare, the rigging worn and frayed to the point of uselessness, and the sea leaking in as quickly as it was pumped out. But incredibly, during the three voyages that Cook had commanded, not one man died of scurvy, although it must be added that his potions were not very effective against scurvy in themselves; his insistence on dry quarters and cleanliness of person and the use of fresh fruits and vegetables whenever possible were the important elements. As Villiers rightly claims, "Cook had performed what was, in the eighteenth century, a miracle."

The curious thing is, for all of the man's enormous abilities as a shipmaster, navigator, explorer, and leader of men, we know very little about Cook the person; it may be that only another seaman could understand him. Perhaps it is enough for the rest of us to look at a map of the Pacific Ocean and see in its vastness the dedicated explorer who translated it into some of the best sea charts ever produced by the hand of man. The English-speaking world can well be proud of James Cook, Sea Captain.

JOHN PAUL JONES
"I have not yet begun to fight!"

JOHN PAUL JONES

John Paul Jones (1747–1792) was born John Paul in Galloway in southwestern Scotland; he entered the British merchant marine in 1761, aged about thirteen, took up a life of slaving and trading in the West Indies, but was forced to leave in 1773 when he killed, in self-defense, a mutinous seaman in Tobago. He then settled in Virginia and changed his name to John Paul Jones. On the outbreak of hostilities between England and the American colonies in 1776 Jones joined the Continental Navy as a lieutenant; a year later he was appointed captain of the sloop *Ranger* (Congress established the United States Navy only in 1794).

After a cruise to France in the *Ranger* late in 1777, Jones met Benjamin Franklin in Paris; Franklin ordered Jones to cruise the British Isles and harry the enemy. Although he destroyed very little shipping, his shore raids set the cat among the pigeons as far as the English were concerned. Jones had better luck in action with HMS *Drake*, which he encountered off Belfast. He took the *Drake* as a prize and got her safely to Brest, where he exchanged his English prisoners for Americans who had earlier been captured by the English, having by now exasperated the British so much that he became known as the "Yankee Pirate."

The French then gave him command of the *Bonhomme Richard*, an old East Indiaman, accompanied by a small squadron, all flying the American ensign. The group sailed from Lorient on August 14, 1779, and Jones headed into the North Sea, intending to intimidate Edinburgh, but he ran into a convoy being escorted from the Baltic by HMS *Serapis*, Captain Richard Pearson, and HMS *Countess of Scarborough*. The engagement that followed—the Battle of Flamborough Head, September 23, 1779, watched by a huge crowd on the chalk cliffs overlooking the Yorkshire coast—proved to be one of the most bitter and hard-fought naval actions of the eighteenth century, and it established John Paul Jones as a hero in American folklore.

Pearson saw to it that his convoy escaped to the north, then turned to engage the lighter-armed *Bonhomme Richard* while the *Countess of Scarborough* closed with the French frigate *Pallas*. *Serapis* hammered the *Bonhomme Richard* with a raking broadside, then some of her men tried to board her, but the fires on the American vessel prevented this. The two warships, lashed together with grappling irons, fought literally muzzle to muzzle, with the *Bonhomme Richard* finally reduced to only two workable guns. It was now night, with a full moon, and the crowd ashore watched mesmerized as the two warships tore at each other's vitals.

In the heat of this terrible battle Pearson called out to Jones to ask if he had struck his colors, to which the American captain gave his now famous reply. At that moment, when all seemed lost, *Serapis* burst into flames and Pearson was forced to surrender. Nevertheless, the *Bonhomme Richard* was so badly damaged that she sank two days later, and Jones had to transfer across to the *Serapis*; the *Bonhomme Richard* had lost 150 killed and wounded, the *Serapis* 128.

When John Paul Jones entered Paris he was feted as a hero. Some months later, in 1780, he returned to America, where Congress gave him command of the *America*, a seventy-four-gun ship, but in 1782 Congress presented the vessel to France because a peacetime American navy seemed too expensive a proposition. Jones spent much of the rest of his life in France seeking employment as a naval officer; for a while he fought in the Russian Black Sea fleet but various intrigues against him ruined his prospects.

He died in Paris on July 18, 1792, shortly after being appointed by President George Washington as American consul in Algeria. France gave him a state funeral, and he was buried in the Protestant cemetery on rue Granges-aux-Belles. In 1905 his body was exhumed and taken to America by U.S. warships and reinterred in the chapel of the U.S. Naval Academy at Annapolis. He is remembered for his superb seamanship and indomitable courage and fighting abilities.

LORD NELSON

"Nelson, born in a fortunate hour for himself and for his country,
was always in his element and always on his element."

G. M. TREVELYAN, *A HISTORY OF ENGLAND*

Horatio Nelson (1758–1805), first viscount and British vice admiral, England's best-loved and certainly most famous seagoing commander, joined his uncle's ship HMS *Raisonnable* at the age of twelve. After a variety of experiences at sea, including service in the West Indies, the East Indies, and the Arctic, Nelson was made lieutenant at age nineteen. He fought in the American Revolution and was made post captain at the astonishingly young age of twenty-one.

In 1787 he married the widow Frances Nesbit and almost immediately found himself on half pay because of the greatly reduced needs of the peacetime navy. This he endured for five years, until the war with Napoleonic France began in 1793 and he went back to sea, this time in command of HMS *Agamemnon*. It was during this period that he was blinded in the right eye, a wound that later gave rise to the famous incident at the Battle of Copenhagen (see below).

His courage and initiative against the Spanish in the Battle of Cape Saint Vincent on February 14, 1797, earned him a knighthood and promotion to rear admiral of the Blue Squadron; he was already an honorary colonel of marines, having spent some time fighting the French on Corsica. Later that same year he attempted to take a Spanish treasure ship at Tenerife in the Canary Islands, but his forces were repelled and Nelson himself was so badly wounded in the right arm that it had to be amputated.

When he had recovered Nelson was sent to the Mediterranean under Jervis (Earl Saint Vincent) to search for a French fleet that was carrying armaments for an unknown destination. On August 1, 1798, he found Napoleon's fleet at anchor in Abukir Bay near the mouth of the Nile; the battle that followed—known as the Battle of the Nile—ended with the almost complete destruction of the French forces.

It was this engagement that led directly to Nelson's notorious affair with Lady Hamilton. At Naples, where he had taken part of his squadron after the battle at Abukir, Nelson was much feted as the savior of Italy; and it was while he was being looked after by Sir William Hamilton, the British minister, that Nelson formed a liaison with Hamilton's wife, Emma, which duly developed into a lifelong love affair that became the scandal of England, if not of all Europe, such was Nelson's fame. When he returned to England (still in the company of the Hamiltons, Sir William himself apparently neither seeing nor sensing anything amiss in his domestic arrangements), Nelson found his own marriage somewhat less than viable; nevertheless Fanny (Frances Nesbit) refused to make a public issue of what already was within the public domain, and her husband continued to support her financially until his death.

Nelson was immediately sent as second in command under Admiral Sir Hyde Parker (1739–1807) to the Baltic to confront a coalition of northern powers, the fighting arm of which was the Danish fleet. (This was the same Hyde Parker who in 1797 had been admiral commanding at the West Indies Station when HMS *Hermione* raised bloody mutiny against Parker's favorite, Captain Hugh Pigot; see HMS *Hermione* Mutiny, chapter 9.) While Nelson was busily attacking the Danish fleet, Parker signaled for him to break off the action. Because his ships were in a dangerous situation in shoal waters, however, Nelson—peering through his telescope with his blind eye at his commander's ship—refused even to see the signal and continued his attack. As a result of his actions in this engagement and because of his clever handling of the armistice terms with Denmark, Nelson was made commander-in-chief instead of Parker, who in turn was recalled to England.

Nelson became commander of the Mediterranean Fleet in 1803 as vice admiral of the Blue Squadron, with his flag on HMS *Victory*. Two years later, on October 21, 1805, the great battle for which Nelson is best remembered unfolded off Cape Trafalgar on the southwestern coast of Spain, where he met and defeated the Franco-Spanish fleet under the command of Napoleon's admiral, Comte de Villeneuve (Pierre Charles Jean Baptiste Silvestre, 1763–1806).

The engagement, during which Nelson himself was mortally wounded on the quarterdeck of the *Victory* by a French sharpshooter on *Redoubtable*, annihilated the French forces and gave England almost total control not only of the English Channel but also of the Mediterranean. This action was perhaps the last great fleet encounter in the classic days of sail (see The Age of Sail, above).

It was during this momentous battle that Nelson hoisted the most famous signal in British maritime history. Lieutenant John Pasco (1774–1853; later rear admiral) was Nelson's signals officer on the *Victory* at the time. As the British fleet sailed into action Nelson turned to Pasco and said, "Mr. Pasco, I wish to say to the fleet, *England confides that every man will do his duty*. You must be quick, for I have one more signal to make, which is for close action." Pasco asked if he could use "expects" instead of "confides" because "expects" already had its own signal flag, whereas "confides" would have had to be spelled out with eight extra hoists. "That will do; make it directly," replied Nelson, and thus this most famous of signals found its place in maritime legend.

Despite his intemperate and prolonged relationship with Emma Hamilton (a woman already known for her many other affairs), and even keeping in mind his share of failure and misfortune in battle, and his one uncharacteristic dishonorable treatment of a surrendered prisoner (he court-martialed and hanged at the yardarm the Neapolitan Commodore Francesco Caracciolo), Nelson ranks as perhaps the greatest and best loved of England's naval commanders.

As an enduring testament to Nelson's memory his flagship HMS *Victory*, a first-rate ship of the line, is kept at Portsmouth, restored to the condition in which she fought under his command. Here she lies, in Kemp's words, as "a permanent memorial to Nelson, Trafalgar, and to the British Navy as a whole" (see First Rate, chapter 7).

9

A MURMURING OF MEN

Some mutinies have become famous despite the fact that little or no blood was shed, as in the one on HMS *Bounty* in 1789, and in the mutinies at Spithead in 1797, the Nore shortly afterward, and the German High Seas Fleet in 1918 (see in this chapter).

If an entire ship's company was implicated in a mutiny it was the ringleaders who were hanged (the term *ringleader* derives from the custom, originating with French sailors, of submitting to their officers a petition of complaint in circular form—the ring—so that the name of the leader could not be singled out; the leader was, of course, known to the men, hence he became known as the ringleader).

Perhaps the most persistent single underlying cause of mutiny was the brutal treatment often meted out to seamen by uncaring zealots: captains and/or officers who believed that the only thing a sailor clearly understood was a rope's end across the back when given an order or an extravagant dose of the cat for some act of insubordination. In his *Two Years Before the Mast* (first published anonymously in 1840) Richard Henry Dana describes a flogging given by a tyrant of a ship's captain:

> *"Can't a man ask a question without being flogged?"*
>
> *"No," shouted the captain, "nobody shall open his mouth aboard this vessel but myself"; and began laying the blows upon his back, swinging half round between each blow, to give it full effect . . . "If you want to know what I flog you for, I'll tell you. It's because I like to do it!—because I like to do it!—it suits me! That's what I do it for!"*

THE *BATAVIA* WRECK AND MUTINY

> *"And the islands . . . gray and gnarled, home of*
> *gull and clicking crab, seal and screeching gull,*
> *gale-blasted, weather-whitened, wave-lashed, ageless."*
>
> HUGH EDWARDS, *ISLANDS OF ANGRY GHOSTS*

The islands Edwards refers to are the Houtman Abrolhos, a scattering of low-lying coral outcrops and reefs about 40 miles off Geraldton on the Western Australia coast and stretching northward parallel to the coastline for perhaps 60 miles.

In 1629 the Abrolhos Islands were the scene of a bloody mutiny and massacre that have few if any parallels in maritime history. The island group was given the name Abrolhos by the Dutch captain Frederik de Houtman in 1619; it means "keep your eyes open," these islands being every bit as dangerous for mariners as the Tuamotu Archipelago in the Pacific. The word *abrolhos* is Portuguese, not Dutch, and it refers to any low-lying collection of marine rocks, reefs, pinnacles, etc. (Note, for example, the Abrolhos Shoals off the coast of Brazil, so named by Portuguese navigators in the sixteenth century.)

The *Batavia* was the newest and one of the largest vessels in the Dutch East India Company, the famous VOC (Vereenigde Oostindische Compagnie), set up in 1602 to coordinate all Dutch trade in Southeast Asia. On October 27, 1628, she sailed with three other vessels from Texel in Holland (known at that time as the United Provinces) on her maiden voyage to the East Indies, under the command of Francisco Pelsaert, a high-ranking official in the VOC. The skipper was Ariaen Jacobsz, and the under-merchant was Jeronimus Cornelisz. She carried some three hundred people—soldiers, sailors, and families—and a rich cargo including ivory, a casket of jewels, and a dozen chests of coins.

Two men, Jacobsz and Cornelisz, were the catalyst for the bloody events that followed. At the Cape of Good Hope Pelsaert had to reprimand both men for their drunken and generally obstreperous behavior. After leaving the Cape the *Batavia* became separated from the other three vessels. Coupled with this, Pelsaert unfortunately spent most of his time below, thus giving Jacobsz and Cornelisz opportunity to sow dissent and dissatisfaction among the crew—never a difficult task on a sailing ship on a long voyage. The conspirators planned to take control of the ship before it reached its longitude for altering course to the north, turn it into a pirate ship, and thereafter seek their own fortune (in this regard see also Pirates, chapter 14).

However, such was not to be. For all of his skill as a navigator, Jacobsz failed to exercise the extreme caution needed on this Australian coast, where there is scarcely a break in the offshore rocks and reefs that infest its entire western section from Cape Leeuwin in the south to North West Cape in the north. During high tide on the night of June 4, 1629, the *Batavia* ran hard onto a reef lying off one of the Abrolhos islands. While the ship was being pounded to pieces, most of the people on board struggled through the surf and across the jagged rocks to seek refuge on two small islands; meanwhile, those who had been planning mutiny looted the ship's stores for weapons, alcohol, and whatever else might come in handy later.

Pelsaert commandeered the longboat and searched for water on the mainland, but the barren coast yielded nothing; then he took with him Jacobsz and most of the ship's officers and VOC officials and headed north for the port of Batavia (now Jakarta) with the intention of raising the alarm and having a rescue ship return to the area. On July 7, after sailing for twenty-nine days and covering some 1,500 miles, Pelsaert and his group reached the Javanese port, where Governor Coen immediately put Pelsaert in charge of the *Sardam*, with instructions to rescue the survivors and recover the treasure. Jacobsz was thrown into prison for his navigational failure.

The survivors, meanwhile, were already rapidly diminishing in number. Cornelisz had taken charge of the group on the Abrolhos, planning to kill all those who had no place in his future life of piracy and then overpower the rescue ship that Pelsaert was sure to bring back. With this in mind he persuaded Corporal Wiebbe Hayes to take his forty-six soldiers and search for water on the outlying islands, while first leaving their weapons behind with him. Hayes and his men agreed, and as soon as Cornelisz had taken them to the islands in the boats that had been built from the ship's timbers, the bloodshed began.

Within a few weeks some 125 passengers and crew had been summarily put to death by Cornelisz and his followers, the women raped before having their throats cut, while the more comely of them were kept by the mutiny leaders as concubines. Some of the men escaped on bits of timber and brought news of the massacre to Hayes, who then had his men make weapons from what wood they could find to add to the few muskets they had retained. Realizing that Cornelisz would have to deal with his soldiers sooner or later, Hayes built a square low-walled fortress from the rocks that littered the islands (it still stands on West Wallabi Island).

The mutineers did indeed attack but were beaten off twice by the more experienced soldiers, with Cornelisz being captured in the fray. The remaining mutineers mounted a third attack, but the sudden and dramatic arrival of the *Sardam* forestalled them. As they sat offshore in their boat and watched the rescue vessel drop anchor, they realized that they had only one last desperate chance of survival. Wiebbe Hayes, too, understood what was going on in their minds, and as the oars of the mutineers dug into the water he and four of his men manned the small boat they had stolen and both boats raced madly for the *Sardam*—the one to warn it, the other to attack it.

Hayes intercepted Pelsaert, who had taken a boat to the highest island in the group (now East Wallabi), to warn him of the mutiny. Pelsaert returned immediately to the *Sardam*, had her guns prepared and the crew armed, and forced the mutineers to surrender. They were secured on board by ropes and chains, most of the chests of coins and jewels were retrieved by divers, and then the mutineers were put to trial.

What followed was almost as horrific as the reign of terror that Cornelisz himself had instituted. According to Dutch law at the time, if there was a strong presumption of guilt Pelsaert was free to use torture to extract confessions. This took ten days.

Eight of the mutineers convicted of a number of brutal murders were executed by hanging on Seal Island. Both Cornelisz's hands were chopped off first, four others had only the right hand detached, and the remaining three were hanged with both hands intact. Others found guilty of various other crimes were keelhauled, flogged, or marooned.

This last was the fate of two of the mutineers, Wouter Loos and a boy named Jan Pellegrimsz (or Pelgrom de By), and they were never heard of again. It is possible that these two landed safely on the mainland coast to the east, because there are persistent stories of light-skinned Aborigines later along the Western Australia coast, which would make Loos and Pellegrimsz Australia's first settlers, some 159 years before Sydney Cove was established in 1788.

When Pelsaert returned to Batavia he was not well received, despite having recovered most of the company's treasure. Questions were asked concerning the legality of the trial and executions; doubts were raised about his own probity regarding VOC property. Within a year he was dead, broken in health and spirit by all that had happened. Jacobsz was tortured during his two years in prison, but he resisted making a confession; what eventually happened to him is not known.

For a long time the exact site of the wreck of the *Batavia* was unknown until in 1960 a skeleton was unearthed on Beacon Island in the Wallabi group. Within a few years other skeletons, skulls, bones, and various items of ship's gear and equipment were found by the highly successful *Batavia* Expedition led by Hugh Edwards.

HMS *BOUNTY* MUTINY

"The secrecy of this mutiny is beyond all conception . . .
The possibility of such a conspiracy was ever
the farthest from my thoughts . . . Christian in particular
I was on the most friendly terms with."

CAPTAIN WILLIAM BLIGH

The story of HMS *Bounty* and the mutiny that took place on her on April 28, 1789, while in the South Pacific is perhaps the best-known instance of a body of men rising up against a captain they perceived as a harsh and arbitrary disciplinarian. We must thank the novelists and Hollywood for much of this perception, incomplete though such a judgment almost certainly is. The captain, William Bligh, was a man of his times, and he and his actions must be judged by the standards of the eighteenth century, not the twentieth or twenty-first. Those searching for evidence of a hell ship will not find it in HMS *Bounty*; one would do much better to consider HMS *Hermione* (see below).

The *Bounty*, originally a merchant vessel, was bought into the British navy and, after suitable fitting out, dispatched to Tahiti in the Society Islands in the South Pacific where she was to take on board a cargo of breadfruit seedlings destined for the West Indies. It was hoped they would there become adapted to the climate and in time serve as a cheap source of food for the Negro slaves working on the sugar plantations (according to one Spanish seafarer, breadfruit sliced thin and "roasted on board ship . . . seemed very good. It tasted like baked chestnuts").

After six months in Tahiti collecting and stowing breadfruit seedlings, the *Bounty* sailed westward, with many of her crew no doubt wallowing in the depths of melancholy at having to leave so splendid a place—or, rather, at having to abandon the extraordinarily compliant women who lived there. Near Tonga in the Friendly Islands group, Fletcher Christian, smarting under what he perceived as the tyrannical and abusive discipline imposed by Bligh, led an uprising against the unhappy captain. Christian was joined by perhaps half of the crew of forty-five in forcing Bligh and eighteen of the men still loyal to him overboard into the ship's launch, and they were set adrift with only nine inches of freeboard.

It would appear that the particular incident that precipitated the mutiny had to do with coconuts, though there is little doubt that Bligh's notorious lack of tact and the ignoble suspicions he harbored concerning the men under his command provided ample fuel for the resentment that boiled over on that fateful day. Kennedy tells us that a journal belonging to James Morrison, the *Bounty*'s boatswain, was discovered in Australia in 1934; the following quotation from this journal makes an interesting contrast with Bligh's quotation above.

In the Afternoon of the 27th Mr. Bligh Came up, and taking a turn about the Quarter Deck when he missed some of the Cocoa Nuts . . . which he said they were stolen and Could not go without the knowledge of the Officers, who were all Calld and declared that they had not seen a Man touch them, to which Mr. Bligh replied "then you must have taken them yourselves," and ordered Mr. Elphinstone to go and fetch every Cocoa nut in the Ship aft . . . He then questioned every Officer in turn concerning the Number they had bought, & Coming to Mr. Christian asked Him, Mr. Christian answered "I do not know Sir, but I hope you don't think me so mean as to be Guilty of Stealing yours." Mr. Bligh replied "Yes you dam'd Hound I do—You must have stolen them from me or you could give a better account of them—God dam you, you Scoundrels, you are all thieves alike" [Morrison then describes the officers' outrage, and the subsequent seizure of the ship and the casting adrift of Bligh and his followers the next day] . . . "No, Captain Bligh [said Christian], if you had any Honor, things had no(t) come to this; and if you Had any regard for your Wife & family, you should Have thought on them before, and not behaved so much like a villain . . . I have been in Hell for this Fortnight passed and am determined to bear it no longer . . . I have been used like a Dog all the Voyage."

What followed then has become one of the classics of maritime history. For all his faults, real and supposed, Bligh was a first-rate navigator and, it would appear from the details available of the magnificent open-boat voyage that he was obliged to make, also an equally adept leader of men when it came to group survival. The fact of the matter is that under very trying conditions of incessant heat, storm, wet, thirst, and hunger, Bligh got himself and his eighteen followers safely to Timor, a distance of nearly four thousand miles, with his crew remaining all the while a disciplined unit. From Timor Bligh returned to England, then lost no time in alerting the British admiralty about what had happened. The British navy then dispatched HMS *Pandora* to find the mutineers and bring them back to England for trial.

Meanwhile, the mutineers made plans for their escape from admiralty attentions. They sailed the *Bounty* back to Tahiti, where most of the crew (including the men who had refused to join the uprising) elected to live ashore. Christian realized that the navy would try to hunt them down if Bligh or any of his men had survived, so he and eight of his followers, together with their Tahitian women, and accompanied by six Tahitian men and three more women (making twenty-seven in all) set off in search of a remote and unknown island. Eventually they settled in 1790 on Pitcairn Island, an uncharted island in the southeastern Pacific and, like Tahiti, a veritable paradise. Nevertheless, because of the vagaries of human nature, within a decade of sequestered life on this jewel of an island only one man and ten women, together with many children, were left alive; of the sixteen dead original settlers, fifteen had perished by violent means.

When the *Pandora*, Captain Edward Edwards, reached Tahiti in 1791, fourteen of the mutineers (some of whom later proved innocent) were captured and imprisoned in a small cell constructed on the quarterdeck, with each man being placed in irons as well; naval wit immediately christened this holding cell Pandora's Box.

Unhappily, while making her way back to England the ship was wrecked on the Great Barrier Reef during a dark and stormy night near the tip of Cape York in far northern Queensland. Some of the prisoners were freed to help man the pumps, one of which then failed, and it soon became clear that the ship was doomed. In the mad scramble to get clear of the foundering vessel, only a few prisoners were freed from the box; one of them was drowned as the ship went down and three others were killed by the gangway that fell on them. Many of the crew perished as well.

Captain Edwards, the surviving hands, and ten prisoners took to the ship's boats and, in a curious replay of Bligh's experience two years earlier, followed that man's route to Timor, reaching Koepang (or Coupang) on September 18, 1791. They were subsequently taken to Portsmouth, where, notwithstanding their very unpleasant experience in the *Pandora*, the prisoners were immediately court-martialed, three of their number being found guilty and hanged forthwith.

In 1808, after eighteen years of a lonely sojourn, the remaining survivors on Pitcairn Island were discovered by the American sealer *Topaz*, Captain Mayhew Folger. In about 1830 a British frigate visited the island and found there one Seaman John Adams (aka Alexander Smith), the only mutineer left alive. Curiously, the frigate's captain did not arrest Adams and take him back to England; perhaps at last the navy was beginning to absorb something of the new and enlightened philosophy of the age.

William Bligh's career did not suffer unduly from the contretemps on the *Bounty*; in 1801 he fought as a commander under Nelson at the battle of Copenhagen, and four years later, in 1805, was appointed governor of New South Wales. Here his testy nature and overly authoritarian approach to all matters professional and private earned him the hatred of those he had to work with. The outcome was yet another mutiny, in 1808, this one led by Major George Johnston, who kept Bligh imprisoned until 1810. Bligh returned to England the following year and was promoted to rear admiral; Johnston on the other hand was court-martialed and dismissed from the army.

HMS *HERMIONE* MUTINY

"The Evidence saw a great quantity of blood in the Cabin window
and at the afterhatch leading from the Gun Room.
He heard repeated groans and screeches from the officers."

"DEPOSITION OF JOHN MASON, FORMER CARPENTER'S MATE
IN HIS MAJESTY'S FRIGATE *HERMIONE*"

The world is thoroughly familiar with the story of Captain William Bligh and the mutiny in 1789 on HMS *Bounty*. Nevertheless, no blood was shed in this affair, no man was made to walk the plank in supposed piratical style (see Pirates, chapter 14, for comment on this alleged practice), and no hated officer was hoisted aloft to dangle from the yardarm at the end of a rope.

A far less widely known, but infinitely more bloody, mutiny is the one on HMS *Hermione* in 1797, the year of the famous mutiny at Spithead and the Nore and only eight years after the one on the *Bounty* (see Spithead and the Nore Mutiny, below). The *Hermione* affair is in fact the bloodiest uprising ever to take place in the British navy, her captain and nine of his officers being variously butchered with axes, wounded or killed by other means, and then thrown overboard. The mutineers shortly thereafter handed the ship over to the Spaniards on the north coast of South America (known then as the Spanish Main; see On the Spanish Main, chapter 7). During the following ten years the navy hunted down and hanged twenty-four of the sixty or so who had been active in the mutiny; the remaining conspirators disappeared into the murk of history.

The reason behind this extraordinary tale of wholesale slaughter lies not with winsome maidens beckoning coyly from some tropic isle, as we find with the men on the *Bounty* in the South Pacific, nor does it have anything to do with grievances about pay and conditions of service, as expressed by the entire Channel Fleet during the Spithead mutiny in the same year. What set the *Hermione* afire with revolt was the excessive tyranny and brutality of her captain, Hugh Pigot, age twenty-seven, a man who Pope states was "possibly the cruelest captain in the service," and "with two others [not named] . . . the worst in the Royal Navy's recorded history."

In an age when British laws ashore permitted the hanging of a person for stealing a handkerchief or a loaf of bread (a punishment in fact rarely carried out), the power wielded by a captain in the British navy in his endeavors to maintain discipline afloat is not surprising. As Pope points out, when Pigot took his first command of a frigate at age twenty-five he possessed "more crude, naked power over any one of his seamen than the King over his whole nation." This power was placed in his hands by the Articles of War, under which he could order a man to be flogged and, under certain conditions, condemned to death. The king could do neither of these things. Truly was it said that a naval captain was "master under God."

Pigot's cruel and tyrannical nature almost certainly sprang from the indulgent upbringing given him by his blustering, autocratic, and arrogant Uncle George in Ireland at a time when Englishmen in that unhappy isle behaved, in the main, with a thoroughly thoughtless contempt for the Irish laboring beneath the English yoke.

Consequently, when young Pigot entered the navy in 1782 at age twelve and sailed with his admiral father to the West Indies, the boy was given every respect due to his privileged position but none of the training that a midshipman's berth might have instilled into his character. Thus the younger Pigot quickly noted how authority was wielded, sometimes without restraint; and as he progressed through promotion he himself acquired these symptoms of power, without ever understanding its real function or learning how to use it judiciously.

In short, Hugh Pigot became a despot and a fanatical flogger. During a fourteen-month period in his first command, HMS *Success*, Pigot ordered *at least* 105 dozen lashes with the cat-o'-nine tails for offenses including drunkenness, contempt, neglect of duty, uncleanliness, disobedience, and theft. Two years later, on board HMS *Hermione*, he would flog a man for being last down from the yards, for stopping momentarily while going aloft, for failing to run on deck when given an order, and so on. When three sailors aloft fell to their death in their rush to avoid being last down from the yards, Pigot regarded their broken bodies with sneering disdain and ordered, "Throw the lubbers overboard!" It was probably this callous indifference that finally decided Pigot's fate.

All seamen welcomed discipline, but they invariably rebelled against tyranny. Good order and discipline are as necessary for the crew of a naval ship as sound masts and sails are for the ship itself; but as a loving parent does not discipline a child with rough oaths and a stinging hand at every turn, neither does a wise captain tyrannize his men with vile invective and an ever-ready rope's end with the cat to follow. Such a vessel under such a man is what seafarers call a hell ship, and under Pigot the *Hermione* soon became a seething den of bitter resentment.

It is surprising, however, that two years passed before matters came to a head. Shortly before midnight on Thursday, September 21, 1797, in the waters of the Caribbean Sea and a day after the three sailors had fallen to their deaths, the more resentful of the crew sat around a bucket of rum in the fo'c'sle, drinking and arguing about what should be done. Then they struck. A number of them overpowered the marine sentry outside the captain's cabin, rushed inside and attacked Pigot with swords and hatchets, and finally heaved him, drenched in blood, through one of the stern windows into the sea below. Most of the remaining ship's officers, including a young midshipman (a boy named Smith), were dealt with in a like manner. By the end of that night's work the captain and nine officers had been tossed overboard, dead or dying.

Then, thinking that the Spanish would welcome them as deserters willing to hand over a British man-o'-war, and having already set the ship's remaining officers adrift with provisions, the mutineers sailed the *Hermione* to La Guaira (or Guarira) on the Spanish Main, in what is now Venezuela. Here they were treated with indifference bordering on contempt (which promptly turned to horror when the authorities later learned what had really happened).

The mutineers soon lost confidence in the Spanish, believing that they might well be handed over to the British—in which case their fate would be a foregone conclusion—and by various means most of them got away from the West Indies. Some went to the American colonies, some to the Continent, some joined foreign vessels, and one or two stayed behind and made a life in this Spanish possession.

The Royal Navy, meanwhile, spent ten years tracking down the fugitives. Of the thirty-three mutineers who were subsequently caught or who gave themselves up, twenty-four were hanged and one was sent to a penal colony. But by various means more than a hundred of the *Hermione*'s crew were able to evade capture and subsequent trial by the authorities.

In 1799, two years after the mutiny, the *Hermione* herself (renamed by the Spanish *Santa Cecilia*) was retrieved by Sir Edward Hamilton in command of HMS *Surprise* in a famous cutting-out expedition in Porto Gabello harbor, about a hundred miles west of La Guaira. In the ensuing battle the cost to Hamilton's men was eleven injured, of whom four were severely wounded, but none killed; the Spanish, on the other hand, lost 119 dead and 231 prisoners, to which must be added fifteen seamen who had jumped or fallen overboard. The *Hermione/Santa Cecilia* was fittingly renamed *Retaliation*, then *Retribution*.

So ended a saga of tyranny, treachery, and derring-do as bloody as one might ever hope to find.

Spithead and the Nore Mutiny

"On the 14th April, 1797, Lord Bridport, the admiral,
unsuspicious of the mutiny, making a signal to prepare for sea,
the seamen of his own ship, instead of weighing anchor,
ran up the shrouds, and gave three cheers."

Belsham, "Great Britain"

Spithead is the name of the stretch of water that lies between the naval base of Portsmouth on the south coast of England and the Isle of Wight in the English Channel; it is an extensive anchorage that was much used by the British channel fleet in the eighteenth century. It is also the scene of the great mutiny of 1797, when the entire body of English seamen refused to take the fleet to sea during the war between England and France (1793–1801) until their demands had been met.

The grievances of the men concerned pay, bad food, and conditions of service. The conditions for the most part involved greater access to shore leave. It was not at all unknown for a seaman to be abroad in a man-o'-war for years in, say, the West Indies Station, to find that when he returned to England—usually in the hope of seeing his wife and family, who often had to shift for themselves in the way of food, etc., because of admiralty rules about paying-off—he was then subject to the Impressment Service, the notorious and much-feared press gang (see below).

By means of this wretched device for manning His Majesty's ships, our anxious sailor could well find himself nabbed the instant he set foot ashore and thence carried off to another warship at that very moment making ready to sail for foreign parts, where he might easily remain for several more years.

There was much substance to this particular grievance, as we see in the following letter from 1794:

> *Honored Sir:*
>
> *I take this liberty to acquaint you that my husband John Hunter the carpenter of your ship the* Queen *and hath been in her during the course of the voyage for which I have received four month's money of Mr. Blackburn and the fifth month was due yesterday. But Mr. Blackburn refused to pay me . . . I had a letter from Spithead from my husband dated the 6th and they sailed the 7th . . . I have five small children and nothing to support them on but what comes from my husband . . .*
>
> *Your humble servant Margaret Hunter*

In addition, the rate of pay for seamen needed adjusting. Since 1653 it had been set at twenty-four shillings a month for an able seaman; nearly 150 years later it was still the same. No seaman's dependents could survive on this rate of pay, given the tremendous social upheavals that coursed through England in this era.

As to the food the admiralty provided to the many thousands of seafarers who, despite all adversity from both friends at home and foes abroad, managed to extend and maintain British influence around the world, it was worse than abysmal (although it must be said that the admiralty did not stint its seamen; however putrid and rotten and maggot-ridden most of the victuals were, there was a lot of it).

Ship's biscuit (a bread known as hardtack, baked ashore by contractors, sometimes many years earlier) was part of the staple diet, along with the weevils that invariably infested it and the rat urine that permeated it (even the rats permitted by the British admiralty to lodge on board navy vessels had to be fed). Before eating hardtack, the seaman rapped it firmly on the mess table in order to dislodge the maggots that had long ago taken up residence therein.

The other staple diet was salt meat, commonly pork, fish, and "beef," with the strict proviso that no seaman ever believed at any time that he closed his jaws around *beef* as such—what was provided to him as salt beef by some canny contractor ashore was instead widely held to be horse meat. Indeed, the cask containing "salt beef" was known as the harness cask, and many a tale has been told in the fo'c'sle of a horseshoe here and a nail there being discovered lurking within the seaman's portion of dinner. Richard Henry Dana, in his *Two Years Before the Mast*, the classic account of life at sea, gives us the American view of the "beef" that was their fare afloat.

> *"Old horse! Old horse! What brought you here?"*
> *"From Sacarap to Portland pier*
> *I've carted stone this many a year:*
> *Till, killed by blows and sore abuse,*
> *They salted me down for sailors' use.*
> *The sailors they do me despise:*
> *They turn me over and damn my eyes:*
> *Cut off my meat, and pick my bones,*
> *And pitch the rest to Davy Jones."*

Naturally, scurvy was an ever-present danger on long voyages, and it is a vastly curious wonder that in the eighteenth century the authorities knew little about its prevention and cure, whereas when Saint Brendan set out on his long voyage in the sixth century he took with him the roots of blue sea holly for the very purpose of preventing the scourge of scurvy (as related earlier). Seamen suffered severely from this disease, despite the fact that it was easy to prevent and simple enough to cure. When Anson crossed the Pacific during his circumnavigation in the early 1740s, scurvy claimed the lives of a dozen men each day on the *Centurion*, while her companion vessel the *Gloucester* lost all but seventy-seven men and boys out of a crew of more than four hundred, all to scurvy.

The seamen at Spithead, then, had good cause to mutiny, and the admiralty was quick to realize this: the rate of pay for seamen was immediately increased, better provisioning was implemented, and greater access to shore leave was permitted.

However, within a short time another mutiny broke out within the fleet anchored in the Nore, a sandbank in the Thames estuary and also the name given to the naval port of Sheerness. As with the Spithead affair, the mutiny of the Nore was ostensibly intended to secure better pay and conditions of service for seamen, but because all these aims had already been achieved by the recent mutiny of the Channel Fleet, the admiralty refused to countenance the claims of the mutineers. The Nore ringleaders were isolated and the leader, Richard Parker of HMS *Sandwich*, and twenty-four of his followers were court-martialed and hanged at the yardarm forthwith.

Given that the Spithead incident had already dealt with the seamen's grievances, it is difficult to know what Parker and his accomplices thought they might achieve; perhaps they should have given more thought to the consequences so eloquently described a hundred years later by Oscar Wilde:

It is sweet to dance to violins
When love and life are fair;
To dance to flutes, to dance to lutes
Is delicate and rare;
But it is not sweet with nimble feet
To dance upon the air.

In 1917 the German High Seas Fleet mutinied because of a mixture of boredom, poor food, inept handling of the men, and propaganda; two of the mutineers were given very short shrift by means of execution on the spot. A year later mutiny broke out again in the fleet's big ships at Wilhelmshaven and Kiel, spelling doom for the fleet's capacity as a fighting force and leading directly to the defeat of Germany in World War I.

THE PRESS GANG

"They heard that the press-gangs were out."
FREDERICK MARRYAT, *PETER SIMPLE*

Ever since medieval times the British crown had claimed the right and the legal power to physically force able-bodied men into the defense of the realm by means of the press gang. By the time of Elizabeth I the needs of the navy had grown so great that recourse was made to passing the Vagrancy Act, which rendered all disreputable persons liable for impressment in the fleet. In time of war, towns and districts were required to provide a certain number of men for the service. This naturally led to local jails being quickly emptied by sheriffs and mayors who knew a good thing when they saw it—the opportunity not only to ease the financial burden of maintaining the inmates but also to rid the district of them altogether, along with other malcontents and agitators who so far had escaped being jailed.

This law remained unchanged until well into the eighteenth century, by which time the naval authorities were complaining so bitterly about the wretched quality of the men entering the fleet that the crown was obliged to make much-needed changes in its recruitment policy.

If these laws had been repealed earlier, England might have retained her American colonies, but the navy persisted in pressing what they called British subjects from the merchant ships belonging to the colonies, thereby causing such bitterness that the practice added to the weight of resentment that eventually led to the War of 1812 (it was not at all rare for a British warship to sometimes forcibly impress U.S. citizens, thus fueling American indignation).

However, England very nearly destroyed herself by her own means, without having to call on her American colonies to assist in the process. So poor was the quality of men that had been forced by the Vagrancy Act into the Royal Navy that inevitably mutiny festered in the lower decks; this eventually erupted in 1797 with the men's mutinous declaration at Spithead and the Nore (see above) that the fleet would not put to sea, thereby bringing England close to the brink of national disaster.

The press gang during the days of the wooden navy in Britain was for the most part made up of seamen or former seamen, who under the command of a naval lieutenant went ashore to scour the seaports (and often the towns farther inland) for men. Those who were thus "pressed" into naval service were paid for their services, but at a lower rate than enlisted men or volunteers. The system lasted until the mid-1800s, at which time conditions of service began to improve enough to attract volunteers in suitable numbers.

The word *press* in this context comes not from the French *presser* and the Latin *pressare*, to squeeze, as we might have expected, but instead is from the Old French *prêt*, a loan, *prêter*, to lend, and the Latin *praestar*, to warrant, authorize, or sanction, in this case, a sum of money given to a recruit. This was known as *prest money*, the amount being a shilling, and the man who accepted it was deemed thereby to have entered into a legal contract to serve the king (hence the origin of the military phrase "to take the king's shilling" as a way of describing the act of joining the army).

Confusion with the English word *press*—squeeze—arose because, as far back as the 1200s, the English kings had the power to compel certain seaports to provide ships and crews for their interminable wars with the French (the most stable collection of ships and men belonged to Dover, Hastings, Sandwich, Hythe, and Romney, known today as the Cinque Ports). The king could thus arrest or detain for his own use those ships and seamen. The term in use at the time was the Old French *empresser*, to commandeer or arrest; but it quickly became confused with *imprest* (sometimes *emprest*), which was money lent in advance, the "prest money." The man who accepted it was thenceforth a pressed man, from "prest man," someone to whom money had been lent or advanced. Etymologically, the two words—*prest* and *pressed*—are completely unrelated.

No matter what the landsman's occupation—whether a businessman, in a profession, or a mere laborer, married or single, father or no—he was knocked on the head if he resisted the attentions of the press gang and then carried unconscious aboard the receiving ship, there to remain until eventually the ship was paid off or the war came to an end. In addition, he had no leave and no pay until the end of the ship's commission, no matter how many years this might last.

It was not unknown for a bridegroom and half the male wedding guests to be carried off at the church door by the very efficient net of the Impress Service. Tattooed and bowlegged men were especially vulnerable, as these characteristics were deemed to be surefire indications of the seafaring man. Many a tailor, too, found himself, willy-nilly, suborned into the king's service instead of safely back in his own shop making clothes. The practice of the press gang was so widespread, not to mention feared and detested, that children in the eighteenth and early nineteenth centuries played their own games of press gangs.

This method of recruitment—for both army and navy—was as common in France and Russia as it was in England, the usual source of manpower being jails, taverns, and the ragtag groups of vagabonds to be found in every shire; one may easily imagine the fighting qualities of such dregs of society. As the eighteenth-century proverb had it, "One volunteer is worth two pressed men."

10

BIG SHIPS AND BATTLES

The story of empire is fundamentally the story of the use (and, frequently, the abuse) of sea power. All the great trading nations, such as the British, the Dutch, and the Portuguese—not to mention the Arabs, the Phoenicians, and the Romans of two thousand years ago—have relied, necessarily, on their being able to support two classes of shipping: first, the trading vessels that carried cheap goods to their respective colonial markets (the Dutch in the East Indies, for example) and then returned with the valuable products of these markets; and, second, the warships to protect this merchant shipping.

It was trade that provided the engine for colonial expansion, and it was trade that drove the rapid expansion of shipbuilding, the extraordinary development of weaponry toward the end of the 1800s, and the emergence of the ironclads in the twentieth century. Two types of vessel mark this period of intense development: the warship (for example, the *Sydney* and the *Ark Royal*, see below in this chapter); and the passenger liner (for example, the *Queen Mary*, see below); and while the liner has virtually disappeared as a result of the aviation industry (although one notes the emergence of the cruise ship), the man-o'-war is still with us, and is likely to remain so.

RMS *TITANIC*

"I felt I simply had to get away from the ship.
She [the Titanic*] was a beautiful sight . . .*
Smoke and sparks were rushing out of her funnel . . .
The ship was turning gradually on her nose . . .
The band was still playing. I guess all of them went down."
HAROLD BRIDE, RADIO OPERATOR

The story of the sinking of the RMS *Titanic* on the night of April 14, 1912, is well known, even to those born fifty years or more after she went down. ("RMS," for Royal Mail Steamship, was a mark of distinction for a shipping company that carried the mails abroad.)

The ship is legendary both for the size of the catastrophe and the overweening pride in the ship's capabilities that led her builder, and the owner, the White Star Line (properly, the Oceanic Steam Navigation Company Ltd.), to allow her to sail with lifeboats that could carry, if fully laden, only half of those on board. (There were no lifeboat drills during the five days of her fateful voyage, an act of negligence that led to substantial improvements in future shipping practices.)

The scale of the tragedy was enormous:

- the number of men, women, and children who perished (1,500 people, give or take, depending on which authority is consulted)
- the size and magnificent appointments of the vessel (at 46,328 tons and 882 feet long she was at the time the largest and most luxurious ship in the world, her name deriving from the Titans, the children of Uranus and Gaea, all of them mythical beings of prodigious size and strength)
- the individual acts of heroism and cowardice while she was sinking
- the fact that this was the maiden voyage of a vessel widely regarded as virtually unsinkable

All these factors worked together to generate a worldwide wave of shock and horror that was recaptured seventy-three years later when the remains of the *Titanic* were discovered in 1985. Gazing at the wreck on the ocean floor, one of those who discovered it had these thoughts: "It is a quiet and restful place—and a fitting place for the remains of this greatest of sea tragedies to rest."

While steaming from Southampton to New York at 22 knots in seas known to have floating ice, the *Titanic* sank shortly after midnight on April 15, 1912, after hitting an iceberg several hours earlier, about 95 miles south of the Grand Banks of Newfoundland. She had already received four warnings from other vessels of ice ahead, but for some reason the last of these—describing an ice field that lay right across her track—was never passed on to the captain, Edward J. Smith. Captain Smith, in the best traditions of the sea, is presumed to have gone down with his ship; at least he was never seen again, although reports have him variously swimming to a lifeboat and passing in a baby, then moving away when told there was no room for him; shouting at the milling mobs through his megaphone, "Be British!" whatever this might mean (but see HMS *Birkenhead*, chapter 11); or shooting himself.

It is morbidly interesting that despite the prolific expansion of sea travel in the late nineteenth century and especially in the early twentieth century, on ships operated by a number of famous companies sailing under the flags of, among others, Britain, America, France, and Germany (see RMS *Queen Mary*, below), the first International Convention for Safety of Life at Sea was not held until 1913, in London. One hopes that the survivors of the *Titanic* disaster were thereby reassured.

HMS *Ark Royal*

"In the meane season the Lord Admirall of England in his ship called the Arke-royall, all that night pursued the Spaniards."
EMANUEL VAN METERAN

The *Arke-royall* that served as the flagship for Lord Howard of Effingham in the historic routing of the Spanish Armada in 1588 (see below) was originally built in 1587 (fifty-five guns) by Sir Walter Raleigh and named *Ark Ralegh*. Her name was changed to *Ark Royal* when Elizabeth I bought Raleigh's ship; she was the first vessel of this name to serve in the British navy (she was rebuilt in 1608 and renamed *Anne Royal*, forty-four guns).

Three other Royal Navy ships of this name have all been aircraft carriers. The first of the series was completed in 1914, but in 1934 she was renamed *Pegasus* so that a new carrier to be launched in 1937 could take the original name (it was this second *Ark Royal* that the Germans insisted they had torpedoed and sunk during World War II, but other sources indicate that she went down while under tow). The third vessel of that name is still in service.

RMS *Queen Mary*

*"Walking up the street to my house, I felt I was the man.
I mean, I was one of the few who was building the Queen Mary.
You had a great sort of feeling that you were doing something."*
SHIPYARD WORKER, 1967

"On the *Queen Mary*, there was no covered deck space where you could sit and look at the sea . . . In 1963, only forty-two [passengers] took their own manservants or maidservants with them at the special rates traditionally offered by the company." These remarks reflect the experiences of an English journalist, John Rosselli, who with his wife and two children crossed the Atlantic on the *Queen Mary* and the *Queen Elizabeth*, one way on each, traveling tourist class.

The early 1960s were an interesting time for travelers because this was the dawning of the era of international jet travel. You could board a very large aircraft and cross the Atlantic in little more than six hours or so, whereas the *Queen Mary*, steaming at her service speed of about 30 knots, took four and a half days. But exciting as the jet age might be, its advent meant for many the death of a more noble era, when going abroad by ship was an intensely exciting and bewildering affair of bookings and boardings, tickets and streamers, watching the pier recede in a tumult of farewells and ships' sirens, and then learning to navigate one's way around a vast new world—and a moving one at that. While it lasted, it was reckoned to be one of life's great experiences.

The "Two Queens," as the Cunard Line's *Queen Elizabeth* and *Queen Mary* were affectionately known to people on both sides of the Atlantic, long enjoyed among travelers an unequaled reputation for speed and comfort. Others swore by the elegant French liners *Île de France* and the *Normandie* as the high points of luxury and service. It was an era never to be repeated, when the ports of Southampton, Le Havre, and New York were, from the turn of the century to the end of the 1960s, the destinations for the greatest liners the world has ever seen.

The *Queen Mary*, perhaps the greatest of these passenger ships, was launched on September 26, 1934, with a displacement of 81,237 tons (her later sister ship the *Queen Elizabeth* had a gross tonnage of 82,998) and set out on her maiden transatlantic voyage on June 1, 1936. For two years the *Queen Mary* alternated with the French Line's *Normandie* as holder of the Blue Riband, an unofficial but coveted trophy for the fastest crossing of the Atlantic. Then from 1938 until 1952 she was the undisputed ruler of the Atlantic waves, having to give way only when the SS *United States* steamed across the "pond" at a record speed of just over 36 knots.

When World War II broke out, the *Queen Mary* was converted to a troopship able to carry 8,000 men; she was based in Sydney until April 1943. Later she spent her time ferrying troops across the Atlantic, carrying up to 15,000 men on these shorter voyages. After the war she again took up her role as a passenger liner, but the economics of world travel had changed: it was now the time of the jet aircraft.

In 1967 Cunard decided that the "Two Queens" were losing far too much money, and the decision was made to scrap them, with the *Queen Mary* to go in September of that year and the *Queen Elizabeth* the year following. In September the

Queen Mary put out into the Atlantic from New York on her last scheduled voyage, while at the same time her sister ship *Queen Elizabeth*, then the largest ship on earth, dropped her moorings and left Britain to make the opposite crossing.

At 2:20 in the early hours of September 25, 1967, the two great ships met in mid-Atlantic for the last time, the lights on both ships blazing in the predawn gloom, their air horns sending out thudding blasts, as they saluted each other in farewell across the dark waters. On the bridge of each ship the captain raised his cap as the two famous liners foamed past each other. Only a few passengers on each ship had stayed up to watch, but it was a sight they would never forget, and one that would never be seen again.

Cunard then sold the *Queen Mary*, thirty-one years old and still one of the two largest ships in the world, to American interests. She was berthed at Long Beach, California, where she was converted into a tourist museum, hotel, and civic center and may still be seen.

HMS *DREADNOUGHT*

*"A fully equipped Duke costs as much to keep up
as two Dreadnoughts, and Dukes are just as
great a terror, and they last longer."*
DAVID LLOYD GEORGE, BUDGET SPEECH

In 1906 Britain launched HMS *Dreadnought*, a battleship of a more powerful type than ever built before (*battleship* derives from the old sailing navy term "line-of-battle ship," from the days when fighting sail went into battle in a fleet formation known as line astern, with the largest ships, the first rates, at the forefront and the smaller ships, the sixth rates, bringing up the rear (see First Rate, chapter 7).

Probably the first ironclad battleship to see service was the steam-powered timber-built *La Gloire*, launched by France in 1859. Armed with thirty-six 163 mm guns and capable of steaming at 13 knots, she immediately rendered obsolete the wooden navies that for hundreds of years had ruled the seas of the world. England replied very smartly with the all-iron HMS *Warrior*, fitted with heavier guns and capable of higher speeds. Clearly, the race was on.

In 1861 John Ericsson's ironclad USS *Monitor* introduced the revolving turret, in this case mounted with two guns, but her speed was low—about 4 knots—and she was said to be unseaworthy. When rifled barrels, high-explosive shells, heavy armor plate, and steam propulsion were introduced into naval warfare in the mid-nineteenth century, the three-deckers of the wooden navy suddenly became seriously outdated and outgunned.

Ironclads had been built by Britain and France before the end of the century, but it was German naval rearmament, combined with the dictates of imperialism and the rapid expansion of trade, that provided much of the impetus for a radical change in the design and construction of capital warships. (Capital ships are those regarded as the most important in a nation's fleet.) The later use of steel led to the introduction of the battleship, the dreadnought, and the super-dreadnought in the navies of the world.

The new technology of torpedoes, the airplane, the submarine, wireless telegraphy, steam turbines, and internal combustion and diesel engines added to the need for change. For some time naval architects and armament designers had experimented with guns of mixed calibers on capital ships, but the problems of giving accurate ranging to guns of different capabilities and then determining their errors from the "splash" produced, encouraged builders to try installing batteries of a single caliber. To everyone's astonishment, it became clear that the heaviest guns could land their shells at ranges of almost 10 nautical miles with surprising and uncomfortable accuracy.

Japan, Russia, and the United States laid down plans for the construction of all-big-guns battleships, but Britain was first to make such plans reality: HMS *Dreadnought*, built in only eight months and launched in 1906, thus immediately rendering outdated all other battleships in the world and setting new standards for supremacy at sea. She displaced some 17,900 tons, carried an armament of ten 12-inch guns, and with her Parsons turbines could steam at a maximum of 21 knots, making her in every respect a superior weapon of war.

Naturally, vessels like these cost a great deal of money, but despite much private and public unease at the expensive nature of these monsters, Britain immediately built six more while Germany brought forth four. By 1918 there were forty-eight dreadnoughts in the British navy and twenty-six in the German imperial fleet. Germany then diverted her resources to submarines, which became particularly effective instruments of war.

When the Washington treaty on the limitation of naval armament was signed in 1921, guns of 16-inch caliber had become the norm, armor plate could be a yard thick, and steaming speeds of 30 knots or more were possible. Curiously, the acquisition of such fearsome platforms that could rain untold Armageddon on the enemy hordes led the maritime nations to be ever more reluctant to commit these machines to frontal engagement. The Battle of Jutland (see below) was only a brief and indecisive engagement between the British and German dreadnought battleships, due in considerable part to the terrible effectiveness of the torpedo, one of man's more ingenious devices of destruction.

Nevertheless, World War II saw the belligerents taking to the field with battleships of dreadnought design and proportions; indeed, many of those that had served in the First World War were dusted off, modified, and thrown into the fray, where their heavy guns were found to be very effective for shore bombardment. On the other hand, the aerial bomb began to emerge as a serious threat to all naval vessels, although the Japanese, in a moment of desperation fired by nationalistic zeal and a misdirected concept of tactics, expanded the notion of aerial bombing by using kamikaze planes against Allied shipping—a terrifying but ultimately useless weapon of war.

It was soon discovered that battleships without air cover were highly vulnerable to attack by enemy aircraft, as witness the loss of the newly built HMS *Prince of Wales* and the older HMS *Repulse,* both of which were sunk by Japanese planes off Malaya in December 1941. The effectiveness of air power on shipping had been amply demonstrated by the Japanese at Pearl Harbor earlier that same month. The Japanese capital ships *Yamato* and *Musashi* (the biggest battleships ever built) displaced 63,720 tons, carried nine 18-inch guns with a range of 27 miles, and could steam at 27 knots.

The last engagement between battleships as such took place on October 25, 1944, during the Battle of Leyte Gulf, in the Philippines, when six U.S. battleships destroyed the Japanese *Yamashiro.* By 1980 only the U.S. Navy retained any of these capital ships, fitting them with missiles and other paraphernalia which, combined with their immense size, doubtless added something to their impressiveness.

The warship had entered a new era when Billy Mitchell, a brigadier general in the U.S. Army and a passionate advocate of air power, convinced the U.S. Navy in 1921 to let him demonstrate the potency of attack from the air. The battered German dreadnought *Ostfriesland,* a survivor of the Battle of Jutland, was anchored about 65 miles off the coast of Virginia and was then subjected to bombing by planes from the army and navy. Despite much damage she remained afloat, and a navy captain gloated, "they're not going to sink this ship."

But shortly after midday the *Ostfriesland* was hit repeatedly with 2,000-pound bombs, and a short time later she rolled onto her beam ends, paused, then slid below the surface, whereupon "Admirals and captains wept openly." One imagines that in weeping for the loss of a ship—any ship—these sailors were also lamenting the end of an era, when the mighty battleship could now be demolished by a machine held together with canvas, wire, and glue, and not much else.

The age of the aircraft carrier had arrived.

THE SPANISH ARMADA

"The miraculous victory achieved by the English Fleete,
under the discreet and happy conduct of the right honourable,
right prudent, and valiant lord, the L. Charles Howard,
L. high Admirall of England, &c. Upon the Spanish huge Armada
sent in the yeere 1588. for the invasion of England."

EMANUEL VAN METERAN

"It was the expedition which the Spanish King . . . set forth and undertooke against England and the Low Countreys." So opens an almost contemporary account of the huge fleet assembled by Philip II of Spain for the purpose of invading England "to the end that he might subdue the Realme of England, and reduce it unto his catholique Religion."

The word *armada* refers to any fleet of ships, airplanes, or other means of transport available in large numbers; it is from the Italian *armata*, "equipped with arms," a fighting force, and is also the source of our word *army*. Most commonly "armada" is associated with the Spanish Armada, a fleet of 130 vessels organized in 1588 for the invasion of England and the subjection of its citizens to Roman Catholicism. This fleet, ironically enough, was called by the Spaniards *la felicissima armada*, "the most fortunate fleet," and *la invincible armada*, "the invincible fleet."

Under the command of the Duke of Medina, the fleet left Lisbon on May 28, 1588, bravely bound for England, but it made such poor progress that twenty days later it had sailed no farther than Corunna (La Coruna) on the northwest coast of Spain, a distance of somewhat less than 350 miles. Here the fleet repaired and reprovisioned itself and a month later took to the field again, as it were, this time determined to overcome all obstacles and force its way through the English Channel so that it might embark the army of the Prince (or Duke) of Parma, who was in the Low Countries, and with this considerable combined force (it would total some 30,000 men) invade England and introduce the English to the benefits of the Spanish religion.

Alas! the curmudgeonly English had other ideas. The Spanish fleet was first sighted by the English on July 19 off the southwest coast, thereby (so we are told) disturbing Sir Francis Drake's game of bowls. During that night the Plymouth squadron of the English fleet, under Lord Charles Howard (Howard of Effingham) slipped out into the Channel. Meanwhile, at Dover another squadron under Lord Henry Seymour kept watch for the army of the Prince of Parma. For six days the tall Spanish galleons worked their way up the Channel, all the while enmeshed in a running fight with the lower and more maneuverable English vessels. Some Spanish ships were lost: two were sunk directly in battle, one blew up, another lost her bowsprit and foremast in a collision, while yet a fifth drifted onto the coast of France. All was not auguring well for *la felicissima armada.*

At last the Spaniards were able to fetch Calais, the appointed place for embarking the Prince of Parma and his men. There they anchored, but unhappily the prince was not there to meet them. Howard's squadron—now joined by Seymour's from Dover—dropped anchor half a mile to windward of the Spanish fleet and set about harrying the Spanish. The following night Howard sent eight fireships in among the tightly packed galleons, a move the Spaniards did not greatly care for, so they cut their cables and in much haste, not to say confusion, made urgent sail downwind toward the French town of Gravelines, about 20 miles east of Calais.

Here a major action developed in which the Spaniards did not do well at all. Three of their best galleons were lost to battle, and alarmingly the rest of the fleet was being driven by the English and the most unhelpful southwest wind toward the shoals off the Dutch coast. Suddenly the wind backed, allowing the Spanish to claw their way off the shallows and out into the Channel.

But what to do? Medina's fleet was now short of provisions and very low on ammunition, the English were hovering around him in force, invasion was now impossible without the Prince of Parma's army, and the fleet could not hope to fight its way back down the Channel. Medina therefore had no recourse but to make his way home to Spain as best he could. And "as best he could" meant that only sailing north around Scotland and then down the west coast of Ireland would offer any hope of survival.

So they set off, pursued as far as the latitude of the Firth of Forth by Howard, who then left the Spanish to the less than tender mercies of the increasingly bad weather, the always terrible reefs and rocks that girded Scotland and Ireland, and—for those Spaniards not yet gathered unto the bosom of God by these wretched pitfalls along the way—there were the rough-and-ready natives of those distant regions who could be relied upon to deal firmly with destitute strangers cast up all at once on their shores. Many Spanish vessels were wrecked on these barbarous coasts, their contents pillaged, and their crews slaughtered as they struggled ashore.

Some of these ships survived as if by a miracle. The *Don Juan*, Admiral Juan Martínez de Recalde, negotiated Blasket Sound off the tip of County Kerry in southwest Ireland in a magnificent display of seamanship, the Sound being a terrible millrace during a storm, with the navigable channel less than a thousand yards wide and fiercely a-boil when the 3-knot tide was running through it. Furthermore, the *Don Juan* had been holed at the waterline during the battle in the English Channel more than a month earlier.

To many a Spanish sailor it must have seemed a profoundly less than happy end to a more than splendid cause. Of the great fleet of 130 ships that had set out from Lisbon in so grand a manner, only 67 ships returned to tell the sorry tale, their crews broken and starving, their vessels battered almost beyond recognition by battle, storm, and tempest, and with more than half of their comrades dead by various means. Meteran states at the conclusion of his account of this epochal event:

> *Thus the magnificent, huge, and mighty fleet of the Spaniards (which themselves termed in all places invincible) such as sayled not upon the Ocean sea many hundreth yeeres before, in the yeere 1588 vanished into smoake; to the great confusion and discouragement of the authours thereof.*

THE BATTLE OF COPENHAGEN

"Time, off o' Cop'nhaïgn, Nels'n comed an' crep his waïy in—...
we worn't n' more 'n skittleses, th' waïy they bowled us over."
STEEN STEENSEN BLICHER, "TIME, OFF O' COP'NHAÏGN"

The island of Zealand (Sjælland) almost completely straddles the entrance to the Baltic Sea from the North Sea; on this island is the Danish port of Copenhagen; between it and Sweden is the Øresund (The Sound). Copenhagen is thus sited in an important strategic position. In Danish the city's name is København, literally "merchant's harbor," from the fact that the locality, ever since it was first occupied some six thousand years ago, has been a trading center for the entire Baltic region.

In 1800 the northern powers of Russia, Prussia (at that time a state in northern Germany), Denmark, and Sweden—all with earnest French backing—formed an armed coalition of mutual defense in answer to British insistence that its navy had the right to search foreign vessels at sea for contraband, for British seamen (those held prisoner as well as those who had deserted the navy), and for whatever else it chose. The British response to this Scandinavian impertinence was, naturally, to send a large fleet of warships—some fifty-three in all, including eighteen line-of-battle ships—to the Baltic early in 1801 in order to teach the locals a salutary lesson in the God-given rights of imperial powers.

In any case, Britain had important trade interests in the Baltic. Because of her difficulties with France during the French Revolutionary Wars and the Napoleonic Wars from about 1793 to 1815, Britain needed to ensure the flow of naval supplies from that northern region (mast timber particularly, tar, and other necessary goods). The former owners of those goods were not to be permitted to interfere with Britain's urgent need of them.

Admiral Sir Hyde Parker was the commander-in-chief (the same who, three years earlier, had been admiral commanding in the West Indies Station when HMS *Hermione* raised bloody mutiny against Parker's favorite, the altogether unpalatable Captain Hugh Pigot; see HMS *Hermione* Mutiny, chapter 9). Second in command was Horatio Nelson (see Lord Nelson, chapter 8). Parker's brief was to persuade Denmark to withdraw from the league within twenty-four hours; should Denmark refuse, he was to ensure that her forces were, one way or another, prevented from being brought into play. Denmark declined the offer.

Parker then sent his fleet against the Danish fleet at Copenhagen, with Nelson in command. For their part the Danes put up such a stiff and determined resistance that Parker, fearful of inordinate British losses, signaled Nelson to break off and retreat. Nelson famously feigned ignorance of his chief's signal, asserting, as he put his telescope to his blind eye, that he had a right to be blind sometimes, whereupon he pressed the attack and finally overcame the enemy's defenses by bombarding Copenhagen.

Nelson then offered an armistice to the Danish authorities. The practical Danes accepted Nelson's overture, not least because of their reluctance to see the rest of their cities blown up and their entire naval force sent to the bottom of the sea. There was an additional factor at work: an alliance with Russia was not really in accord with Danish national temperament. Besides, Denmark had just received news that Tsar Paul, one of the architects of the alliance against Britain, had—happily or unhappily, as the case may be—recently been assassinated. With the new tsar, Alexander I, unwilling to continue a policy of hostility toward Britain, an unaccustomed peace was the natural outcome of this northern adventure. Parker was recalled by the admiralty and Nelson replaced him as commander-in-chief, much to everyone's satisfaction.

Six years later, in 1807, the Danes, unaccountably forgetful of the Nelson touch, allowed themselves to be suborned once more by the pesky French. Yet again sensing a threat to her Baltic trade, Britain mounted another expedition to the north, this time with soldiers under Lord Cathcart embarked on the fleet commanded by Lord Gambier. Once more Copenhagen was bombarded, and so serious were the resulting fires and damage that the Danes capitulated. The usual armistice was arranged, this time with the proviso that most of the Danish fleet had to suffer relocation to British ports, an arrangement that no doubt suited Britain's needs admirably.

Alas! still the Danes persisted in allying themselves to French interests, this time by building privateers (see Pirates, chapter 14, for the origin of this term) and gunboats with which the French harassed British sea trade until the end of the Napoleonic Wars in 1815. At this time Sweden found herself on the winning side and as a result she gained control over Norway, which had been united with Denmark since the Middle Ages—a heavy price indeed for Denmark to pay for her wandering allegiance.

THE BATTLE OF JUTLAND

"On the afternoon of Wednesday May 31 [1916],
a naval engagement took place off the coast of Jutland."
BRITISH ADMIRALTY COMMUNIQUÉ

The Battle of Jutland, called by Germany at that time the Battle of the Skagerrak, fought on May 31, 1916, between the British Grand Fleet (Admiral Sir John Jellicoe) and the German High Seas Fleet (Vice Admiral Reinhard Scheer), was the largest naval engagement of World War I. Each side also had an advance force of battle cruisers, cruisers, and destroyers, the English force being under the command of Vice Admiral Sir David Beatty and the German under the command of Vice Admiral Franz von Hipper.

The area of battle lay about 75 miles west of Jutland, the continental peninsula of Denmark reaching north into the Skagerrak, which is the eastern arm of the North Sea between Denmark and Norway. This was the only occasion during the war when the main fleets of both sides entered hostilities with each other. It was the last fleet action worldwide in which air power played little part. In all, some 99 German warships confronted 149 British warships, the final outcome being that Britain was left in undisputed control of the high seas for the next twenty years.

For the first two years of the war, Britain had blockaded the German High Seas Fleet base in Wilhelmshaven to such effect that the constant pressure encouraged the German naval command to attempt to entice part of the British Grand Fleet into a trap where they could destroy enough of it to relieve the blockade.

On May 30 Hipper's advance squadron of five German battle cruisers, cruisers, and destroyers slipped their moorings and went to sea, with the High Seas Fleet following 60 miles astern; but the British, already informed by intelligence of German activity, had two hours earlier committed Beatty's squadron of six battle cruisers, some cruisers, and a number of destroyers to the North Sea. Beatty did not know that the main German fleet was at sea, and when he sighted Hipper's advance force the following afternoon, May 31, Hipper and Scheer were equally unaware that the British were in the vicinity.

Hipper then attempted to lure Beatty into the hands of the German main force. Beatty lost two battle cruisers in the engagement with Hipper's squadron, but when his scouting cruisers then spotted the High Seas Fleet, Beatty immediately swung north, drawing the Germans after him—straight into the waiting arms of Jellicoe and his twenty-eight battleships. Beatty thereupon hammered Hipper's force, severely damaging three of his four battle cruisers. Just after six in the evening, Jellicoe formed line astern and steamed across the head of the approaching High Seas Fleet (the classic naval action known as "crossing the T") and poured a deadly rain of 12-, 13.5-, 14-, and 15-inch shells into Scheer's fleet of twenty-two battleships. In the gathering gloom Scheer turned away to the west, thus permitting Jellicoe to insert his force between the Germans and their ports.

Scheer returned to the battle, but with the fading light behind him he was at a disadvantage because Jellicoe's guns could profit from the silhouettes the German fleet offered. Again Scheer had to disengage; but alas! Jellicoe, confident that he could find, engage, and annihilate the enemy the next morning, shaped a course that, unknown to him, allowed Scheer to escape into the night.

Poor night action skills on the part of the British contingent, inadequate reporting to Jellicoe from those of his ships that did manage to close with German elements, and, perhaps most damningly of all, inexplicable failure on the part of the British admiralty to pass on to Jellicoe their radio intercepts that revealed the precise course Scheer had taken—all these contrived to allow Scheer's forces to traverse the cleared channel in the mined sea off Heligoland and reach port more or less safely. The Germans now believed that they had outwitted and outmatched the British forces.

For his part Jellicoe was steaming homeward, headlong into controversy that raged for years: why hadn't he taken the opportunity to pursue and completely destroy the enemy after "crossing its T," instead of being content to steam southeast on a sort of watch-keeping mission, only to find that come the morning he had the North Sea to himself, the Germans having already packed up and gone home?

The German press reported overwhelming victory, the jubilant kaiser visited his ships, Scheer was promoted to full admiral, Hipper to admiral—all of which news the British admiralty received most glumly, having had no battle report from Jellicoe himself, who was otherwise immersed in the details of getting his ships home safely. By the time Beatty's battle cruiser anchored at the naval base at Rosyth, in Scotland, rumors of disaster had already swept the country, and Beatty's men were greeted with—and much astonished by—a hostile reception from the locals.

When finally Jellicoe submitted his report it listed, as per admiralty instructions, losses suffered by the British but not those of the Germans; and while he did not report defeat, neither did he claim victory. As far as the admiralty was concerned, Jellicoe's report was substantially the same as the earlier German communiqué that had trumpeted complete victory. The admiralty then released a statement that reported, with considerable blandness, the fact that there had been a "naval engagement" off Jutland, together with a list of British losses and the advice that German losses had been "serious." There was word of neither triumph nor debacle.

Three hours after he had brought his remaining dreadnoughts to anchor in Scapa Flow, north of Scotland, Jellicoe advised the admiralty that his ships would be ready to sail into battle again if given four hours' notice—but still he offered no account of enemy losses. Confusion reigned supreme throughout the kingdom. The press sought a scapegoat, and given Beatty's devil-may-care reputation and the fact that of all the groups at Jutland his had suffered the greatest losses in both ships and men, the mantle of scorn soon settled on Jellicoe. But this was an unfair assessment, although sadly there were too few people in authority able to recognize this.

British losses were in fact greater than German: 6,097 English killed compared with 2,551 German; 510 English wounded to 507 German wounded; 14 English ships lost at 111,000 tons compared with 11 German ships at 62,000 tons. Nevertheless, as Jellicoe bravely and rightly said, "A victory is judged not merely by material losses and damage, but by its results."

Only three times more did the German fleet take to the high seas, and on each occasion these were brief excursions that amounted to nothing useful. Toward the end of 1918 disaffection had taken such a hold within the crews of the High Seas Fleet in Wilhelmshaven that mutiny broke out, and the German cause finally collapsed.

Jellicoe's actions at Jutland were subsequently vindicated when, shortly after the mutiny, Beatty received the surrender of the greater part of the High Seas Fleet.

Perhaps the true meaning of the Battle of Jutland was never better expressed than by the following report in a New York newspaper: "The German fleet has assaulted its jailer, but it is still in jail."

THE SINKING OF HMAS *SYDNEY*

"Joe and I were sitting on the verandah . . .
about dinnertime when we heard strange loud noises . . .
away over the coast and across Dirk Hartog Island . . .
a lot of heavy boom-booming . . . with flashes and flares
plainly visible . . . suddenly there was a huge explosion
and burst of heavy black smoke . . . it was
quite some time before we heard about the Sydney."

IVY MALLARD

The Australian light cruiser HMAS *Sydney* was sunk with all hands on the evening of November 19, 1941, not far off the central west Australian coast, as a result of a close-range gun battle with the German raider *Kormoran*, which was disguised as the Dutch merchantman *Straat Malacca*.

Both ships went down in the engagement; all the *Sydney*'s 645 officers and men perished (until this engagement *Sydney* had never lost a man in action, despite having been attacked some sixty times), while 317 of the *Kormoran*'s crew of 397 survived to give the only firsthand account available of the battle. It would seem from Ivy Mallard's remarks (above) that she is one of the few Australians to have heard or seen anything of this naval battle.

Sixteen months earlier the *Sydney* had covered herself with glory in the Mediterranean when she sank the Italian cruiser *Bartolomeo Colleoni* off Crete on July 18, 1940. Her loss to the *Kormoran* was therefore a profound blow to the Australian navy (as it was also to the Australian public at the time: her destruction accounted for more than 35 percent of all Australian navy seamen lost during the whole of the war), and in the sixty years since she was sunk a bitter controversy has developed concerning how and why such an efficient ship and crew could have been trapped by a raider in that fashion.

Theories accounting for her loss have included an incompetent command on board the *Sydney* and a Japanese submarine lurking in the area before Pearl Harbor and Japan's declaration of war against the Allies shortly afterward. Government censorship at the time created the widely held suspicion that there was a cover-up involved, to the effect that Britain had broken the Japanese naval codes, knew that the attack on Pearl Harbor was imminent, and therefore counseled silence on Australia's part so the Japanese raid could take place and therefore draw America into the war as an ally of Britain.

To this end a parliamentary inquiry was begun in Canberra early in 1998, aimed at establishing once and for all the circumstances surrounding the sinking of the *Sydney* and, if at all possible, determining the resting places of the wrecks of both ships.

The three hundred or more survivors from the *Kormoran* came ashore north of Carnarvon in two steel lifeboats, each about 28 feet long; clearly, it would have been a very cramped journey (Lieutenant Gösseln of the *Kormoran*, some of whose report appears below, also mentions rubber rafts). They landed not many miles apart on the coast and were soon found by stockmen and then taken into custody by Australian army authorities.

In due course rumors arose concerning a supposed movie-camera film taken by the Germans of the action between the two ships, later buried secretly in or near the coastal cave at Red Bluff, along with the *Kormoran*'s logbook. Even if this had been done, the storms of winter and the cyclones of summer since 1941 would have demolished many times over any film and written record buried in the wildly shifting margins of that turbulent coast.

Following is a portion of the eyewitness account of Lieutenant Joachim von Gösseln, who was on the bridge of the *Kormoran* during her engagement with the *Sydney*:

> *It is November 19, 1941. The German auxiliary cruiser* Kormoran *is following a course some 150 miles south-west of Carnarvon, Western Australia . . . the mine crew is busy during its watch, going over the preparations for an attempt on the following night to mine the harbor of Fremantle [some 400 miles further south] . . . suddenly the bridge messenger bursts in and announces to the skipper: "Ship sighted to starboard!" . . . From the speed with which the enemy was changing position as well as by instinct, Captain Detmers knew that this time he was not dealing with a merchant steamer . . . We changed course to turn away . . . The enemy, which has been recognized as a light cruiser, comes within range of our masked guns. We hoist the Dutch flag and maintain our course . . . The* Sydney *[asks] "What ship?" . . . we, as slowly and ceremoniously as possible, hoist the answer: "Straat Malakka". . . . The* Sydney *is 1000 to 1500 yards away . . . "Give me your secret signal" calls the signal man from the bridge of the* Sydney. *Captain Detmers quickly weighs the problem. "Well, Gösseln, there is nothing left to do," he says to me. Now in a matter of seconds the drama unfolds. The cue: "Down gun masks." The German naval ensign is sent aloft . . . the Dutch flag is hauled down . . . from the hatches rise two guns which are swung out . . . Simultaneously two ack-ack guns rise up on their hydraulic hoists. Still there is no shot from the* Sydney. *They do not seem to have grasped the spectacle of the transformed merchant steamer . . . we break out a 37 mm gun. On the bridge opposite we can see the shots hitting among the white uniforms . . . A direct hit! A gun aboard the* Sydney *is struck. Two torpedoes*

*leap from our tubes . . . Salvos two and three follow . . . .Opposite us
a turret gun has gone into action. The first shell whistles overhead and
splashes in the water to our leeward. They have completely forgotten to
allow for the short range . . . The* Kormoran *shudders as a shell hits
her . . . An oil bunker is hit . . . A few seconds later there follows an
explosion and flames shoot up from the engine-room skylight. Our
shells continue to explode on the* Sydney *without ceasing. Now there
is a mighty explosion as a torpedo hits* Sydney *just forward of her
bridge. The* Sydney *is sinking with her bow in the water, and it looks
as though she is going to the bottom . . . now her bow rises from the
sea, and she shakes off the mass of water . . . the* Sydney *changes course
and bears down on us, striving to ram us with her remaining strength.
We can only keep firing, for our engines are now out of commission . . .
Suddenly, there is a loud shout on deck . . . torpedo tracks are sighted
coming towards us . . . The* Sydney *falls away on our port side, but
our shells continue to explode. Slowly, the distance between the ships
widens, and the Captain orders: "Cease fire." Aboard the* Kormoran
*the fire spreads. The explosion in the engine-room has taken heavy toll
of the personnel . . . The burning ship has no way on. The fire-fighting
equipment is destroyed . . . How long will it take for the fire to reach
the munitions and the 300 mines we are carrying? With a heavy heart
Captain Detmers gives the order: "Abandon ship!" [A] boat is loaded
up to the last place and shoves off from the side. The wounded are
gathered in our largest rubber boat, and some water and biscuit passed
in. A second rubber boat is similarly filled . . . I remove my shoes, then
take off my jacket, folding it carefully, lay my cap in the middle of the
pile, and blow up my swimming jacket . . . I decide to swim in the
direction taken by the life boats . . . I see some forty yards distant one
of our life boats. . . . Hands pull me aboard. . . . We can see the*
Kormoran *some thousand yards away. It seems to us that the fire
has subsided a bit. I turn around towards the* Sydney. *Away in the
distance I can see a fire on the water. From time to time there is a
sudden glow, probably explosions of munitions. Then the* Kormoran
*explodes. Flames and clouds of smoke rise to the sky, and even where
we are we can hear the splashing of shell fragments on the water.
Within a few seconds our proud ship has disappeared under the waves.
Dark night and silence now reign where a few hours earlier gunfire
had so suddenly disturbed a quiet day. The battle itself had lasted perhaps
twenty minutes to half an hour. By 11 P.M. we had lost sight of the
burning* Sydney. *Heavy torpedo damage and the many 5.9-inch shells
she had taken precluded her reaching the safety of the coast. Not one
man of her brave crew of 42 officers and 603 men was saved.*

So sank the *Sydney.*

11

DEATH AND DISASTER

G oing to sea can be a hazardous venture. Your ship may be wrecked and you could go down with it. Alternatively, you might manage to scramble into a lifeboat, but if you are a great distance from the nearest land or your lifeboat is ill-equipped with food and water, you might as well have drowned in the first place. Failing that, you may be cast ashore on the proverbial deserted island, with little or no food and water.

If there are others sharing your predicament, there is the very real possibility of having to address "the delicate question which": who shall die in order that others may live? Philbrick puts it this way: "For as long as men had been sailing the world's oceans, famished sailors had been sustaining themselves on the remains of dead shipmates." Anyone interested in exploring this particular theme might consult Neil Hanson's *The Custom of the Sea,* a vivid and literate account of the famous trial concerning cannibalism after the sinking of the British yacht *Mignonette* in 1884; or—in another sphere of activity—Paul Piers Read's *Alive: The Story of the Andes Survivors.*

This chapter discusses examples of appalling shipwreck; cannibals who felt they had no alternative; and murderous criminal chaos in time of disaster. It ends with a brief commentary on man's inhumanity to man (a cliché, to be sure, but as with all clichés it conceals more than just a modicum of truth).

USS *SCORPION*

*"Under water men shall walk,
Shall ride, shall sleep, and talk."*
ANONYMOUS, "THE PROPHECIE OF MOTHER SHIPTON"

Mother Shipton was famed as a prophetess and witch more than three hundred years ago. She was born "phenomenally ugly" in a cave in Yorkshire in 1487 or 1488, of peasant parents, baptized as Ursula Southiel (or Sowthiel or Southill), in 1512 married a Tony (or Toby) Shipton, builder, and died in 1561. The evidence for both her existence and skill at foretelling the future is about as reliable as that pertaining to any of the astrologers found in women's magazines today. Her first prophecy, published in a pamphlet in 1641, foretold the death of Cardinal Thomas Wolsey (1475–1530) and others, and she is credited with having predicted airplanes, the steam engine, the telegraph, the end of the world in 1881, and other such marvels, including submarines; a *Life and Death of Mother Shipton* appeared in 1677.

The U.S. Navy nuclear submarine *Scorpion*, 3,000 tons, Commander Francis Slattery, and nearly a hundred men disappeared some four hundred miles west of the Azores in the North Atlantic in May 1968; three months later her wreckage was discovered on the seabed and photographed by the research ship *Mizar.* She was lying at a depth of some 10,000 feet, her hull evidently crushed (technically, imploded) as a result of overwhelming external water pressure.

The *Scorpion*, launched in 1959, had a year earlier undergone an extensive overhaul in the naval shipyard at Norfolk, Virginia, and then successfully completed a number of sea trials. In March 1968 she was attached to the U.S. Sixth Fleet in the Mediterranean and two months later set out to return to Norfolk. On May 21, when she was about 250 miles west of the Azores, she transmitted a routine progress signal and that was the last message the world had from her.

In due course a search was put into operation, but of course nothing was found, except that her top-secret code name, Brandywine, was intercepted on May 29, with hasty radio intercepts putting her some 100 miles off the Norfolk coast. Eventually this was treated as a hoax, although it is curious that anyone outside naval operations should have access to the code name of an American warship, and a nuclear submarine at that. Clark claims that *Newsweek* magazine asserted at the time that the U.S. Navy possessed audiotapes of *Scorpion* being crushed, with a verbal message describing what was happening.

What brought about the demise of the *Scorpion*? No one can know for sure. It was likely the usual combination, in varying degrees, of bad weather, human error, and structural or mechanical failure, events that have accounted for lost ships and planes ever since people began building them. But this has not deterred The Bermuda Triangle (see chapter 16) adherents, who have advanced the following certainties to account for the loss of this vessel:

- ◆ the *Scorpion*'s company was probably abducted by a UFO, with the submarine left behind as not worth anything, even as scrap metal
- ◆ an Atlantean crystal-laser ray gave her a fatal zapping from a bunker deep in the seabed of the Atlantic (see Fabled Atlantis, chapter 16)
- ◆ the *Scorpion* stumbled into a parallel universe and, coupled with the antimatter that as everyone knows infests these places and the nuclear forces she was running on anyway, she simply atomized (as, unhappily, did the men in her); this is a theory favored by a subgroup of these otherworld enthusiasts (the wreckage that the *Mizar* photographed remains unexplained in this theory)

HMS *ROYAL GEORGE*

"Toll for the brave—
The brave! that are no more:
All sunk beneath the wave,
Fast by their native shore."

WILLIAM COWPER, "ON THE LOSS OF THE ROYAL GEORGE"

The loss in 1782 of the first-rate HMS *Royal George* is one of maritime history's best-known examples of a ship capsizing with great loss of life. (Two other better-known capsizes involving many lives lost are the *Vasa*, or *Wasa*, a wooden warship built in Sweden—she sank at the outset of her maiden voyage in 1628; and the *Mary Rose*, built by Henry VIII. In going out to engage the French fleet off Portsmouth in 1545, the *Mary Rose* was swamped through her lower deck gun ports—she sank almost immediately, losing almost her whole complement of some four hundred men.)

On August 29 the *Royal George* was lying at Spithead with almost all of her crew on board, together with a large number of women and children. Admiral Richard Kempenfelt had hoisted his flag in the vessel, which belonged to the fleet under the command of Lord Howe, who was planning for the speedy relief of Gibraltar. In the midst of these preparations the *Royal George* capsized and sank, drowning some eight hundred people, including Admiral Kempenfelt.

It appears that the ship was being given a "Parliament heel" in order to bring about some repairs to her timbers just below the waterline, which involved heeling her over until her lower gun ports were just above the level of the sea. (A Parliament heel is a makeshift way of careening a vessel; it is carried out by running all the guns to one side so she heels sufficiently; the name probably came about during the time of Cromwell's Parliament, 1653–58, when the procedure was in wide use. Other sources suggest that the name comes from the British navy's traditional contempt for Parliament, that institution being regarded as nothing more than a debating society in contrast to the strict discipline of naval life.)

The court martial that followed did not sheet home the blame for the disaster to a single cause, but it is likely that because of the state of her timbers (many of which were known to be decayed) a frame collapsed, thus allowing the lower tier of gun ports to be submerged. (In his poem—see above—Cowper attributes the loss of the *Royal George* to a "land breeze," a very unlikely scenario, but Cowper was not a sailor.) A great deal of water entered the ship very quickly, and down she went.

In 1848, some sixty years later, parts of the wreck were blown up and some sections were brought to the surface by means of the closed-suit diving apparatus invented by Augustus Siebe in 1830, which heralded the era of deep-sea diving.

THE *GILT DRAGON*

"Then rose from sea to sky the wild farewell—
Then some leap'd overboard with fearful yell."
GEORGE GORDON, LORD BYRON, "DON JUAN"

Late on the night of April 28, 1656, the *Gilt Dragon (Vergulde Draeck)*, Captain Pieter Albertsz, drove headlong onto the reefs near Ledge Point on the west Australian coast, some 72 miles north of present-day Perth. At the time the *Gilt Dragon*, sailing in company with other Dutch vessels bound for the port of Batavia in the East Indies, had a king's ransom of gold and silver in her hold. The ship was a total wreck (the other vessels reached the East Indies without mishap). Only three years earlier she had been purchased and equipped by the VOC (Vereenigde Ostindische Compagnie), the United Dutch East India Company, for the purpose of trading between the Netherlands and the East Indies. This was only her second voyage. The question the Dutch in Batavia began asking was: what happened?

Some months after the shipwreck a number of exhausted men in a longboat from the *Gilt Dragon* who were on the point of dying from thirst and starvation pulled into Batavia harbor and reported to the VOC office, whose records state the following:

> *There arrived here from the Southland [Australia; see chapter 4]*
> *the cockboat of the yacht [from the Dutch* jaght, fast] *the* Gilt Dragon
> *with seven men, to our great regret reporting that the said yacht had*
> *run aground on the said Southland in 30°40' on April 28 [a private*
> *source states 31°13'], that besides the loss of her cargo of which nothing*
> *was saved, 118 men of her crew had perished, and that 69 men who*
> *had succeeded in getting ashore were still left there.*

A number of rescue operations to "the Southland" were mounted by the VOC, but to no effect, although one discerns a somewhat piously hopeful note in the company's final report of August 21, 1660, which states: "Now that all the missions have been fruitless we will have to give up, to our distress, the people of the *Gilt Dragon*, who have found refuge in the Southland." It is a sad irony that each ship sent to find possible survivors of the *Gilt Dragon* disaster lost numbers of their own men to various causes. The exact site of this wreck remained unknown for three hundred more years, when in 1963 a party of local spearfishermen discovered some wreckage and artifacts that later proved to be from the *Gilt Dragon*.

Beatty tells us that "a few years back" a boy discovered a small cave "on a lonely part of the coast"; it contained the very old skeleton of a white man and some forty Spanish and Dutch coins dating to no later than 1648. Beatty wisely makes no connection between these remains and the *Gilt Dragon*, probably because this coast has been the graveyard of dozens of vessels that had miscalculated their longitude and discovered their sad error only when they and their ships were being pounded into very small pieces by the terrible reefs waiting for them. (The boy who discovered the bones and coins was named A. Edwards, and the site was Cape Leschenault, at latitude 31°19' S.)

Beatty adds that in 1875 two British navy geographers engaged on a survey of the western Australian coast some 12 miles north of where the *Gilt Dragon* was wrecked came across a ring of stones about six feet in diameter in the bush and some distance inland (how far inland is not stated). The ring struck them as peculiar, particularly because the stones were such that "they must have been carried in from the coast." Since then, says Beatty, "another man, a Mr. Stokes, a grazier, has stated that he saw the ring of stones when searching for lost sheep."

Subsequent searches over the years have failed to find this elusive ring of stones beneath which, Beatty believes, "the treasure, or the clue to it, is buried." One can only bow gravely at such ineluctable certainty (the likelihood that these stones were the remains of an Aboriginal campsite does not seem to have intruded itself into Beatty's thinking).

The mystery about the fate of a number of seafarers—mostly Dutch—who had survived shipwreck on this coast during the sixteenth and seventeenth centuries is subjected to a reasoned argument by Gerritsen as to the likelihood of their having been absorbed into local Aboriginal groups.

See also The *Batavia* Wreck, chapter 9, for an account of the extraordinary brutality that followed another shipwreck on this most dangerous of coasts.

HMS *BIRKENHEAD*

"But to stand an' be still to the Birken'ead *drill*
Is a damn' tough bullet to chew,
An' they done it, the Jollies—'Er Majesty's Jollies—
Soldier an' sailor too!"

RUDYARD KIPLING, "SOLDIER AN' SAILOR TOO"

The loss of HMS *Birkenhead* off Simonstown in South Africa in 1852 gave rise to the expression "Remember the *Birkenhead*!" as a rallying cry of encouragement and inspiration in time of great danger.

The frigate HMS *Birkenhead*, launched in 1845, was the first iron ship to enter the British navy; she was intended to be a warship, but the admiralty had her fitted out instead as a troopship. After a number of trooping voyages she sailed for South Africa with her crew and 487 officers and men of the 74th Highlanders and their women and children.

The *Birkenhead* struck a submerged rock off Danger Point near Simonstown, South Africa, on the morning of February 26, 1852. As the ship began to sink in waters known to be shark-infested, the soldiers were drawn up in ranks on deck to enable the women and children to be got away safely in the lifeboats. The discipline and steadiness of the men as they remained to meet certain death became a byword for courage and self-sacrifice for the good of others. The regiment lost 454 men. The rock on which the ship struck is known today as Birkenhead Rock.

RMS *LUSITANIA*

"On entering the war zone tomorrow,
we shall be securely in the care of the Royal Navy."

CAPTAIN WILLIAM T. TURNER

So spoke the captain to his nervous passengers shortly before their ship was sunk by a German U-boat in the North Atlantic in 1915.

RMS *Lusitania*, 31,500 tons, was built by the Cunard Line in 1906. In an early indication of her qualities she captured the Atlantic Blue Riband in 1907 by crossing from Liverpool to New York at a speed of nearly 24 knots, and she continued monthly sailings between these two ports after the outbreak of war in 1914. (The vessel was named for a province of the Roman Empire, a region roughly corresponding to the Portugal of today.)

Before she left New York on May 1, 1915, the German authorities in the United States published a warning that ships of Great Britain and her allies would be attacked by submarines in the war zone and advised passengers not to sail. The millionaire Alfred G. Vanderbilt was said to have been told, "Have it on definite authority the *Lusitania* is to be torpedoed. You had better cancel passage immediately."

The warning was not regarded as serious (certainly not by Cunard officials, who publicly denied that warnings of any kind had been received), and apparently the British admiralty did not send radio warnings to the *Lusitania* on May 6 that there was German U-boat activity in the approaches to southern Ireland. According to the ship's sailing orders, she should have been steering a zigzag course and had been instructed to keep off the land, but these instructions were ignored.

At 2:15 P.M. on May 7 a torpedo struck *Lusitania*'s starboard side, fired from the German submarine *U-20* (Captain Walther Schwieger). She sank rapidly (her bow was already on the seabed when her stern lifted clear of the water), and because she was listing so heavily and was at so steep an angle with her bow down when she sank, it was extremely difficult to get her lifeboats away. Thus 1,198 people died, including Alfred G. Vanderbilt. There were 761 survivors. One of these, a young American, McMillan Adams, who helped try to launch some of *Lusitania*'s lifeboats, wrote that "the staff Captain told us that the boat was not going to sink, and ordered the lifeboats not to be lowered." It took only eighteen minutes for the *Lusitania* to settle on the seabed.

One theory has it that the second explosion came from the detonation of contraband cargo (although the *Lusitania* was not herself armed, she was certainly carrying a cargo of munitions). It was also claimed that she was deliberately ordered into the path of the submarine by Winston Churchill, who was at the time first lord of the admiralty, and by Sir John Fisher, first sea lord, in an attempt to bring the United States into the war (the same notion was advanced after Pearl Harbor in 1941). Former President Theodore Roosevelt said of this sinking that it was "piracy on a vaster scale than the worst pirates of history," but doubtless this was an overstatement, possibly because 124 Americans were among the 1,198 people lost.

Germany claimed that the *Lusitania* was an armed merchant cruiser carrying troops from Canada, but London insisted that she carried no troops and no guns and that her only war cargo was 5,000 cases of cartridges; it is also possible that her cargo included a quantity of fuses in addition to the ammunition. Nevertheless, despite this quantity of munitions in her hold, it was contrary to the rules laid down at the Hague Convention of 1907 for such a vessel to be sunk without first boarding her to establish the fact that she was carrying contraband and then making provision for the safety of her passengers and crew.

The U.S. government's passionate protest to Germany included the following remarks.

> *[The government of the United States] confidently expects, therefore, that the Imperial German government will disavow the acts of which the government of the United States complains, that they will make reparation so far as reparation is possible for injuries which are without measure, and that they will take immediate steps to prevent the recurrence of anything so obviously subversive of the principles of warfare for which the Imperial German government have in the past so wisely and so firmly contended.*

The tone of this diplomatic note conceals the bewilderment and fury that erupted in the United States at this apparently senseless act of war; the press referred to the sinking as "a deed for which a Hun would blush, a Turk be ashamed, and a Barbary pirate apologize." Racial and ethnic slurs aside, one can only sympathize with the sentiments expressed. Despite the medallions cast in Germany commemorating the sinking of the *Lusitania* that showed her decks crammed with guns and aircraft, it would have been perfectly clear even to pro-German workers on the docks of New York that the vessel was virtually harmless.

SS *WARATAH*

"Let another's shipwreck be your sea-mark."
SEVENTH-CENTURY PROVERB

The SS *Waratah* disappeared off South Africa late in July 1909, with the loss of all 211 persons on board—no bodies, lifeboats, wreckage, or shipboard items of any kind were ever found, making this one of the best-known examples of a ship lost entirely without trace (but compare this incident with the sinking of HMAS *Sydney* in 1941, with the loss of the entire crew, 645 men; chapter 10).

The *Waratah* was a British cargo-passenger vessel launched only a year earlier, operated by the Blue Anchor line on the run between England and Australia by way of the Cape of Good Hope. That she was not fitted with wireless was not unusual for that time when radio was still very new, although no doubt the subsequent court of inquiry might have wished that a radio telegraphy facility had been installed.

This vessel was named from *waratah*, the Aboriginal word for the bright red flower of the shrub, genus *Telopea*, found in eastern Australia (the waratah is the floral emblem of New South Wales, not the national flower of Australia, as Clark mistakenly claims). Under the command of Captain Ilberry, the *Waratah* was on her second round-trip, having sailed from London in April 1909. When she reached Australia she landed her passengers at Sydney, loaded some 6,500 tons of cargo, then set out for Durban, South Africa, where she took on coal.

At Durban an interesting incident occurred. A businessman by the name of Claude G. Sawyer, who had booked his passage home from Australia to England, suddenly left the vessel. He took himself and his luggage ashore despite the fact that he had no business affairs to attend to in Durban. Hardwick says passengers watched him go down the gangplank, then tapped their heads with their fingers to signify what they assumed to be the state of Sawyer's mind. Hardwick adds, "For they had heard the reason for Mr. Sawyer's departure. He had had recurrent bad dreams. Night after night the vision that had come to him in his bunk had terrified him into wakefulness."

The ship then left for Cape Town, eight hundred miles away, on the evening of July 26; the following day she overtook the *Clan MacIntyre* on the same course—and that was the last time the *Waratah* was seen. Two days later the *Clan MacIntyre* reported that the weather had been unusually bad, with fierce winds and "tremendous seas" (it was the Southern Hemisphere winter); nevertheless, she and other vessels in the area had come through safely. The master of the *Clan MacIntyre* told the board of inquiry that when she was sighted on July 27 the *Waratah* was not listing and neither was she rolling unduly in the heavy weather. The reason for her complete disappearance has never been satisfactorily explained, although there were persistent rumors that the vessel was unstable.

When the *Waratah* was posted missing, Sawyer appeared at the inquiry and explained the nature of these dreams. In them he is leaning on the rail and staring out to sea. A blood-spattered knight dressed in armor and mounted on a horse suddenly rises out of the waves, holding aloft in one hand his sword and in the other a blood-soaked rag, all the while apparently trying to shout something to Sawyer. The message seems to be, "The *Waratah*! The *Waratah*!," then the phantom knight disappears. Hardwick assures us that nobody now laughed at Sawyer's story—he was, after all, the only survivor, and that by inexplicable default.

But note this statement made to the English newspapers at the time by the *Clan MacIntyre*'s chief officer, C. G. Phillips, who had exchanged signals with the *Waratah* when they sighted each other (Phillips later became commodore of the Clan Line, an indication of his reputation for being capable and level-headed):

> *A gale of hurricane force had been lashing the seas when the* Waratah *passed us. Some hours after I had sent the signal to the liner I was standing on the bridge when I sighted a sailing vessel. There was something strangely old-fashioned about her rig. As I watched her I noted with astonishment that by some extraordinary means she was sailing with comparative ease into the very teeth of the gale.*
>
> *I'm not a superstitious man, but I know my seafaring lore. The rig of the strange craft immediately brought to mind the legend of the* Flying

Dutchman . . . *the phantom ship held me spellbound. It disappeared in the direction taken by the* Waratah, *and I had a feeling it was a sign of disaster for the liner.*

Hardwick tells us that in the "second half of the twentieth century" a pilot in the South African Air Force reported that while flying over the sea just off the coast he had seen, very clearly, the outline of a ship lying on the bottom, close in to the shore. Hardwick says that the pilot "recognized" the wreck as the *Waratah* (it is not clear how he achieved this feat, the ship in question having already been submerged for more than fifty years), but subsequent efforts to locate it again failed.

Some thirty or forty years ago a popular writer of drama and mystery wrote a story about a cargo liner that ran into some of the very bad weather that often attends a passage through the Mozambique Channel, that strait of unruly water between Mozambique on the east coast of Africa and the island of Madagascar. The Agulhas Current sweeps south through this relatively shallow channel against the prevailing southerly winds, a confluence of events that can bring on mountainous waves. The author has his ship encounter seas so fiercely steep that an underwater mountain is momentarily revealed in the troughs, with a huge cavern in its side into which the vessel is driven headlong, to be immediately engulfed forever by the raging ocean.

Many years later, the story continues, an air force pilot, in search of the wreck of the ship in which his father had been an officer, discovers this very same underwater cavern during a terrible storm, brings his aircraft safely alongside the ship's hulk that he discovers therein (exactly how he achieves this underwater miracle remains a mystery), and a meeting is thereby effected between long-lost father and lately landed offspring. The remainder of this story is, naturally enough, something of a blur.

Supposedly, this yarn might be taken as an explanation of the fate of the *Waratah*, proving yet again (if indeed such proof is needed) the truth of Fabian's observation in *Twelfth Night*: "If this were play'd upon a stage now, I could condemn it as an improbable fiction."

(Note: Late in 1999 a report appeared in the press that the remains of the *Waratah* had at last been found off the East African coast.)

THE WHALER *ESSEX*
"The cannibals that each other eat;
The anthropophagi."
WILLIAM SHAKESPEARE, *OTHELLO*

Cannibal is from the Spanish *canibal, caribal,* the Spanish version of Caribe, the name of the fierce and warlike Indians first encountered by Columbus in the Caribbean Sea (see chapter 8). The Carib people were noted for their practice of eating human flesh; their name probably means "strangers."

Cannibalism is one of humankind's greatest taboos, the idea of eating one of our own kind filling us with horror and revulsion. The fact is that most of us have never experienced the extremities of thirst and starvation; we have often been very hungry, even famished, but never starving enough to contemplate seriously the prospect of eating human flesh to permit ourselves a chance of survival. The literature of the sea is well signposted with accounts of otherwise decent folk who, driven to the extremities of starvation, have done this very thing (the story of the *Mignonette*, 1884, is a case in point).

Perhaps the most famous incident of cannibalism at sea is connected with the Nantucket whaler *Essex*, Captain George Pollard, which on the morning of November 20, 1820, was repeatedly rammed and then sunk by an enraged sperm whale in the vast South Pacific. The crew of twenty took to the sea in three open boats, but only eight men in two of these boats survived the ordeal; the third boat under the second mate disappeared.

The captain commanded one of the boats and Owen Chase, first mate (who a year later, in 1821, gave an account of this sinking), commanded the other. On February 18 Chase and his men were rescued by the English brig *Indian*; Captain Pollard and one other survivor still in his boat were picked up by the American whaler *Dauphin*; both sets of survivors arrived at Valparaíso, Chile, within three weeks of each other. Such was the suffering of the men in Chase's boat during the ninety days that followed the sinking of the *Essex* that when one of their number died they agreed immediately with the first mate that they should eat their comrade's flesh.

Captain Pollard's account of his own experience was even more chilling. After having exhausted the meager supplies they had managed to take off the *Essex*, they too were forced to eat the bodies of their comrades who had already died. But when these were consumed it became obvious to the remaining men that lots would have to be cast to determine who might be sacrificed for the sake of the others. By this method Owen Coffin, the cabin boy and Pollard's first cousin, was chosen; he was barely sixteen years old. Pollard said to him, " 'My lad, my lad, if you don't like your lot, I'll shoot the first man that touches you.' The wretched boy hesitated a little; then, quietly laying his head down upon the gunnel of the boat, he said, 'I like it as well as any other.' "

Such were the conditions faced by men whose livelihood was founded in and bounded by the sea, when the drawing of lots for an act of cannibalism was, of necessity, one of the customs and usages of seafaring. The story of the ramming of the *Essex* became the basis for the climax in Herman Melville's *Moby-Dick*, when the great white whale turns his fury on the whaler *Pequod* and sinks it (see Moby Dick, chapter 4).

THE *WILLIAM BROWN*

"It isn't important to come out on top.
What matters is to be the one who comes out alive."

BERTOLT BRECHT, *IN THE JUNGLE OF CITIES*

One cannot peruse the literature of shipwreck without sooner or later having to deal with the question of survival: who in the group shall die in order that the remainder might live? The following story illustrates some of the difficulties involved.

On the night of April 19, 1841, the *William Brown*, Captain George Harris, was sunk by an iceberg some 250 miles southeast of Newfoundland. The captain, eight seamen, and one passenger took one of the two lifeboats; the mate and the remaining crew and some thirty passengers filled the remaining boat, a longboat. About half the passengers, perhaps three dozen men and women, went down with the ship. It was clear from the shouted conversation between Captain Harris and the officers that they would have to do something to lighten the overloaded longboat; then the captain's boat drifted out of sight.

The longboat was leaking, and within a short time they were among ice flocs again. The mate, Francis Rhodes, told his men that they would have to lighten the boat if any of them were to survive. The seamen understood Rhodes perfectly, and that night they threw a number of passengers into the sea. Some of the victims accepted their fate; one, Frank Askins, fought wildly against his executioner, Alexander Holmes; and another, James MacAvoy, asked for five minutes in which to prepare himself. He then said his prayers, stood up, buttoned his coat, and jumped overboard. The two sisters of Frank Askins went next, one because she insisted on joining her brother, the other because she was forced over.

The dreadful business went on throughout the night. The seamen gave no quarter on account of blood ties: uncles and nieces, brothers and sisters, even the guardian of an orphaned child—all were thrown overboard in order to save the remainder in the longboat. Rhodes, the man who had set this affair in motion, apparently became sickened by the wholesale killing, but he intervened on only one occasion to reprieve a husband and his wife who had insisted on going down with him.

Ironically, the last passenger had hardly disappeared beneath the ice-cold waters when one of the seamen spied an American ship, the *Crescent*, heading toward them. The captain, George Ball, hauled the survivors on board and the ship sailed to Le Havre, France, where the British and American consuls took statements from everyone in the longboat concerning the whole affair. Interestingly, a few of the surviving passengers defended the sailors and what they had done, but other passengers were less forgiving.

For a time there was a furor in the press, but the authorities in England and America decided that prosecution would serve no purpose—the seamen in the longboat had merely been following the custom and usage of the sea. However, when some of the passengers reached Philadelphia a few months later they circulated a tale that the Irish Catholics on the boat had been heaved overboard in order to make room for the Scottish Protestants.

Naturally, this accusation aroused some powerful feelings; a trial was held and Alexander Holmes was formally charged with the murder of Frank Askins. He was found guilty of manslaughter instead and given a recommendation of mercy, with six months' hard labor in jail. Because he had already been locked up for that period before the trial, Holmes was immediately set free, but he must have been sorely puzzled about the justice of it all. Hadn't he, after all, simply obeyed his captain's powerful hints concerning who should survive and who should not?

As for the captain, he and his men in the other lifeboat were picked up six days after the *William Brown* had gone down. They had all suffered some frostbite but that was all, and there was no question of prosecuting Captain Harris; he had broken no law.

For a detailed discussion of cannibalism as a "custom and usage of the sea" read Neil Hanson's *The Custom of the Sea*, a detailed account of the fate of the *Mignonette*'s crew in 1884.

WRECKER'S COAST

"Not that they shall, but if they must—
Be just, Lord, wreck them off Saint Just
. . . Soul nor sailor mean we harm.
But our blue sky is their black storm."
DONALD MICHAEL THOMAS, "SONG OF THE CORNISH WRECKERS"

For a long time the coast of Cornwall was notorious for its fraternity of wreckers, dismal souls who late at night would hang a lantern from the neck of a hobbled horse and lead it along the cliff tops overlooking the Atlantic. To a vessel out at sea the bobbing lantern would seem for all the world like the riding light of a ship at anchor, which would mean a snug harbor or safe waters at the least. Not a bit of it.

Lured in by the light, an unwary ship would soon find herself driving onto the rocks above which the wreckers waited, certain to find among the dead sailors and smashed wreckage in the foaming seas a goodly collection of pieces of cargo, ship's gear, and other items that would fetch a price already paid for in blood. According to local legend, the curious who search along that coast may still see a phantom wrecker, especially in Priest Cove, where on a stormy night he can be glimpsed in the breakers clinging to a ship's spar before disappearing in the thrashing foam, a suitably endless fate for one of life's least noble workers.

The coast of Kerry, on the southwest portion of the Irish Republic, was also noted for its wreckers, and a local legend tells of the fate of some who dared too much. In the early eighteenth century a party of wreckers found a large vessel wedged into the rocks that lie off the coast; it had lost its masts and was, apparently, abandoned. Watched by their companions on the cliffs, the scavengers pushed off in their boats and discovered to their intense excitement that the ship was a Spanish galleon, her holds full of silver ingots and other costly cargoes. They scrabbled to loot everything in sight, and when their boats were heaped to the gunnels with treasure they began the long pull back to shore.

Alas! As if in terrible retribution for their thievery, a monster wave rose up and thundered down on the luckless men, burying them and their boats in a mountain of roaring water and foam. When the wave had swept back out to sea and everything had cleared, the boats and the men in them had disappeared forever. It is said that each year, at the same time, a giant wave hurls itself upon that very place.

12

NAVIGABLE WATERS

I t would be no exaggeration to say that two of the world's greatest feats of engineering are The Panama Canal and The Suez Canal (see below). Nevertheless, by the ineluctable forces of irony these two immeasurable boons to international shipping were the direct cause of the rapid demise of man's most beautiful creation, the full-rigged ship (see, for example, The Clipper Ships and The Windjammers, chapter 8).

Anthony Trollope, the English novelist, wrote in 1859 (the very year Ferdinand de Lesseps began work on his "impossible project," a canal joining the Mediterranean to the Red Sea), "I have a very strong opinion that such a canal will not and cannot be made." Ten years later the job was completed and the Suez Canal extracted its first tolls from marine traffic.

And ten years after that, Britain had finally come to its senses, realizing at last that the canal was not only fated to be a going concern but would also reflect a great deal of unnecessary glory on the French. Benjamin Disraeli, British prime minister at the time, advised Queen Victoria that she now owned a goodly portion of the canal because he had completed the purchase of Britain's soon to be immensely valuable shares in the venture.

THE AMAZON RIVER

"She towered, fit person for a queen
To lead those ancient Amazonian files."

WILLIAM WORDSWORTH, "BEGGARS"

The Amazon is the South American river of enduring fame. Every traveler who visits the region is obliged to note the appropriate statistics. For example, the Amazon drains an area as large as the continental United States; it contains one-fifth of all river waters on the earth; and every year it dumps five billion tons of sediment into the South Atlantic, where it muddies the ocean up to two hundred miles from the coast.

Originally, the Amazon was known as Río Santa María de la Mar Dulce (literally, "River Saint Mary of the Calm Sea"), so named by the Spanish explorer Vicente Pinzón, who first discovered this vast waterway in 1500 and ascended it for some fifty miles from the coast. It also became known at the same time as Mar Dulce, Rio Grande, and El Ryo Maranon.

It was renamed the Amazon after a battle when the Spanish explorer Francisco de Orellana (about 1490–1546) made the first descent of this river from the Andes to the sea in 1541. During this incredible feat of endurance, Orellana found himself engaged in a savage battle with Indian tribes near the village of Obidos, where he saw women fighting alongside the men.

As a result of this observation, Orellana renamed the river the Amazonas, in honor of the tribe of fierce warrior women celebrated in antiquity. These were the original Amazons of legend who, according to the Greek historian Herodotus in the fifth century B.C., inhabited ancient Scythia, a large area now in eastern Europe and Asiatic Russia (some writers of this period also mention an even much older nation of Amazons living in Africa). According to the ancient legends of the Greeks (of whom Herodotus was but one of a number who retold this story), these women—the Amazons—fought many fierce battles with the Greeks; the famous hero Achilles was said to have slain the Amazon queen Penthesilea when these female warriors were trying to help the besieged Trojans. These mythical women were said to cut off their right breasts so they could draw their bows more easily; thus the word *Amazon* is claimed by the classical writers to derive from the Greek *a*, without, and *mazos*, breast.

No men were kept in this society of Amazons; when male captives were taken in battle they were sometimes required to mate with the women, immediately following which happy event they were put to death (there is an enduring legend that one impertinent warrior welcomed death after mating had been achieved, but in return insisted that he be dispatched by the ugliest woman in the tribe; it is said that he lived to tell his tale). Sons born of these encounters were either immediately killed or sent back to the neighboring tribe that had supplied the fathers. When girls reached puberty they were subjected to a mastectomy by having one breast burned off.

It seems, however, that the story is nothing more than that, a myth invented by the ancient Greeks to account for the barbarians who lived far beyond the borders of the known world. There is also the distinct probability that it is a variety of the familiar tale of a distant land where everything is done the wrong way round. Thus in the land of the Amazons it is the women who do the fighting, which in all other societies is normally men's business.

The habitat of the Amazons becomes even more remote in the telling, according to the development of Greek geographical knowledge at the time. Homer's *Iliad* places them in Phrygia (in the northwest of present-day Turkey), where Priam, king of Troy, meets them. When the Black Sea was colonized by the Greeks, an area much more remote than Phrygia, it is this region that becomes the home of the Amazons. One of the traditional labors of Hercules was an expedition to secure the girdle of the queen of the Amazons and bring it to Eurystheus.

The myth has certainly been with us for a long time and was believed by educated men in what we might call modern Europe; Dr. Johnson in his *Dictionary* (1755) said: "The Amazons were a race of women famous for valour, who inhabited Caucasus; they are so called from their cutting off their right breasts, to use their weapons better."

The Amazons are now firmly entrenched in the literature, despite our strong misgivings about the authenticity of their origin. Tennyson referred to them in "The Princess": "Glanced at the legendary Amazon / As an emblematic of a nobler age."

There was, indeed, a band of female warriors known as Amazons kept as a personal guard by the king of the French Protectorate of Dahomey in Africa in quite recent times, but they were "Amazons" in name only. The use of the term today varies. Western Europeans think of a mannish sort of woman, what we would call a virago, a violent or bad-tempered female (from the Latin *viraga*, a woman of manly courage, *vir*, man). Americans envision a tall, athletic woman, physically strong and graceful to boot.

THE PANAMA CANAL

"It is absolutely indispensable for the United States to effect a passage from the Mexican Gulf to the Pacific Ocean; and I am certain that they will do it."
JOHANN WOLFGANG VON GOETHE, *CONVERSATIONS WITH ECKERMANN*

The first proposals for cutting a canal through the Isthmus of Panama came in 1523 from King Charles V of Spain (1500–1558; reigned 1516–56), when as a result of Spanish interest in Central America following Columbus's fourth voyage to the region (1502), he put forward plans for a canal that would link the Atlantic Ocean with the Pacific Ocean, but nothing came of it. Three hundred years later the German scientist Baron von Humboldt (1769–1859) lent his considerable reputation to such a notion, despite the fact that there were significant differences in mean sea levels as well as in tidal ranges between the two bodies of water: at the Atlantic end of the canal the extreme tidal range is 3.05 feet, while at the Pacific end it is 22.7 feet.

After Ferdinand de Lesseps had conquered the Egyptian desert to build the Suez Canal (see below; it was opened in 1869), he then set about performing the same miracle at Panama (which politically was a part of Colombia); he planned a sea-level canal to be constructed by the French Panama Canal Company, but financial and engineering problems proved to be too daunting.

At the same time, Adolphe Godin de Lépinay de Brusly, a French engineer who had made a thorough study of possible sites throughout the Isthmus, strongly advocated a canal at Panama based on a series of locks, with a dam on the Chagres River on the north side of the continental divide and another on the Rio Grande on the south side, the lakes so formed to be then connected to their respective oceans by locks. A massive channel would then have to be cut through the divide itself to join the lakes (in the case of a sea-level canal, the excavation needed would be unbelievably stupendous). In 1889 de Lesseps's company had to withdraw, but by then it had seen the wisdom of a high-level lock system.

In the mid-1800s Nicaragua, about 320 miles west and north of the present Canal Zone, was highly favored by the United States as the site for an interocean canal, with access to the Pacific by means of the navigable San Juan River that flows from the Caribbean Sea to Lake Nicaragua, and thence to the Pacific by a shortcut through the narrow strip that separates the lake from the west coast of Nicaragua. International politics of that time, however, resulted in a deadlock between the United States and Great Britain, since the Mosquito Coast at the eastern terminus was under British control. In any case, when three American entrepreneurs completed a 48-mile railroad across the Isthmus of Panama in 1855, having overcome tremendous engineering difficulties, Nicaragua became a less favored site for a canal.

In 1898, when the Spanish-American War broke out, USS *Oregon*, ordered to Cuba from San Francisco, took some weeks to get there by way of Cape Horn (see chapter 7). This incident encouraged the United States government to take a greater interest in the idea of a canal that could link these two oceans and thus avoid the dangerous, not to say very lengthy, voyage by way of the Southern Ocean. Clearly, the Panama railroad would offer great advantages for the building of such a canal.

The American government, which regarded an Isthmian canal as "virtually a part of the coastline of the United States," then resorted to the Monroe Doctrine of 1823, which in broad terms stated that the North American continent was not available for colonization by any European power. From this position it logically followed that any canal across the Isthmus would by that very fact be under the possession and control of the United States government.

After the de Lesseps effort collapsed, the Americans set up a commission in 1899 to investigate the cost of buying out the French holdings and constructing a canal under its own steam. The figures proved to be equally as daunting as the physical obstacles of the region. The French were asking for their property nearly three times the amount the Americans had assessed it at (in rounded U.S. dollars, $110 million as against $40 million). The commission thereupon swiftly recommended the site in Nicaragua.

Subsequent negotiations with Great Britain in 1901 induced that European power to recognize "the exclusive right of the United States to construct, regulate and manage any Isthmian canal." The rules of operation were those adopted for the Suez Canal: the canal would be open to all vessels, whether of commerce or war, of all nations, with equitable tolls for everyone.

Bearing in mind that the American preference for the Nicaraguan site was common knowledge, it was no surprise to anyone when the (French) Panama Canal Company promptly let it be known that their holdings in the Isthmus would immediately be made available to the American government at the figure initially determined by the Americans ($40 million). The U.S. commission just as promptly cancelled its original recommendation of Nicaragua and now advocated the Panama site as the most practical and feasible available.

To this end President Theodore Roosevelt set in motion the machinery by which he might acquire from Colombia sufficient Panamanian territory in which his government could exercise, in perpetuity, political and operational control over the canal that he proposed should be built there. This happy state of affairs was finally achieved by the Spooner Act in 1902, but only after a great deal of heated debate. The Colombian senate, meanwhile, objected strongly to the terms of the subsequent treaty with the United States, and matters did not look at all promising. The Panamanians, concerned that the canal might after all be built in Nicaragua, started a revolution (not a difficult achievement in Latin America) against the government of Colombia. This erupted on November 3, 1903, the warship USS *Nashville* having magically appeared at Colón just one day earlier.

Colombian troops were thus dissuaded from crossing the border, and Panama thus gained its independence (as Roosevelt himself said in a moment of candor concerning this affair, "Speak softly and carry a big stick—you will go far"). A few weeks later the United States and Panama signed a treaty that, in line with the Spooner Act, gave the American government exclusive use of and sovereign powers over the Canal Zone through which the canal was to be built, with Panama itself denied all such rights in this zone. The treaty was formalized on May 4, 1904, the date subsequently celebrated every year in the zone as Acquisition Day. Work began in 1904, but significant progress was not made until 1908, when the U.S. Corps of Army Engineers was given control of all construction.

The obstacles that faced the builders were formidable. The region was endemically unhealthy because of yellow fever and malaria, the terrain was mountainous and difficult, local rivers were torrential, and the heat was exquisitely enervating. In 1906 opinion had become divided over what kind of canal to build—sea-level or high-lock; much argument ensued until Congress finally resolved the impasse by adopting the high-level system. The canal, long since regarded by many as one of the greatest engineering feats in history, was finally opened to international traffic on August 15, 1914, two weeks after World War I had broken out.

THE SUEZ CANAL

"And here not far from Alexandria,
Whereas the Terren and the red sea meet,
Being distant less than ful a hundred leagues,
I meant to cut a channel to them both,
That men might quickly sail to India."

CHRISTOPHER MARLOWE, *TAMBURLAINE*

Marlowe was not of course the first to suggest that a channel be cut through the Egyptian desert to link the Mediterranean with the Gulf of Suez and thence with the Red Sea and, ultimately, with trading nations in Asia. The idea had been put into practice some four thousand years earlier, when a canal was dug joining the Great Bitter Lake to a branch of the River Nile, thus assuring an exit to the Mediterranean, with another channel excavated between Great Bitter Lake and the Red Sea. The Pharaoh Necos (also Necho, Nechos) probably used this route when, according to Herodotus, he sent an expedition of Phoenician sailors on a circumnavigation of Africa (see Hanno the Navigator, chapter 3).

When the Persian king Darius the Great (about 522–486 B.C.) conquered Egypt, he restored and enlarged the canals that the pharaoh had caused to be built, as did the invading Romans and later the Arabs. But by then other trade routes to the east had been opened up—notably the famed Silk Road that reached across Asia Minor and the Middle East to China—and the canals fell into disuse.

By the end of the fifteenth century the Cape route to India had been discovered, and Frenchmen began to debate the possibility of digging a channel across the

Suez isthmus so that trade with India and the Far East could be instituted. Accordingly, Napoleon Bonaparte (1769–1821, self-crowned emperor of France in 1804) occupied Egypt in 1798, and his engineers studied the possibility of a sea-to-sea canal. However, it was believed at the time that the levels of the two seas differed by as much as 30 feet, and it wasn't until nearly sixty years later, in 1853, that the French engineer Linant de Bellefonds proved that no such difficulty existed.

Now the world was to meet the Frenchman Ferdinand de Lesseps (1805–1894), *diplomate extraordinaire.* De Lesseps spent some years in Egypt as a member of the French diplomatic service, his charm and intelligence guaranteeing him access to important figures in the Egyptian government. During his period there he studied the reports that had been written about a canal across the isthmus, and when he retired the political situation in Egypt was such that he was able to interest the government in such a project. By 1856 there was formed the Compagnie Universelle du Canal Maritime de Suez, the charter of which, among other things, proclaimed that the canal was to be a neutral passageway open to all merchant shipping regardless of nationality; furthermore, ninety-nine years after it was opened for navigation, outright ownership of the canal was to revert to the Egyptian government.

The British, of course, vigorously opposed the whole idea, believing—not entirely mistakenly—that the canal scheme implied even grander designs by the French. De Lesseps countered with a generous offer of shares to all European nations, as well as to the United States. Britain and America declined to take them up. France came out of it with more than half the issue of shares, whereby Britain was able to confirm, by her own foolish default, her worst expectations: France was now a major shareholder in a project that, if successful, would promise that country nothing but brilliant wealth and undying national glory.

De Lesseps pressed ahead. On April 25, 1859, he dug a spadeful of sand to mark the site of the northernmost exit of the canal, Port Said. The British persisted in being troublesome. Work proceeded slowly. Port Said itself began to rise out of the marshes around Lake Menzala. British lobbying continued to interfere with the work force, conditions, national politics, and so on, but finally de Lesseps saw his vision come to fruition: the Suez Canal was formally opened on November 17, 1869, the triumphal procession along the canal being led by the French imperial yacht *Aigle* itself, the Empress Eugénie regally waving at the spectators. Britain, now recognizing a fait accompli when she finally saw one in front of her very nose, belatedly joined in the celebration of de Lesseps's genius.

The canal, which is about 100 miles long, was originally excavated to a depth of some 26 feet, with a navigable bottom width of about 72 feet, but the subsequent development of tankers and bulk carriers over the years has forced the company to widen and deepen the waterway or risk losing the substantial income generated by this strategically and economically important shortcut to and from the Mediterranean.

But while the undoubtedly splendid canal promised an exciting new era in trade and traffic with Asia, it also meant the end of the beautiful square-rigged ships, as mentioned (see chapter 8). Steamers could now reach the Indian Ocean and western Pacific regions without having to establish expensive coal-bunkering ports along the African coastline; they made their cargo rates increasingly competitive with sail and their delivery times quicker and more reliable. By the beginning of World War II a chapter—a long and glorious chapter—of man's enduring affair with the sea had finally come to an end with the demise of the last working deep-water sailing ships engaged in freight carrying.

13

CASTAWAYS
AND SURVIVORS

Marine literature is awash, so to speak, with tales of shipwreck and catastrophe, death and disaster being the lot of most who come to grief at sea or who are cast ashore by their colleagues. Some are spared the agonies of death by starvation or—what is infinitely worse—by thirst. Others are lucky: rescuers find them before it is too late. Then there are those courageous souls who attempt to save themselves.

Simmons reminds us that "the figure of the castaway is one of the most powerful in our literary heritage." Saint Paul shipwrecked on Malta, Ulysses loafing around for ten years on Nausicaa's beach, the much-disillusioned Gulliver mooning about on Lilliput, or the hapless Ancient Mariner in Coleridge's poem—all endure trials and tribulations in their newfound isolation (see The *Odyssey*, chapter 4, and *Gulliver's Travels*, chapter 3).

The following accounts are but a sampling of the difficulties awaiting the unwitting castaway.

ROBINSON CRUSOE

"It's so utterly out of the world!
So fearfully wide of the mark!
A Robinson Crusoe existence will pall
On that unexplored side of the Park—
Not a soul will be likely to call!"

WILLIAM PLOMER, "A SHOT IN THE PARK"

Robinson Crusoe by Daniel Defoe (1660–1731), one of the world's great classics in the literature of the sea, deals with the experiences of a sailor cast away on a (supposedly) deserted island. It was published in 1719 as *The Life and Strange Surprizing Adventures of Robinson Crusoe*.

The story was founded partly on Dampier's *Voyage Round the World* (1697) and still more on the adventures of one Alexander Selkirk, as communicated to Defoe by Selkirk himself (see Simmons 1993 for an interesting discussion of Selkirk's experience). Crusoe's shipwreck and adventures and his discovery of the famous footprint in the sand—that of his man Friday—are all wonderfully told, but Defoe's notion of civilized man alone and face to face with unadorned nature made his story an imperishable part of world literature.

Alexander Selkirk (originally Selcraig; 1676–1721) was the seventh son of John Selcraig, shoemaker and tanner of Largo, Fifeshire. In 1695 Alexander ran away to sea; in 1703 he joined William Dampier (1652–1715) in a privateering expedition to the South Seas as sailing master on the *Cinque Ports*.

The following year the *Cinque Ports* put in at Más a Tierra Island, the largest of the Juan Fernández group, which lies some 400 miles west of Chile. There Selkirk had a dispute with his captain, Thomas Stradling the buccaneer ("a sullen, irascible, incompetent, and unpopular leader"), and at his own request Selkirk was put ashore with a variety of tools and supplies, including powder and shot (many more goods than the Indian William had; see below). Before the ship left he begged to be taken aboard again, but Stradling refused, leaving Selkirk marooned on the island, which was well stocked with wild goats, fruits, and rushing streams of clear water.

Here he remained alone for a little over four years until in January 1709 Captain Woodes Rogers (who in 1718 became governor of the Bahamas with the task of stamping out pirates), in company with that indefatigable explorer Dampier, stopped at Más a Tierra to take on fresh water. It is said that when Selkirk came out of the forest to hail the ship's boat drawn up on the beach, the seamen were frightened out of their wits. Rogers reported that Selkirk, clad in his goatskins, looked "wilder than the first Owners of them."

Rogers made Selkirk his mate and later gave him command of one of the prizes that he and Dampier had taken on their privateering cruise. Selkirk returned to England and was back at Largo in 1712; in 1717 he was again at sea, and in 1721 he died of fever while master's mate of HMS *Weymouth* on the West Africa station. It is unlikely that Selkirk was aware that barely two years earlier an obscure writer in London had produced a best seller based on his, Selkirk's, own experiences. In 1868 a memorial tablet was erected on the island of Más a Tierra at a point called Selkirk's Lookout.

Defoe was probably familiar with several versions of Selkirk's account of his adventures, and he certainly added many incidents from his own imagination to his tale about Crusoe, presenting it to the public as a true story. The thoroughly convincing account of the shipwrecked Crusoe's successful efforts to make a tolerable existence in his solitude reveals Defoe's genius for vivid fiction, suggesting that *Robinson Crusoe* may readily claim to be one of the first English novels.

Crusoe tells us how, with the help of a few stores and utensils saved from the wreck and by the exercise of infinite ingenuity, he builds himself a house, domesticates some wild goats that roam the island, and makes himself a boat. A visit by some cannibals causes him much unease, but he is able to rescue a native from certain death at their hands; this man he later names Friday. Finally an English ship hoves in sight, its crew being in a state of mutiny; the mutineers are subdued and Crusoe and Friday are rescued.

The book had an immediate success with the public and inspired many imitations, such as *The Swiss Family Robinson*. In 1719 (the same year he published the original story) Defoe followed it with *The Farther Adventures of Robinson Crusoe*, in which Crusoe revisits his island in company with Friday, but as they prepare to leave again they are attacked by a hostile band of natives in canoes and Friday is killed in the subsequent battle. The expression "Man Friday" (and later "Girl Friday") entered the English language in modern times to describe an assistant who performs a wide variety of menial tasks.

Marooning was a popular way of dealing with a sailor who didn't fit in within the scheme of things; the offending man was simply put ashore on an isolated island—occasionally with a few provisions, but more often without—and left there to die; very few survived. Selkirk lived not only because Más a Tierra provided ample food and water, but because he had the wit to adapt to changed circumstances.

One other man—a Mosquito Indian named William from the Caribbean coast of Nicaragua—had been left behind on this island in about 1680, some twenty years before Selkirk, although this had been an accident whereas Selkirk's marooning was deliberate. William survived on Más a Tierra for nearly four years, proving in the process to be particularly adept at looking out for himself. He was rescued in 1684 by Captain John Cook.

Originally a maroon was a Negro who lived in Dutch Guiana and the West Indies; it comes from the French *marron*, which in turn is an abbreviated form of the Spanish *cimarron*, wild and untamed. A maroon was thus someone who normally lived in the wilds. Later the word came to be used as a verb, so that "to maroon" someone was to cast him ashore on some wild and desolate island and let him fend for himself.

ICEBOUND BY NORTH

"Obscurest night involved the sky,
Th' Atlantic billows roared,
When such a destined wretch as I,
Washed headlong from on board,
Of friends, of hope, of all bereft,
His floating home forever left."

WILLIAM COWPER, "THE CASTAWAY"

The island of Spitzbergen lies in the Barents Sea to the far north of Sweden, within 10 degrees of the Pole. It is a bleak and barren country, taking its name from the frozen mountains that rear up like spikes into the leaden sky.

In 1743 a Russian vessel set out for the Greenland whale fishery with fourteen men aboard. Within a few days the ship was beset by ice near an island called Little Broun, just off the east coast of Spitzbergen. Because of the imminent danger that they all faced, four of the crew—Alexis Himkof, Iwan Himkof, Stephen Scharapof, and Feodor Weregin—were sent ashore to search for a hut that it was believed had been built the previous year.

Provided with a musket, twelve charges of powder and ball, an axe, a kettle, about twenty pounds of flour, a knife, and a tinderbox, the men eventually completed the dangerous journey to the island across the shifting, wind-driven ice. To their great joy they discovered the hut that same day, although it was now in a very sorry state of disrepair. After an uncomfortable night sheltering from a storm they hurried back to the shore to tell their comrades about their good fortune. Imagine their astonishment and alarm when they found only the open sea, completely free of ice, and not a sign of their ship. It had disappeared utterly.

Horrified at the prospect of never being able to leave the island, the four men returned to the hut. They shot a number of reindeer, using up all their powder and ball in the process, and prepared the flesh and hides for the coming winter. They then made a bow and two spears from driftwood, and with these they attacked and killed a polar bear, at great peril to themselves, thus providing themselves with extra meat for food, and sinews for a bowstring.

By forging nails and bits of iron collected from driftwood they made some serviceable arrows that enabled them over the next six years to kill some two hundred and fifty reindeer, large numbers of foxes, and ten more polar bears. Bears repeatedly tried to enter the hut in order to attack and eat the men, so nine of the ten were killed in self-defense. The men deliberately hunted only one bear.

For suitable clothing, necessary in such a vigorous climate, the men treated the reindeer hides with water and fat until they were softened sufficiently for sewing into garments. A needle was forged from a nail, and with reindeer sinews for thread they worked up some jackets and trousers that could protect them from the winter cold. What concerned them most was the knowledge that their families would have no idea what had happened to them. As one year succeeded another and still their situation remained hopeless, the men resigned themselves to dying on this remote island.

Unwilling to take the necessary precautions against scurvy (by drinking hot blood from the reindeer and eating wild celery, or scurvy grass), Feodor Weregin soon fell victim to the disease, and for six years he suffered dreadfully and died only weeks before his three companions were rescued (see Scurvy, chapter 7).

In August 1749 another Russian ship came into sight. The captain had intended to spend the winter on West Spitzbergen, but contrary winds and currents had forced him to the coast of East Spitzbergen, near which lay the island of Little Broun, where the three castaways were marooned. The ship took the overjoyed men, together with their vast hoard of animal hides and fat and the few tools that had insured their survival, and landed them at the Russian port of Arkhangelsk six weeks later. Alexis Himkof's wife was present when the vessel arrived, but, ironically, so overcome was she by his miraculous appearance that she fell into the icy water and only narrowly escaped drowning.

The three survivors were surprisingly healthy considering their long ordeal, and for some time they enjoyed a measure of fame before disappearing into obscurity.

POON LIM

"Alone, alone, all, all alone
Alone on a wide wide sea!
And never a saint took pity on
My soul in agony."
SAMUEL TAYLOR COLERIDGE, "THE RIME OF THE ANCIENT MARINER"

Of all the accounts throughout history of this man or that woman surviving the elements—of being trapped deep in a mine because of a rockfall or being isolated on a mountain in bad weather because of injury or lost in the desert with dwindling supplies—by far the greater number of survival situations have to do with being at sea. War, of course, is a prolific source of survival stories afloat, especially World War II, which managed to infiltrate virtually every navigable stretch of ocean worldwide.

The following account of Poon Lim comes from an incident in that war. It is not the most dramatic story in the literature, nor by far the most harrowing. There has been many a peacetime ocean voyage that ended in people's being cast onto the broad bosom of the ocean with little more than a brief prayer and even fainter hope. Tony Bullimore's ordeal in the Southern Ocean in early 1997 is one such; his story is told in *Saved*. Also, the gripping tale told by Dougal Robertson in his book *Survive the Savage Sea* has become well known.

But the story of Poon Lim, the steward from Hong Kong, although it lacks the ordeal of being hounded and harried by bad weather, crippling thirst, and hungry sharks—seemingly in equal proportions—manifests a curious dignity and quiet courage not always encountered in tales of survival. It reveals that rare human quality that Ernest Hemingway probably had in mind when he defined courage—"guts" was the word he used—as "grace under pressure."

Poon Lim possessed that kind of grace. He was a twenty-five-year-old steward on the *Ben Lomond* at the time it was torpedoed in the North Atlantic on November 23, 1943, about 750 miles off the Azores. Most of the rest of the crew died in the explosion or drowned soon afterward; Poon Lim makes no mention of seeing survivors. He struggled to get away from the sinking ship, found a raft, and pulled himself onto it.

The flat lifesaving raft was about 6 feet square, with a short post at each corner and two containers of survival rations secured onboard, one at each end. One held water and the other some food such as chocolate, barley sugar, biscuits, fish paste, and a bottle of lime juice (see Scurvy, chapter 7, for the importance of lime juice at sea). There were also some yellow-smoke flares and a Very pistol with cartridges.

Poon Lim had lost his shoes and shirt (possibly from the force of the torpedo blast); his trousers and sweatshirt were soaked with oil, so he washed them in seawater and spread them out to dry, then he lay down to sleep. Cold rain woke him up during the night, and he discovered that his trousers had been washed overboard. In the morning he inspected his provisions and decided to ration himself to two biscuits per meal, or six for the day. Fortunately, Poon Lim was in good physical condition when his ship sank; he had played a lot of basketball and soccer in his youth and had been a keen fisherman.

After many days of adjusting himself to his new situation, he realized he would have to try to catch fish if he were to survive. He found a length of rope on the raft, unraveled its strands, and spun himself a finer line more suited to fishing. The hook was a problem: there were none in the survival kit, an odd omission, one would have thought; however, he managed to fashion one from the fastener on one of the smoke flares. For bait he made a paste from biscuit crumbs but, as one might have expected, the sea immediately washed it off. Barnacles had begun to grow beneath the raft, however, so he broke them open and used the flesh inside as bait. Poon Lim caught a small fish, which he then cut up as bait for something larger; this proved to be a shark of about ten pounds, the entrails and blood of which he used for enticing some whiting closer to the raft; he was able to scoop a few of them onboard. In the manner of his home village he split the fish open and strung them up to dry ("[I] felt very pleased with myself," he said later).

His darkest day came when a steamer hove close enough that he fired off his Very lights and smoke flares, certain that the vessel would see the curious conflagration in midocean and come over to investigate. Nothing of the kind. The steamer carried on as before. Poon Lim, anxious to make the best of things, began singing. By means of dredging up from memory all the Chinese opera he could remember, meanwhile encouraging a gaggle of trusting fish to edge even closer to the raft and thence into his less than tender mercies, he managed to cheer himself.

Occasional rain kept him from undue thirst, and in humid weather he used the water can as a condenser. After about a hundred days of this very literally hand-to-mouth existence, the fish disappeared and his supplies of dried fish were consumed. Things did not look good ("I struck a bad patch," he said). On the fifth day of this foodless period some seabirds settled on the raft. Poon Lim waited until nightfall, whereupon he caught thirteen of them but, presumably to save the shipwrecked mariner from the evils of superstition, Providence promptly permitted one of them to escape. Some of them he ate raw on the spot, some he kept for bait.

By trial and error he discovered the art of dibbling (a method of catching small fry, still used on the far north coast of Australia); one simply jigs the baited hook up and down until the fish become sufficiently enraged that they investigate the annoyance, whereupon one of them—one hopes—gets too close to the action. Poon Lim was now so hungry that he ate these fish raw.

The raft had long been in the grip of a current moving westward; Poon Lim noticed that the water had changed color and that some of the fish were very similar to salmon. In fact he was approaching the mouth of the Amazon River. As if to underline all the more his now increasingly desperate straits, a number of ships passed at a distance, then disappeared over the horizon.

A few days later an airplane suddenly appeared overhead, dropped a flare, then flew off again. A Brazilian fishing vessel then bore down on Poon Lim and took him back to its home port. (Another account states that Poon Lim greeted his rescuers with a humble bow.) He was able to walk ashore, but his trials on the raft had weakened him, and he spent a month and a half recovering in hospital. "I was a bit thin when I landed," he said, "but I never had a headache the whole time I was on the raft and I had slept soundly every night."

When he was repatriated home by way of England, Poon Lim was summoned by King George VI to tell his story. The Chinese steward from Hong Kong had been at sea on the raft, alone, for 133 days.

HERBERT KABAT

"I would define true courage to be a perfect sensibility of the measure of danger, and a mental willingness to endure it."
GENERAL WILLIAM TECUMSEH SHERMAN, *MEMOIRS*

In October 1942 the destroyer USS *Duncan* was sunk by a Japanese ship near Guadalcanal in the western Pacific, off the northeast coast of Queensland, Australia. The senior surviving officer, Lieutenant Herbert Kabat, organized the abandon-ship procedure. Only two lifeboats were available because the others had been previously used to help another sinking ship, so the remaining crew made do with life jackets. Kabat tied a couple of cans together that, with his life jacket, would keep him afloat; he was certain planes and rescue ships would find them in the morning.

At dawn he saw a large formation of aircraft overhead, and as he contemplated his inevitable rescue he suddenly became aware of a sharp scratching sensation in his left foot. When he lifted it out of the water he was horrified to discover that it was pouring blood. A shark had bitten him.

Kabat naturally enough panicked; he had no weapons and he knew that sharks were very dangerous once they scented blood. The five-foot-long shark charged once more, but Kabat warded it off with a great deal of kicking and splashing. As it moved in for its next pass Kabat raised his right arm high into the air and thumped it repeatedly across the head.

The shark swam out of range. Kabat then noticed that he had lost part of his left hand to the ravening creature. Realizing that he had to conserve his energy, he floated quietly, all the while watching the shark for its next approach. Fifteen minutes later it attacked again. This time the open jaws had almost seized him when Kabat brought his fist down on the beast's nose and eyes again and again. Nevertheless, the shark managed to remove some flesh from his left arm. More attacks followed. The big toe of his left foot was dangling, a piece of his right heel was gone, and his left elbow, hand, and calf had been torn open. Kabat's greatest fear was that the shark would attack him from below: against this angle of approach he had no defense. American warplanes passed overhead and some of the pilots waved to him; meanwhile, the shark swung in for another pass and once more Kabat lost some portion of his body as he hammered away with fists and feet.

Then he saw a ship, and as he kept a wary eye out for the shark he waved and screamed frantically for help. To his great joy a lifeboat pulled away from the destroyer and began picking up other survivors in the area, and then, unbelievably, only two hundred yards from him, it turned back to the ship, was hoisted aboard, and the vessel disappeared over the horizon. No one had seen him.

In his excitement and subsequent anguish Kabat had forgotten the shark; now it attacked yet again, and this time his left thigh was slashed to the bone. He had by now lost a lot of blood and was feeling groggy. Kabat contemplated finishing it all by slipping off his life jacket and quietly drowning, but his willpower kept him going. He was determined to defeat the shark, one way or another.

The shark rushed him once more just as an airplane began diving over his position; when he had beaten the animal off he saw a destroyer steaming toward him. Someone waved at him from the ship's deck. As he paddled furiously toward the vessel he heard a savage zing! near his head; five or six sailors were shooting at the shark, which alarmed Kabat greatly because it was still very close to him. He was convinced that a bullet would finish him off before the shark did, but within minutes a boat had pulled away from the destroyer and Kabat was quickly hauled over the side.

Herb Kabat spent fourteen months being treated for his many wounds. He lost no limbs, but there were deep scars on his body testifying to his terrifying ordeal.

"I was," he said, "amazingly fortunate."

JOHN CALDWELL

"There's nothing half so sweet in life
As love's young dream."

THOMAS MOORE, "LOVE'S YOUNG DREAM"

John Caldwell, an American sailor in the U.S. merchant marine at the end of World War II in 1945 finds himself ashore in Sydney, Australia, where he meets a Melbourner named Mary. Events faithfully follow the path laid down by Providence, and within a short time they are married. But three days later, because of the postwar demand for competent seamen, John is obliged to join a ship for New Guinea and Borneo, a round-trip of six weeks. Neither Mary nor John knows that it will be more than eighteen months before they see each other again.

On the return voyage from New Guinea Caldwell's ship is diverted at the last moment to Manila, and in short order he is steaming across the Pacific to the Panama Canal, the West Indies, Honolulu, Yokohama, and Shanghai, back to Panama, on to England, and finally to New York City, where he is allowed to sign off. This is where Caldwell's troubles really begin.

Because of the urgent needs of the Allied shipping nations, there is nothing available to take him back across the Pacific to Australia. He hitchhikes to San

Francisco: nothing. New Orleans is the same, so he jumps a ship to Panama, where he attempts to stow away aboard a Dutch vessel bound for Indonesia, but he is soon caught and thrown into jail in Panama. After a short period of imprisonment Caldwell buys a 29-foot yacht called *Pagan* so as to "sail the bloody thing back to Australia," and by the end of May 1946 he is ready to leave on his transpacific voyage home to his beloved Mary.

The interesting thing about all of this is that Caldwell knows absolutely nothing about sailboats. Despite his experience in the merchant marine he is entirely ignorant of the art of sailing and the mysteries of navigation, but he has found a book called *How to Sail*, and Mary is still waiting for him in Australia, so off he goes.

Caldwell's departure from the yacht club in Panama would have had even a landlubber shrieking with despair. With the engine running and the tiller firmly lashed he goes forward to clear away the anchor and chain from the foredeck, but somehow he manages to fall overboard with the anchor still in his hand. Happily, he remembers to let go of the iron weight that is taking him to the bottom of the harbor, regains the surface, and begins swimming after *Pagan*, which is now motoring vigorously around the harbor on a dragging anchor.

The boat hits a mooring, sheers toward the swimmer, and Caldwell is able to haul himself aboard—and then, with the motor still running, the anchor down, and the tiller lashed as before, *he hoists sail in the freshening breeze* . . . and promptly runs aground. As the writer Negley Farson sadly admits in his introduction to Caldwell's book *Desperate Voyage*, this is "one of the most fool expeditions ever undertaken." And all for Mary.

Caldwell teaches himself seamanship and navigation by sailing around the Galápagos Islands, about a thousand miles out into the Pacific, from where he writes Mary that he is "on a small ship with a small crew headed your way"; then he sets out on his long voyage to faraway Australia, accompanied only by two kittens. He does not say how he manages to post the letter.

Five months after leaving Panama *Pagan* is dismasted in a hurricane. Caldwell sets up a jury rig and, weak from starvation and thirst, he shapes a course for Samoa, where he can have repairs done. But his navigation gear has been lost or damaged in the storm and he misses his landfall. For thirty-six more days he struggles on across the wastes of the western Pacific. There is a foot of water in the cabin from a leak that he can't find, and his drinking water is now almost gone.

He manages to catch a triggerfish (a foul dish at the best of times), fries it in hair oil, and eats every bit of the creature: flesh, skin, scales, head, and bones. Caldwell then makes a bow, attaches some nails to strips of pine for arrows, and after many hours of weary effort kills a seabird, which he promptly tears apart and wolfs down even before it has finished kicking. Hunger so crucifies him that he boils up a shoe, cuts the leather into strips, greases them with hair oil (with which he seems well sup-plied), and swallows the lot. Eventually he drinks the remaining hair oil when his water supply runs out.

Finally, Caldwell is wrecked on the island of Thuvatha in the Fiji group, six thousand miles out of Panama and still two thousand miles from his beloved Mary, who is still patiently waiting for her husband to return, from exactly where she knows not. Gradually he is nursed back to health by the islanders, and many weeks later he is taken off by a trading schooner and landed in Suva on Viti Levu (Fiji). With much difficulty Caldwell makes his way to Sydney by military aircraft. Mary is waiting by the airstrip and in his own words "a thousand dreams had come true . . . my trials on the sea were far away."

Almost sixty years on, the Caldwell family operates a sailing resort on Palm Is-land in the Grenadines Saint Vincent group in the West Indies. John Caldwell himself died in 1999. Life on Palm Island, as John once told me, was magic. He had hoped to salvage the wreck of *Pagan*, which still lies half-buried on the beach on Thuvatha, in memory of "the joys of youth and adventure."

TROPIC ISLAND HELL

"Why do you look on us, and shake your head,
And call us—orphans, wretches, cast-aways?"
WILLIAM SHAKESPEARE, *RICHARD III*

To be marooned is not quite the same as to be cast away, although the practical difference between the two is negligible. When marooned, one is deliberately set ashore by one's fellows on an isolated island as a punishment for some perceived transgression against the common weal (see Robinson Crusoe, above; for an acci-dental marooning see Icebound by North, above). But to be cast away, one need only be shipwrecked on some reef, island, promontory, or some such—an entirely involuntary affair brought about usually by bad weather, bad management, or per-haps bad luck.

In either case one may fetch up on what the public commonly calls a "desert island," which doubtless should be "deserted island." There was once a popular BBC radio program, *Desert Island Disks*, in which well-known figures were asked to name phonograph records they would like to have with them if fate were to deliver them to the aforesaid "desert island." No mention was ever made of the need for electric-ity, but no matter—"desert isles" were known for being models of paradise where all one's wishes were realized (see, for example, Hy Brasil, chapter 2).

A modern example of a group's being cast away is the case of the seventeen men from Tonga who in 1962 ran onto the Minerva Reef in the South Pacific during heavy weather; the story of their survival during the next three months, their terrible hardships, and the deaths that followed before the survivors were finally rescued is superbly told by New Zealand writer Olaf Ruhen in *Minerva Reef* (1973).

This entry on castaways, however, concerns neither severe hardship nor death; neither does longed-for rescue figure in its telling (at least, not the kind of rescue one usually associates with the aftermath of being shipwrecked). Rather, it is about a man and a woman who—very inadvisedly, as the reader quickly discovers—agree to spend a year together on an island in Torres Strait (between Australia's Cape York Peninsula and Papua New Guinea) in a sort of man-and-wife arrangement wherein they would pursue the supposed delights of a Robinson Crusoe existence on a deserted tropical island, entirely free of outside assistance.

As Simmons points out, Lucy Irvine and her companion were not true castaways but rather beachcombers, which is an entirely voluntary activity (although the genuine beachcomber engages in as little activity as possible beyond that required to beg sustenance from others or somehow derive it from the environment). Irvine met her companion Gerald Kingsland in London (both are English) through a classified advertisement. Kingsland, who saw himself as a writer, wanted a "wife" to spend a year with him on a tropical island, it being his notion—and hers—that such a life would be paradise. Alas! as Kahlil Gibran reminds us, the fear of hell is hell itself (while the longing for paradise is paradise itself). Reality and fantasy hover severally somewhere between the two.

Irvine, born in 1956, had by the early 1980s already experienced many of the ups and downs of life (the title of her autobiographical *Runaway*, 1986, gives some insight into her character). Kingsland, born in 1930, was twice her age (and also twice married) when they took up residence on Tuin Island in 1982. Both agreed to breathe life into their joint fantasy by setting up in self-sufficiency on some isolated and uninhabited island and to heck with the rest of the world. For a while, anyway.

Their practical resources did not, sad to relate, match their private rhapsodies. They had only enough money for two one-way air tickets from England to Australia, and consequently precious little was left for supplies and other practical necessities. In addition, the Australian government was tiresomely prudish about the whole thing, being most unwilling to allow an unmarried couple to set up house on one of its precious islands; a marriage—even one of convenience—was insisted upon before they were permitted to establish domestic relations on Tuin. This "marriage" probably contributed to the emotional difficulties that eventually, in conjunction with some of the daunting problems of living on a flat, dry, and damned hot island in the Arafura Sea some 10 degrees south of the Equator, led to the rift that made social relations between these two laughably mismatched people a veritable hell.

For some time their home was a two-person tent, and given the understanding that Kingsland had come to (with himself, be it noted), it was only natural for him to assume that living in such close quarters would be sufficient enticement for Irvine happily to assume the conjugal duties of a proper wife.

Irvine, for her part, was having none of it. While she gradually immersed herself in the business of exploring the island, a place she later came to love, and searching for fruits, coconuts, and fish (an exhausting task that took up most of each day, as little sustenance was available), Kingsland fumed at her intransigence and fretted over her lengthy absences from camp; in fact, according to Irvine he angrily assumed that she had found a lover out in the bush somewhere, and he railed at her for being unfeeling and "unfair."

Luckily, native islanders from nearby Badu Island visited them some months after Irvine and Kingsland had set up camp. These people were friendly and helpful (and, indeed, they later proved to be a godsend to Kingsland). They built a proper shelter for the "castaways," showed them the art of weaving palm leaves, and regularly brought them food and water. When the health of the two Crusoes began to deteriorate, the natives brought two nurses over to attend to them, and indeed this outside medical and nutritional support allowed them to remain where they were.

When the islanders discovered that Kingsland was something of a genius with motors, his immediate future was settled. There was a steady and increasing demand for his services as mechanic for the fishing-boat motors and other mechanical devices that they used in their daily lives. Kingsland's skills became important to them all. He changed from being, in Irvine's view, a rude, obnoxious, boorish man to one who was "lively, resourceful, confident."

When Irvine returned to England after her year on Tuin, Kingsland remained behind, happily becoming absorbed in the local community. He had, it seems, found peace and paradise at last. One wonders what happened to the restless Irvine. Her story of their island adventure, *Castaway* (1983), became a best seller and was the basis of a film.

14

AT ODDS WITH THE LAW

For some reason, the profession of Pirate (see below) has long had a fascination for young men (and, let it be said, for some young women, as we shall see). Certainly the life of a pirate seemed to hold forth the heady prospect of a kind of personal freedom (although from what, one is not sure, because very few pirates ever found themselves free of the vigorous attentions of the authorities). One might indeed sail the balmy seas of the Spanish Main (see chapter 7) or plow across great oceans, but in truth it was a dreary dreadful life—a life, to paraphrase the philosopher Thomas Hobbes, that was poor, nasty, brutish, and short.

Pirates and their near cousins Buccaneers (see below) led a life that was, at the very best of times, dull, boring, and replete with hunger, quarrels, and disease, with the promise that sooner or later it would all come to a grisly end at the end of a rope or on the point of a sword.

Very few pirates ever made good. Tales abound of vast treasure buried on some forgotten coral strand, but for the most part these are only stories, conjured up by those who would a-roving go. The only gold that most pirates garnered for themselves was in the form of a pair of earrings, and even then they had to throw one of them into the sea before embarking on their chosen profession.

It was indeed a wearisome life.

PIRATES

"If I were to advertise in my paper tomorrow
for fifty young men to go on a pirate ship
and for five men to work on my farm,
there would be five hundred applications for the
situation on the pirate ship and not one for the farm."
HORACE GREELEY

The Latin *pirata* is from the Greek *peirates*, *peirao*, attempt, assault—thus *pirate*, synonym for vice, cruelty and plunder, one who marauds and pillages. Horace Greeley was no doubt right: for some curious reason the life of the pirate has always held some sort of appeal for the romantically minded. The reality of such a life, however, was an altogether different matter.

Piracy can be said to have begun the moment man first set out to sea on a log raft or in a dugout canoe, for others would soon follow suit, and if there is one quality that people of all nations share, it is avarice, the longing to possess what another person owns. What easier and quicker means of obtaining satisfaction than by relieving the other fellow of his burden—if necessary, by force? So was piracy born.

No sea was free of this plague; wherever trade flourished, so did piracy. The ancient Greeks complained bitterly of pirates in the Mediterranean, especially the Barbary corsairs (from Berber, the people who occupied much of the coast of north Africa), as no doubt the Phoenicians did before them, and so even further back into prehistory. As a young man, Gaius Julius Caesar (about 100–44 B.C.) was sailing to Rhodes to study law when his vessel was boarded by "Sea Peoples" and he was kidnapped and held for ransom. His friends paid the money but Caesar immediately put together some warships and pursued the pirates; when he captured them he crucified every man jack of them, as he had earlier warned them he would do.

In 67 B.C. Pompey (106–48 B.C., Roman general and a member of the first triumvirate) cleared the region of the pirate menace by dividing the entire Mediterranean and the Black Sea into a number of sectors; then he placed a commander in charge of each and attacked all but one of the sectors, the remaining untouched area being Cilicia at the east end of the Mediterranean, north of Cyprus. The pirates not captured elsewhere eventually fled to Cilicia, where Pompey's concentrated fleet soon routed them out and finished them off.

But for the next two thousand years the western and eastern Atlantic, the English Channel, the North Sea, the Indian Ocean, the Caribbean, the Gulf of Mexico, the west coast of South America, not to mention the extensive coastal waters of Africa and Asia—all experienced the havoc and misery of pirates intent on securing plunder in any form (including of course securing their fellow man, who for a handsome profit would be sold off into slavery if the market was handy). And pirates are still with us, as the waters around Singapore, Borneo, Indonesia, and the South China Sea bear witness.

The Golden Age of piracy (if the term can be used in this context) spanned the late seventeenth and early eighteenth centuries, when the West Indies and the Indian Ocean became infested with these sea rovers (from the Dutch *zee roover*, one who practiced piracy, hence "to rove"). This is the period that springs to mind when we talk of pirates. When "Charles Johnson" (very likely Daniel Defoe, 1660–1731) published his *General History of the Robberies and Murders of the Most Notorious Pyrates*, the public learned a great deal about that particular trade. Robert Louis Stevenson (1850–1894) used this book as one of his sources for *Treasure Island* (1883), thereby delivering generations of schoolboys into the exciting but somewhat sanitized hands and habits of Pew the blind pirate, Long John Silver the buccaneer, Ben Gunn the marooned pirate, Jim Hawkins the narrator, and others. It is a romantic and adventurous yarn, but that's all it is; the real story of piracy is altogether different.

The Jolly Roger, the so-called skull and crossbones, a white skull on a black background with crossed thigh bones beneath it, is now an almost comical term for the flag that pirates were said to fly; in any case, it is difficult to authenticate. Kemp tells us that "there is no evidence that such a flag was ever flown by a pirate ship at sea"; yet *Pirates* shows just such a flag used by Captain Edward England, who pillaged the Caribbean and then the Eastern Seas (the Indian Ocean). Most pirate captains designed their own lurid flags, intended to strike terror into the hearts and minds of their prospective victims. It is true, though, that skeletons—whole or selected parts thereof—were a constant feature. The most common pirate symbol was simply a plain black flag flown on the mainmast head.

Why were pirate flags named Jolly Roger? There are two theories about its source. One is that the term comes from the French *joli rouge* (French for "pretty red," blood?), perhaps a reference to the red banner that the early privateers used to fly. The other possible explanation is that from the sixteenth to the nineteenth centuries *roger* was a colloquialism for sexual intercourse. Roger was a common name given to bulls; and "roger" was long a slang term for the penis. "To bull" or "to roger" was to lie with a woman, often vigorously, and usually in the nature of rape. It is well known from the literature of the period that pirates treated the women they captured with violence and contempt: females were usually rogered at the rail, then thrown overboard. Clearly, the romance of pirating was of a sadly blighted sort.

It has long been a feature of stories about the "brethren of the coast" that prisoners who failed to please were made to "walk the plank." A plank was run out over the side of the vessel, and the victim, arms usually bound, was encouraged by a cutlass to step out along it and then off the end to a watery grave. But along with the familiar piratical trappings of a raucous parrot perched atop the shoulder of a leering layabout sporting a villainous eye patch and noisily swigging from a jug of rum spiked with gunpowder, we can safely consign the notion of "walking the plank" to where it properly belongs: the heady realm of imagination. There is nothing in the accounts written about—and by—pirates indicating that prisoners were ever dispatched by this means. True, they were routinely tossed over the side to the sharks if no further use could be found for them or hanged or run through with a sword, set on fire, pelted with broken bottles, and so on; but "walking the plank" remains some writer's fevered flight of fancy.

On the other hand, marooning was a common way of dealing with malcontents among the crew. This is the custom of putting someone ashore in an isolated place that offered no opportunity for escape. The person put ashore became a castaway, that much-loved figure of romantic literature of the sea (for an accidental marooning, see Icebound by North, chapter 13).

One of the most famous examples of an intentional marooning concerned the Scot Alexander Selkirk (1676–1721), who was left, at his own request—he had quarreled violently with the captain—on the island of Más a Tierra in the South Pacific, about 400 miles west of Chile. He was put ashore in 1705 and rescued in 1709. The incident formed the basis of Daniel Defoe's famous novel, *Robinson Crusoe* (see a brief account of Crusoe's experiences in chapter 13).

Selkirk was lucky. Many a man punished by marooning simply died of thirst or starvation, often after losing his mind on some remote and barren cay or islet. Or he could be cast adrift on a raft in midocean with a few necessities of life or with none at all (see HMS *Bounty* Mutiny, chapter 9, for an account of seafarers cast adrift and the extraordinary seamanship that saved them).

The true story of pirates is a sorry tale of long periods of heat, boredom, and dreadful food, relieved only by bouts of drinking (when liquor was available) and the very occasional but always ferocious descent on some vessel unlucky enough to be in the same area. A pirate's future was universally precarious, his end invariably grim. The world's seafaring nations had long declared war on the "brethren of the coast"; navies scoured the seas to seek them out, to put the renegade ship to the torch and the pirate to the sword or the hempen rope (or, if he were convicted in England, secured to a stake at Execution Dock in Wapping, East London, there to be slowly and satisfactorily drowned by the rising tide, his corpse later hung high in chains as a suitable warning to others—see, for example, William Kidd, below).

Privateers were men and ships licensed by nations at war with each other, their purpose being to act as a kind of naval auxiliary, with an official commission—known as the letter of marque—to attack and loot enemy shipping. Many a privateer was in fact manned by pirates who, for the nonce, saw an opportunity for some legal plundering, and many an otherwise honest privateersman, dazzled by the sometimes unbelievable loot that was available, turned pirate for an opportunity to further improve his station in life.

These privateers were often known as men who had gone "on the account"; that is, they could supposedly account for themselves if questioned by the authorities, in that they could show an official "license," the letter of marque. Some of them were merely buccaneers, a term that later encompassed true pirates and their ilk but that earlier referred to the chiefly French and British woodsmen living on the Spanish-held island of Hispaniola in the Caribbean, trying to earn a living of sorts by curing wild beef and pork and selling it to passing ships (see Buccaneers, below). When the Spanish set about suppressing this trade and ousting these squatters from the island, the buccaneers naturally took umbrage at such treatment and sought redress by harassing Spanish shipping. This quickly (and naturally) degenerated into piracy because of their habit of plundering Spanish vessels in times of peace as well as in times of war. Thus the buccaneer was increasingly seen as an out-and-out pirate and dealt with as such. No longer could he plead that he was "on the account," as he might have been able to do when privateering; thus the distinction between privateers and pirates was always difficult to establish, and many a judge didn't trouble himself with the exercise—he ordered the man hanged forthwith.

BUCCANEERS

"I enlisted with a boucanier *named Kulescher . . .*
and with him I led the rough life of the boucaniers. *"*
LOUIS ADHÉMAR TIMOTHÉE LE GOLIF, *THE MEMOIRS OF A BUCCANEER*

The Spanish entered the West Indies both as pirates and as colonizers. Christopher Columbus had founded the town of Isabela on the island of Hispaniola on his second voyage in 1493, establishing the first permanent European settlement in the Caribbean. (Hispaniola, earlier Santo Domingo, is the former name of the Dominican Republic, which takes up the eastern two-thirds of the island, Haiti being in the western third.)

This invasion by the Spanish gave rise to the buccaneer. In the early days of piracy in the Caribbean, privateers were known as buccaneers, from the French *boucaner*, derived from the Carib Indian *boucan*, meaning to meat cured by by placing it on a *barbacoa* (see below) and smoking it over a greenwood fire. They gained this name from their widespread but illicit trade in boucan meat.

These buccaneers were men who, although not quite pirates, still had tendencies that were decidedly piratical. For some two hundred years they infested this area, plying their trade in boucan and other valuable commodities, such as rum and salt. They were made up mostly of Protestant sea rovers from England, France, and the Netherlands, all of whom haunted the Caribbean in the seventeenth century, united in their intense opposition to the Catholic Spanish, the colonial masters of the New World.

By the early seventeenth century, Hispaniola had become almost completely depopulated of native peoples as a result of Spain's oppressive colonial policy. The island then became overrun by immense herds of wild cattle and pigs, and consequently it was an excellent place for the provisioning of ships by smugglers and similar kinds of sea rovers. The few natives remaining on the island were skilled in the art of the boucan, that is, preserving animal flesh without using salt, which was both very scarce and costly.

Because the Spaniards refused to recognize the right of other nations to establish settlements or even conduct trade in the Caribbean, outsiders who tried to do so found themselves constantly at war with the Spanish authorities. From these conditions arose the buccaneer, outlawed trader in smoked or cured meat, occasionally a planter, and frequently a sailor and hunter—a roving, bold, unscrupulous and often savage entrepreneur of the Spanish Main (see On the Spanish Main, chapter 7).

Buccaneering developed into a profitable venture, so much so that in 1630 a fortified storehouse for boucan meat was built by the English and French on the small island of Tortuga. The Spaniards attacked this settlement in 1641 and massacred everyone they found. Open war was then declared against the Spanish, and when in 1655 the English navy captured the island of Jamaica from Spain, the by now very large bands of buccaneers had ample secure harbors as bases for their operations against their common enemy.

However, the fierce and unscrupulous behavior of the Welshman Henry Morgan, leader of the buccaneers against the Spanish settlements throughout the Caribbean, caused a public outcry in England. Morgan was eventually captured, transported home, and clapped into the Tower of London. Ironically, years later he was freed, appointed lieutenant governor of Jamaica, and entrusted with the task of suppressing the very buccaneers he had once so successfully led in their pillaging of the West Indies.

The outbreak of war between England and France in 1689 doomed the bond of unity that had kept the buccaneers of these two nations together in their schemes of aggression against a common foe. It was inevitable that they should take opposite sides in this war. Their power and influence gradually dissipated as they turned on each other, and within a few years the whole Caribbean fell under the influence of government control exercised by European nations anxious to establish a foothold in the region.

The terms *buccaneer* and *filibuster* are usually regarded as synonymous, but while the former is more commonly used, the French *boucanier* and *flibustier* describe activities quite distinct from one another, though both means of earning a living were often followed by the same man at different times ("filibuster" is from the Dutch *vrijbuiter* and the Spanish *filibustero*, "freebooter," one who obtained his plunder or booty "for free"). Many of the cattle-hunting *boucaniers* subsequently took to the sea to hunt the Spaniards, and similarly many of the *flibustiers* took to hunting the cattle; some men did both, hence the confusion between these two words.

Spain had secured to herself all of the rich new countries bordering the Caribbean Sea. Although nominally at peace with the other maritime nations of Europe—France, the Netherlands, and England—she rigidly excluded those nations from establishing colonies in her area of influence. Moreover, these colonies were supposed to deal only with Spain in a trade that was usually extortionate, and to enforce this monopoly the Spanish authorities ruthlessly seized any vessel caught within the Spanish Main. Such a state of affairs could not be tolerated by Dutch, English, and French shipmasters, who were aware of the wealth that awaited them in the Spanish colonies. While their governments conveniently looked the other way, these sea captains set out to capture Spanish ships, sink any that might interfere, and bring back great wealth from New Spain.

Ultimately such men became generally known as buccaneers, but one from Holland was first called a *vrijbuiter*, literally a "free robber" or corsair. This, because of its sound and its resemblance to the English words *free* and *booty*, became *freebooter*. In French, however, it became first *fribustier* and later *flibustier*. These French forms were rarely used by English writers, who favored *freebooter* or *buccaneer* in writing about the pirates of the sixteenth and seventeenth centuries.

Buccaneer and *barbecue* have an interesting connection with each other, springing as they do from the same period of bloody history of piracy and freebooting in the Caribbean of the old, wild, seafaring days. *Barbecue* came into English from the Spanish *barboka* or *barbacoa*, which in turn derived from the Haitian *barbacoa*, a framework of sticks over a fire on which meat could be grilled. The word originated with the Tupi tribe in Brazil and was then taken to Haiti by early travelers in the region—goldminers, slavers, soldiers of fortune, and such. A definition of a *barbacoa* was given by a Frenchman who had been in Brazil in 1557: "a wooden gridiron, whereon the cannibals broile pieces of men and other flesh."

The importance of the buccaneers in history lies in the fact that they opened the eyes of the world to, on the one hand, the hopeless corruption of the Spanish colonial government of that era; and, on the other, the enormous possibilities of commerce if conducted along the right lines. From these factors arose the West Indian possessions controlled by the Netherlands, England, and France, whose collective colonial influence is still seen in this region.

EARRINGS FOR CUTTHROATS

"A man who is not afraid of the sea will soon be drowned."
J. M. SYNGE, *THE ARAN ISLANDS*

Males today who wear an earring—or perhaps indeed a jeweler's whole tray of rings not to mention chains artfully threaded through the nose, ears, eyebrows, etc.—are frequently looked on askance as if their virility were in doubt. The odd thing about this is that gold earrings were once commonly worn by pirates of old, and one would have been reckless indeed to bring into question the virility of any of these adventurers.

It was once the custom of seafarers to place a golden earring in the ear, and the practice was still common at the turn of the twentieth century. When a young man embarked on his first voyage he quickly learned the rules, regulations, and lore of the sea and the custom that required him to take out an insurance policy against drowning. This was achieved by buying two gold earrings (either ashore or from some other seaman on board, but the rings had to be real gold), cutting one of the rings through and spreading it slightly, then carefully piercing one's ear with it. A witness was then required to accompany the young man to the port side of the vessel (the left side), where the uncut ring was cast into the deeps with the words "Protect me, O Davy Jones," while at the same time the cut ring was threaded into the man's ear again and closed (see Davy Jones's Locker, chapter 19).

The idea was, of course, that Mr. Jones would be suitably mollified with a gift of gold (the custom strikes the observer as a kind of wedding; see Launching a Ship, chapter 19), and indeed the policy worked, because many a salt lived to a ripe old age, thereby proving—if ever proof were needed—that it was entirely possible to prevail upon Davy Jones for protection from drowning (and from those unfortunate enough to have drowned anyway, there seems to be no record of complaints).

HENRY EVERY

"A pirate is an enemy to all humanity."

PIRATA EST HOSTIS HUMANI GENERIS—LEGAL MAXIM

Henry Every (1655–1697; also known as John Avery and Long Ben Avery) was an English sea captain, probably the most famously villainous pirate within his own lifetime. His exploits were the subject of a very popular play in London, *The Successful Pirate*. Daniel Defoe, in his endless mania for matters piratical, seized on him as the prototype of the eponymous *Captain Singleton* (1720).

Every learned honest seamanship as a boy, but by the age of forty he had become a pirate. His early occupations are vague, but he is known to have been a slaver on the Guinea coast of Africa in the 1690s. In 1694 he instigated a mutiny as first mate on the *Charles II* out of Bristol, bound for the Caribbean. Every took command, renamed the ship the *Fancy*, and set out for the Eastern Seas (the western part of the Indian Ocean, off the east coast of Africa) to make his base in Madagascar, whence for the next two years or so he plundered and ravaged everything in sight.

In 1695 he was at the entrance to the Red Sea, hoping to waylay the Mogul treasure ships that regularly sailed to India. Here he intercepted the *Fateh Mohamed*, a vessel of considerable size but dubious courage, acting as escort to the treasure ship *Gang-i-Sawai*. When Every boarded the *Fateh Mohamed* she yielded some £50,000 in gold and silver (a considerable fortune in those times) whereupon, much encouraged, Every and his men chased the bigger and better armed *Gang-i-Sawai*.

Astonishingly—considering that the Mogul ship carried 62 guns, some five hundred musketeers, and about six hundred passengers—Every finally overcame their resistance. His reward, for the loss of about twenty of the *Fancy*'s crew, was more than £325,000 in gold and silver and a plentiful supply of girls and women. The passengers were immediately tortured for their valuables. The men were then butchered and the females met the fate that was usual at the hands of pirates.

Flushed with prodigal wealth, Every then turned his hand to slavery again. He filled his ship with a human cargo and set out for the Bahamas, where Nicholas Trott, the English governor, when suitably bribed, welcomed them one and all; but he could not issue pardons. Every changed his name to Benjamin Bridgeman and, with most of his men, sailed back to Ireland and England—a desperate ploy, as was soon evident. When shiftless seamen lavish gold and silver on simple country folk in payment for their necessaries, someone is bound to wonder. Certainly the local sheriffs did. Eventually some twenty-four of Every's men were arrested on suspicion of piracy; six were hanged and the others found themselves in the Caribbean colonies again, this time as convict laborers.

But Every evaded capture, and to all intents and purposes he also evaded the subsequent scrutiny of history. He simply disappeared into obscurity. Whether he lived comfortably on the proceeds of his crimes or eked out a miserable existence as a pauper, we do not know; but he left a legacy that excited the envy and admiration of seamen throughout Britain. For years afterward the Eastern Seas were thick with pirate vessels anxious to extract their share from the great Mogul fleet.

WILLIAM KIDD

"Said Cap'n Morgan to Cap'n Kidd:
'Remember the grand times, Cap'n, when
The Jolly Roger flapped on the tropic breeze,
And we were the terrors of the Spanish Main?' "
JOHN HEATH-STUBBS, "GREAT BLACK-BACKED GULLS"

Captain William Kidd (1645?–1701) might well have uttered these words himself as he ascended the gallows on the mud flats by the Thames at Wapping; this was his sentence, not for piracy, but for murdering another man (what's more, the rope broke and Kidd had to be strung up once again). He had a fearful reputation as a cutthroat of the worst kind, but in fact he shed less blood and captured fewer prizes than almost any other outlaw of the seas. Nevertheless, Captain Kidd has today a fearful reputation as a bloodthirsty piratical rogue of the deepest dye. Nothing could be further from the truth; his downfall lay in his choice of friends rather than in his choice of trade.

Kidd was born (probably in Greenock, Scotland) in about 1645. We know little of the first forty-five years of his life, but by the early 1690s he was a wealthy and respected merchant sea captain living in New York, with an elegant brick house on the corner of Pearl and Hanover Streets in Manhattan and other properties elsewhere. He had married and was known to be devoted to his wife and children.

When piracy in the Eastern Seas (Indian Ocean) was rampant, and preying on the great Mogul's fleets to India had reached unendurable proportions, the governor of New York and New England, Lord Bellomont, at the urging of Colonel Robert Livingston, a prominent New Yorker, offered Kidd (both Kidd and Bellomont were in London at the time) a privateering commission to wipe out these pirates and thereby participate in a share of captured booty. The proposed (and anonymous) financial backers for the expedition were England's most powerful men: the first lord of the admiralty, the secretary of state, the lord keeper of the great seal, and the master general of ordnance. Even the king, William III, was to put up £3,000, although this aspect of the deal fell through.

William III then issued Kidd two commissions that would supposedly give an official cast to the central matter, which was the private money-making venture directed against pirates. One was a letter of marque, which licensed him as the commander of a privately owned vessel to operate against France, England's enemy at the time, whereby he could legally capture and confiscate their vessels and all goods in them. The other was a commission giving Kidd the authority to pursue and seize certain pirates, together with their ships and everything in them.

Kidd was now faced with a number of problems. He had to sell off some of his interest in the affair to raise his share of the expenses, and he knew that there were very few French pirates in the Eastern Seas, and in any case his crew was not really up to an engagement with such cutthroats. But his main problem was the knowledge that the line between privateering with a letter of marque and piracy was very thin indeed, not often readily recognized by courts of law; and privateer crews had a habit of turning to piracy if treasure was not soon forthcoming.

The venture got off to a bad start. When his specially built ship *Adventure Galley* was launched on the Thames in December 1695, with a selected crew of reliable men on board, Kidd omitted to salute a British navy ship at Greenwich. The navy thereupon responded with a warning shot, at which point Kidd's crew—who were aloft at the sails—derisively showed and slapped their backsides. Naturally, navy tradition took umbrage at this ill-mannered display, and Kidd's ship was immediately boarded by a press gang that carried off his best men, replacing them with navy rejects. One doesn't insult the British navy with impunity.

The incident highlighted the poor judgment, coupled with bad luck, that dogged Kidd for the rest of his days, of which precious few remained to him anyway. When his ship was in the vicinity of Cape Town, Kidd somehow offended the commodore of a navy squadron, who then threatened him with the press gang, forcing Kidd to sneak away at night. At Madagascar he antagonized an East India Company ship over the issue of who had the right to fly the navy pennant. The merchant ship offered to board him forthwith, so once again our erstwhile privateer, by now apparently quite puffed up with self-importance, fled to the Comoros Islands north and west of Madagascar, there to careen his vessel and clean her hull. Here fifty of his men very soon died of disease.

More than a year had passed since Kidd's ship had been launched; so far no one had garnered even one penny from the project. It is not surprising that some of the crew began agitating to turn pirate themselves.

In August 1697 the *Adventure Galley* sailed north, and Kidd planted himself at the mouth of the Red Sea to await choice pickings: if French, well and good, because the letter of marque protected him; if not, then they were far enough from home so that no one would ever know or care—or so Kidd's crew urged.

The fleet out of Mocha (a port in what is now southwestern Yemen, famous for its Arabian coffee) appeared on the horizon. Kidd slipped in among it, but he was noticed by the English ship *Sceptre*, a well-armed East Indiaman. The *Adventure Galley* fired a broadside at a large Moorish ship, the *Sceptre* fired at the *Adventure*

Galley, and Kidd turned tail and ran. With such a poor showing on his part, it is no wonder that his crew exerted great pressure on him to join in with their plans. And this is exactly what he did.

A few weeks later Kidd boarded a Moorish vessel off the west coast of India, whence he took as plunder a bale of coffee, a sack of pepper, the English captain (as pilot), and the Portuguese mate (as interpreter). The news of this outrage spread from port to port, and from that moment on Kidd was regarded by the local authorities as pirate proper rather than pirate chaser. Three months later, again off the Indian coast, Kidd boarded the *Loyal Captain*, a merchantman, although he knew it was an English vessel; after inspecting her papers he let her go on her way. His crew was furious. A row broke out between Kidd and his gunner, William Moore. Words were exchanged. Kidd smashed a heavy bucket against Moore's head, and the man died the next day.

Things had now come to a sorry pass. At the end of November Kidd took another Moorish vessel by inducing it to show French colors; it proved to be sailing under the protection of a French pass, but this was meaningless. Kidd had committed an act of piracy. He sold its cargo ashore, dividing the money with his men (clearly against the provisions of his English contract), and set out for more prizes. He took traders as fast as they appeared, but all he gained for his troubles was what you might find as stock in any general store across India: rice, beeswax, butter, bales of cloth, and so on.

Then Kidd captured the *Quedah Merchant*, a fat prize from Bengal (but, unknown to Kidd, sailing under the command of an Englishman, a Captain Wright, with a French pass). Using his French flag ruse yet again he took its cargo, sold some of it ashore, and set off for Madagascar with the officers of the *Quedah Merchant* on board the *Adventure Galley* and his captured ships following in convoy. When eventually Kidd discovered the captain's nationality he was greatly alarmed and wanted to hand the *Quedah Merchant* back to Wright, but Kidd's crew refused.

They reached Madagascar (on April Fool's Day 1698) and anchored at Saint Mary's Island. Across the harbor lay the *Mocha Frigate*, a pirate ship, Captain Robert Culliford. Kidd suddenly remembered his commission and was all for taking her, but his crew yet again howled him down. They divided their spoils, then all but thirteen of them deserted to Culliford, but not before sacking Kidd's prize vessels of their guns and supplies and threatening Kidd himself with an early death. Finally Kidd realized that his only option was to promise Culliford that he, Kidd, would do him no harm in the future. Culliford left for a cruise and Kidd set about preparing the *Quedah Merchant* for the voyage home.

Meanwhile, the British East India Company in Surat complained to the Lords Justice in England about Kidd's depredations. His erstwhile backers, now the center of a thrilling political scandal of national proportions, set the navy on him and ordered the governors of the American colonies to arrest and prosecute Kidd if he showed his face there.

So when in April 1699 Kidd dropped anchor at Anguilla in the Caribbean, he discovered to his horror that the whole world was aching to have his head. He thereupon decided to go to Boston where, he believed, Governor Bellomont would give him necessary protection. Kidd bought a fast trader, the *Antonio*, transferred his treasure to its hold, left the *Quedah Merchant*—now dangerously slow and too easily recognized and outsailed—at Hispaniola (the island today comprising Haiti and the Dominican Republic), and set out.

Nearly three years after leaving England, and with most of his original crew either dead or gone a-pirating, Kidd had arrived home an outlaw, his life at stake. He anchored in Oyster Bay, on the north side of Long Island and made contact with the governor, who masterfully induced Kidd to enter Boston. Kidd meanwhile disposed of his loot in various places (particularly on Gardiner's Island at the eastern end of Long Island, where it was reputed that some £14,000 of treasure was dug up in the nineteenth century), and was briefly reunited with his wife and two daughters.

Kidd's interview with the governor was unsatisfactory. He handed over to Bellomont the French passes that he believed exonerated him from any charge of piracy, but a month later, on July 2, 1699, Kidd was arrested and clapped in irons by the man who had been the chief mover behind the voyage in the first place, Bellomont, who now referred to Kidd as a "monster." Nearly all his dispersed treasure was then tracked down and shipped to England.

Six months later Kidd followed, secured below in a navy ship. He was thrown into the infamous Newgate prison and left to rot there for more than a year: old, sick, alone, and losing his mind. In March 1701 he appeared before the House of Commons, where by insisting on his innocence (he was relying on the two French passes from the Eastern Seas being offered in his defense) he lost the chance to implicate his political backers.

By the time he appeared for trial at the Old Bailey he had been in prison nearly two years. His French passes had disappeared (the one for the *Quedah Merchant* resurfaced in the British public record office in 1920, more than two centuries too late). What's more, the £50 that the admiralty had set aside for Kidd's defense counsel was delayed, and his counsel did not appear until an hour or so before the case began. After two years of waiting for his trial Kidd had only one brief consultation with his counsel on the very morning that things got under way.

Things were not looking good. Court rules required that only Kidd himself could cross-examine witnesses, and Kidd being what he was—politically clumsy, truculent, and naively convinced of his innocence—it was clear that only a miracle could save him. The jury speedily convicted him of the murder of the gunner, William Moore. He and others were even more smartly found guilty of piracy. The sentence of death was a foregone conclusion, which must have brought a profound sense of relief to milords who had earlier urged this silly man on his profoundly ill-advised cruise against pirates.

After Kidd died on the gallows at Wapping (the second attempt now being successful), his body was taken down and covered in tar, then bound with chains and the skull enclosed in a metal cage so the bones would stay in place after the flesh had rotted away, and the whole reeking ensemble was hoisted at Tilbury Point as a suitable warning to others sailing in and out of the Thames. Apparently it remained visible for many years.

Mrs. Kidd and family took his death hard, but eighteen months later Mrs. Kidd married a prominent politician and spent a long and comfortable life in New Jersey. Kidd's two daughters married and had families of their own. Governor Bellomont died in Boston three months before Kidd met his end. As for the captain's legendary treasure, it is most unlikely ever to be found because there isn't any left, several of his convicted shipmates—having been pardoned and set free—immediately hieing themselves off to the American colonies to recover their buried spoils.

EDWARD TEACH ("BLACKBEARD")

"Pirates, when they chance to cross each other's crossbones,
the first hail is—'How many skulls?' "
HERMAN MELVILLE, *MOBY-DICK*

Melville might well have been speaking of Edward Teach, or Tach, Tatch, Tash, Thatch, Thach. (Daniel Defoe, English novelist, essayist, and indefatigable chronicler of pirates, claimed that Teach's real name was Drummond.)

This was the notorious pirate widely known as Blackbeard from his habit of wearing only black clothing and interlacing his full and ragged beard with black ribbons and lengths of smoking slow match (pieces of cord or rope soaked in saltpeter, used for firing off cannon, the "great guns"). Across his shoulders were slung bandoliers, each fitted with a number of pistols.

Blackbeard was in truth a fierce and awesome spectacle, but he was not the greatest of the many pirates who infested the West Indies. That honor (if honor is not too jarring a word in this context) belongs to Bartholomew Roberts (1682–1722), who captured four hundred or more ships and established a remarkable discipline over his crews. Neither was Blackbeard the most successful in terms of booty, Roberts and Henry Every surpassing him in this. But Blackbeard was certainly the best known and one of the most widely feared, and with his uncouth manners and outlandish appearance and his face perpetually wreathed in smoke through which his fierce black eyes glared balefully, he gave every appearance of being verily a fiend from hell, a notion that he took great care to cultivate.

Blackbeard was a prodigious drinker, as were virtually all pirates. (On the other hand, Roberts drank nothing stronger than tea, went to bed early, observed the Sabbath strictly, and never gambled—truly, a paragon of virtue in any society, piratical or no.) Blackbeard was impetuous and violent, extremely competitive, and an inveterate bigamist who delighted in sharing his "wife" of the moment with his crew (his last bride, a girl of barely sixteen, was forced to entertain half a dozen or so men after spending her first night with Blackbeard).

As with most pirates, we know very little about the background of Drummond/Blackbeard. Defoe says he was born in Bristol (the date is unknown), others claim that it was Jamaica or Virginia; it is also thought that Blackbeard learned his seamanship on board a British privateer in the West Indies during the War of the Spanish Succession (1702–13, or 1701–14), and that when peace was declared he turned to piracy, as did many a seaman after a spell of privateering. He was tall, very strong, and much admired for his bravery: all in all, well fitted to be a leader among the piratical riffraff that numbered in the tens of thousands worldwide in the early eighteenth century.

In 1716 Blackbeard captured a large French merchant ship in the Caribbean and renamed her *Queen Anne's Revenge*. Then he sailed out of Nassau and into history. It is a measure of his grotesque personality that although he died fighting little more than eighteen months later, he is still remembered as perhaps the most bloodcurdling piratical figure in all history. During most of 1718 he was the scourge of shipping up and down the Atlantic coast of the American colonies, ably helped by the governor of North Carolina, Charles Eden. This worthy granted Blackbeard a pardon under one of the Acts of Grace promulgated from time to time by the British government in a bid to rid the seas of pirates, as they were bad for trade. And trade was the clue to Eden's tolerance. North Carolina had virtually no export commerce at all.

Thus armed with Eden's pardon (granted in return for a share of any spoils that Blackbeard might secure), our pirate ravaged whatever colonial shipping fell into his hands. He blockaded Charleston, the capital of South Carolina, and seized a number of vessels, along with a member of the governor's council and his four-year-old son, both of whom he offered to kill forthwith if the governor failed to give the pirate ship much-needed medical supplies (Blackbeard and his men were likely suffering from raging syphilis).

Eighteen months after leaving Nassau, Blackbeard had taken some twenty prizes between Virginia to the north and Honduras far to the south. He now had a fleet of four pirate ships and some four hundred men under his command and access to Governor Eden in North Carolina for refits and provisioning. It must be said that the good folk of North Carolina detested the rum-sodden pirates, who every time they landed there behaved with impeccable loutishness. It was the trade they cared for, not the traders.

Still Eden stayed his hand. Perhaps, like Macbeth in his bloodied rampage for the throne of Scotland, the governor was so steeped in avarice that to repent now would have been as tedious as to carry on. But others were less considerate. The governor of Virginia, one Alexander Spotswood, was by now thoroughly fed up with Blackbeard's depredations up and down the American seaboard, and he determined to be rid of the man once and for all, with or without the approval of his legislative council. It turned out to be with neither their approval nor their knowledge.

Spotswood had learned that Blackbeard was planning to set up a fortified camp on the Ocracoke Inlet in North Carolina. Caring not a fig for the diplomatic niceties involved, and with the help of the captains of the warships HMS *Pearl* and HMS *Lyme*, both then on the James River in Virginia, Spotswood secretly supplied the navy crews with two shallow-draft sloops.

On November 17, 1718, Lieutenant Robert Maynard and Midshipman Baker set sail, each in command of a sloop. Four days later they entered Ocracoke Inlet, anchored at dusk, and waited for daylight. Blackbeard, by means of information from the corrupt collector of customs in North Carolina, had been expecting them, but, oddly, he did nothing that night to prepare for the battle that was inevitable the next day. Instead he and his men drank and caroused the night away.

Battle was joined at daylight. Both sloops grounded on sandbars as they tried to work closer to the pirate vessel. Blackbeard slipped off down the channel and Baker tried to block him, whereupon the pirate ship swung and fired a heavy broadside, killing Baker and several of his crew. Maynard and his men closed the distance with their oars and the pirate fired again, with great effect. Then Blackbeard came alongside and boarded the sloop with his howling men; the two crews crashed together head on, and a fierce hand-to-hand fight erupted.

In the thick of it all Maynard and Blackbeard found themselves face to face. Both fired their huge pistols point-blank at each other. Probably because of his heavy drinking the previous night and earlier that very morning, Blackbeard's hand was somewhat less than steady and his shot missed. It cost him his life, though not immediately. Maynard's ball plowed into Blackbeard's body, but the man didn't seem to be aware of it. He had now worked himself up into his customary rage. Roaring wildly and bellowing oaths and curses, he smashed Maynard's cutlass in two with his own and was about to finish off the hapless lieutenant when one of Maynard's men luckily appeared from behind and ran his sword through Blackbeard's throat. Still the giant figure fought and howled, while spouting great gouts of blood. While navy men hacked and shot at him he pulled out another pistol, cocked and aimed it, then slowly toppled forward and fell to the deck, dead. It was all over.

Ten navy men were killed, along with ten renegades; all nine surviving pirates were wounded. Maynard had Blackbeard's head cut off and the much-mutilated body heaved overboard into Ocracoke Inlet; the head was then hung from the bowsprit of his sloop, and they set out for Virginia. The trophy must have made an interesting, not to say arresting, sight as the ship sailed into port.

Blackbeard's demise marked the end of piracy along the Atlantic seaboard. Unaccountably, Governor Eden survived the resulting scandal, but justice of another sort was served three years later when he died of yellow fever.

ANNE BONNY

*"There is no fouler fiend than a woman
when her mind is bent to evil."*

HOMER, THE *ODYSSEY*

Whether Anne Bonny was naturally evil is perhaps debatable, but it is certainly true that she and Mary Read, another notorious female pirate, were formidable companions in battle.

Irish-born Anne was the illegitimate child of a respectable lawyer, William Cormac, and Peg Brennan, the family maid (her dates of birth and death are unknown but she was actively "on the account" as a pirate when captured in 1720; see Pirates, above, for the term "on the account"). Cormac immediately decamped to Charleston in South Carolina with mother and child, where he set up as a merchant and became very wealthy.

Either because of her father's fortune or because of her spirited temperament, Anne at the age of thirteen or fourteen was much sought after as a marriage prospect. She was known for her hot temper, having even at that tender age given a thrashing to a young fellow who had tried to rape her. She later married badly, falling in with a worthless layabout named James Bonny, who carried her off to New Providence, the notorious pirates' den in the Bahamas. When James offered to inform on the pirates to the new governor, Woodes Rogers (himself a one-time privateer), Anne left him in disgust and attached herself to one John ("Calico Jack") Rackham (or Rackam), a pirate who had (temporarily) set aside his trade in return for a royal pardon (he had earned his nickname because of the colorful cotton clothes he affected).

When her husband James complained to the governor about the liaison, Anne and Calico Jack made plans to go "on the account" together, Rackham being already widely known for his infatuation with the woman. She and Rackham then took command of a fast merchant vessel, and the two became a serious nuisance in the Caribbean, plundering everything in sight. On one occasion they were pressing experienced seamen from a Dutch ship (see The Press Gang, chapter 9) when Anne took a fancy to a handsome Dutch fellow, but sadly he proved to be neither Dutch nor fellow, being instead one Mary Read, a lady with her own interesting background (see below). Rackham then took Mary Read into his own crew, whereupon she fell in love with a young sailor. But the romance was given little time to blossom.

In October 1720 a British navy sloop chanced upon Rackham's ship in Jamaica waters. Calico Jack and most of his men were too desperately drunk to fight and they hid below, but Anne Bonny and Mary Read fell to with a will and put up a terrifying show against the navy, but it was little use. Those not already killed were captured, put to trial as pirates, and sentenced to death. Both Anne and Mary—being pregnant—pleaded their bellies, which automatically earned a stay of execution until each woman's child was delivered. However, Mary Read died of fever before she was brought to term. What happened to Anne Bonny is unknown. Like Henry Every, she simply disappeared into the mists of time.

MARY READ

"Of all the wild beasts on land or sea, the wildest is woman."
MENANDER, *SUPPOSITIO*

Had Menander lived two thousand years later and met Mary Read and Anne Bonny he would have had no reason to change his mind about "woman." When Mary and Anne fought side by side to take a merchantman or mounted a desperate rearguard action against a British navy sloop in 1720, no one would have thought them other than fierce oath-spitting bloodcurdling rum-guzzling outlaws of the sea; they both were indeed quite as wild as pirates come.

Mary Read was born presumably in England (the year of her birth is not known); she died in jail in Jamaica in 1720 after a life of considerable excitement and adventure. Like Anne Bonny, Mary was of illegitimate birth; her mother concealed this from her relatives by dressing the girl in the clothes of one of her sons who had recently died. This suited Mary's temperament, and for most of the rest of her life she wore only men's clothing. She entered the British navy as a cabin boy on board a man-o'-war, then became a soldier in Flanders during the War of the Spanish Succession (1702–13).

Eventually she wearied of the military life, despite her love of fighting; in any case, she had fallen in love with her tent mate, a Flemish youth who persuaded her to marry him (one marvels at the stratagems she must have devised in order to conceal her gender from the thousands of other soldiers around her). They set up a tavern in the Netherlands, Mary for the first time in her life dressing as a woman. Sadly, her husband soon died of a fever, and Mary—by now accustomed to making her way in the world dressed as a man—joined a Dutch ship and sailed off to the Caribbean. Here she met John ("Calico Jack") Rackham and Anne Bonny when she was summarily pressed into service on board their pirate ship. Mary agreed to sign pirate articles (and, unknown to her at the time, thereupon sealed her own fate).

15

SEA FANCIES

I n 1789, Hester Thrale-Piozzi recounted the story of how one fine day she took a young woman of twenty-seven—who until then had spent her whole life entirely in London—on a visit to the coast of Sussex. When asked if she were surprised at the sight of the sea, the girl replied:

"It is a fine sight, to be sure, but . . ."

"But what? Are you disappointed?"

"No, not disappointed, but it is not what I expected when I saw the ocean."

"Tell me, what did you expect to see?"

"I expected," the girl said, *"to see a great deal of water."*

Alas! that is exactly what all sailors see: not only a great deal of water, but very frequently too much of it for too long. Yet if you go to sea for your livelihood, you may see a great many things other than just "a great deal of water."

As every sailor of old knew (and this may well also apply to many modern-day mariners), there are things to be encountered at sea that would have confounded the philosophy of *Hamlet*'s Horatio (see, for example, chapter 17, Sea Monsters, for a discussion of this perennial topic).

MERMAIDS

"Since once I sat upon a promontory,
And heard a mermaid on a dolphin's back
Uttering such dulcet and harmonious breath
That the rude sea grew civil at her song,
And certain stars shot madly from their spheres
To hear the sea-maid's music."

WILLIAM SHAKESPEARE, *A MIDSUMMER NIGHT'S DREAM*

Thus speaks Oberon, Shakespeare's king of the fairies, echoing a belief that has stood seafarers in good stead for thousands of years, mermaids having a history that goes far back into antiquity. Their description reflects the wish list of sailors since time immemorial: "Voluptuously naked from waist up, fish-scaled and fish-tailed from waist down, forever combing her tresses on some sea-rock." (Gordon imparts the interesting and apposite information that "the Greek and Roman words for comb, *kteis* and *pecten*, are also terms for the female pudenda".) Mermaids commonly come equipped with gold or green hair, comb and mirror ready to hand (which would seem to support Fool's remark in *King Lear*: "For there was never yet fair woman but she made mouths in a glass").

Bearing in mind the aversion seafarers traditionally harbor for women at sea, it is curious that such workaday men should be so beguiled by a scaly half-human marine enchantress whose female charms are dubious indeed (see Kemp and German for illustrations of some particularly unalluring mermaids). Perhaps it is simply that sailors who wax lyrical about these creatures have been at sea too long. Be that as it may, worldwide evidence attests to the frequent appearance of marine creatures called "maids of the sea" and to a universal male yearning for their company, despite oft-repeated warnings that mermaids spell nothing but doom for seafarers reckless enough to pursue them, with death by shipwreck and drowning their inevitable lot.

Historically the mermaid descends from undines (Latin *unda*, wave), water sprites. In European folklore an undine could attain human form if she married a mortal; and if she had a child by him, she would thereby acquire a soul, bringing with it the privilege of suffering the pains and pangs that are the common lot of humanity.

Other sea-dwelling creatures with a recognizable human form have established themselves in myth. The Irish believed that the Formorians were a race of demons who lived in the sea, and the ancient Babylonians told of Oannes, the fish-tailed god who rose from the sea each day in order to give humanity the benefit of his accumulated wisdom (a pleasing contrast with Aegir, the Norse god of the sea, whose wife Ran used a net to snare sailors from passing ships and thereby drown them).

The ancient Syrians worshipped a sea deity called Atargatis, a half-and-half fish-woman whose power came from the moon, the controller of tides. In one hand she held a musical instrument called a plectum (not to be confused with a plectrum) and in the other a moon-shaped mirror in which she could admire her beauty. She attracted the devotion of seafarers because she had the power of abating storms and calming rough seas with her sweet singing, a skill that has been one of the enduring characteristics of mermaids throughout history.

The mermaid of lore was long the pelagic symbol of Aphrodite, the Greek goddess of love and beauty (and, of course, desire), who emerged from the ocean, that vast womb of nature that Gordon reminds us is "the source of all biological desire, tempting the weak spirit" (*Aphro-geneia*, the "foam-born"). It is not surprising, therefore, that the early Christian church earnestly taught that the mermaid-siren complex represented nothing more than the devil's endless tempting of man with the lure of lust, to be resisted at all costs if one valued one's compact with God and subsequent reward in heaven.

Plato, who lived about four hundred years before the birth of Christ, declared that the sirens' song was "music of the spheres . . . an irresistible heavenly harmony" (see also Sirens, below, and The *Odyssey*, chapter 4, for an account of sirens in antiquity).

In fact, the song of sirens and mermaids was nothing but the cries of seals, dugongs (sea cows), and manatees, which to seafarers far from home and perhaps bored witless by the tedium and hardships of a long voyage, appeared to be sea creatures of bewitching human female aspect, whose plaintive call as they dived promised Fiddler's Green (see chapter 19) itself to the overimaginative sailor. As Kemp remarks, "The attitude of the female dugong when suckling her young takes on a particularly human appearance."

Belief in mermaids has been so strong throughout human history that enterprising individuals have not scrupled to display specimens to an ever-gullible public. In 1825 a mermaid from Japan was exhibited at Bartholomew's Fair in London; but as Kemp informs us, close inspection revealed that the creature was in fact a woman with the skin of a large fish artfully stitched to her skin (one marvels at her stoic endurance of the discomfort so occasioned).

SIRENS

"Next, where the sirens dwell, you plough the seas."
ALEXANDER POPE, "HOMER'S *ODYSSEY*"

Sirens are the mythical half-woman, half-bird creatures famous in classical literature for their supposed ability to so bewitch men with the sweetness of their song that the listeners forgot everything else and died of hunger. The sirens encountered in Homer's *Odyssey* were the virgin daughters of Phorcys, a Greek sea god who was the putative grandfather of the Hesperides, and Scylla (for accounts of the charms of this particular femme fatale, see Scylla and Charybdis, chapter 1, and The *Odyssey*, chapter 4).

According to Homer, the sirens lived on an island situated somewhere between Aeaea, the home of Circe, and the lair of Scylla the sea monster, who earlier had suffered the wrath of Circe by becoming enamored of the handsome fisherman Glaucus, with whom Circe herself became infatuated when he approached her for a love potion to secure the affections of Scylla. Circe thereupon regularized the situation by turning Scylla into a hideous monster, anchoring her in the Straits of Messina, and then applying her own not inconsiderable wiles to Glaucus.

The sirens, who earlier had lived in a forest by a riverbank, had issued a challenge to the Muses to engage in a singing duel, but the former lost the encounter, whereupon they abandoned their forest habitat and took up quarters on the rocky coast of southern Italy. Here they spent their days roosting and singing endlessly so as to infatuate all who might be sailing past; the bones of those men who had already succumbed to these oratorical enticements lay in large moldering heaps nearby.

It is here that Odysseus meets them. Circe had warned Odysseus of the dangers posed by these creatures, urging him to stop the ears of his men with wax after first ordering them to bind him to the mast of his ship. This permitted his men to concentrate on rowing, at the same time making them immune to the frantic entreaties of Odysseus, who desired above all things to stop and go ashore to meet the creatures who were making such sweet song.

Jason and the Argonauts were protected from this danger by the singing of Orpheus, whose voice was said to be so sweet and compelling that even inanimate things were moved to tears by it (see The Argonauts, chapter 4). It had been ordained that the sirens were to live only until someone proved immune to their song. At the successful passing of Odysseus, therefore, or because of the compelling countermusic of Orpheus aboard Jason's vessel the *Argo*, the sirens were immediately changed into rocks, and the hazard hitherto posed to sailors was removed forever.

The Lorelei

"Oh, train me not, sweet mermaid, with thy note,
To drown me in thy sister's flood of tears:
Sing, siren, to thyself, and I will dote."

WILLIAM SHAKESPEARE, *THE COMEDY OF ERRORS*

Lorelei is the name of a steep rock about 430 feet high, situated on the right bank of the River Rhine, not far from the town of Saint Goar. It is noted for two things: its remarkable ability to reflect an echo and its being the traditional haunt of a siren (see Sirens, above) who could lure to destruction anyone on the river.

The story goes that a maiden, despairing because of a faithless lover, climbed the rock and threw herself to her death in the river below, where she became a siren and exacted retribution of all passing fishermen, in the meantime combing her hair with a golden comb (an attribute of all mermaids) and singing wild songs. Men who chanced to see her immediately lost their reason and their sight, while those within hearing distance of her beautiful voice were thereby condemned to forsake their ordinary lives and spend eternity in her company.

The name is from the Old High German *Lur*, and the Modern German *lauern*, to lurk, be on the watch for; an opera called *Die Lorelei* was written by Max Bruch and produced in 1864.

Selkies

"The Irishman is an imaginative being.
He lives on an island in a damp climate,
and contiguous to the melancholy ocean."

BENJAMIN DISRAELI, "SPEECH ON AYLESBURY HUSTINGS"

A selkie in Celtic mythology is a seal that has taken human form for some reason. This is, however, not just any seal: seals with this power of transformation were the "fallen angels," the children of Eithne and her female court, drowned by Eithne's father Balor, one of the less likable of the Irish pantheon of personalities. (*Selkie*, *selky*, *silky*, are sixteenth-century variants of the Scottish *selch*, a seal, especially the imaginary sea creature that resembles a seal in the water but is able to assume human form on land.)

Selkies were said to inhabit the Caithness region in northern Scotland. When a female of these seal people decides to take human form, she takes care to hide her seal skin as carefully as possible, since if a man found it he could demand that the selkie marry him (though why he might want to do so is not clear). If the now married selkie finds her seal skin again, she immediately leaves her home, husband, and children and heads for the sea. Children with webbed hands or feet were, naturally enough, said to be selkie-born.

HALCYON DAYS

"Thus lovely halcyons dive into the main."

WILLIAM COWPER, "TABLE TALK"

Colloquially, halcyon days are times of peace and prosperity. The expression comes from *halcyon*, the Greek word for kingfisher (*hals*, the sea, and *kuo*, to brood on). It was believed by the ancients that in mid-December, just before the coming of winter proper, the kingfisher laid her eggs on a nest of seaweed that she built on the surface of the sea, wherein she incubated her eggs for about fourteen days (some accounts have it that the eggs incubated in seven days and the mother then fed her young for the next seven). During this period the sea was said to remain calm and unruffled so as to allow the incubation to proceed uninterrupted. Seamen traditionally look forward to the kingfisher's season of breeding because it heralds the onset of good weather—that is, the end of winter will not be far off.

The story is told of Ceyx, who married Alcyone, the daughter of Aeolus, king of Thessaly, a region in the eastern part of modern-day Greece. Ceyx and Alcyone were so happy together that they compared themselves to Zeus and his wife Hera. Naturally enough, Zeus took umbrage at their hubris (overweening pride, which in the Greek way of things always led to the comeuppance known as nemesis), and he forthwith changed the happy couple into kingfishers. As a mark of his fairness, however, Zeus commanded the sea to remain calm during the period in which Alcyone incubated her eggs.

Ovid (?43 B.C.–A.D. ?17, Roman poet) gives a different account of this legend. According to him, Ceyx was shipwrecked and drowned while on his way to consult an oracle. Alcyone, knowing the havoc winds could wreak at sea, had done all she could to dissuade Ceyx from his purpose, but to no avail. When her husband failed to return, Alcyone, all unknowing of his death, spent many days in prayer for him. Touched by Alcyone's devotion to her husband, Juno (the Roman equivalent of Hera) sent a message to Somnus, the god of sleep, asking him to send a dream to Alcyone that would reveal to her the truth about Ceyx. Somnus charged his son Morpheus with the task. Morpheus then assumed the form of Ceyx and appeared to Alcyone in her sleep, to tell her that he was, alas, dead.

In the morning Alcyone went down to the headland where she had earlier said farewell to Ceyx and, finding his body by the shore, she cast herself into the sea to be with him, whereupon the gods—exercising a compassion for which they were not universally known—changed both into kingfishers.

> *Every year there are seven days on end when the sea lies still and calm;*
> *no breath of wind stirs the waters. These are the days when Alcyone*
> *broods over her nest floating on the sea. After the young birds are*
> *hatched the charm is broken; but each winter these days of perfect*

peace come, and they are called after her, Alcyon, or, more commonly, Halcyon days.

KING CANUTE

"Kings are happy in many things, but mainly in this: that they can do and say whatever they please."

SOPHOCLES, *ANTIGONE*

Canute (Canute the Great, King Canute of ocean-tide fame, about 994–1035, sometimes rendered as *Cnut, Cnutr, Knut*) was the Danish king of England 1016–35, Denmark 1018–35, and Norway 1028–35.

When he was about fifteen, Canute sailed for England with his father, Sweyn Forkbeard, king of Denmark, and took part in the battles that resulted in the conquest of Wessex. On the death of his father in 1014, Canute was forced to flee England on the return of King Ethelred, who had earlier been exiled to Normandy. Canute was back a year later with a large Danish fleet, and after a number of battles he secured the rule of central England (Mercia) and the north. Both Ethelred and his son Edmund died in 1016, and Canute was then elected king of all England.

Canute proved himself to be a wise and astute administrator. Because he was a foreign ruler, he was able to remain apart from the tribal jealousies that normally govern mankind's behavior toward their fellow men. At the same time he was careful to align himself with the church, and he even took the unusual step of banishing his Danish wife and two sons to Denmark and then marrying Emma, the widow of King Ethelred. Canute pursued a policy that favored the English rather than the Danish; he sent home all his soldiers and ships, keeping only a bodyguard of Danish sailors, and he took care to restore churches and confer benefactions.

Canute was in fact probably the wisest and most effective king Saxon England had yet experienced. Naturally, he attracted a good deal of flattery, not to mention sycophantic attention, from some of his courtiers and followers, and it is these blandishments that lie behind the incident that has fixed Canute in popular imagination—though his actions have been seriously misinterpreted by many.

The following story was first told by Henry of Huntington (about 1084–1155), archdeacon of Huntington, in his *Historia Anglorum* (about 1130) and was picked up by Raphael Holinshed (died about 1580), that indefatigable chronicler of English history, both true and fabled.

Huntington wrote that by way of rebuking his courtiers for their incessant and unavailing flattery, Canute one day betook himself down to the edge of the sea, planted his throne on the wet shingle, sat down, and waited for the tide to come in. When eventually the tide duly followed its instincts, Canute hurled commands and imprecations at the sea, ordering it to stay its movement and obey the lawful commands of the nation's king. The tide, for its part, was soon lapping halfway up the royal shanks. Wisely, the king retreated.

Presumably he left it to his watching court to make what deductions they might (possibly not a prudent move on his part). What is clear is that popular history has made its own conclusions, the essence being that Canute was indulging a monumental delusion of grandeur in trying to assert his kingly authority over the powers of nature—trying to prevent the tide from coming in.

Nothing could be further from the truth. The wily old monarch was simply demonstrating to his retinue of sycophants the futility of attempting certain things: on his part, commanding the tide to be still; on theirs, expecting their king to be swayed by flattery.

16

MYTH AND MYSTERY

E ver since sailors first went to sea and returned from places no landlubber ever heard of, mariners have been telling their hoary tales of adventure—ghost ships sailing the tempest-tossed ocean, astonishing people in far-off lands, and sights far stranger than fiction. Seamen often misunderstood or misreported most of what they saw, and in any case their yarns would change a little with each retelling until over the course of time these stories often became regarded as tall tales of fantasy and much-embroidered truth.

The *Flying Dutchman*, for example, has been sailing the seven seas for well over three hundred years now, and the versions of her particular history are many: with every telling her rig changes, as do her color, size, and shape, not to mention the identity of the captain. On the other hand, the details concerning the *Mary Celeste*, one of the more notable of seagoing mysteries, are too well established be changed; what happened to her, and why, is a conundrum that has never been solved.

Seagoing mysteries abound in the literature, as we would expect, given the profoundly superstitious nature of seafarers the world over.

FABLED ATLANTIS

"Atlantis represents Man's dreams of the perfect world . . .
a vision of eternal summer and plenty, even . . . of immortality."
MICHAEL HARDWICK AND MOLLIE HARDWICK,
THE WORLD'S GREATEST SEA MYSTERIES

Atlantis (also Atalantis, Atlantica) is the subject of one of the enduring legends of the sea that, like the so-called Bermuda Triangle (see below), has powerfully exercised the mind and imagination of the scholarly and the credulous alike. The name Atlantis is from the Greek Atlantikos, the adjectival form of Atlas, a son of Poseidon.

Atlantis was a legendary island or continent in the Atlantic Ocean, itself known earlier as the Straits of Gades, the old name for Cádiz. Atlantis was situated somewhere west of the Pillars of Hercules—that is, the Rock of Gibraltar and, directly opposite on the northern coast of Africa in present-day Morocco, the fortress of Ceuta.

Plato wrote in *Timaeus* in about 350 B.C. that Egyptian priests had told Solon (Athenian statesman, about 638–558 B.C., one of the Seven Sages of Greece) that there was a far-off land called Atlantis that was larger than Asia Minor and Libya (Africa) combined, and that beyond it lay an archipelago of lesser islands. In a companion volume Plato had Critias (his maternal great-grandfather) present a history of this ideal commonwealth; its civilization was said to be advanced, and it was thought to have flourished some nine thousand years before the rise of the Greeks. Critias related that soon after the armies of Atlantis had overrun most of western Europe (except for Athens, which withstood the assault by forging an alliance with the other Greeks), it was destroyed by an earthquake and then obliterated by the subsequent upheaval of the sea. Nothing remained except a series of shoals on the seabed.

In the words of Critias (who even as he introduced the story to his listeners commented to them that his tale "was a strange one"):

At a later time there were earthquakes and floods of extraordinary
violence, and in a single dreadful day and night all your fighting
men were swallowed up by the earth, and the island of Atlantis was
similarly swallowed up by the sea and vanished.

Critias explained that when the gods divided up the earth, Poseidon was given Atlantis. He then fathered by Cleito five sets of twins who subsequently ruled the island; the first of these kings was a twin named Atlas, from whose name the island and the surrounding ocean took their identity. The land was well favored, with all kinds of wild and domestic animals, ample timber for building, and an abundance of foodstuffs; Plato (by way of Critias) even added elephants, which thereby bestowed on the island a splendidly exotic flavor. The temple consecrated to Poseidon and Cleito, some 200 meters long and 100 meters wide, was a veritable treasure house of gold, silver, and ivory (among other things, the statue of Poseidon inside the temple reached to the roof and was made of solid gold); in like manner the king's palace was astonishing to behold.

There is much more to whet the appetite of anyone anxious to emigrate to what was obviously a Utopia beyond the wildest dreams of the most jaded suburbanite: moats and canals (with bridges over all), hot and cold springs, richly decorated public buildings, gardens, gymnasia, temples, a track for horse races, and dockyards and ships. The island proper was surrounded by a large moat, then further ring islands, and finally a city wall covered in bronze beyond which a wide canal led to the sea. In this connection one cannot help thinking of El Dorado, the fabulous city of gold once believed to exist somewhere on the Amazon River in South America. Also, it is interesting that Sir Thomas More's Utopia was an island.

How much of the legend of Atlantis is due to Plato's imagination and to what extent it is based on records that no longer exist is impossible to determine; what is clear is that medieval writers—who received their account of Atlantis by way of Arab geographers—certainly believed it was true, not least because of Plato's authority and, in turn, because of the authority invoked in his use of the much-revered Solon.

This "lost" civilization of the deeps has been identified with other well-known mythical islands such as the Greek Islands of the Blessed (otherwise known as the Fortunate Isles), the Portuguese Isle of Seven Cities (also known as the Isle of Antilia), the Welsh Avalon, Hy Brasil (see chapter 2), Saint Brendan's Island, the island of Lyonnesse (see chapter 2), the lost Breton city of Is (known also as Ys), and other equally idyllic but elusive sanctuaries such as the French Îles de la Très-Verte and its Portuguese counterpart Ilha Verde.

So deeply entrenched in popular belief was the legend of Atlantis that this mythical isle of plenty even appears, in a modified form, in the story of Saint Brendan, the Irish saint who was also known as Brendan the Navigator and Brendan the Bold. Brendan encountered much that was marvelous (and, let it be said, much that was plain fantasy) during his seven-year voyage in search of the Land of the Saints (see Voyages of Saint Brendan, chapter 3).

Homer, Horace, and others posited two Atlanticas, one known as the Hesperides and the other as the Elysian Fields, both supposed to be the abodes of the blessed, although it is not clear in what way these two islands differed, nor exactly what considerations determined a posting to one or the other (see The Hesperides, chapter 2). Plato, not otherwise known for his geographical accomplishments, stated that it was but an easy passage between one of these Atlanticas and other islands that lay near a continent greater in size than Europe and Asia—thought by some writers to be a clear pointer to what is now called North America.

These legendary islands were dutifully placed on the charts and maps of the fourteenth and fifteenth centuries, and several voyages of discovery were mounted to find them . . . alas! to no avail (as late as the mid-nineteenth century Atlantis itself, this time in the form of Ilha Verde, was positioned with commendable exactitude at 44°48' North, 26°10' West, but so far it has eluded all scrutiny, having no doubt already sunk without trace beneath the waves).

Modern geology has shown that the now-submerged coastline of western Europe did at one time more nearly approach the North American mainland, thus fueling increased speculation concerning the supposed existence of "lost Atlantis"; but despite the fact that this submergence took place in geologically prehistoric times, there are still enthusiasts who insist that the story of Atlantis is in fact more than the product of some ancient writer's lively fantasy (for an example of a modern writer's overheated imagination, see Berlitz 1976).

So pervasive has been the legend of Atlantis that even as late as the eighteenth century its credibility was debated by serious scholars and, it must be said, accepted by intellects as formidable as Voltaire and Montaigne.

More recent work by archaeologists and others has placed the likely origin of this fabled "lost continent" in the eastern Mediterranean, where much of the ancient island of Strongyle (known today as Stromboli), was destroyed by catastrophic volcanic action and submerged by the sea in about 1500 B.C. It is known that the Minoan Empire, based on Crete, suffered an overwhelming disaster at about the same time; hence the strong presumption that Atlantis and Strongyle were one and the same. (In fact, recent techniques in dating have established that Minoan Crete was overrun by early Greeks in about 1500 B.C.)

Francis Bacon (1561–1626), English essayist and philosopher, wrote a fable called *The New Atlantis* (unfinished at his death and published a year later). In it he described the ideal social conditions on an imaginary island called Bensalem, somewhere in the Pacific, where the people devoted their energies to the cultivation of the natural sciences (one is reminded here of Jean-Jacques Rousseau's concept of the "noble savage").

Ashley (1984) reports that Edgar Cayce (1877–1945), a self-styled prophet who lived in Virginia, is said to have offered a detailed and elaborate history of the "lost city of Atlantis," predicting that it would rise again in 1968 or 1969. Therefore in

1968 the world (or at least that portion of it most receptive to revelations of this nature) was astonished to learn that "ruins" had been discovered on the seabed off the coast of Bimini, an island near the Bahamas in the Caribbean. It was confidently claimed by excited commentators and "experts" that the ruins consisted of "massive pillars" (no doubt belonging to a "temple"), and that there were clear signs of "ancient roadways" and "massive walls," etc.

The ancient myth of Atlantis (or so it seemed to the faithful) had at last found its apotheosis beneath the otherwise indifferent waves of the West Indies. Certainly Berlitz (1976) thought so. In his somewhat breathless account of the submerged "ruins" at Bimini, which he regards as Atlantean, he writes enthusiastically of "sunken walls," "foundations," "roads," "docks," "stone pillars," a "great arch," "underwater pyramids," "concentric circles" of rock suggesting an "American Stonehenge," and other "man-made structures," such as "a 100-foot wall" on the sea bottom off Venezuela and "roads" or "causeways" lying off Yucatán and Honduras.

Clinching his case, Berlitz reports "evidence" of a "submerged building complex" covering more than ten acres lying on the seabed north of Cuba and explored, he says, with "Russian assistance." Furthermore, he reminds us of the "fact" that in "what may or may not be an extraordinary coincidence," these "prehistoric remains" lie within the Bermuda Triangle (see below), the site of the apparent and widely reported disappearance over the years of many boats, ships, and aircraft—a mystery Berlitz suggests may be solved by supposing an "advanced Atlantean civilization" which possessed "laser power sources." As an indication of his unabashed enthusiasm for mystery, Berlitz concludes his presentation of the "evidence" for Atlantis thus: "There were indeed cultures before our own 'time span' of 3500 B.C. to the present. One of these . . . was the one we call Atlantis."

But others may prefer the caution expressed by Burman:

> *The Platonic legend of Atlantis can be considered in three ways: as a description of a real lost world, as a vision of an ideal city, or as the first piece of pure science fiction. While the third seems more likely, the first has had more currency through the centuries.*

The Russian mystic Helena Blavatsky (1831–1891), cofounder of the Theosophy movement, advised the world before she died that a book exists that survived the many vicissitudes visited upon Atlantis; this tome of Atlantean wisdom, she said, now rests somewhere safely—but elusively—in Tibet.

THE BERMUDA TRIANGLE

*"Where once
Thou call'dst me up at midnight to fetch dew
From the still vex'd Bermoothes."*
WILLIAM SHAKESPEARE, *THE TEMPEST*

Bermoothes (also Barmudas) is an old word for the Bermudas, a group of islands in the Atlantic about 640 miles east of Cape Hatteras in North Carolina. A British possession since 1612, the islands were named by the Spanish in 1519 for the Spaniard Juan de Bermúdez, the first recorded discoverer (1515) of the group, who called them the Islands of Devils (known by the English as Isles of Divels) because of the strong winds and fierce seas encountered there.

At one time they were known as the Somers Islands, from Sir George Somers (or Sommers), who was wrecked on the islands in 1609 in the *Sea Venture*. The account of the wreck that was published a year later by Silvester Jourdan, one of the crew, is thought to have been the inspiration for Shakespeare's *The Tempest* (1611?). "The still vex'd Bermoothes" (see quote, opposite) was probably suggested by Sir Walter Raleigh's description in his *Discoverie of the Large, Rich, and Beautiful Empire of Guiana* (1596), wherein Raleigh complains of the "hellish sea, for thunder, lightning, and storms" of the Bermudas.

The so-called Bermuda Triangle is one of those enduring mysteries guaranteed to capture the interest of those who believe in the existence of Atlantis. The Triangle is an area of the western Atlantic roughly bounded by a triangle incorporating Bermuda, Puerto Rico, and Melbourne on the coast of Florida (not to be confused with the Golden Triangle, a Euclidean notion of quite different significance). Berlitz defines it as "an area between Florida, the Sargasso Sea, and Bermuda," the significance here being the Sargasso Sea, another region of much-touted mystery and dread (see The Sargasso Sea, chapter 7).

The Bermuda Triangle is notorious for the large number of ships and aircraft said to have been lost there without trace of wreckage or survivors; many of these disappearances were preceded by reports of unusual fog, instrument failure, sudden loss of power, strange sea conditions, and so on. Enthusiasts favor explanations in terms of unknown forces (see above for Berlitz's theory that the ancient Atlanteans possessed laser technology); other-dimension displacement, whereby entire ships and aircraft are sent packing to "another world" by means of electromagnetic anomalies; and of course UFOs (sometimes invisible, a very handy attribute), those hardy stalking horses of mayhem and mystery.

The triangle has long been a powerful symbol of mysticism and otherworldliness, as in the cabalistic charm *abracadabra*, the letters of which used to be arranged on a piece of parchment in the form of a triangle and hung around the neck so as to ward off illnesses such as ague, toothache, flux (diarrhea), and so on. The triangle is, of course, the familiar and powerful symbol of the Christian Trinity (God the Father, God the Son, and God the Holy Spirit). Also, the concept of three is the perfect number of Pythagoras (about 582–500 B.C., Greek philosopher and mathematician), expressive of beginning, middle, and end.

This area in the Caribbean is also known among aficionados as the Devil's Triangle and the Limbo of the Lost. Attempts have been made to dub the sea immediately east of South Africa as the Devil's Triangle in fitting commemoration of the *Flying Dutchman* (see below) and the SS *Waratah* (see chapter 11), but it seems that it is the Caribbean that retains its death grip on the imagination (and the credulity) of a certain section of the reading public.

The concept of a Bermuda Triangle was first proposed by Vincent Gaddis in a 1964 article in *Argosy* magazine about the mysterious disappearance of a group of U.S. Navy bombers over the Caribbean in 1945 (the now-famous Training Flight 19). But the myth had taken off much earlier, so to speak, and has been sustained ever since by a formidable list of disappearances dating back to 1800 and coming to a halt (presumably temporarily) in 1976, including planes and ships of every description.

Training Flight 19 will serve as an exemplar of these disappearances. Five Grumman Avenger navy torpedo bombers comprising Training Flight 19 took off from Fort Lauderdale in southeastern Florida at 2:00 P.M. on December 5, 1945. The weather was not good; in fact, it worsened and a tropical storm developed. Each plane carried three men, to make a total of fifteen (except that one of them, Corporal Allen Kosnar, had earlier reported sick, having apparently had a premonition not to fly on that day); most, but not all, of the men were inexperienced trainees. The flight was to last two hours.

At about 3:45 P.M., not long before the flight was due back at Fort Lauderdale, the leader (Lieutenant Charles Taylor, a veteran flyer) radioed the control tower at Fort Lauderdale to say that he and his men were lost—"We seem to be off course. We cannot see land"—and when the tower advised him to head due west Taylor replied, "We don't know which way is west. Everything is wrong . . . even the ocean doesn't look as it should." Inexplicably, Taylor then handed leadership of Flight 19 to Captain George Stivers, who added his (garbled) radio message to the effect that they were "hopelessly lost."

Radio reception from the planes was bad and fading; the control tower could barely make out frantic messages saying that the compasses and gyros in the aircraft were "going crazy." Gordon reported that these radio messages "cannot be traced beyond a 1962 magazine article," indicating either that the messages were subsequently lost or destroyed by the authorities or that they didn't exist in the first place. Berlitz said that "their base . . . could overhear their intercom conversations although the pilots could not hear the base."

At about 4:30 P.M. a rescue aircraft was sent out, a well-equipped Martin Mariner flying boat with thirteen experienced men aboard, Lieutenant Harry Cone in command. Cone subsequently gave two position reports, then disappeared: the crew and their plane, larger than a Flying Fortress bomber, simply vanished into thin air. At about 7:00 P.M. the control tower picked up a very faint message from Flight 19: "FT . . . FT," part of its agreed call signal; then silence. Nothing more was heard from, or of, these six aircraft and twenty-seven men.

The Martin Mariner, because of its function as an air-sea rescue plane, normally had to carry a prodigious amount of fuel; consequently, fire and explosion were particularly real hazards. It may be significant that the master of the oil tanker *Gaines Mills*, steaming in that very area, reported that he had seen "a ball of flame descending into the ocean at about 8:00 P.M." He investigated but found neither wreckage nor bodies. Although this is not conclusive proof, it seems likely that the "ball of flame" was the Martin Mariner.

There is no ready explanation for the disappearance of the five Avengers of Flight 19, although every avenue has been examined, including, of course, the notion of UFOs. Clark said that a Florida radio ham gave evidence that, having tuned in to the radio transmissions between Flight 19 and Fort Lauderdale, he heard these last words from Taylor: "Don't come after me. They look like they're from outer space"—a wonderful scenario for a film, which of course is just what happened when Stephen Spielberg made his film *Close Encounters of the Third Kind*, wherein thirty years after their disappearance the five Avengers are discovered neatly arranged in a remote desert, each in perfect condition, and Taylor and his men jauntily step out of a flying saucer, quite undamaged and having aged not one whit.

Other theories have been advanced to account for this puzzling disappearance:

- The men of Flight 19 were involved in a fraudulent plan to extend their flying time by deliberately going off course so as to accumulate more flight pay.
- A Lieutenant Robert Cox, in the air over Fort Lauderdale at the time and in good radio contact with Taylor in Flight 19, and believing from Taylor's remarks that he appeared to be over the Florida Keys, advised him to fly north until he was over Miami, when Fort Lauderdale would then be only 20 miles farther north. Unhappily, Taylor was at this time almost certainly far out to sea over the Grand Cays, which Clark tells us look very much like the Florida Keys; Cox's advice thus would have set him on a course into the Atlantic.
- The air-sea rescue base at Port Everglades, as well as six other radio stations in the region, got a fix on the position of Flight 19, putting it some 150 miles north of the Bahamas but without informing the flight itself, leaving Taylor believing that he was much farther south, thus encouraging him to fly variously east and north—that is, farther out to sea.

Eventually Flight 19 disappeared, in every sense; and although pieces of aircraft wreckage (some containing human bones) have turned up from time to time off the Florida coast, there has been nothing to identify these items with Flight 19. Clark reported that in 1987 some wreckage unmistakably from an Avenger was found 20 miles west of Key West, but no claim has been made that it is from Flight 19.

However, Gordon tells us in a tantalizingly cryptic note that "in 1991 the remains of the flight [Flight 19] were located on the seabed" (no other details are given). He attributes the loss of the five Avengers to "an inexperienced crew, rough weather, poor radio conditions, [and] a flight leader un-corrected when wrongly thinking he was off course. A storm blew up, night fell, the planes ran out of fuel and ditched in heavy seas which tore them apart."

It is difficult to argue with this conclusion, but it is also clear from Clark's account of the Bermuda Triangle that, if reports are to be believed, stranger things have gone on there. There are accounts of aircraft entering peculiar cloud formations and/or disappearing from radar tracking screens, then landing safely but with their onboard clocks and watches all having lost exactly the amount of time during which the plane had vanished from the radar screens.

Then there is the experience of Bruce Gernon. He was a private pilot who on December 4, 1970, while flying with his father in a Beechcraft Bonanza A36 from Andros Island to Palm Beach flew into an enormous elliptical white cloud, causing all the plane's instruments to malfunction; he headed the plane for a hole in the cloud, found himself in a sort of tunnel, experienced a total loss of gravity, then flew clear of the cloud to find himself over Palm Beach. One might reasonably dismiss this as hallucination, except that when he landed Gernon discovered that he had cut half an hour off the usual time for the 200-mile trip, that his aircraft had actually flown 250 miles, but used only a fraction of the fuel normal for that journey, and that he had covered that distance at something over 320 miles per hour in an aircraft with a maximum cruising speed of 195 miles per hour.

Many other examples of strange disappearances and anomalous atmospheric conditions in the Bermuda Triangle have been recorded. One need only peruse the Berlitz list spanning the period 1800 to the time of publication of his book in 1977 for evidence that a lot of ships, planes, and people have come to grief in this area, a good many of them disappearing without trace.

Much of this mayhem can be blamed on bad weather. Cape Hatteras, on the coast of North Carolina and almost due west of Bermuda, is notorious for the storms and violent seas often encountered in that part of the Atlantic, and clear-air turbulence has brought tribulation, not to say destruction, to many an aircraft. The east coast of South Africa is also well known for its bouts of bad weather, especially in the Mozambique Channel, where the Agulhas Current can often produce the most ferocious of seas (see SS *Waratah*, chapter 11, for the complete disappearance of a large vessel and all aboard her, through bad weather).

Some of these disappearances, of course, were caused by human error: it is not difficult to become totally disoriented in certain kinds of weather conditions, the "whiteout" experienced by travelers in regions of snow and ice being a familiar example; and of course mechanical failure has been known to visit disaster upon both ship and plane with distressing regularity. It seems, too, that there may well be some forms of electromagnetic anomalies and high-level weather disturbances not yet properly understood by science that could be responsible for the otherwise unexplained events so firmly linked with the seas and skies of the Bermuda Triangle.

On the other hand, it would appear to many to be drawing a spectacularly long bow to invoke extraplanetary forces as a means of accounting for the mysteries said to be peculiar to this part of the Atlantic. While there is still much to be learned about those otherwise prosaic concepts of time and space, we do not need quite yet to embrace with uninhibited enthusiasm the notion suggested by Berlitz that some of the forces touted by adherents of sci-fi are at work. In his own words:

> *On the other hand, the very absence of survivors or wreckage could*
> *be explained, according to many who believe that unknown forces*
> *are at work within the Triangle, by the possibility that the craft and*
> *occupants did not necessarily go down into the ocean, but rather up*
> *into the sky, through a reversal of gravity or by collection of extraterres-*
> *trial entities—through disintegration as a result of encountering an*
> *extremely high magnetic field or a field of ionization, the latter perhaps*
> *in turn caused by pathways of extraterrestrial spacecraft.*

This is the nub of the argument: the unseemly haste with which commentators invoke "extraterrestrial entities" and "extraterrestrial spacecraft" to account for the so far unaccountable; that, in short, spacenappers are at work ("It is likely that intelligent entities are questing in outer and inner space").

They need not come from space, of course. Berlitz's writings on Atlantis show that he is an enthusiastic advocate for the possibility that "The onetime existence of Atlantis and the present day existence of the Bermuda Triangle are two of the ocean's outstanding mysteries," where the "seismic, tidal, or perhaps cosmic forces that overwhelmed the once populated lands now under the sea may still be at work after thousands of years."

Sadly, the truth may be somewhat more prosaic. A newspaper reported that a British scientist claimed to have solved the mystery that surrounds the Bermuda Triangle. Geologist Ben Clennell told the British Association Festival of Science in Cardiff that the disappearance of planes, ships, and people in large numbers without trace was caused by large bubbles. He explained that these bubbles result from methane gas excreted by bacteria from beneath the ocean bed; underwater landslides trigger the release of the gas as hydrates, a crystalline mix of methane and water ice, which then float to the surface (there was evidence, he said, of a very large quantity of hydrates in the area).

Clennell said that the effect of the apple-size bubbles could be disastrous because a release of a large quantity of methane would so reduce the density of seawater that any ship in the immediate area would sink like a stone. When the gas hydrates reached the surface, they would create a serious hazard to planes flying overhead because of the release of highly combustible methane gas into the atmosphere; this would be fatal for aircraft because their engines would almost certainly burst into flame when they came into contact with it.

Perhaps it is so.

THE FLANNAN ISLES

"We seemed to stand for an endless while,
Though still no word was said,
Three men alive on Flannan Isle,
Who thought, on three men dead."

W. W. GIBSON, "FLANNAN ISLE"

The Outer Hebrides islands lie some 30 miles off the northwest coast of Scotland, the most northerly being Lewis; 20 miles west of Lewis are the Flannan Isles (also known as the Seven Hunters), named for Saint Flannan, who lived a solitary existence there in the seventeenth century. In December 1900 the Flannan Isles were the focal point of a strange occurrence, a disappearance that has never been solved.

The Flannan Isles comprise a group of cliffy rocks, of which Eilean Mor, about 500 yards long and perhaps 200 yards wide, is the largest. Because of their position these rocks increasingly became a hazard to coastal shipping, so a lighthouse was built on Eilean Mor in 1899, 75 feet high, fitted with a light powerful enough to be seen 40 miles out to sea. There were two landing places, which had to be blasted out of the rock itself: one on the western edge of the island and the other on the eastern edge, with steps cut into the cliff and rope and tackle set up for hauling supplies to the top.

The light was manned by four men, three at a time, each man on duty for six weeks followed by two weeks ashore. Stores and mail were brought to the lighthouse every two weeks by the steamer *Hesperus*; also on board was the fourth man rotating back in from his shore leave.

On December 6, 1900, Joseph Moore left on the *Hesperus* for his spell ashore, leaving behind Donald McArthur, Thomas Marshall, and James Ducat. Moore would have been due back on December 20, but bad weather kept the steamer away, and it wasn't until December 26 that Moore was able to make the trip. He was worried on two counts: first, the delay in the steamer's return meant that the three men in the light had to go without their Christmas mail and provisions; and second, for the past few days the light itself had not been lit, always a matter of concern for mariners at sea and for the authorities ashore.

When the *Hesperus* anchored off the eastern edge of the island and a boat put in for the landing stage, Moore had further cause for worry—there was no one there to meet them, which was unusual, as the fortnightly steamer was something of an event for the men in their otherwise solitary existence.

Moore clambered up the steps in the cliff and inspected the lighthouse. It was empty. Nothing was out of place. As with the cabin on the *Mary Celeste* (see below), the interior of the lighthouse was a model of orderliness. The machinery that drove the light, the lens, the lanterns and their wicks—all had been properly serviced. The three men had simply vanished, without leaving behind any clue pointing to panic, disaster, or distress. The last entry in the log was for 9:00 A.M. on December 15, and it was later confirmed by coastal shipping that this was the date when the light ceased to burn. Curiously, the foul-weather gear belonging to Marshall and Ducat was missing, but McArthur's was still in place.

Moore inspected the landings. The eastern landing was still in good order, but the landing on the western edge of the island showed signs of severe storm damage, the iron handrails running up the cliff steps badly twisted and some torn out of their sockets. The log showed that there was bad weather on December 12 and 13 but that the next two days at least were calm.

Where had the three men gone, and why? Their disappearance has never been solved and now, a century after the event, it never will be. But a possible answer lies in the discovery (not noticed earlier, since the lighthouse had been operational for only a year) that when the weather was settled, the sea at the west landing would, without warning of any kind, often suddenly rear itself into a giant wave and batter the clifftop a hundred feet above. The phenomenon is well known, being probably an unlucky accumulation of ocean swells. These king waves, as they are called on the west Australian coast, have dragged many a fisherman off an ordinarily safe rock and flung him into the sea, drowning or battering him to death.

It is likely that this is what happened to Marshall, Ducat, and McArthur when they, for some reason we can never know, took themselves down to the west landing.

THE *FLYING DUTCHMAN*

"The sea never changes and its works, for all the talk of men,
are wrapped in a mystery."

JOSEPH CONRAD, *TYPHOON*

Cornelius Vanderdecken

Of all apparitions the mariner may encounter at sea, none is more famous nor more full of foreboding than the *Flying Dutchman*. As with nearly all legends of note, there is more than one version of this story (see below), but perhaps the most commonly accepted one tells of the Dutch skipper Captain Cornelius Vanderdecken, who, on a voyage home to the Netherlands from Batavia in the era of Admiral Maarten Tromp (1597–1653, perhaps Holland's most famous seaman), ran into foul weather in the latitude of the Cape of Good Hope.

After many weeks of thrashing hopelessly westward the crew begs Vanderdecken to wait until the weather moderates, but the Dutchman is adamant: he intends to carry on. Then God appears in the midst of a particularly violent gale; the crew throw themselves to the deck (seamen have always been pious, albeit hopelessly naive, unlettered, and sometimes coldly brutal) but Vanderdecken remains standing on his poop deck, defying the Almighty, going so far as to fire his pistol at the vision in the clouds and swearing by Donner and Blitzen (a teutonic oath, *Donner und Blitzen*, "thunder and lightning," somewhat stronger than the English "hell's bells") that despite God's wrath he would beat his way into Table Bay, where Cape Town lies.

God, willing to accept only so much impious passion, exacts retribution on the Dutchman by making him sail the seas "forever without rest." No sooner are the words out of Vanderdecken's mouth than the vessel founders beneath him, leaving only a phantom ship condemned to sail for all eternity, beating back and forth in a (futile) attempt to reach Table Bay.

Rogers's account has it that the ghost ship sails with only Vanderdecken and one other man as crew, "and he a monster." Other variations include the *Flying Dutchman* pursuing other ships until they are overtaken, whereupon Vanderdecken can be seen leaning across the rail of his quarterdeck, holding aloft a letter and screaming that he wishes to have it posted. But nobody will accept the commission, it being a firm belief among sailors that to do so would doom them to perpetual bad luck; hence the universal insistence among seamen that the phantom ship, if ever sighted, be given the widest possible berth. Another belief is that any seaman setting eyes on such a ship will be struck blind. Rogers remarks that there has been no dearth of witnesses who insist that they themselves have laid their very eyes on this ghost ship as it endlessly battles its way round the Cape of Good Hope—the Cape of Storms in the old parlance.

Other similar stories include the German legend that has a Herr von Falkenberg and the devil on board his ship as they sail forever around the North Sea without so much as a rudder, let alone a helmsman, while the devil is playing dice with von Falkenberg for his soul, the German captain having apparently once committed a murder. (Coleridge uses the same motif in "The Rime of the Ancient Mariner," wherein the mariner sights a ghost ship on which two figures, "Life" and "Death in Life," throw dice for his soul.) Wagner's operatic version of this story, *Der fliegender Holländer* (1843), allows Vanderdecken to go ashore once every seven years so that, if he can find a woman who can love him, he will be released from his awful curse. A Dutch legend has the ghost of van Straaten, a Dutch seaman, as master of the *Flying Dutchman.*

Kemp suggests the legend may ultimately derive from a Norse saga in which the Viking Stöte steals a ring from the gods, his skeleton later found wrapped in a robe of fire and seated at the base of the mainmast of a black ghost ship. However, the reported sighting in more or less modern times of this most famous of maritime apparitions by a person noted for his sobriety of character must give us pause, at least to shake our heads in wonder rather than in dismissal.

In 1881 Prince George of Britain, later George V, the "sailor king," was making a flag-showing cruise round the world in a squadron under the command of Vice Admiral the Earl of Carnarvon in the *Inconstant.* The squadron visited Melbourne in June and Sydney in July 1881. At four o'clock on a morning in early July 1881, in the Southern Ocean, south of the southeastern tip of Australia, the lookout on the corvette HMS *Bacchante* reported a strange sight, what seemed to be a spectral ship crossing the bows of the *Bacchante.*

Bridges quotes from the ship's log:

> *The* Flying Dutchman *crossed our bows. A strange red light, as of a phantom ship all aglow, in the midst of which light the masts, spars, and sails of a brig two hundred yards distant stood up in strong relief. ["On arriving there, no vestige nor any sign whatever of any material ship was to be seen either near or right away to the horizon, the night being clear and the sea calm."] Thirteen persons altogether saw her, but whether it was Van Diemen, or the* Flying Dutchman, *or who else, must remain unknown. The* Tourmaline *and* Cleopatra, *which were sailing on our starboard bow, flashed to ask whether we had seen the strange red light.*

It is interesting that two other vessels in company with the *Bacchante* also saw something. One notes another incident, too: the lookout who first spotted the phantom ship died six hours later in a fall from the foretopmast crosstrees to the deck, and the Hardwicks tell us that at the next port—presumably Sydney—the admiral of the squadron became fatally ill (and our ancient mariner would have nodded knowingly: hadn't thirteen people claimed to have seen the apparition?).

In 1911 a whaler, the *Orkney Belle,* is said to have encountered this phantom ship in Icelandic waters, "her sails swelling in a non-existent breeze, her bows almost ramming the side [of the *Orkney Belle*]. Then, from her depths, three bells sounded and, heeling to starboard, she drifted away."

Bernard Fokke

There are, according to maritime legend, not one but two vessels hammering back and forth in the seas around the Cape of Good Hope. This second *Flying Dutchman* (the name has long since become a generic description for spectral ships) was under the command of one Bernard Fokke, a Dutch sailor in the latter half of the seventeenth century, notorious for his reckless courage and boastful manner. Fokke let it be known that no other vessel afloat could beat his, and to make good this claim he encased his ship's masts in iron so they could withstand the heavy press of sail that he customarily crowded on, a procedure that, he claimed, enabled him to make the Rotterdam–East Indies passage in ninety days by way of the Cape of Good Hope (this compares more than favorably with the six months that were still common for ships making the run from England to the Australian colonies in the eighteenth and nineteenth centuries).

Inevitably Fokke overreached himself; in an effort to beat his own record for this route he is said to have made a compact with the devil: sailing supremacy in return for his soul. The story is that when he died, Fokke and his ship vanished into thin air, destined to reappear until the end of time in the seas he once ruled, battling endless gales as his ship tries to forge ahead and is just as relentlessly driven back, with Fokke accompanied only by his bosun, cook, and pilot from earlier and perhaps happier days.

Bridges adds this note:

> *Whether the phantom ship be that of Vanderdecken or of Fokke, the fact remains that nine-tenths of all reported appearances of phantom ships are between the fortieth and fiftieth latitudes [south of the latitude of the Cape of Good Hope]. Nor has the age of steam killed the tradition, for rarely a year passes without some vessel sighting one of these ghostly wanderers of the ocean.*

Both these accounts are maritime versions of the theme of the Wandering Jew; also see the SS *Waratah*, chapter 11, for a phantom of a different kind.

The *Mary Celeste*

> " 'Wouldst thou'—so the helmsman answered,
> 'Learn the secret of the sea?
> Only those who brave its dangers
> Comprehend its mystery.' "
> HENRY WADSWORTH LONGFELLOW, "THE GALLEY OF COUNT ARNALDOS"

Perhaps the best-known maritime mystery, and certainly the most puzzling, is the case of the *Mary Celeste*. The name of the vessel is often rendered as *Marie Celeste,* as we find it in Bridges and in many other sources, perhaps from the notion that because "Celeste" looks French, then "Marie" is its proper consort, the foreign touch supposedly adding something to the mystery; but in fact it is *Mary Celeste*, a point Brewer acknowledges, though he persists in discussing the vessel as *Marie Celeste*. Indeed, the owner of this vessel at the time—there were seventeen owners in all— is reported by Bridges as referring to the vessel as the *Marie Celeste*, thereby adding to the confusion. The Hardwicks quote documents from the official record held by the U.S. Department of State, in which it is perfectly clear that the vessel's name was *Mary Celeste* and no other.

The Hardwicks also show that this confusion over the name can be sheeted home to the then unknown writer Dr. Arthur Conan Doyle (1859–1930), who in 1883 published in the *Cornhill Magazine* a story titled "J. Habaluk Jephson's Statement," which purported to be a confession by the sole survivor of a massacre on board a vessel called the *Marie Celeste*. Although the story was a fiction, so many credulous readers took it to be a factual account of the earlier events of 1872 that a Solly Flood, at that time the advocate general at Gibraltar, issued a public statement to the effect that Conan Doyle's story was just that: a story. Nevertheless, the name of Doyle's invented vessel, *Marie Celeste,* has remained firmly lodged in the memories of many writers, publishers, and newspapers.

The facts behind this story are simple enough; it is interpreting them that has challenged the imagination of novelists and script-writers, as well as the accumulated experience of marine investigators.

The Hardwicks say that the *Mary Celeste* was a brigantine, but according to Kemp she was a hermaphrodite brig of U.S. registration, 280 tons. (*Hermaphrodite* means a two-masted vessel that is square-rigged on the foremast and fore-and-aft rigged on the mainmast—fitted with a gaff mainsail—with a square topsail set above the mainsail, a type also known as a brig-schooner. A *brigantine* is square-rigged on the foremast and fully fore-and-aft rigged on the mainmast. A *brig*—or, rather, the true brig—is fully square-rigged on both foremast and mainmast.)

The *Mary Celeste* was found on December 5, 1872, by the British brigantine *Dei Gratia,* Captain David Morehouse, in the Atlantic some 350 miles or more to the east of the island of Santa María in the Azores, due west of Gibraltar. The ship, under the command of Captain Benjamin Briggs (accompanied by his wife and small daughter), had loaded 1,700 barrels of alcohol in New York and then set sail on November 5, 1872, with seven crew, bound for Genoa. She never arrived.

When the *Dei Gratia* sighted her, the reduced sails of the *Mary Celeste* were set for the starboard tack and for somewhat heavy weather, yet she was making easterly headway on the port tack in a light breeze. It was obvious that something was wrong, so the captain of the *Dei Gratia* sent Deveau the mate and another seaman to board her.

They found her abandoned, with "her only boat gone," as Kemp says; the Hardwicks report that "the other boat still hung from its davits"; see below for Bridges's account of the last owner's remarks concerning boats on the *Mary Celeste*. They also found a frayed or parted painter (mooring rope for a ship's boat) hanging over the stern, the sounding rod lying by the ship's pump (used for measuring the depth of water in the bilges), two upper sails blown out, some running rigging in a tangle, the two small fore-and-aft hatches and the galley hatch lying aside, and the main cabin skylight open. The cargo and the main hatch over it were untouched and secure (but, as was later determined, nine casks of alcohol were either empty or damaged).

Brewer adds the information that the ship's sextant, chronometer, and register were also missing (these would be items certain to be taken off by a captain in an emergency), and Bridges tells us that "Proof of the haste in which she had been abandoned appeared in the fact that the breakfast of the captain, his wife, and child had been left half consumed." Kemp does not mention these "facts" as reported by Brewer and Bridges. The Hardwicks admit that the "popular version" insists that "in the cabin the table was laid for a meal and three cups of tea, still warm, stood on it as well as a boiled egg with the top cut off and an unfinished plate of porridge . . . the [galley] range had been raked out recently and was warm, like the tea." It is very likely, say the Hardwicks, that this account of domestic detail is inaccurate; they do report, however, that a cat was found in the cabin, fast asleep and apparently quite undisturbed by recent events.

What were originally thought to be bloodstains on the deck and railing and on a cutlass in the cabin (all of which, according to some fevered theorists at the time, pointed to mutiny and murder—or at least piracy) proved to be nothing more sinister than wine stains and rust. The *Dei Gratia* put a salvage crew aboard the empty vessel, and they sailed her to Gibraltar, arriving there December 13. The subsequent marine court of inquiry canvassed a number of theories to explain the mystery of the *Mary Celeste,* including one that presumed mutiny, piracy, *and* murder; another that supposed collusion between the masters of the two vessels for the purpose of claiming salvage money; a third that had a giant squid failing to get out of the way in sufficient time to avoid a collision; and so on. At the end of the inquiry, say the Hardwicks, Captain Morehouse and his crew were paid £1,700 salvage money.

Despite the ingenuity of interested parties in constructing a variety of lurid explanations to account for the mystery, only two practical suggestions make some sort of sense. The first supposes that the nine damaged casks were the result of a minor explosion of alcohol vapor, which might have persuaded the captain and crew to launch the boat immediately, board it, and let it fall astern of the vessel on a long

Myth and Mystery 271

painter; if the ship's cargo failed to explode they could pull themselves back to their ship. Alas, the painter parts, the ship sails on, and those on the boat cannot row hard enough to catch up. Against this is the fact that the deck beams above the cargo show no sign whatsoever of fire or smoke. However, this is the explanation favored by J. H. ("Captain") Winchester, the owner of the *Mary Celeste* at the time.

The second theory has a waterspout hitting the vessel, causing such extreme variations in local atmospheric pressure that a great deal of water is sucked up the pump well from the bilges (which even at the best of times have water in them) and out onto the deck; this could easily lead the crew to believe that the vessel had sprung a very serious leak (the sounding rod found on deck suggests that the depth of water in the bilges had been checked). The crew set the boat over the side, board it, the painter parts, but the vessel remains afloat and makes too much headway for the crew to overtake. They all then perish at sea.

As if to underline yet again the belief held among virtually all seafarers that some ships are forever unlucky, the *Mary Celeste* pursued an unhappy and unprofitable career for the next thirteen years (a significant period in the reckoning of any seafarer), with a succession of sixteen further owners, J. H. Winchester presumably having sold her immediately after the board of inquiry hearing in Gibraltar in 1872. She met her end in 1885 by being deliberately wrecked on a reef in the Caribbean, whereupon her owner made a (false) claim for insurance.

That was the end of the *Mary Celeste,* brig/brigantine, but the beginning of a literary industry devoted to solving what had become, and bids fair to remain, the world's greatest sea mystery (but see also Flannan Isles, above, for a story of comparable curiosity; also SS *Waratah*, chapter 11, for an account of the complete peacetime disappearance, without trace, of a large ship and all on board, and The Sinking of HMAS *Sydney*, chapter 10, a large war vessel sunk off the west Australian coast without survivors or any trace of wreckage).

In 1913 a group of writers concocted a theory that some smugglers abducted the crew of the *Mary Celeste* in order to swell their own depleted numbers. In another explanation, an unknown phenomenon causes everyone on board to go mad, whereupon they all leap into the sea (the captain has wit enough to take—God knows why—the ship's chronometer with him). Yet again, one of the crew on the *Mary Celeste* loses his reason, poisons all on board with suspect coffee, then jumps overboard, again, with the ill-fated chronometer.

The *Strand* magazine startled the world with the publication of some "old papers" left by a "survivor" from the *Mary Celeste*, discovered by one A. Howard Linford, schoolmaster, wherein all except this survivor are drowned in a freak accident. In January 1914 the *Liverpool Weekly Post* ran a story telling how an officer in the merchant marine, while a young apprentice, had discovered a message in a bottle written in German, which when translated told a story about a small steamer, stricken with a dying crew, boarding the *Mary Celeste* so as to abduct its men (for what purpose is not disclosed).

In 1917 a Chippy Russel, chemist in Shrewsbury, admitted to being Jack Dossel, bosun of the *Mary Celeste.* In 1924 a Captain H. Lucy surfaced, saying that in the South Seas he had met a bosun called Briggs of the *Mary Celeste,* who had told him a tale of boarding a nearby derelict ship, finding a large sum of money therein, and then abandoning their own vessel.

A book by Laurence Keating in 1929 revealed to a waiting world the story of John Pemberton, cook on board the *Mary Celeste* and one of seven men Keating knew to have survived. Pemberton described how Mrs. Briggs, the captain's wife, had driven the mate Hullock to distraction with her piano playing (there was in fact a harmonium on the *Mary Celeste* when boarded by the *Dei Gratia*). When this instrument toppled during a storm and killed Mrs. Briggs, the captain went berserk, then disappeared, presumably overboard (whether or not he took the now popular chronometer is not stated). Hullock assumed command and became dictatorial, fighting broke out, and Pemberton the cook was next to take over; Hullock deserted to the Azores, along with Chippy Dossel or Russel (the Shrewsbury chemist, see above). The *Dei Gratia* appears on the horizon. All is now apparent: it is a conspiracy to falsely obtain money for the salvage of the *Mary Celeste*; but unhappily for author Keating, the names he uses for the crew of this vessel are not at all those known to the board of inquiry at Gibraltar in 1872.

The Hardwicks tell us that when the *Mary Celeste* was finally wrecked on a Cuban (or Haitian) reef in 1885, investigators discovered that the barrels of molasses in her hold contained nothing but seawater. Given this subterfuge at the end of the vessel's life, it is not at all surprising that all the subsequent "accounts" of her strange circumstances thirteen years earlier are equally as empty of substance.

THE SCHOONER *JENNY*

"Avaunt! and quit my sight! let the earth hide thee!
Thy bones are marrowless, thy blood is cold;
Thou hast no speculations in those eyes
Which thou dost glare with!"

WILLIAM SHAKESPEARE, *MACBETH*

In the mid-1800s, in the waters of the Southern Ocean between Australia and Antarctica, there occurred an incident that even the most jaded observer of the affairs of this world would have to call curious, if not downright macabre.

On September 22, 1860, Captain Brighton of the whaler *Hope* entered into his logbook the fact that a whale had been sighted and chase given, but when they had drawn close to the ice barrier, the whale had given them the slip. An hour later Brighton wrote another report that later would stun and mystify all those familiar with the sea. He had just come on deck when the nearby endless wall of ice began breaking up with a tremendous thunder and crashing of huge frozen cliffs collapsing into the sea; happily, the *Hope* was some hundreds of yards away from the fracas and, provided she didn't drift any closer, was thought safe. Suddenly some of the crew gave a shout and pointed in alarm and terror—a ship was slowly floating out of one of the chasms that had opened up in the disintegrating walls of ice. Its decks were wreathed with ice and snow, its sails hanging in tattered and frozen shreds, its rigging broken and rotten, and the vessel itself crushed and splintered, but still she floated.

What terrified Brighton's men was the crew of the wreck in front of them: seven men standing upright and encased in steel-hard ice, like so many statues of stone. Some of the *Hope* crew cried out in fear, "The *Flying Dutchman!*" but Captain Brighton reassured them; then he called for a boat to pull him across; he clambered aboard and went below to see what he might find. When he opened the master's cabin door he was confronted with a man sitting at his desk with pen in hand and seemingly about to write in the logbook in front of him; it was clearly the captain of the stricken ship. Brighton immediately spoke to him, but the fellow remained perfectly silent, being in fact dead and frozen solid to boot. Captain Brighton then checked the log on the desk. The ship was the English schooner *Jenny*, last port of call Lima, Peru, and the final entry read, "No food for 71 days. I am the only one left alive."

It was dated May 4, 1823. For some thirty-seven years the *Jenny* had remained hard and fast, crushed and imprisoned within the unrelenting walls of the ice barrier of the Antarctic. In another cabin was found the body of a woman, no doubt the captain's wife; like all the rest, she was perfectly preserved by the fierce cold of that terrible region.

The crew of the *Hope* gave the nine bodies a proper sea burial, and when he returned to England some months later Captain Brighton passed on to the admiralty the logbook and the unusual story of the ice-bound *Jenny*.

USS *CYCLOPS*

"Ships are but boards, sailors but men."
WILLIAM SHAKESPEARE, *THE MERCHANT OF VENICE*

Perhaps the disappearance of the USS *Cyclops*, a collier attached to the U.S. Navy during World War I, ranks as one of the best-known maritime mysteries in the history of American shipping. (Clark unintentionally introduces an even greater mystery in his account of this incident: he has this ship disappear in April 1918, although he says it was not built until 1919 and "launched in May of the following year"; for the sake of some sort of credibility the *Cyclops* is now assumed to have been built in 1916, since it is clear from the rest of Clark's account that the ship did go missing in 1918.)

The *Cyclops* was a large vessel for its time, being some 20,000 tons deadweight and widely touted as unsinkable; but on her maiden voyage she was found to roll and pitch badly, a criticism also leveled at the *Waratah* by experienced seamen (see SS *Waratah*, chapter 11). Her captain was a German, Georg Wichmann, who—probably as a result of anti-German feeling then common—had changed his name to George Worley. Clark tells us that Worley's indifferent ship handling often resulted in minor damage to the vessel and that he was less than inspiring in his navigation: the *Cyclops* was often seen approaching an intermediate port of call from the very direction of her ultimate destination. He was also apparently eccentric, often wandering around his ship clad only in his underwear and a bowler hat. Clearly, these are not idiosyncrasies guaranteed to sink a ship, but when she did disappear, these aspects of his character, along with suspected design faults in the ship, possible inefficient loading, and bad weather, did not give George Worley a glowing posthumous reputation as a competent mariner.

In January 1918 the *Cyclops* left Norfolk, Virginia, and steamed to Bahia (presumably to Salvador, in fact, at that time the port for the Brazilian state of Bahia) with coal for the USS *Raleigh*. At Rio she loaded manganese ore and then returned to Bahia, where she took on passengers and then left for Baltimore, Maryland, on February 21, with an unscheduled stop in Barbados (date not indicated by Clark). The day after she left Barbados she was seen in midocean by the passenger liner *Vestris*, and that was the last contact the *Cyclops* and all aboard her had with the world. She had disappeared without a trace, with—as they say in these cases—all hands.

Ten days after the due date for the ship to arrive at Norfolk, the U.S. Navy set a search in motion, but nothing remotely identifiable with this large ship was ever found. Because the *Cyclops* had disappeared in Caribbean waters, the Bermuda Triangle (see above) was enthusiastically invoked by those who saw an ineluctable connection between this incident and that area, not to mention the maritime periodical that opined that the *Cyclops* had been dragged to a watery grave by a giant squid (see Monster Kraken, chapter 17, for a brief history of the significance of these creatures in maritime experience and literature).

There were other theories, of course: Captain Worley sailed the *Cyclops* to Germany or the crew mutinied and seized the ship (at the time of this incident, some of them were in the ship's brig for serious misdemeanors) and so on. All of these "explanations" ignore the inescapable probability that somewhere at sometime at least one of the 304 people on board the "seized" vessel when she disappeared would have spoken up about desertion or mutiny. It is far more likely that the *Cyclops*, like many another ship in the history of seafaring, ran into bad weather, and through an unhappy combination of poor design, careless distribution of cargo, indifferent seamanship, and a murmuring and unhappy crew, broke up and sank immediately.

That there was no trace of this catastrophe is, like the *Waratah* incident (and, in a somewhat different context, like the *Mary Celeste*, above), the real mystery. We don't need to resort to occult powers to "explain" things (see Fabled Atlantis, above, for theories involving "occult powers" and "advanced technology").

17

SEA MONSTERS

Sea serpents, or sea monsters, have for a very long time been all the rage among otherwise sober seafarers. (Indeed, considering the question of sobriety, it is interesting to note that innkeepers throughout Scotland have done little to dispel the widespread conviction that Loch Ness harbors its own sea monster.) Belief in these fearful creatures of the deep reaches back far beyond recorded history. In Scandinavian mythology, a worm known as Midgårdsormen, which lived at the bottom of the sea, was of such a size that it stretched right round the world—truly a most formidable creature.

The curious thing about sea serpents and other monsters of that ilk is that a number of them have been attested to by some otherwise trustworthy people, as we see below.

MONSTER CADDIE

"Ingratitude . . .
More hideous when thou show'st thee in a child
Than the sea-monster."
WILLIAM SHAKESPEARE, *KING LEAR*

Caddie (sometimes Caddy) is the nickname of the sea creature that has continued to mystify folk who live along the coast of British Columbia—or its descendants have, anyway. It takes its name from the nonce word *cadborosaurus, saurus* from the Greek *saura*, lizard, and *cadboro* from Cadboro Bay, which lies within the provincial capital Victoria, on Vancouver Island.

Sightings of a strange animal living in the straits and sounds of this region of western Canada apparently go back to prehistoric times, since they are recorded in the myths and legends of the Salish Indians who have occupied British Columbia and the northwestern United States for a considerable period. The coastal Salish speak of a friendly beast known by the Sechelt Indian name of T'chain-ko, said to have been seen at a number of places along this coast but particularly in the straits between the British Columbian mainland and the many offshore islands. There have been sightings of a strange sea creature as recently as the late 1970s, but Caddie's credibility seems to be founded on a series of sightings made on the coast of the lower mainland between 1932 and 1934.

(The Salish of the British Columbian interior may also be responsible for the story of Ogopogo, the monster or serpent that is claimed to inhabit the otherwise entirely beautiful and innocent Lake Okanagan in the British Columbian interior; if not the Salish, then the British Columbian government tourist authority may be responsible. A report in a local paper in Victoria, British Columbia, suggests that Caddie and Ogopogo are related species.)

On October 8, 1933, Major W. H. Langley, a well-known barrister and at that time clerk of the British Columbia legislature, while sailing off Cadboro Bay in the early afternoon with his wife, saw a large creature "nearly eighty feet long and as wide as the average automobile" wallowing around in the water. It was as large as a whale, but its serrated back and greenish-brown color precluded that beast as a possibility; anyway, said Major Langley, he'd once spent time on a whaling ship and could therefore be relied on to know his whales. A report of Langley's sighting was published in the Victoria *Times Colonist*, which encouraged one F. W. Kemp to admit that he, too, only a year earlier and in the same location, had seen what was very likely the same monster, but had—probably sensibly, since he was an otherwise reliable employee in the provincial archives—kept quiet about it for fear of ridicule. Kemp and his wife saw the creature's serrated back, which closer to the tail "resembled the cutting edge of a saw"; its color was greenish-brown.

During the next two years there were reports of dozens of sightings up and down the coast by fishermen, steamer captains, quarry owners, an accountant with the Canadian Pacific Railway, and a gaggle of important folk on a steam yacht. All agreed on the animal's appearance: a long looped body with a slender neck, perched on top of which sat a head much like that of a cow or a camel.

In February 1950 no less a personage than Chief Justice James T. Brown of the King's Bench, Saskatchewan, laid his professionally doubting eyes upon what had come to be known as Caddie, and was convinced. Readers who have checked other accounts of sea serpents and monsters in this collection will be impressed with the number and undoubted probity of many of the witnesses who happened to be in the right place at the right time. Perhaps Democritus (about 460–370 B.C., Greek philosopher) knew more than he was letting on when he said, "Nature has buried truth at the bottom of the sea."

CAPTAIN M'QUHAE'S MONSTER

"Neither in the case of monsters which are born and live,
how quickly soever they die, will it be denied that they will rise again."
SAINT AUGUSTINE, *ON FAITH, HOPE, AND CHARITY*

On August 6, 1848, HMS *Daedalus*, Captain Peter M'Quhae, was in the South Atlantic between the Cape of Good Hope and the island of Saint Helena, on passage from the East Indies to England. At about 5:00 P.M. M'Quhae, Lieutenant Edgar Drummond, and William Barrett, sailing master, were pacing the quarterdeck when suddenly a seaman reported a strange object off the starboard beam. The officers stood at the rail and peered at the water; what they saw prompted the captain to exclaim, "This must be that animal called the sea-serpent." When *Daedalus* reached London Captain M'Quhae submitted a description of the creature to Admiral Sir W. H. Gage, as follows.

> *It was discovered to be an enormous serpent, with head and shoulders*
> *kept about four feet constantly above the surface of the sea, and as*
> *nearly as we could approximate by comparing it with what our main-*
> *topsail-yard would show in the water, there was at least sixty feet of the*
> *animal a fleur d'eau [showing above the surface], no portion of which*
> *was, to our perception, used in propelling it through the water, either*
> *by vertical or horizontal undulation. It passed rapidly, but so close*
> *under our lee quarter that, had it been a man of my acquaintance,*
> *I should have easily recognized his features with the naked eye; and it*
> *did not, either in approaching the ship or after it had passed our wake,*
> *deviate in the slightest degree from its course to the southwest, which it*
> *held on at the pace of from twelve to fifteen miles per hour, apparently*
> *on some determined course.*

The diameter of the serpent was about fifteen or sixteen inches behind the head, which was, without any doubt, that of a snake; and it was never, during the twenty minutes that it continued in sight of our glasses, once below the surface of the water; its color, a dark brown, with yellowish white about the throat. It had no fins, but something like the mane of a horse, or rather a bunch of sea-weed, washed about its neck.

The objectivity characteristic of ships' officers who are accustomed to describing and analyzing dispassionately what they see is obvious. Although doubters immediately suggested floating seaweed or a giant python or crocodile that had lost its bearings as explanations for the *Daedalus* sighting, it is difficult to imagine British naval officers of long and wide experience being fooled by such comparatively familiar creatures.

As with the supposed activity of UFOs, the "mystery" of the Bermuda Triangle, and various excited predictions of Atlantis rising again (see chapter 16), there is a tendency to dismiss all such sightings as interesting products of susceptible minds. But it is probably worth remembering that the coelacanth, known to ichthyologists as Old Fourlegs and said to have been extinct for some 60 million years, was caught in a fisherman's net off East London, South Africa, in 1938, much to the astonishment of science worldwide.

HAIPHONG MONSTER

"[In Along Bay] There were islands that took on
grotesque human profiles, others that looked like
crouching frogs, sugar loaves and ships under sail . . .
it was as though the architectural giants of the world,
grown senile, eaten with age and weather,
had been dumped down here to crumble quietly away."
CROSBIE GARSTIN, "THE DRAGON AND THE LOTUS"

In April 1904, in the Bay of Along, not far from the port of Haiphong in what was then called Indochina (now Vietnam), the French gunboat *Décidée* was showing the colors (and the guns that went with them) to those citizens who had been chosen to live under the comfort and protection of the French flag, when the entire ship's complement laid their corporate and unbelieving eyes on what was at the very least a most unusual creature. One can do no better than record here the French commander's (translated) official report to the admiral of the Indochina station:

I was standing on the bridge when my attention was directed to a round dark mass in the water about three hundred yards to port. I took it to be a rock, but on seeing it move, presumed it was an enormous turtle four or five yards in diameter. Soon afterward it rose out of the

*water, and by the undulatory movement that followed, I saw that I
was in the presence of an enormous sea monster shaped like a flat-
bodied serpent about one hundred feet in length. It appeared to have
a soft black skin covered with marbled spots, and the head, which
rose about sixteen feet out of the water, closely resembled that of an
enormous turtle with huge scales. It blew up two jets of water to a
height of about fifty feet. It moved slowly through the water at a speed
of about eight knots, and when one hundred and fifty yards from the
gunboat, plunged beneath it like a submarine, reappearing on the surface
about four hundred yards away. A number of the officers and crew
watched the monster, which gradually disappeared from view. After it
had gone Lieutenant Lagresville, one of the officers of the gunboat, said
that when cruising off this part of the coast in 1898 in the gunboat*
Avalanche *he had seen a similar—possibly the same—creature.*

Not only is one impressed with the detail of this reported observation (what
we might expect from an experienced naval officer, anyway), one is amazed at the
compressive force that could send two jets of water fully fifty feet into the air. On the
one hand, we might be compelled to regard this as a spouting whale (the dimensions
are not unusual for that species) being sighted by *perhaps* overenthusiastic naval personnel; on the other hand, the "flat-bodied serpent" description might remind us
of the forward-projecting "tail" of the giant squid or decapod (see below). It must be
pointed out, though, that the "soft black skin" of the creature does not fit easily with
the "huge scales" said to be on its head.

MONSTER KRAKEN

*"As if the Kraken, monarch of the sea
Wallowing abroad in his immensity
By polar storms and lightning shafts assailed
Wedg'd with ice-mountains here had fought and fail'd,
Perish'd—and in the petrifying blast,
His hulk became an island rooted fast."*

JAMES MONTGOMERY, "GREENLAND"

The Kraken is the fabled sea monster said to have been sighted frequently off the
coast of Norway; it was apparently quite capable of dragging the largest ships to
the bottom and simply by submerging itself it could suck a vessel to its doom by
means of the whirlpool it thereby created.

Brewer says that the Kraken was first described by Erik Pontoppidan in his *Natural History of Norway* (1752; Pontoppidan, 1698–1764, was bishop of Bergen at
the time). "Kraken" is probably from the Old Swedish *kraken* and the Danish *krage*,
stump or stem of a tree, from a claimed resemblance to the infamous and decidedly uncouth monster. Mercatante says Pontoppidan described this creature as
"a mile and a half wide." Clearly, even allowing for regional variations in what

constituted a proper Christian mile, this was a beast of no mean proportions. Pontoppidan's assertion that the creature's "discharges turn the sea murky" point to the likelihood that the dreaded Kraken was nothing but a giant cuttlefish.

The sea monsters of Scandinavia were of a peculiarly clerical bent: they seemed regularly to manifest themselves to seagoing clergy. Hans Egede, a Norwegian missionary (1686–1758) and later bishop of Greenland, described in 1741 a monster seen in those waters:

> The Monster was of so huge a Size, that coming out of the Water its Head reached as high, as the Mast-Head; its Body was as bulky as the Ship, and three or four times as long. It had a long pointed snout, and spouted like a Whale-Fish; great broad Paws, and the body seemed covered with shell-work, its skin very rugged and uneven. The under Part of its Body was shaped like an enormous huge serpent, and when it dived again under Water, it plunged backwards into the Sea and so raised its Tail aloft, which seemed a whole Ship's Length distant from the bulkiest part of its body.

Kemp says that according to one of the stories, the Kraken spends its time sleeping on the seabed and feeding on huge seaworms now and then, and when the fires of hell warm the ocean beyond the point of comfort (as determined by Krakens), the beast will rise to the surface and die.

Other accounts have it lounging around on the surface like an island. In 1555 Olaus Magnus (1490–1557), the Catholic archbishop of Sweden, said this monster had skin that looked so much like beach shingle that seamen were often beguiled into landing on it and cooking their food (a curious action, one would have thought, since all voyaging vessels were equipped with their own galleys for just such a purpose). There is an illustration in *Encyclopedia of World Mythology* showing a section of the North Sea in a sixteenth-century marine chart where a large sailing vessel has set its anchor into one of these monsters, two seamen meanwhile busily cooking a meal over a fire on the creature's back—clearly, an indication that the Kraken is regarded as being so huge that its particularities cannot be distinguished. Woodcuts of this nature, embellished with many dire warnings, were common on early sea charts for hundreds of years.

Archbishop Magnus was something of an historian, and because of the reports and descriptions that he appended on his maps he also became the authority of his time on fabulous sea monsters, his drawings of which were copied and passed on by other writers and mapmakers. He described a local monster, the Soe Orm, in the following terms:

> A very large Sea-Serpent of a length upwards of 200 feet and 20 feet in diameter which lives in rocks and in holes near the shore of Bergen; it comes out of its cavern only on summer nights and in fine weather to destroy calves, lambs, or hogs, or goes into the sea to eat cuttles,

lobster, and all kinds of sea crabs. It has a growth of hairs of two feet in length hanging from the neck, sharp scales of a dark brown color, and brilliant flaming eyes.

Clearly, this is a sea monster with a difference: it has developed the characteristics of an amphibian in order to satisfy a very comprehensive diet.

Mercatante tells us of a bishop (a Danish priest, according to Kemp) who, returning by sea to his own country, spies what he thinks is an island; he goes ashore and celebrates Mass, and it is only when he boards his ship again that he realizes that the island is in fact a Kraken, idly floating on the surface of the sea (see Voyages of Saint Brendan, chapter 3, for an account of a similar incident).

Rogers makes the sensible suggestion that the Kraken was in fact a gigantic squid or octopus; he mentions the fact that Frank Bullen (an English whaling captain; his book *The Cruise of the "Cachalot"* is an interesting account of nineteenth-century whaling) once saw a large sperm whale attacking an octopus—it may have been a squid; both were the natural prey of these whales, which they almost equaled in size. Kemp shows a late-eighteenth-century engraving of a large vessel being overwhelmed by a Kraken, which the artist has depicted as a giant octopus (although its eyes are curiously situated at the roots of two of its tentacles).

Rogers also records that in 1873 two fishermen were attacked by an octopus in Newfoundland waters; they managed to drive it away by chopping off two tentacles. Later measurements indicated that the creature would have been some 80 feet across its spread-out diameter, a compelling bulk.

Interestingly, Rogers insisted that the sperm whale, the famous cachalot, is capable of swallowing a man, and he included an authenticated account, one of a number of such, in his book *Ships and Sailors* (see, for example, Jonah and the Whale, below, for just such an account). The sperm whale will actually devour a giant squid, and sections of the tentacles of those creatures are at least as thick as a man—all of which makes the story of Jonah's three-day sojourn in the belly of "a great fish" not at all difficult to swallow.

The English writer John Wyndham (1903–1969) created a Kraken that was very much alive in his science-fiction novel *The Kraken Wakes* (1953), in which the beast bursts into life and wreaks destruction on everything it encounters.

It is likely that the Kraken and the sea serpent are in fact the giant squid known as *Architeuthis* (see below), examples of which have been discovered in the past century afloat and washed up on beaches, especially in cold climates. The sea serpent sighted from HMS *Daedalus* (see Captain M'Quhae's Monster, above) may well have been *Architeuthis* swimming on the surface with its flattened broad-arrow tail that actually precedes the animal as it moves through the water, looking for all the world like a huge snake—the quintessential description of the sea serpent of myth.

In 1861, while approaching Tenerife in the Canary Islands off the northwest coast of Africa, the French steamer *Alecton* came across a giant squid on the surface of the sea. The commander, Lieutenant Bouyer, reported that it was up to 18 feet long with a head shaped much like a parrot's beak (characteristic of the giant squid), arms 5 to 6 feet long, and colored brick red; it looked like a "colossal and slimy embryo [that] has a repulsive and terrible appearance." This was in fact *Architeuthis*, the giant squid, specimens of which were found on beaches in Newfoundland in the period 1870–80, some of the bodies being over forty feet long. Then, for reasons unknown, the creatures disappeared from the waters of Newfoundland and relocated themselves to New Zealand, whence they wandered to sites as disparate as Iceland, Norway, South Africa, and Cape Cod.

Examination of carcasses shows that *Architeuthis* has the largest eyes in the animal kingdom (as large as the hubcap of a car, as Richard Ellis colorfully puts it), indicating that they live at great depths in the ocean. The suckers on each of their ten arms are each equipped with a ring of teeth that can immovably grip prey; where the arms meet at the head there is an enormous beak used for ripping flesh from creatures as large as sperm whales, though the whales are believed to dive to prodigious depths to seek, in return, their favorite food, the giant squid.

But one thing is certain: no amount of scientific explanation, nor even the production of suitably gigantic carcasses as tangible proof, will convince those who prefer shivery myth and mystery to the plain austerity of everyday fact.

LOCH NESS MONSTER

"Beautiful Loch Ness
The truth to express . . .
Your scenery is romantic
With rocks and hills gigantic
Enough to make one frantic . . .
. . . you are most beautiful to behold
With your lovely landscape and water so cold."
WILLIAM MCGONAGALL, "LOCH NESS"

The Loch Ness Monster is the world-famous creature said to inhabit Loch Ness in northern Scotland. The search for the monster has probably consumed more money, time, and newspaper space than attempts to prove the existence or otherwise of UFOs. Loch Ness, the largest body of fresh water in Great Britain, is about 23 miles long, nearly two miles wide, and measures 754 feet at its deepest point.

Legend has it that the loch, or lake, was not always there; instead there was a pleasant valley containing a well which, whenever its cover was removed, provided an unlimited supply of sweet water, the flow ceasing only when the cover was replaced. One day a woman who was fetching water from the well heard her child screaming in her crib; she ran quickly to see what was the matter, in her haste dropping the cover on the ground. The well overflowed, filled the valley, and drove out the people living there, who cried as they fled, "Tha loch nis ann!" ("There is a lake there now!"), hence the name Loch Ness.

In April 1933 two men who happened to be driving along the shore of Loch Ness reported sighting a strange creature swimming along the surface; it was some thirty feet long, had two humps and a head like a snake at the end of a long neck, and also had two flippers attached at the midsection of its body. (Gordon offers the intriguing information that the two "discoverers" of Nessie, as its nickname became, were local hoteliers; see also a similar comment by Wannan in The Bunyip of the Billabongs, below.)

Following a somewhat hysterical press report (the hysteria has abated not a whit in the succeeding decades, with periodic sightings doing nothing to diminish the creature's shape or embellishments), other observers also "saw" the monster. Within the following six months more than twenty sightings of the creature had been duly reported, and thus an industry was born. Scientific expeditions have been mounted on, around, and in Loch Ness, sophisticated photographic and sonar surveillance has probed every nook and cranny of the lake waters, and still Nessie refuses to reveal herself—or themselves, popular sentiment declining to entertain the notion of only one bizarre loathsome worm infesting these murky northern waters.

Reports of a monster in this otherwise innocent and pleasant stretch of water date back to the sixth century A.D., when Saint Columba apparently battled the wretched beast and brought about its defeat by means of a bout of concentrated prayer and a stern warning (there is no record of Nessie's ever harming anyone over the past fifteen hundred years). This is precisely what any Christian community would have wished for; and, one dares suppose, legendary tales of battles between the forces of Good and the forces of Evil must always bring about the defeat of the evil usurper, even if only as a temporary measure until the next conflict comes.

RATTRAY HEAD MONSTER

"The 31 of August [1583] . . . there passed along
betweene us and towards the land which we now forsooke
a very lion to our seeming, in shape, hair and colour . . .
sliding upon the water with his whole body . . .
yawning and gaping wide, with ougly
demonstration of long teeth, and glaring eies . . .
roaring or bellowing as doeth a lion."

RICHARD HAKLUYT, *VOYAGES AND DOCUMENTS*

Rattray Head is about forty miles north of Aberdeen on the east coast of Scotland. Early in the 1900s J. Watt, the chief engineer of the steam trawler *Craig Gowan*, Captain Ballard, reported to the captain that a "large animal" was following astern of their vessel; the captain duly investigated and subsequently made his report. Bridges gives us Captain Ballard's interesting account:

> *On reaching the deck I found several of the crew looking over the weather rail. On joining them I saw a very large animal of a dark colour, which seemed racing with us, but which was about fifty feet to windward. I have often seen whales, but I at once saw the animal was not a whale but some sea monster, the like of which I have never seen in my life. As it rose several portions of the body were visible at the one time. It seemed to snake its way through the water, showing repeated portions of a brown body. The animal was now uncomfortably near. We could even see that the skin was covered with some substance like a rough coating of hair. Securing the furnace rake [used for setting the fires in the boilers] to a stout line I threw it at the animal, but it fell short. I again tried; this time the rake landed across the animal's back and we suddenly drew the line. The monster raised its body (the fore-part) clean out of the water and made direct for the* Craig Gowan. *I plainly saw the monster rise up until its head was over our gaff peak [the upper part of the steadying sail commonly used in trawlers], when it lowered itself with a motion as sudden as lightning, carrying away the peak halliards and sending the gaff, sail and all, down on deck. The utmost consternation ensued among the crew and it was a time before we got matters squared up. The animal had then entirely disappeared and we did not see it again.*

One is somewhat surprised at the boldness, not to say rashness, of those folk who take it into their heads to offer violence to what they universally describe as a large "monster" of unknown habits and preoccupations. A perusal of the literature seems to indicate a ready willingness of people to fire guns and whatnot at these strange creatures of the sea rather than make off in the opposite direction with all decent haste.

CAPE COD MONSTER

> *"Captayne Gosnoll comaunded the shallop to be trymmed out and went a shore, where he perceaved this Headland to be parcell of the Mayne and sondry Islandes lying amost rownd about yt, whereupon thus satisfied he repayred abourd agayne, where during the tyme of his absence which was not above 6 howres, he found the shippe so furnished with excellent Cod-fish . . . This headland therefore they called Cape-Cod."*
> WILLIAM STRACHEY, *THE HISTORIE OF TRAVELL INTO VIRGINIA BRITANIA*

The Cape Cod Monster was sighted by the crew of the U.S. Coast Guard survey steamer *Drift*, Captain Platt, on August 29, 1878, a few miles off Race Point, Cape Cod, in southeastern Massachusetts, on a clear and calm day. In fact, the day was hot enough that the crew were, according to Bridges, "lounging in the shade of the sails," which indicates the *Drift* was an auxiliary steamer. Suddenly there appeared sticking up from the sea an object for all the world like the spar of a sailing vessel; it rose for about fifteen feet above the surface and simply stayed there, in full view of all aboard the *Drift*.

The "spar" was some two feet thick at the upper end, and although it had manifested itself about a quarter mile from the vessel the air was so clear that it was immediately obvious that this was no ship's yard or mast suddenly risen from the depths. The object then curved over and sank into the water; the entire crew waited in some excitement, certain that they were seeing a fabled sea monster or serpent at work, so to speak. In half an hour it reappeared, this time rising to a height of some forty feet and looking for all the world like a gigantic worm, with an evenly cylindrical body that was dark brown in color; neither mouth nor eye was visible. Then the "spar"—now a "worm"—curved over once again and slid back into the depths, but this time in doing so it revealed a dorsal fin some fifteen feet long.

Captain Platt reported to the superintendent of survey in Washington what he and the crew had seen, but according to Bridges, for various reasons—mostly those to do with public ridicule—this report did not see the light of day until it was published eight years later, 1886, in *Science*. Unhappily, Bridges does not cite the exact date of publication, but the other details of his account, such as the names of the survey vessel and the captain, together with the date of sighting, suggest that the witnesses were, like those on HMS *Daedalus*, a reliable lot (see Captain M'Quhae's Monster, above).

CAPE SÃO ROQUE MONSTER

"Swift Scamander roll thee to the deep,
Whose every wave some wat'ry monster brings."
ALEXANDER POPE, "HOMER'S *ILIAD*"

Cape São Roque (Cabo de São Roque) lies on the northeast coast of Brazil, some 250 miles north of Recife (formerly Pernambuco) and about 5 degrees south of the Equator. On July 8, 1875, the London-registered sailing ship *Pauline*, Captain George Drevar, carrying a cargo of coal from northern England to Zanzibar on the east coast of Africa, encountered three large sperm whales. These creatures had moved close enough to the vessel that they attracted the very close attention of all on board.

Without warning (and of course to everyone's intense amazement) "suddenly there arose from the deep a gigantic serpent which wound itself in two coils around the largest of the whales, which it proceeded to crush in the fashion of a boa-constrictor. The hapless whale plunged and lashed frantically, but all in vain, and as the giant coils tightened, the horrified men in the *Pauline* heard the ribs of the great whale cracking with reports like those of a small cannon. Soon whale and serpent together plunged into the depths and were seen no more."

Naturally enough, Captain Drevar's report of this incident was met with the skepticism that is usual when God-fearing folk are confronted with something beyond the compass of everyday experience. Why, people asked, should it be a serpent of the sea when a giant squid would serve, particularly since such creatures are known to prey on whales? Because, Bridges replies, giant squid do not have the powers of constriction attributed to a serpent built along the lines of an enormous boa constrictor such as the one encountered by the *Pauline*.

Anyone who shares my doubts about Bridges's confident assertion might review the Monster Kraken, above.

HALIFAX MONSTER

"As for Halifax, its well enough in itself,
though no great shakes neither . . . the people,
the strange critters, they are all asleep.
They walk in their sleep, and talk in their sleep,
and what they say one day they forget the next,
they say they were dreamin.' "
T. C. HALIBURTON, *THE CLOCKMAKER, OR THE SAYINGS AND DOINGS OF SAMUEL SLICK*

From time to time Bridges makes detailed reference to specific dates of sea serpent sightings, and often he gives us the names of people involved; what I call the Halifax Monster is a good example of his attention to correct details (though one might regret that this exactitude is not more frequent throughout his book).

On May 15, 1833, a boat set out from Halifax, Nova Scotia, bound for a popular fishing spot; aboard were Captain W. Sullivan, Lieutenant A. Maclachlan, Ensign G. P. Malcolm, and Lieutenant B. O'Neal Lyster, all of the British army, together with Henry Ince and Jack Dowling, the latter an old salt from the Royal Navy. Not much fishing seemed to be done because when we meet them the officers were firing their rifles at some grampuses (a harmless and quite innocent blunt-headed creature that somewhat resembles a dolphin).

At some time during this diversion Dowling, the former navy man, called out (I give Bridges's actual words here; otherwise they could easily be attributed to something from Gilbert and Sullivan): "Oh, sirs, look at that! I've sailed in all parts of the world and seen some rum sights, but this is the queerest thing I ever see!" And of course the "queerest thing he ever saw," about 150 yards away, was a sea serpent, or at least the very large head of one of these apparently increasingly common creatures, rising about six feet above the surface and with a neck "as thick as the trunk of a moderate-sized tree," colored brown and white in an irregular fashion.

Captain Sullivan, in his report of this encounter, opined that "There could be no mistake, no delusion, and we were all perfectly satisfied that we had been favored with a view of the true and veritable sea serpent, a creature which has been generally considered to have existed only in the brain of the Yankee skipper." Unlike the good folk of Halifax described by Haliburton (see quote previous page), these six citizens seemed to be very much awake.

WHALER *DAPHNE*'S MONSTER

"The serious student of abnormal psychology
will find 'the whalemen' markedly interesting;
it is my own conviction, reached after reading hundreds of
logbooks and sea journals, that the old whaling vessels
had more than their arithmetical proportion of madmen."
CAPTAIN C. B. HAWES

Strangely, very few whaling men have made reports of sea serpents—curious, because these men were at sea for prodigious periods of time and were to be found in every ocean of the world. However, Bridges does include in his chapter on sea serpents a report from the American brig *Daphne*, Captain Henderson, which in September 1848 met with a sea monster some 1,200 miles north of the earlier *Daedalus* sighting (see Captain McQuhae's Monster, above).

This creature surfaced about forty yards away from the *Daphne* (apparently not a large vessel, crewed by only nine men), with a head rather like a dragon's and equipped with huge glaring eyes and a body at least a hundred feet long. Given the obvious size of the monster and the only too apparent insignificance of the *Daphne*, what Captain Henderson did next might have signaled the man's personal courage, but it certainly underlined the danger of precipitate action: he loaded a small cannon with nails and bits of iron and fired the charge point-blank at the monster's head.

The creature reacted immediately. In the words of Bridges, "The serpent immediately reared its head and plunged violently with its body, and turning made off at the rate of 15 to 16 knots an hour." (Anyone sensitve to nautical matters will immediately note that this is a lubberly expression: *knots* already means nautical miles per hour; see Of Knots and Logs, chapter 7.) Bridges very much doubts that the creature was a large ribbon fish, a basking shark, a whale, or an octopus (in which last category he presumably also includes the giant squid).

NAHANT BEACH MONSTER

"There has always been something a little difficult
between myself and Massachusetts, some incompatibility."
H. G. WELLS, *THE WAY THE WORLD IS GOING*

Nahant is the name of a beach close to Swampscott in Massachusetts. John Marston, fisherman of that town, claimed his place in history by being the first to witness an unusual event. At about eight o'clock on the morning of August 3, 1819, Marston was walking along Nahant beach when his attention was attracted by a disturbance in the water about two hundred yards offshore; then to his no doubt considerable amazement (mixed very likely with a frisson of alarm), the head of an enormous serpent broke the surface of the water and stared at him.

Marston spent twenty minutes staring back at the apparition until he realized that unless he gathered a few witnesses no one would believe his story. In no time at all he had two hundred citizens of Swampscott down on the beach and gaping at the sea serpent as it roamed the bay in an apparent search of fish for breakfast. When the beast suddenly headed for the shore the gathered crowd turned and ran off in terror lest the creature be of a mind to include them in its early-morning feed.

Among the watchers were some of the more notable citizens of the town, including the Honorable Amos Lawrence, Samuel Cabot (presumably a scion of the clan Cabot of Boston), and James Prince, the local U.S. Marshal. From these sober folk emerged an agreed description of their aquatic visitor: dark brown and 80 to 90 feet long; there were some humps (alternatively, serrations) on its back, and it moved through the water "faster than a whale." Notwithstanding this last characteristic, some whaling vessels chased the creature and one of them, for some inscrutable reason, fired a cannon and apparently hit it, whereupon it dived and very sensibly swam out to sea.

Bridges advises the reader that his "records" include several accounts of sea serpents showing themselves in the cold and deep waters off Maine and Massachusetts and British Columbia, as well as, of course, in Norwegian waters, which last might be regarded as the historical home of sea monsters in general (and perhaps hysterical home as well, see Monster Kraken, above). One of Bridges's records is an account of an actual attack on a vessel by a sea serpent, an event not frequently encountered, apparently—and indeed, thankfully; see Rattray Head Monster, above.

JONAH AND THE WHALE

"The story of the whale swallowing Jonah,
though a whale is large enough to do it,
borders greatly on the marvelous;
but it would have approached nearer to the idea
of miracle if Jonah had swallowed the whale."

THOMAS PAINE, *THE AGE OF REASON*

Jonah was one of the minor prophets of the Old Testament (in the New Testament his name is usually rendered as Jonas). His claim on our attention and his subsequent established place in seafaring folklore arises from God's having commanded him to take himself to Nineveh, the ancient capital of Syria in the east, in order to reform its wicked ways. Jonah, however, is not of a mind to follow this particular instruction, no doubt fearing a disagreeable reception from the recalcitrant citizens of thoroughly unwholesome Nineveh, so he alters his sailing orders and heads west for Tarshish (or Tarsish), an ancient city said to be located in southern Spain, the place from which Solomon was accustomed to obtain his gold and silver and other valuable commodities.

A great tempest blows up on the way to Tarshish, and the sailors, fearing the worst (the Mediterranean can mount a very respectable storm indeed) and learning of Jonah's function as a servant of God—albeit a rather truculent and disobedient servant at that—immediately heave him over the side, straight into the gaping maw of a "great fish," said to be a cousin of Leviathan; the New Testament and folklore report this "fish" as a whale. (Interestingly, this incident is likely the source of the well-known and widely practiced superstition held by seafarers: priests are most unwelcome on board ship.)

Jonah then lies in the fish's belly for three days. At the end of this time the fish—or whale—regurgitates Jonah onto the shore. By now somewhat chastened, Jonah immediately hurries off to Nineveh and carries out the task God had earlier laid on him. He then forswears seafaring, and much later reappears in the Bible.

What concerns us here is the dispute that has raged among scholars and seafarers ever since: first, could a sea creature have a gullet large enough to swallow a man whole? And second, would a man unfortunate enough to have been gulped down by such a creature survive the experience? That is to say, wouldn't the animal's digestive juices quickly begin their corrosive work on him, and even if he didn't drown in the fluids, wouldn't there be a good chance he'd quickly expire anyway, as there is very little fresh air in a whale's stomach at the best of times?

These questions have usually been met with the response that the throat of a whale (indeed, the throat of any other sizable creature in the sea) is not large enough to admit a human figure. However, Rogers refutes this: "If Jonah was swallowed by a whale, the cachalot is the guilty party, for he has a throat that will admit the passage of objects the size of a man, without difficulty . . . There are well-authenticated accounts . . . of men being swallowed by sperm whales." The Hardwicks agree with Rogers, recounting an example of just such an incident.

In 1891 the American whaler *Star of the East* was cruising the equatorial Pacific in search of the increasingly elusive sperm whale, which is normally completely harmless to mankind. (But see The Whaler *Essex*, chapter 11, and Moby Dick, chapter 4, for accounts of what an angry whale can do.) The coxswain of one of the *Star*'s longboats was James Bartley. A whale had been sighted and harpooned and Bartley's boat and excited crew went after it, with the coxswain standing in the bow, another harpoon in his hand. The whale, apparently maddened by pain, turned and charged the pursuing boat, and the shock of the impact caused Bartley to topple forward, and before anyone had time to do anything he fell straight into the whale's open mouth. The animal, no doubt just as surprised as Bartley, immediately shut its enormous jaws and sounded. Both whale and man vanished beneath the sea. Bartley's crew rowed smartly back to their ship, very much sobered by what they had witnessed.

The next day the body of a recently dead male sperm whale appeared, floating not far from the *Star of the East*; it was a very large beast, probably a hundred tons. The *Star* spent two days flensing the beast—stripping it of its valuable blubber—then left the carcass to the sharks; it was of no further commercial use. As the carcass drifted off, someone on the ship remarked that perhaps this had been the whale that had swallowed Bartley, of recent memory; it even seemed to have a wound corresponding to where the *Star's* first harpoon had been thrown.

Somewhat reluctantly, the flensers began the wearisome job of slicing into the whale's body so they could get to the stomach. When at last they cut it open they could see inside a great mass of shrimp and other small creatures, along with a large lump of something vaguely human shaped. Finally it was dragged out of the awful stinking mess of stomach and the horrified crew found themselves gazing on the blood-soaked body of their erstwhile coxswain, his face purple and drawn tight in apparent horror.

It took five hours to bring James Bartley back to something resembling life, and even then he seemed raving mad, screaming and thrashing around so much that he had to be lashed to his bunk. He babbled endlessly about the fire that had been consuming him, and no wonder—a whale's body temperature is higher than man's, and someone confined in the stomach of such a creature would have felt as though he were being cooked in an oven. This is not to mention the truly dreadful ordeal of being entombed without hope of release, as well as being cooked alive, all this in addition to the certainty of suffocation as the whale's digestive machinery ground endlessly on. Here is an extract from Bartley's account of what happened to him:

> *I remember very well from the moment that I jumped from the boat . . .*
> *I felt myself drawn downward, feet first, and I realized that I was*
> *being swallowed by a whale . . . a wall of flesh surrounded me . . .*
> *suddenly I found myself in a sack much larger than my body, but*
> *completely dark. I felt about me; and my hand came in contact with*
> *several fishes, some of which seemed to be still alive, for they squirmed*
> *in my fingers . . . Soon I felt a great pain in my head, and my*
> *breathing became more and more difficult. At the same time I felt*
> *terrible heat; it seemed to consume me, growing hotter and hotter.*
> *My eyes became coals of fire in my head, and I believed every moment*

> *that I was condemned to perish in the belly of a whale. It tormented*
> *me beyond all endurance, while at the same time the awful silence of*
> *the terrible prison weighed me down. I tried to rise, to move my arms*
> *and legs, to cry out. All action was now impossible, but my brain*
> *seemed abnormally clear; and with a full comprehension of my awful*
> *fate, I finally lost all consciousness.*

It is not surprising that after this experience Bartley could not bear to be left alone. Furthermore, not only did he never go whaling again, he refused even to look at the sea.

Orcs, Whales, and Leviathan

"An island salt and bare
The haunt of seals and orcs, and sea-mews clang."
JOHN MILTON, "PARADISE LOST"

The orc was a fabled sea monster much feared for its ability to devour humans, somewhat like the Kraken of Scandinavian fame; "orc" was also the name sometimes used earlier for the whale. The word (from the Latin *orca*, large sea creature) is usually rendered today as *orca*, which we understand to mean the killer whale. Science today refers to the creature as *Grampus orca*, "grampus" alluding to its loud and heavy breathing.

The orca or killer whale is known for its ferocity in attacking prey such as fish, seals, porpoises, and dolphins; it is a determined and voracious hunter. When seeking whales, orcas hunt in packs; they have been known to combine as a group in Antarctic waters to break ice floes from below so as to topple their prey into the water; this prey may include humans. The orca is equipped with large conical teeth and a formidable attitude, making it worthy of great respect.

The whale was regarded in Christian folklore as a symbol of the devil, the sea creature thought able to lure fish into its maw by wafting its sweet breath over its prey (sad to report, a whale's breath resembles nothing so much as the morning exhalations of a dog with a severe halitosis problem). It was believed that the devil lured folk into sin by the same means. The whale also, of course, symbolized the power of the sea; hence it stood for regeneration as well as the grave. Thus Jonah "dies" by being swallowed by the whale, whose jaws are the "gates of hell," but the creature's stomach ("hell") is also the womb, so his final regurgitation after three days is a "rebirth."

Leviathan is the Hebrew name for a monster of the sea. Leviathan is female, while Behemoth, another water creature of unappetizing aspect found in Hebrew literature, is male. Job 41:1 seems to be referring to a crocodile ("Canst thou draw out Leviathan with an hook? or his tongue with a cord which thou lettest down?"). Psalm 104:26 suggests the whale ("There go the ships: there is that leviathan, whom thou hast made to play therein"). Isaiah 27:1 makes clear that leviathan is a sea serpent.

Leviathan is thus the equivalent of Tiamat, the Sumerian cosmic serpent that represented chaos, and also of Typhon (also known as Typhoeus), in Greek mythology a hundred-headed monster and father of the winds (the word *typhoon*, the violent hurricane encountered in east Asian waters, is from a different source, although its spelling was influenced by Typhon; see Trade Winds, chapter 7). All in all, leviathan is something of great size usually associated with the sea, such as whales and ships.

THE BUNYIP OF THE BILLABONGS

"Certain large fossil bones . . . have been referred by the natives . . . to a huge animal of extraordinary appearance, called in some districts the Bunyup [sic]."

W. WESTGARTH, *AUSTRALIA FELIX*

In the folklore of the Australian Aborigine, a *bunyip* is a roaring, man-eating monster that lives in lakes and swamps and billabongs, waiting in the dead of night to grab his unwary victim and drag him or her down to the bottom, where he then eats the poor wretch (there is one important caveat: this large, black anthropophagous amphibian was said to much prefer women and children in his diet, a piece of information that Wannan says was reported to him by Aboriginal males "with some satisfaction").

(Note: Anyone suffering the grave disadvantage of not having been born in Australia is probably unaware that a *billabong* is a pool of water that has been separated from the main stream, usually during the dry season. In the northern reaches of the continent, billabongs are the haunt of crocodiles, filefish, leeches, and, of course, bunyips that have migrated from the south.)

The bunyip loomed large in the traditional beliefs and stories of Aboriginal groups in many different parts of Australia, particularly in the eastern states, where there were large and relatively permanent bodies of water compared to the more arid areas of the western third of the continent (there are, nevertheless, also some accounts of this creature in Western Australia).

Although its name might vary from tribe to tribe, the bunyip's appearance and habits were essentially the same: it was large, black, often hairy (some versions describe the creature as furry, others as feathered). It possessed enormous baleful, shining eyes, was given to making bellowing or booming noises in the middle hours of darkness, and preferred to emerge on moonlit nights to catch and noisily dine on whatever luckless human prey came within reach.

Many colonists and a number of scientists throughout the nineteenth century believed in the existence of this Australian werewolf, although accumulated experience should have told them (and certainly ought to have informed the Aborigines themselves, since there is strong evidence that they have inhabited the Australian continent for at least 60,000 years) that there are no large dangerous animals indigenous to this country.

Nevertheless, the Sydney *Morning Herald* reported on June 19, 1847, that a bunyip had been sighted on the Murrumbidgee River in southeastern New South Wales, "about as big as a six months old calf, of a dark brown color, a long neck, a long pointed head, large ears, a thick mane of hair from the head down the neck, and two large tusks." An account appeared in the Wagga Wagga *Advocate* (south-central New South Wales) on April 13, 1872, in which a group of settlers watched "a bunyip swimming in a lagoon." A year later this creature, or one of its cousins, was seen quietly disporting itself in a lake in the same district.

Wannan makes a laconic point—curiously, echoed by Gordon concerning the Loch Ness Monster (see above):

> *My own experience with bushmen and their tales suggests that bunyips are usually seen in swamps near bush shanties [rough huts where "sly grog" was sold—that is, liquor]. They are never seen by men going to shanties, only by men on their way home.*

18

WRAITHS OF THE SEA

Richard Garrett makes a telling point when he quotes the British statesman Edmund Burke on "the lucrative business of mystery." Writers in this genre—the mystery story, and in particular the murder mystery—have never lacked an audience. Garrett goes on to wonder why we are "in love with the apparently unexplained," a conundrum that insists on being resolved.

The curious thing is—or so it seems to me—that we are often disappointed when we discover a solution that explains completely what was heretofore a wonderful mystery. People often prefer to have and hold an enigma, an inexplicable puzzle. When the crop circles that littered the corn and wheat fields of England in the late 1980s were finally revealed as a simple (and most effective) hoax, there was a hue and cry from believers in the widely supported theory that a number of UFOs were kindly leaving messages for humanity (an old standby: see, for example, Fabled Atlantis, chapter 16).

The previous chapter deals with sea monsters, more than a dozen of them, all with various curious aspects and many reported by some very sober citizens indeed. Garrett states that out of some six hundred reported sightings of sea serpents and monsters, at least four hundred seem to be genuine. And, after all, the sea is very wide and rather deep in places and covers almost three quarters of the earth's surface—is it not reasonable to expect the occasional oddity to turn up from time to time?

CAPES OF VIRGINIA PHANTOM

"At first cock-crow the ghosts must go
Back to their quiet graves below."
THEODOSIA GARRISON, "THE NEIGHBORS"

Not all sea phantoms come from past disasters, such as those caused by evil wreckers and terrible storms. Occasionally an apparition makes itself known to a seafarer, apparently to give timely warning of danger ahead.

Bridges tells of the figure of a drowned man who—or which—manifested itself in the middle of the night to Captain Rogers aboard HMS *Society*, off the coast of Virginia in 1664, with the warning (spoken, one assumes—though it is not a confident assumption) that the captain should go on deck and have the watch cast the lead. This the captain did, only to find that he was well within soundings, the lead showing only seven fathoms (about forty feet), whereupon he immediately tacked into deeper water. At first light he was astonished to find that his vessel was uncomfortably close to the Capes of Virginia (Cape Charles and Cape Henry, forming the entrance to Chesapeake Bay) instead of, as he had earlier supposed, a hundred miles or more out to sea.

Adrian Hayter, a New Zealand yachtsman, in the early 1950s sailed *Sheila* from England to New Zealand by way of the Cape of Good Hope. Shortly after his boat was blown onto Horrocks Beach on the western Australian coast (happily, the vessel was undamaged and later refloated), Hayter gave a talk on his adventures to a group of boys, of whom I was one. A curious incident that Hayter related happened in the South Atlantic. He had turned in, exhausted from dealing with bad weather, knowing that although a group of islands or rocks lay directly ahead on *Sheila*'s course he was still far enough away from them to be in no immediate danger. However, when very much later he awoke and went on deck he was astonished to find that the islands were now dead astern—*Sheila* had apparently sailed round them, then resumed her previous course.

What had saved him from disaster? Vagaries of wind? Of current? One is reminded of Slocum's pilot of the *Pinta* who, it would seem, was of considerable assistance to Slocum when he fell ill after leaving the Azores during his famous circumnavigation of 1895–98 (see Phantom Pilots, below).

One is otherwise reluctant to say more.

GULF OF SAINT LAWRENCE GHOST SHIP

"When Mrs. Brooke upon her Return to England from Quebec
told Mr. Johnson that the Prospect up *the River Saint Lawrence*
was the finest in the World—but Madam says he, the Prospect down
the River Saint Lawrence is I have a Notion the finest you ever saw."
HESTER LYNCH THRALE, *THRALIANA*

The Gulf of Saint Lawrence leads to the Saint Lawrence River, a long stretch of navigable water that spears deep into the seaboard of eastern Canada. The Gulf and the river were for a long time the scene of much shipping activity during the wars of the English and the French as they fought each other for control of this rich maritime region. The Gulf and the river are also noted for their fierce winter storms, and, as we might expect, there are a number of stories of phantom ships seen here.

One of them involves the fleet sent by Queen Anne against the French in the early eighteenth century. When her armada reached Gaspé Bay, an inlet from the Gulf, a great storm fell upon them. One by one the ships were driven onto the rocks, where they smashed themselves into pieces and sank, taking all on board to the bottom. The flagship met her end under the cliffs of Cap d'Espoir (meaning, ironically, "Cape of Hope"). As is common with many of these stories, on the anniversary of this disaster any observer in the vicinity sights the phantom flagship on the storm-tossed waters of the Gulf.

Bridges gives us a suitably colorful description of the destruction that the apparition undergoes:

> *The flagship's deck is seen to be covered with soldiers, and from her*
> *wide, old-fashioned ports lights stream brightly. Up in the bows stands*
> *a scarlet-coated officer, who points with one hand to the land, while*
> *the other arm is round the waist of a handsome girl. Suddenly the*
> *lights go out, the ship lurches violently, her stern heaves upwards, and*
> *screams ring out as she plunges bow-foremost into the gloomy depths.*

This account bears a striking resemblance to an encounter I have seen in Las Vegas, in the forecourt of a casino, between an English man-o'-war and an enemy—one forgets which it was—presented as a tourist attraction/distraction every evening with laughable dialogue and considerable technical skill, this being Las Vegas, after all. I was struck by the very un-naval behavior of the "scarlet-coated officer" standing "up in the bows"—an unheard-of action unless he is there to help fend off enemy boarders, which clearly he is not doing because he has one arm round a woman. *And* on one of Her Majesty's warships.

No wonder an outraged Providence sent a storm to demolish the fleet.

LONG ISLAND SOUND GHOST SHIP

"It was a matter of chance that I should have
rented a house . . . [near] the most domesticated
body of salt water in the Western Hemisphere,
the great wet barnyard of Long Island Sound."

F. SCOTT FITZGERALD, *THE GREAT GATSBY*

Several ghost ships are said to haunt the U.S. East Coast, among which is the *Palatine*, whose appearance in Long Island Sound is regarded by local fishermen as an infallible portent of a terrible storm. In 1752 the *Palatine* was carrying emigrants to New England, but conditions on board were terrible: the captain and the crew were frequently drunk, many of them terrorizing and robbing the passengers. It was probably this slack discipline that caused the ship to pile up on the rocks; then a party of wreckers (who very likely had helped events along with false lights) set about stripping the vessel of everything of value, and when they had finished they put a torch to the hull to remove all trace of their work.

The incoming tide lifted the flaming wreck, and slowly she drifted out into the Sound. Suddenly screams of pain and terror could be heard, and a woman—some accounts have her a young mother who had hidden from the wreckers—appeared on the deck of the burning ship, shrieking for help. Then the deck collapsed and she disappeared in a torrent of flame and sparks; by dawn there was nothing left except a few pieces of floating wreckage. All that remains, it is said, is the ghost of the *Palatine*, which according to local legend can be seen on every anniversary of this event, drifting away from the shore in flames, a spectacle known as the Palatine Fire.

NEW HAVEN GHOST SHIP

"Here's to the town of New Haven,
The home of the Truth and the Light,
Where God talks to Jones in the very same tones
That He uses with Hadley and Dwight."

F. S. JONES, "ON THE DEMOCRACY OF YALE"

As with the *Palatine*, the ghost ship that figures in this legend is a harbinger of disaster. In January 1647 (Bridges is able to give a fairly exact date here, though unfortunately not the name of the ship) a vessel came off the stocks at New Haven, Connecticut, and shortly afterward set sail on her maiden voyage, soon becoming well known as a coastal trader in the region. Five months later, in June, a furious storm fell upon the town and did not abate until late afternoon, leaving a strong wind blowing down the Quinnipiac River and out into Long Island Sound.

When the local fishermen came down to the harbor to check their craft they were astonished to see this coastal trader sailing up the river, straight into the eye of the wind (a feat that, as even any landsman knows, is beyond the capability of ordinary sailing vessels). Word of this amazing event quickly spread, and the townsfolk gathered on the shore to watch as the ship slowly disappeared into the air itself. When all the spectators had collected their wits they agreed that it was a sign that the coaster had been lost in the storm, and in fact she was never seen again.

The story must have been well known, for Bridges quotes a verse from the poem that Henry Wadsworth Longfellow wrote about the incident some two hundred years later, "The Phantom Ship":

> *And the masts, with all their rigging,*
> *Fell slowly, one by one,*
> *And the hull dilated and vanished,*
> *As a sea-mist in the sun.*

GHOSTS OF DEAD MEN

"Vex not his ghost. O, let him pass! He hates him
That would upon the rack of this tough world
Stretch him out longer."

WILLIAM SHAKESPEARE, *KING LEAR*

Bridges reminds us of the old belief among seafaring men that the ghost of a dead sailor will sometimes show itself. There is, for example, the account given by "the late Mr. Marion Crawford" of a specter whose presence was detected in the cabin of a modern ocean liner because the berth was soaked with seawater and littered with seaweed (not an infallible sign of a seafaring ghost, to be sure, but though seawater is readily available to all voyagers who may wish it, seaweed does not come so easily to hand for passengers on a liner).

Almost in the same breath Bridges gives an account of an incident that, he says, took place in about 1910–14 on the *Monongahela*, a U.S. Navy corvette. The paymaster on this vessel—a one-eyed, red-haired gentleman much admired throughout the service for his ability to tell a story—let it be known among his friends that his time was at hand; therefore he vowed that because the ship and its crew had been so good to him in life, he would in death do all he could to return. "You'll find me," he said, "in my old cabin, No. 2 on the port side."

Although none of his shipmates privately believed that "Pay" would reappear among them at some time in the future, in any case his old cabin remained empty for the next three voyages. At the outset of the fourth cruise the new paymaster (whom Bridges identifies only as "Assistant Paymaster S—"), a profound skeptic in matters of superstition, installed his gear in No. 2 cabin. Nothing untoward happened until one night in April, when the *Monongahela* was bound for her home port, the crew were startled to hear some very distressed screaming coming from the vicinity of No. 2 cabin. When nearby crew members rushed there they found S—collapsed on the deck outside his cabin, babbling distractedly about a corpse with one eye and a red beard, lying in his berth.

The men peered cautiously inside. There was of course no corpse on the paymaster's berth, but what did hold their startled gaze were some strands of seaweed scattered across the wet blankets—yet another proof to these seamen (as if any were needed) that the ghost of a sailor who dies aboard his vessel may well return to it.

Another tale that illustrates this same hidebound seafaring truth concerns the private yacht *Mohawk*. The *Mohawk* was lying anchored off Staten Island, and presumably because the weather was fine her mainsail and staysail were left hoisted. But fine weather or not, it is curious that the working sails of a vessel at anchor were allowed to remain standing; what is more, the sailing master had hauled the mainsail boom "midships and secured the sheet to its cleat" (even Bridges allows that the reason for doing this is obscure) before turning in below through the open companionway.

Be that as it may, within a few minutes a sudden squall fell upon the vessel, and in less time than it takes to draw breath to utter these words, the *Mohawk* was slammed over onto her beam ends, water rushed in through the open hatches, and the hapless vessel sank to the bottom, together with nearly everyone aboard her. Eventually she was raised and sold into government service, but the crews that worked her complained incessantly that the ship was haunted by the spirits of those who had drowned in her—every evening the ghost of the sailing master would come rushing from below and throw itself on the cleat that held the mainsheet in a desperate effort to ease the mainsail and so prevent the vessel from foundering.

THE VIKINGS OF SOLWAY FIRTH

"O'er the Wind's ploughing field
Come the Norse coursers!
By a hundred each ridden,
To the bloody feast bidden."
GEORGE DARLEY, "O'ER THE WILD GANNET'S BATH"

Solway Firth, the finger of the Irish Sea that probes deep into the mountains of southwestern Scotland, harbors a legend from long ago concerning two Danish sea rovers or pirates (probably remnants from a Viking raiding party). After a long period of robbing and pillaging the coastal villages and towns of Britain (in the process dispatching a good many of the inhabitants), the two Danes anchored their heavily laden longships in Solway Firth with a view to some local R&R for themselves and their crew. However, a great storm blew up during the night, sinking both ships and drowning every man on board.

Naturally enough, the locals saw this as the work of divine retribution, and it wasn't long before it became an article of faith that on a clear night both longships could be seen sailing silently up the firth, the single square sail of each set in the following breeze and the crew's shields, ranged along the sides, gleaming in the moonlight. But tempting though it may have been for some of the braver villagers to row out and investigate these apparitions, no one dared do so—until, so goes the legend, in the early eighteenth century (some thousand years after the original "incident") two young men took it upon themselves to investigate these strange vessels. They rowed out into the firth, whereupon the two longships suddenly sank, and the rowboat with the young men in it was dragged down by the suction, never to be seen again—a most satisfying legend, all would agree.

The Solway is the scene of yet another boating mishap that ended in tragedy and consequently was immortalized in legend. This is the tale of the spectral shallop (a coastal boat of moderate size), which local history says was ferrying a bridal party across the firth when a rival rammed and promptly sank the shallop. (It is not clear whether the captain of the offending vessel was a rival for the lady's affections or was the operator of a competing ferry service.) Who and how many died in the sinking is not given, but by all accounts the apparition of the bridal shallop is still sometimes sighted out on the waters of the firth, with the ghost of the man who rammed her at the helm. What is more, any vessel approached by this phantom is thereby doomed to destruction.

PHANTOM PILOTS

"I must—I will—Pale phantom cease."

SIR WALTER SCOTT, *ROKEBY*

Slocum's Pilot of the *Pinta*

The pilot of the *Pinta* is the famous phantom Slocum discovered (as he tells us) at the helm of his beloved *Spray* when he fell ill during his now legendary circumnavigation of 1895–98. The *Pinta* was a caravel, one of the three vessels that Columbus commanded on his epochal 1492 voyage of discovery to the westward (the other two were the *Niña*, also a caravel, and the *Santa María*, a nao; see Christopher Columbus, chapter 8).

Slocum had made a stop at Horta, the chief town on the island of Faial (also known as Fayal), the Azores, in the North Atlantic, where generous well-wishers had given him a large supply of plums for the voyage, the American consul-general adding a huge white (fresh) cheese from Pico. After he set out again Slocum feasted on plums and cheese, with dire results.

> *Alas! by night-time I was doubled up with cramps. The wind, which was already a smart breeze, was increasing somewhat, with a heavy sky*

to the sou'west. Reefs had been turned out, and I must turn them in
again somehow [he does this, with considerable difficulty] . . . Then
I went below, and threw myself upon the cabin floor in great pain.
How long I lay there I could not tell, for I became delirious. When I
came to, as I thought, from my swoon, I realized that the sloop was
plunging into a heavy sea, and looking out of the companionway, to
my amazement I saw a tall man at the helm. His rigid hand, grasping
the spokes of the wheel, held them as in a vise. One may imagine my
astonishment. His rig was that of a foreign sailor, and the large red cap
he wore was cockbilled over his left ear, and all was set off with shaggy
black whiskers. He would have been taken for a pirate in any part of
the world . . . "Señor," said he, doffing his cap, "I have come to do you
no harm . . . I am the pilot of the Pinta *come to aid you. Lie quiet,*
señor captain . . . you have a calentura *[a tropical delirium common*
among sailors] . . . You did wrong, captain, to mix cheese with plums.
White cheese is never safe unless you know whence it comes.

The incident is well known, reflecting, no doubt, the fact that Slocum's voyage itself was—and still is—deservedly famous for being the first single-handed circumnavigation of the world. Nevertheless, one must be cautious about accepting Slocum's account at face value. Bearing in mind that he wanted us to believe that he had navigated the *Spray* around the world by way of the Strait of Magellan and the Cape of Good Hope using only an old kitchen clock for his noon sights and thus his position at sea, it is very likely that Slocum was artfully pulling our leg a little. There is little doubt that he was ill—a surfeit of plums have on their own been known to induce much discomfort in persons of all degree—and one is not quite oneself during a delirium. The apparition of the pilot of the *Pinta* was very likely a dream brought on by too much fresh cheese and stone fruit. Besides which, either Slocum spoke excellent fifteenth-century Spanish or Portuguese, or pilots five hundred years ago were uncommonly fluent in nineteenth-century English.

Johansen's Pilots

The Hardwicks tell us that in the last days of August 1900 a Captain Johansen and his fourteen-year-old son, both of Liverpool, were sailing from Gibraltar to America in a small open boat, the *Lotta*, by way of the North Atlantic. About a week into the voyage the father was relaxing in the warm sun of a calm day while his son slept, when suddenly he heard someone speaking and other voices replying, all in a language he did not recognize. The boy woke up and heard the same conversation; neither of them could account for it.

Two days later the boy, who was steering, let go the tiller to free the jib sheet, the weather having turned worse. The *Lotta* immediately swung beam on to the rising seas and would have foundered then and there if four phantoms of men in outlandish costume had not suddenly materialized and set the small boat to rights. One of them (Johansen noted that he had a metal stake instead of a left leg) took the tiller and steered throughout the night, and all the time the men talked to each other and to the Johansens, who could not understand a word of what they were saying. In the morning the weather had improved and the phantoms had disappeared, only to turn up again that evening, during the course of which they seemed to be signaling other vessels nearby. Shortly afterward they vanished again, this time for good.

Had the Johansens had too much sun? Were they disoriented from lack of sleep? The Hardwicks report that the father was "hard-headed, sober and skeptical." If the future king of England could vouch for having seen the *Flying Dutchman* (see chapter 16), it would seem unfair to deny a couple of commoners the same sort of privilege.

19

SUPERSTITION AND BELIEF

P ossibly no group of people has harbored as many superstitions as seafarers. Perhaps the dreadful conditions that went with the seaman's
   calling made it necessary for him to wrap himself round with a multi-
   plicity of beliefs and talismans in an effort to ward off evil. When you
   are at sea far from home and a full gale is blowing your ship onto a
lee shore, there is much to be said for a system of beliefs that offers some sort of
hope, no matter how tenuous.

When there was every chance of dying by drowning, thirst, or shipwreck; being marooned on a desolate speck of coral sand far from the haunts of mankind;
being visited by sheer bad luck in the form of a howling storm off Cape Horn or

a piercing heat-shrouded calm in the doldrums—when death was always at one's elbow in its many different forms at sea, one took great care to placate the gods at every opportunity (note, for example, the curious reason that underpins the otherwise gory and inhumane traditions associated with Launching a Ship; see below).

When only good luck and (one hopes) good management lie between you and a berth in Davy Jones's locker, you are likely to place a good deal of faith in the unfathomable. There are no atheists aboard ship. As the old proverb has it, "The devil divides the world between atheism and superstition."

There are many hundreds—probably thousands—of seafaring beliefs and superstitions; this chapter examines only a few. They are arranged in roughly chronological order: from the building and launching of a ship; the various precautions to be taken for a safe passage; the many instances of the inefficacy of these precautions; until finally ship and crew make their last voyage—the one to the breakers or a storm-tossed reef, another to retirement ashore, and some to Davy Jones's locker.

LAUNCHING A SHIP

"Was this the face that launch'd a thousand ships,
And burnt the topless towers of Ilium?"
CHRISTOPHER MARLOWE, *DOCTOR FAUSTUS*

We are familiar with the custom of breaking a bottle of champagne across the bow of a vessel being launched for the first time, while some director's wife bellows out the ceremonial cry "Bless this ship and all who sail in her!" (The lanyard to which the bottle is nowadays attached was added when a certain lady miscalculated her aim and accidentally struck a spectator, who promptly sued the admiralty for damages.)

The practice derives from an ancient custom: red wine was poured onto the deck of a newly launched vessel and then onto the surface of the sea as a libation to the gods of the ocean, thus apologizing to them for so rudely and abruptly entering their domain (the Romans often used water for this occasion as a symbol of purity, while the Greeks were quite happy to use wine). Red wine was chosen because it is the same color as the human blood once used in these proceedings; champagne gradually replaced wine because, being rather more expensive, champagne was regarded as being that much more appropriate for such an auspicious occasion.

An even earlier ceremony featured a priest, armed with a flaming torch in one hand and in the other an egg and some brimstone (i.e., sulphur, "burning stones" from the Old English *bryne*, burning); these two items would be offered to the deity whose image was carried aboard the vessel being launched. Greek and Roman ships commonly had the image fixed on the bow, and the ceremony at launching was dedicated to it specifically (see Ships' Figureheads, below).

In a once-hallowed practice, the Norse Vikings when they were launching a warship tied their prisoners onto the launchways or skids so that as the hull passed over them the blood from their crushed bodies entered the sea as an offering to the gods—a custom no longer followed, one might be thankful to say, although its demise has certainly subtracted some of the drama and color associated with these events. It was believed that giving the warship's keel a taste of warm blood would guarantee the vessel's future success. Galleys newly launched in the Mediterranean were often christened in like manner, in this case by using domestic slaves.

COIN UNDER THE MAST

"Charon: . . . the dark and grisly old man in a black sailor's cloak,
who ferries the souls of the dead across the river for the fare of an obolos.
The coin was put into the mouth of the dead for this purpose."
SEYFFERT, *DICTIONARY OF CLASSICAL MYTHOLOGY, RELIGION, LITERATURE, AND ART*

It was once a time-honored custom among shipbuilders to place a coin beneath the heel of the mainmast of a vessel they were building as a reminder of that longest and most final of all journeys made by man—the voyage to the underworld. The reference is, of course, to the Greek legend concerning Charon the Ferryman.

Souls of the dead on their way to Elysium were taken across the River Styx by Charon, who charged each soul one obolus (a small coin) for the journey; anyone who did not have the toll money was left behind. To avoid this embarrassment the ancient Greeks adopted the custom of placing a coin in the hand or mouth of their dead, thus enabling that soul to pay Charon the required passage money and arrive safely on the other side. Shipbuilders long ago adopted this custom of offering symbolic protection money in advance to the spirits of the deep by placing a coin under the mast before launching.

SHIPS' NAMES

"He that hath an ill name is half hanged."
JOHN HEYWOOD, "PROVERBS"

Some seamen believe that it is not a good idea to give a ship a name connected in any way with fire, lightning, or storm, or indeed with anything that might spell doom for a vessel at sea; for example, no vessel should be named after an ocean or after the elements. Others hold that a ship should never change her name. But just to confuse matters, the *Norseman*, built in 1893, changed her name no fewer than twelve times in the course of her career, so the rules of superstition apparently didn't apply to her. Sir Francis Drake's ship, too, made a triumphant homecoming in 1580 even though her name had been changed from *Pelican* to *Golden Hind* in honor of Drake's friend and patron Sir Christopher Patton, whose family crest was a golden deer.

Those who scorn such superstition are solemnly reminded of the fate of the *Fiery Cross*, a famous British tea clipper that met her end at Sheerness in 1889 when fire broke out in the cargo of coal. Anyway, not only had her name invoked fire; two years earlier she had been sold to Norwegian owners and renamed, thereby adding to the ill omens. *Lightning*, another clipper of the same era, foundered in 1869 when she caught fire while loading wool in Geelong, Victoria.

The clipper *Aurora*, another vessel named from the elements, was destroyed by fire in 1875 when her cargo of wool caught fire. When Sir Ernest Shackleton took his Ross Sea group to the Antarctic on the Newfoundland sealer *Endurance* in 1914 (she had earlier been the *Aurora*), the vessel was beset by ice for nine months, during which she drifted aimlessly until hopelessly crushed; only Shackleton's superb leadership saved the crew.

Struck by lightning in 1853, the clipper *Golden Light* caught fire and had to be abandoned. The *Fiery Star*, which earlier had been named *Comet*, met her end in 1865 from fire in her cargo of wool while on passage from Moreton Bay, Queensland, to Liverpool.

Many an old seaman would have nodded knowingly at these incidents.

SHIPS' FIGUREHEADS

"At the bows . . . was the ship's figurehead,
either a ramping red lion or a plain white bust,
or a shield, or some allegorical figure suggested by
the name of the ship . . . [the sailors] took
great pride in keeping it in good repair."
JOHN MASEFIELD, "SEA LIFE IN NELSON'S TIME"

There was a time when nearly all sailing ships were fitted with a figurehead at the bow, usually a carved representation of an animal noted for its strength, ferocity, and courage (for example, the lion, the boar) or one of the sea deities (Poseidon) or a creature admired for its grace and stability in the water (the swan) or an animal or deity suggested by the name of the ship itself or, as in many ships built after the eighteenth century, often a representation of the owner or of some notable public figure.

By the mid-nineteenth century a female figurehead was increasingly common, either robed or bare-breasted, often the latter because of the sailor's belief that a partially clad female could calm the sea gods in time of storm and tempest. When steam replaced sail figureheads began to disappear, but they are becoming popular again with a few twentieth-century shipping lines.

Originally the figurehead was carried *in* the vessel, where its purpose was usually twofold, on the one hand a form of religious symbolism and on the other hand an attempt to express the life and spirit of the vessel itself. The earliest seafarers took aboard with them the head of an animal that had been sacrificed to the gods of the sea to insure a safe passage; later a head representing that animal replaced the original sacrifice. Gradually the figurehead found its way into the bows of the vessel, where its eyes could keep a good lookout ahead. As well as carrying a figurehead of a bird, the Egyptians also painted eyes on the bows of a vessel as a double insurance.

The figurehead was commonly erected on the beakhead, the space forward of the forecastle that accommodated archers on the early warships, but when methods of war changed and forecastles fell out of fashion, the figurehead was located at the top of the stem, just below the bowsprit. This meant, especially on a raked clipper bow, that the carved head was always raised, it being an article of faith with seafarers that the eyes of the figurehead needed always to be on the far horizon, constantly keeping a lookout.

It is a curious fact that the heads have been cut off the figureheads of some vessels that have been wrecked, as if to prevent another ship being fitted with an emblem that patently had failed in its duty.

DEPARTURES

"Now Friday came. Your old wives say,
Of all the week's the unluckiest day."
RICHARD FLECKNOE, *DIARIUM*

No old-time tar worth his salt (and many a modern one, too) would have dreamed of setting sail on a Friday, this being the ill-omened day on which Christ was crucified; to do so would have been to invite disaster of one sort or another.

During World War II the Australian light cruiser HMAS *Perth* returned to Australia for repairs after being severely damaged in the Crete campaign in the Mediterranean; when she was seaworthy again she picked up a replacement crew at Fremantle, Western Australia, and sailed for Singapore a few minutes into Saturday, February 14, 1942—the navy having delayed her departure so that she would not have to leave on Friday the 13th. When the *Wellesley* put out to sea from a British port on a Friday in March 1848, she was immediately recalled by the port admiral and made to wait until the following day.

The first Monday in April is also frowned on as a day to begin a voyage because seamen believed it was not only the birthday of Cain but also the day on which he killed his brother Abel. The second Monday in August is also a nonstarter, being the day when Sodom and Gomorrah were destroyed by God's wrath, although it is not clear why mariners should have been anxious on this account. December 31 always found little favor as a departure date because according to tradition (which is to say, a body of irrational belief that is most unwisely ignored), this was the day on which Judas Iscariot hanged himself.

On the other hand, Wednesdays were always favorable days to begin and end a voyage, from the fact that Wodin, the chief god of the Vikings, was the particular protector of all mariners. Our Wednesday is from Wodin's Day, regarded by seafarers as the luckiest day of the week.

THE EYES OF HER

*"In Asia, boats have a large eye painted on
either side of the bow, to ward off the evil spirits."*
BERNARD MOITESSIER, *CAPE HORN*

"The eyes of her" refers to the farthest forward part of a vessel, a reminder of the time when it was common for a ship or boat to have an eye painted on each side of her bow so she could "see" her way safely across the water; anyone familiar with the Mediterranean will have seen many a fishing boat so adorned (see also Ships' Figureheads, above). A boatbuilder or ship's carpenter commonly refers to the bow of a vessel as "up in the eyes of her"—which then raises the question: why is a ship a "she"?

There are at least three possible answers. One is that for all their casual hardness and, sometimes, unthinking callousness, seafarers could often appreciate beauty, especially the inspiring sight of a full-rigged ship under stuns'ls and topgallants heeling to brisk trade winds (see chapter 7) as she plowed her way across the world's oceans ("Sail's a lady, steam's a bundle of iron"—Captain Bromley).

Another answer may have something to do with the fact that a seaman's ship was, for the duration of a voyage, his only haven; he lived in and depended on it for his well-being and safe arrival. That complicated arrangement of timbers and fastenings and spars and rigging that he called a "ship" was all that lay between him and eternity; it looked after him if he took care that all was well with everything that contributed to the safe and proper working of that arrangement. In this way his ship was like a woman: protective, sustaining, and sometimes ultimately self-sacrificing, in much the same way that a mother might be. In the words of that master seaman, Joseph Conrad:

> Yes, your ship wants to be humoured with knowledge. You must treat
> with an understanding the mysteries of her feminine nature, and then
> she will stand by you faithfully in the unceasing struggle with forces
> wherein defeat is no shame . . . if you remember that obligation . . .
> she will sail, stay, run for you as long as she is able.

The third explanation carries probably the greatest historical weight. When a ship is launched, the event is marked with the breaking of a bottle of wine, champagne, etc., over its bow as a libation or offering to the gods of the sea, with Poseidon (see chapter 1) particularly in mind. The vessel is in many senses being offered as a bride to the great ocean; hence the references to it as "she" (see Launching a Ship, above).

GUIDING STAR

"I must go down to the seas again, to the lonely sea and the sky,
And all I ask is a tall ship and a star to steer her by."
JOHN MASEFIELD, "SEA FEVER"

It is still a common practice among some ship designers and builders to have a representation of a star—either carved or cast in some suitable material—set into the end of the bowsprit and in the ends of sail booms.

They are a sign of the old-time seafarer's faith in the Pole Star as the guiding star for his ship (in the Northern Hemisphere), a sort of backup for the eyes of the figureheads once common on the bows of sailing ships (see Ships' Figureheads, above). The stars may also be reminiscent of early seafarers' belief in Castor and Pollux in the constellation Gemini, as protectors of those who go to sea (see Castor and Pollux, chapter 1, and The Argonauts, chapter 4).

THE LODESTONE

"And as if thought had the power to draw to itself, like the loadstone [lodestone],
Whatsoever it touches, by subtile laws of its nature . . ."
HENRY WADSWORTH LONGFELLOW, "THE COURTSHIP OF MILES STANDISH"

"Lodestone" is the mariner's early name for the ship's compass; its properties may first have been discovered by the ancient Chinese. Commonly it is magnetic oxide of iron (magnetite), named from a corruption of *load,* Old English *lad* (pronounced "laid"), way, journey, hence direction, thus *lodestar,* the North Star, Pole Star, of great importance to early navigators, who during the Middle Ages were known as *lodesmen,* while pilotage was known as *lodemanage.* The Laws of Oleron—a set of maritime laws enacted by Eleanor of Aquitaine and introduced into England in about 1190—stated that "if a ship is lost by default of the lodeman, the maryners may . . . bring the lodeman to the windlass or any other place and cut off his head."

It is clear that the lodestone attracted (if one may so use the word) many virtues unto itself, such as its infallible ability—when placed on the pillow—of inducing a wife suspected of having cuckholded her husband to confess her adultery as she lay sleeping. It was also apparently useful as a curative for a number of (unspecified) illnesses, and enjoyed a sound reputation as a contraceptive (exactly how is not known).

Garlic and/or onion was firmly held to be an efficacious but not entirely desirable means of counteracting the attractive pull of the lodestone, which naturally led to a suggested prohibition against seamen being allowed to consume these vegetables while on board ship in case their breath should demagnetize the compass needle.

In Ben Jonson's comedy *The Magnetic Lady* (1631) Lady Loadstone "draws unto her guests of all sorts." The hero of this play is named Compass, Lady Loadstone's steward is Needle, and the lady herself marries Compass's brother, Captain Ironside.

Unlucky Ships

*"He came safe from the East Indies,
and was drowned in the Thames."*

Thomas Fuller, "Gnomologia"

Seafarers the world over are convinced that some ships are lucky and others unlucky and that a number of those in the second category are very unlucky indeed, vessels that no seaman would ever serve in if he had any choice in the matter.

In 1964 the Australian navy aircraft carrier HMAS *Melbourne* collided with HMAS *Voyager*, a destroyer, off the New South Wales coast with the loss of eighty-two men; five years later the *Melbourne* plowed into the destroyer USS *Frank E. Evans* in the South China Sea, and seventy-four men from the *Evans* were lost. Navy men the world over shook their heads and reminded all who would listen of the essential truths that underpin the beliefs and customs of seafaring: the *Melbourne* was an unlucky ship.

Morton tells us of the *Peppercorn*, without question an unlucky ship because fourteen of the treenail holes in her hull were in fact unencumbered with treenails, the long oaken cylindrical pins that secured a vessel's planking to her timbers. One can only marvel that the good *Peppercorn* stayed afloat as long as she did (which, as it turned out, wasn't long at all: the cook managed to set the vessel on fire, and the admiral's ship rammed her; combined with the fact that some of her planks weren't fastened properly, the *Peppercorn* promptly sank—altogether a compelling example of an unlucky ship).

But if there were unlucky ships, there were also lucky ones, vessels that seemed to lead a charmed life. The clipper ship *Torrens*, for example (Joseph Conrad was first mate on her for two voyages in the early 1890s on the Australia–U.K. run), was widely regarded as a lucky ship, her passages being fast and successful and the ship as a whole attracting the benevolence of a smiling Providence. On one occasion the ship had exhausted her supply of lamp oil, when what should be found float-ing far out at sea but a barrel of the very oil she needed. Any seaman would have given a good deal to be able to get a berth in such a vessel.

Luck is not just happenstance; there is an agency that causes luck, good and bad. Sailors commonly considered a Finn—especially what they referred to as a Russian Finn—as a prime suspect when bad luck was in the offing. Finns were fre-quently regarded with suspicion and sometimes fear, since they were known to be wizards with the power of bewitching a ship; it was always wise to keep in their good books because they possessed the ability to call up not only a fair wind but a foul one, too, if they were so minded. If things were going badly on a vessel—she was be-calmed or laboring in heavy weather or the food was rotten or the seams were open-ing up—it was a certainty that a Finn lay somewhere behind it all. If a sailor needed a scapegoat (and he often did, that being the nature of life at sea) and there was a Russian Finn in the crew—why, then, there's your answer. Morton mentions the story of the ship's captain who locked a Finn in the forepeak with the promise that he would be released only when he "changed the wind."

Admiral John Byron (1723–1786) was long known in the British navy as "Foul Weather Jack" because of the bad weather he invariably attracted when at sea, and no seaman ever regarded storms and gales with casual indifference. If bad weather persisted, a scapegoat was sought. On one occasion a young seaman in the *Conrad* was blamed for a storm that had battered the ship for days; his mistake had been to bring aboard a skull to take home as a souvenir of his travels. Morton relates how the boy was permitted to keep the grisly relic only if the wind were to change, and soon (which, luckily for the sake of the boy's memento, it did).

WOMEN ABOARD SHIP

"There's nothing in the world worse than woman—
save some other woman."

ARISTOPHANES, *THESMOPHORIAZOUSAI*

It is a curious fact that seamen have never been happy with the notion of women on board a working vessel, believing that their very presence encouraged the onset of gales and other forms of bad weather (it was a different matter when the ship was in harbor: in the old British navy the women of the port were frequently to be found in the "tween decks," posing as "wives" of the men and seeing to their com-forts; the scandal eventually became too much even for those times, and the au-thorities were obliged to rectify matters).

On the other hand, it was believed by all that a naked woman (actually, the figure of a woman carved in wood) could calm a stormy sea, in much the same way, one supposes, that music is said to calm the savage breast. This is why there were so many figureheads of women in partial undress clamped to the bow of a vessel, baring their considerable charms (the woodcarvers of old sometimes had exaggerated notions of what constituted feminine charms) in such a manner that only the most curmudgeonly of sea gods could have resisted such beguiling blandishment.

Kemp reports that as late as the end of the nineteenth century fishermen in the Firth of Forth on the east coast of Scotland would refuse to go to sea if a barefoot woman happened across their path while the seamen were on their way to their vessel. It would be interesting to track down the origin of this particular superstition; one wonders if this barefoot bane is an echo of a biblical reference.

WHISTLING ABOARD SHIP

"Whistle only when the sun is asleep. An old
sea belief that to whistle in a calm brings fair winds
but to whistle in a wind brings hurricanes."

LEW LIND, *SEA JARGON*

It is known to all seafarers that whistling on board a sailing ship when a fair wind is blowing is an infallible recipe for disaster, usually in the form of a strong and contrary wind at least and a howling full gale at worst, although such a worst case may well include a hurricane or typhoon, whistling being the very undesirable act that it is. The sailor's reasoning behind this prohibition was that if you whistled, the god of the wind might think he was being mocked and would then very likely become furious.

There is also a practical reason for the ban: certain kinds of whistling could easily be confused with the sound of a signal on the bosun's pipe; if mistaken for such, there could be serious consequences for the ship and crew (as, for instance, in a seaman's mistakenly freeing a brace or halyard, and so on).

Whistling softly during a calm, however, is an acceptable way to attempt to awaken Saint Anthony, the patron saint of breezes and winds. It can be useful in that it may bring on a suitable wind, as can gently scratching the backstays or taking an old broomhead and heaving it overboard in the direction from which the wind is desired. On the other hand, a woman who whistles while aboard hardly bears thinking about (and a seaman with any respect for tradition would want to know what a woman was doing on board in the first place—unless she was the captain's wife, of course).

With reference to another method of raising a suitable wind, following is an extract from a journal that Dorothea Moulton Balano, the captain's wife, kept while voyaging on the *R. W. Hopkins*:

> *Sunday, July 2, 1911—Fred heaved his old shoes overboard to bring*
> *wind. A sacrifice to Neptune? It's a tradition going back, I know, and I*

must spend some time in re-studying ancient history to see what I can
find out about Greek and Roman seamen making their sacrifices to get
a fair wind.

RINGING GLASS ABOARD SHIP

"[Evans] put his forefinger on the rim of the glass
in order to cut off the bright, ringing note.
He sat back and let out his breath in a slow sigh.
Upton, fork in hand, stared at him with
a look of baffled inquiry upon his face.
Evans said, in his soft Welsh voice, 'I'd be grateful if
you didn't do that. You see, here in Wales there's a belief
among our old seafaring families that if somebody
accidentally knocks a glass, and you don't stop it ringing,
then somewhere or other a sailor dies at sea.' "

JOHN MANCHIP WHITE, "A SAILOR DIES AT SEA,"
IN *WHISTLING PAST THE CHURCHYARD*

Should someone unthinkingly cause the rim of an empty wineglass to ring in the ship's mess, it will be regarded by everyone present as a knell of doom for some unfortunate sailor who will, it is certain, die by drowning. However, if the ringing is stopped immediately, the assembled company can breathe a little easier—the devil will take two *soldiers* instead.

The sound of ringing glass is likened by superstitious sailors to the church bell that tolls for someone's passing; and it is also echoed in the bell that has for centuries been rung on land to mark a ship lost at sea (the Lutine Bell at Lloyd's that was installed in 1799; see Lloyd's of London, chapter 5).

SHARKS ASTERN

"The shark or Tiberune, is a fish like unto those which
we call dogfishes, but that he is far greater . . . he is
much hated of seafaring men . . . It is the most ravenous fish
known in the sea; for he swalloweth all that he findeth.
In the pouch of them hath been found hats, caps, shoes, shirts,
legs and arms of men, ends of ropes, and many other things."

SIR RICHARD HAWKINS, QUOTED IN *THE BRITISH SEAFARER*

Many older seafarers believed that a shark following a vessel was a sure sign that someone on board was going to die (that is, die somewhat earlier than that unhappy individual might have otherwise; see also Christopher Columbus, chapter 8). The reason most often given was that sharks can "scent" death, an interesting extension of their known ability to scent blood in the water from a great distance.

It was once quite common to see a sailing ship with a shark's fin suspended from the outer end of the jibboom, not so much as a trophy (sailors hated sharks with a passion, as one might expect) but rather as a talisman or warning to other sharks patrolling nearby, so that they might see the fin and, exercising a proper prudence, keep clear. Knowlson quotes the following passage from the biography of a Reverend Bryan Roe, at that time a missionary in West Africa, that illustrates how ingrained in some seamen this belief can become.

> *Two or three sharks, it may be, are following in the vessel's wake, attracted, it would seem, by the fact that there is a sick man lying on board; for the old, weather-beaten, quarter-master confidentially informs the clerical passenger (Mr Roe) that he will soon have a burial job on hand. The quarter-master is always an authority on the subject of sharks. "Them there sharks," he explains, "have more sense in them than most Christchuns. They knows wot's wot, I can tell yer; doctors ain't in it with sharks. I've heard sharks larf when the doctor has told a sick man he was convalescent—larf, sir, outright, 'cos they knew what a blessed mistake he was making. They are following up the scent of a man on board that's going to die, and they'll not leave us until such times be as they get him."*

In fact, it is clear that sharks have long since learned the same lesson that seagulls live by: the certainty that ships are a handy and reliable source of food scraps. (See also Herbert Kabat, chapter 13.)

SHIP'S CAT

"More ways of killing a cat than choking her with cream."
CHARLES KINGSLEY, *WESTWARD HO!*

Most sailing vessels carried a cat for at least two very good reasons: first, they were a familiar reminder of life ashore, allowing the seaman to bestow some affection on another being in a working life that was frequently harsh and unrewarding; and, second, cats were adept at keeping down the rat population—sailing ships were a natural habitat for this rodent.

Consequently seamen often invested the cat with certain powers, one of these being the ability to call up the gale that all sailors knew was kept stored in the animal's tail. If you stroke a cat's fur on a dry day you will feel the discharge of static electricity stored up in the cat's coat; sailors believed that these tiny sparks of electricity were lightning bolts that the cat kept in its tail, and if you allowed the animal to become too frisky, this lightning would release a gale. (See also Whistling Aboard Ship, above.)

COFFINS ABOARD SHIP

"Get the coffin ready and the man won't die."
CHINESE PROVERB

There is no established record of coffins figuring among those many examples of belief and behavior that constitute seagoing superstition, but by the same token there is no doubt that any self-respecting mariner would feel strongly about the presence of a coffin on board his vessel (even modern-day passengers are usually none too eager to fly in a plane carrying a coffin in its hold; carrier practice is to not tell customers of the fact). The following incident illustrates how easily the wellsprings of superstitious belief are tapped.

> *About 12 miles off the West Australian coast lies Rottnest Island. On the night of July 12, 1899, after some days of very heavy weather, the square-rigged ship* City of York, *on passage from San Francisco to Fremantle by way of the Torres Strait, drove onto one of the many reefs that surround Rottnest; eleven men were drowned and the ship became a total loss. At the subsequent marine court of enquiry the reasons for its loss were established, but they do not concern us here; what is of interest is an incident that happened on board before she piled up onto the reef.*

> *It came out—possibly at the enquiry itself, but certainly in the press reports that followed—that while the* City of York *was crossing the Pacific the ship's carpenter, Alex Anderson, had carved a miniature coffin from a balk of wood; why he did this is not known. When some of his shipmates saw what he had done there were murmurings; and when, surprisingly, Anderson went further and began carving a corpse to place in the coffin, there was outright protest and a delegation complained to the captain (Phillip Jones). What happened as a result of this we do not know, and there is no further information available on this matter.*

> *But perhaps we don't need any.*

> *It wouldn't be at all difficult to imagine what the crew members said to the captain, and what their thoughts and feelings were concerning coffins and corpses on board ship; and it is very likely that some individuals expressed their opinions on the incident to the press in the inns and taverns of the Port of Fremantle. They would have muttered something about it being an ill omen to fool around with a representation of a coffin on board ship; and then to carve a wooden corpse for the thing . . . it was no wonder that ship and crew had run into foul weather a couple of days north of its destination. Eleven men dead and gone . . . and the crew would have shaken their heads at the foolhardiness of the carpenter, an experienced seaman, a man who should have known better.*

> *It was perhaps a stroke of irony that Captain Jones was drowned while Anderson survived the wreck [as did the cat that was traveling on board—see Ship's Cat, above]; the coffin and corpse that had upset the crew was washed up on a nearby beach.*

Carrying a corpse on board ship was considered extremely unlucky. When a shipmate died at sea, the sailmaker—usually the one who undertook the task—sewed the body into a shroud of canvas, usually with a roundshot or other heavy object at head and foot to weight the corpse to the sea bottom, and he then finished the job with a stitch through the corpse's nose. This was to keep the seaman's ghost attached to the shroud so that it could never return to haunt his old ship (it was also probably a final reassurance to all that the body in the shroud really was dead—a sail needle rammed through your nostrils is no trifling matter).

Hampshire tells us that HMS *Natal* was for some years after her launching in 1905 considered a lucky vessel, an important consideration for practically all seamen. Ten years later her luck had turned. Shortly after she had taken the body of the American ambassador back to the United States from Britain she blew up in Scottish waters with great loss of life. Furthermore, four salvage firms went bankrupt, one after the other, after they had purchased the wreck of the *Natal*, and the fourth lost their salvage vessel and its entire crew in a storm. When Isambard Kingdom Brunel's *Great Eastern* (launched in 1858) was broken up in 1888, it was claimed that the skeleton of one of the workers who built her had been found between her double plating, which immediately explained to old salts why the vessel had never been successful during her period as a liner on the transatlantic run (the rumor, however, seems never to have been confirmed).

It is no wonder that the crew of the *City of York* were murmuring.

FLOWERS ABOARD SHIP

"Shall I strew on thee rose or rue or laurel,
Brother, on this that was the veil of thee?"
ALGERNON SWINBURNE, "AVE ATQUE VALE"

As you value your life, never take flowers on board ship, for if the crew is of the old school, it is likely that both you and your posies will be smartly heaved over the side. It was a strong article of belief among such men that flowers are solely for funerals—ergo, wreaths were as welcome aboard as women, priests, whistling, and umbrellas (all discussed in this chapter); even twentieth-century submariners are firm on this point.

FLAGS, BAGS, BELLS, AND RAGS

"Superstition brings the gods into even the smallest matters."
LIVY, *HISTORY OF ROME*

For some sailors it is an unlucky omen to repair a flag on a ship's quarterdeck or to pass a flag to a shipmate between the rungs of a ladder (possibly an extension or variation of the very old superstition that warns against walking under a ladder).

For other mariners, black traveling bags are harbingers of misfortune, probably because of the long association between "black" and "death"; there is also a likely echo here of the sailor's distaste for having priests and parsons on board ship, wearing their usually black habiliments. Note, though, that in the old British navy, a seaman often made himself a holdall from a piece of sailcloth he then painted black; in it he would keep his most treasured possessions (including his shore-going rig or clothes); the old expression "to give a young lady his black bag" was the sailor's way of proposing marriage to her.

Kemp reports that for many seamen, to hear bells at sea is a portent of death, no doubt a reflection of the custom ashore of tolling the village church bell to mark the passing of a parishioner. John Donne (1572–1631) in "Meditation" reminds us forcibly of this: "therefore never send to know for whom the bell tolls; it tolls for thee." One wonders, though, if the superstitious seaman was also disturbed by the regular sounding of the ship's bell as it marked the completion of each half-hour period of watch duty afloat. Seamen apparently also feared the sound of a rooster crowing on board ship because of its association with Peter's denial of Christ and the Crucifixion that followed.

When a sailor died at sea, his clothes and other effects were usually auctioned among his shipmates, with the proceeds passed on to any surviving dependents. Nevertheless, many seamen considered it unlucky to wear any of the dead man's clothing until that particular voyage had come to an end.

Other shipboard beliefs include the notion that it is bad luck to leave a hatch cover upside down on the deck, as this is an invitation to fate to deal similarly with the vessel itself. A rope should never be allowed to hang from a beam of any kind for, as every good sailor knows, this is the sign of a gallows.

For some seafarers, to have a dog or any other furry animal aboard will bring bad luck—feathered pets, on the other hand, were always good omens. Nevertheless, there were others who were comfortable with a cat or dog on board; many a captain kept a dog on his ship, and it was not at all uncommon to see a ship's cat stalking the decks (see Ship's Cat, above).

The seaman's life was replete with many different taboos. In the mess no right-thinking seaman would leave a loaf of bread standing upside down (cut side up), this being a clear invitation for the ship to founder. On some vessels it was sternly frowned upon for a seaman to do any sewing while a contrary or unhelpful wind was blowing, otherwise he would "stitch in the wind" and thus prevent it from backing or veering to a more favorable quarter. It is apparently a common belief among seafarers, especially older ones, that a vessel raised from the bottom and put into service again will be haunted by the ghosts of those who died aboard her.

UMBRELLAS ABOARD SHIP

"The rain it raineth on the just
And also on the unjust fella;
But chiefly on the just, because
The unjust steals the just's umbrella."

CHARLES SYNGE CHRISTOPHER BOWEN

A most unwelcome item on board ship was the umbrella. Incidentally, considering the demands of superstition and the subsequent prohibition of so many different articles and practices aboard ship—women, priests, flowers, whistling, ringing glass, and so on—it might be thought surprising that a vessel ever weighed anchor and set sail in the first place.

Umbrellas were frowned upon because by their very nature they were associated with bad weather, and the sailor had no need of climatic elements that refused to cooperate with him in his desire to make a safe and speedy voyage; an umbrella on board ship was therefore quite likely to incite the gods of the ocean into venting their considerable spleen. One wonders if an echo of this belief is the frequent warning against opening an umbrella inside a dwelling.

THE ALBATROSS

"Whales and seals, petrels and albatross."

CHARLES DARWIN, *VOYAGE ROUND THE WORLD*

Sailors have long believed that when one of their shipmates died (went to Davy Jones's Locker; see below), his soul inhabited the body of the albatross, that graceful bird that forever wanders the Southern Ocean. It may follow a ship for weeks at a time, being capable of sustained flight for a very long period. One species of albatross, *Diomedea exulans*, has a wingspan reaching 15 feet:

> *We hauled it [the albatross] over the rail, held it upside down so that some*
> *of the water ran out of its lungs, and set it on deck. Like a swan, the poor*
> *creature was pathetic out of its element, rolling its black eyes reproachfully*
> *at us, and flapping its vast wings. We measured them: from tip to tip they*
> *were eleven feet—perhaps more, for it was hard to extend them.*

It was a dreadful thing to kill such a creature, little short of a crime, and the seaman who did so was often subjected to a fearful penalty, as we see in Samuel Taylor Coleridge's "The Rime of the Ancient Mariner":

> *"Why look'st thou so?" "With my cross-bow*
> *I shot the albatross . . .*
>
> *And the good south wind still blew behind,*
> *But no sweet bird did follow,*

Nor any day for food or play
Came to the mariners' hollo!

And I had done a hellish thing,
And it would work 'em woe;
For all averred, I had killed the bird
That made the breeze to blow.
Ah wretch! said they, the bird to slay,
That made the breeze to blow!"

Coleridge's mariner eventually bitterly repents his actions and finds forgiveness, but he is driven to wander from land to land, telling his tale to all he meets, warning them against cruelty and abjuring them to love all God's creatures.

Brewer says that William Wordsworth had told Coleridge about the experience of the privateer George Shelvocke (1675–1742), who, according to Wordsworth, shot an albatross while rounding Cape Horn in 1720, the ship being dogged thereafter by bad weather; however, Kemp says that it was Simon Hatley, Shelvocke's second in command, who did the deed. Whatever the case, Coleridge used the incident as a partial basis for his famous poem.

Haining tells of a ship beset with endless misfortune, all of which (claimed the crew) was to be blamed on a dead albatross. In 1959 a supply vessel returning from the Antarctic had on board an albatross bound for a zoo in Germany. The bird was put in a cage, but it died soon after the ship set sail. The rest of the voyage to Europe was such a litany of storms, engine trouble, and other disasters that the crew went on strike. The ship had to put into Liverpool, with the captain finally declaring what the crew had known all along: it had been a very bad thing indeed to catch an albatross, let alone imprison it in a cage.

Albatross is from the Spanish and Portuguese *alcatraz*, seafowl, Portuguese *alcatruz*, Arabic *al-qadus*, "bucket of a water-wheel," first applied to the pelican in allusion to the storage capacity of its bill. Portuguese sailors commonly confused the pelican with the albatross, and because they believed that the pocket beneath the pelican's bill was a water pouch, they gave this pelican-like bird the name *algatross*, "water bucket." William Dampier (1652–1715), the English privateer and explorer, introduced the Portuguese term to England, but the fact that the body of this large bird was almost completely white suggested instead to others that *alba*, Latin for white, would be more appropriate—hence "albatross."

Alcatraz, the one-time prison island in San Francisco Bay, opposite the Golden Gate Bridge, is named for the pelicans that used to live there.

OUR FLAT EARTH

"What is the earth but a lump of clay surrounded by water?"
BHARTRIHARI, *THE VAIRAGYA SATAKA*

In a real sense this comment could well have been made by any citizen of ancient times, when mythology and limited experience told them that the known world (the southern and western parts of Europe and the northern fringe of Libya, the old name for Africa) was encircled by Oceanus, which in the Homeric view was a vast river or flood that bounded the earth. Beyond the Pillars of Hercules lay the Western Seas, those distant waters wherein were to be found—if one were sufficiently bold—such reposeful sanctuaries as the Islands of the Blessed, the Isle of Joy, and perhaps even that most elusive haven of happiness, Atlantis (see Fabled Atlantis, chapter 16).

But no one dared the venture, for every seafarer knew that if you sailed beyond the western end of the Mediterranean you would encounter nothing but chaos, that your ship and all aboard her would slip off the edge of the world and plummet into an infinite abyss, to be lost forever (the first voyage of Columbus in 1492 is remarkable for the unprecedented thirty-six days he and his crew spent at sea sailing ever westward; see Christopher Columbus, chapter 8).

What's more, it was very likely that even before you confronted that unhappy end, another one awaited you in the form of huge and terrifying sea monsters whose omnivorous diet embraced human flesh as well as fish, fowl, and good red herring. And should you be lucky enough to survive these not inconsiderable discomforts, there was always the prospect of being broiled alive, because it was common knowledge that the farther off one sailed the closer one approached the sun—the terrors of Cape Bojador on the northwest coast of Africa were sufficient proof of this (see Voyages of Gil Eannes, chapter 3). Far better to stay in home waters.

It is astonishing, then, that despite the absolute certainty of a fearful end awaiting those who braved the unknown seas, there were in fact some hardy souls who did just that (see, for example, Hanno the Navigator, chapter 3). What is even more staggering is that notwithstanding the advances in maritime exploration made 2,500 years ago by men such as Hanno, and in spite of the skill of mapmakers such as Claudius Ptolemy (Egyptian, Greek-influenced mathematician and astronomer; second century A.D.), and the even much earlier conclusions of the Greek mathematician Pythagoras (about 582–500 B.C.) that the earth was a sphere and Eratosthenes (276?–195? B.C., Greek mathematician and astronomer at Alexandria), who calculated the circumference of this sphere to within two hundred miles of its true figure—in the face of all this priceless knowledge, many scholars in the Middle Ages were still warning anyone who would listen of the perils to be encountered in the vast sea of mud that lay only a short distance west of the Strait of Gibraltar.

Boland makes the interesting assertion that by 1200 B.C. the Phoenicians had reached the Pillars of Hercules (they had sailed at least as far as the straits that separate Africa from Europe and had established a colony at Gades, now called Cádiz, on the southwest coast of Spain), making them perhaps the most-traveled and best-informed traders in the Mediterranean. They were known as the Silent People because of their habit of saying nothing about their voyages, since to do so would reveal not only their sources of tin, amber, gold, silver, and so on, but would also give others an idea of the sailing routes to these commercial centers, which included Britain for tin and amber and India (thought to be ancient Ophir) for precious metals, ivory, and other commodities.

They also had discovered the Azores, a group of islands in the North Atlantic about eight hundred miles west of Portugal where, Boland tells us, a pot full of Phoenician coins was found in 1749 on Corvo, the westernmost island in the group, which he says came from the decade 330 to 320 B.C.

The curiousity in this is that, despite all the transoceanic experience that the Phoenicians accumulated during the thousand years before the birth of Christ, very little of it—if indeed any at all, bearing in mind the fanatical secrecy they maintained in their commercial affairs—percolated through to other seafaring nations. It is no wonder, then, that only five hundred years ago most of the civilized world still believed in a flat earth, boiling seas, and huge monsters of terrible aspect.

SAINT ELMO'S FIRE

"Ariel, a spirit of the air, appears as Saint Elmo's Fire
. . . whenever it appeared as a single flame, it was supposed
. . . to bring ill-luck . . . When it came double, it was called
Castor and Pollux, and accounted a good omen."
WILLIAM SHAKESPEARE, *THE COMPLETE ILLUSTRATED SHAKESPEARE*

Saint Elmo's Fire refers to this phenomenon: during a storm brushlike electrical charges from the atmosphere are attracted to various parts of a ship, usually masts, spars, and rigging, causing flamelike lights to appear; they are often accompanied by crackling or fizzing sounds (they also occur ashore around church spires, chimney stacks, aircraft propellers, and so on). The phenomenon is said to be named after Saint Erasmus, a Syrian bishop who was martyred in about A.D. 303, whom Mediterranean seamen came to think of as their patron saint, with the electrical fireball considered a sign of his presence and guardianship. Rogers tells us that the legend comes from the story of a Breton captain who during a storm saved the bishop from drowning; Erasmus, properly thankful, thereafter sent his electrical fireball to sailors as a sign of his gratitude. Others link the phenomenon with Saint Peter Gonzales, a Dominican friar of the late twelfth century who devoted the latter part of his life to improving the conditions of Spanish seafarers.

"Saint Elmo" is an Italian corruption by way of Sant' Ermo or Saint Ermo; other variations include Saint Elemi, Saint Ermyn, Saint Telme, Saint Helm, Saint Anselmo, Saint Helen, Saint Elm, Saint Herm, Saint Clare, Saint Peter, Saint Nicholas, Helen's Fire, Jack-o'-Lantern, and Castor and Pollux. The fireball is also known by Italian seamen and others as *corposanto*, "holy body," from the belief that the light came from the body of Christ. This name also appears variously as corposant, cormazant, comazant, Capra Saltante, Corbie's Aunt, Jack-o'-Lantern, etc.; whaling men referred to it as *ampizant.*

But where sailors may dispute its significance, there is no doubt that many reliable observers have noted its appearance, men such as Vasco da Gama, Columbus, Magellan, and William Dampier. Richard Henry Dana, in his classic *Two Years Before the Mast,* gave an eyewitness account of the phenomenon:

> *Upon the maintopgallant masthead, was a ball of light, which the sailors call a corposant* (corpus sancti), *and which the mate had called out to us to look at . . . For sailors have a notion that if the corposant rises in the rigging it is a sign of fair weather, but if it comes lower down there will be a storm.*

Herman Melville wrote of seeing Saint Elmo's Fire for the first time:

> *About midnight I rose & went on deck. It was blowing horribly—pitch dark, & raining. The Captain was in the cuddy & directed my attention "to those fellows" as he called them—meaning several "Corposant balls" on the yard arms and mast heads. They were the first I had ever seen, & resembled large, dim stars in the sky.*

Seamen generally regarded Saint Elmo's Fire as a good omen, particularly as a sign from Saint Elmo himself that bad weather would soon end. But as is the way with superstitious folk there were contrary views, such as the firm belief that if the supernatural light of a corposant fell on a seaman's face or lurked around his body he would be dead within twenty-four hours; thus very few older mariners dared look such an event in the eye, as it were.

Perhaps there is a grain of reason in all this; perhaps atmospheric conditions preceding a storm are conducive to the appearance of Saint Elmo's Fire. As Rogers says, "The legendary explanation is a pretty one, and if we are wise we are content to leave it at that. The old storytellers at least usually had something on which to build." (See also Castor and Pollux, chapter 1.)

PRIESTS ABOARD SHIP

"Priests and conjurors are of the same trade."
THOMAS PAINE, *THE AGE OF REASON*

Gentlemen of the cloth were never welcome aboard ship by the old-time sailor, who regarded clerical black dress as unduly ominous; priests buried the dead, and the last thing a seaman needed was a reminder of his ever-present mortality (the mariner would have acknowledged that priests performed other functions, too, such as marrying folk and christening their offspring, but for the sailor these were of minor importance compared to the permanent nature of death, especially his own).

There is another dimension to this superstition. When Jonah fled west by ship to Tarshish (see Tarshish, chapter 2), the edge of the known world at that time, in order to evade God's command that he journey east to Nineveh and publicly denounce the wickedness of that city, God sent a great storm as punishment for his disobedience. This endangered the vessel so much that the sailors woke Jonah from his sleep (the wretch had stolen below for safety) and demanded to know why God had sent the storm upon them.

Jonah confessed his responsibility, saying that he was a man of God (of the cloth, as we would say today; he was in fact one of the twelve minor prophets), and begged the sailors to throw him overboard forthwith so they might be saved. They promptly obliged and heaved him into the raging sea, and the storm abated immediately (see Jonah and the Whale, chapter 17). From this biblical example sailors had every reason to resent the presence of clergymen aboard their ship.

EBB TIDE

"The ebb will fetch off what the tide brings in."
J. RAY, *ENGLISH PROVERBS*

For a long time it was widely believed along the east coast of Britain, and very likely elsewhere among people who live by and on the sea, that the ebb tide (the outgoing flow) was the time when those who were close to death finally died, as if it were a natural and proper thing for their own receding life force to join at last the ebbing tide force of the great ocean from which, some would say, we long ago all sprang. As Shakespeare put it in *Henry V*:

> He's in Arthur's bosom, if ever man went to Arthur's bosom. 'A [he]
> made a finer end, and went away an it had been any christom child; 'a
> parted ev'n just between twelve and one, ev'n at the turning o' the tide.

WREN'S FEATHER

"Superstition is the weakness of the human intellect;
it is inherent in that mind; it has always been, and always will be."
FREDERICK THE GREAT, "LETTER TO VOLTAIRE"

One of the more curious maritime superstitions was to be found among some of the isolated seafaring communities. On the Isle of Man, for instance, in the Irish Sea, it was a common belief that to possess the feather of a wren was to insure oneself against perishing by shipwreck and subsequent drowning.

The story goes that there was once a mermaid possessed of such beauty of body and voice that any sailor who heard and saw the lady was irresistibly compelled to follow her into the depths and thus to his death. A certain knight, hearing of this and anxious to do the chivalrous thing by being of service to seamen, discovered how to counteract the creature's charms; but she, wily one, changed herself into a wren and so foiled the fellow's good intentions. Providence, in the person of the gods of the sea, was so outraged at the mermaid's subterfuge that she was condemned to change into a wren on New Year's Day every year. This inspired mariners to institute a wholesale slaughter of wrens for miles around, peaking on New Year's Day itself, as a feather from this attractive and harmless songbird killed on that day was looked upon with especially high regard.

Unhappily for the world of wrens, the efficacy of the charm conferred by their feathers lasted for only one year. At the end of the twelvemonth the slaughter was renewed and the population of these birds was seriously diminished (one would hope the incidence of vamping mermaids suffered a parallel decline).

DEATH BY DROWNING

"He goes a great voyage that goes to the bottom of the sea."
H. G. BOHN, *HANDBOOK OF PROVERBS*

It is a surprising fact that virtually all seamen in the old sailing navies could not swim a stroke to save their lives. In Patrick O'Brian's remarkable fiction series dealing with the Royal Navy of the late eighteenth and early nineteenth centuries, Captain Jack Aubrey is held in considerable awe by his men, not least for the fact that he can swim and has often done so to rescue some clod who had seen fit to fall overboard.

It was a widespread belief among seamen, even into the present age, that he who possessed a caul (the inner membrane that surrounds a fetus, sometimes found on a child's head at birth) was infallibly protected against drowning. Thus it was once common to come across advertisements in the newspapers from seamen willing to pay a sizable sum of money for such an article.

If a seaman was unlucky enough to fall overboard, caul or no caul, the odds were that his shipmates would do little for him. I recall reading some years ago an account of a fisherman falling from his boat into the harbor of a well-known port on the east coast of Britain. The crew of the vessel immediately gathered at the rail but did nothing to help him: no rope was thrown to the desperately floundering man, no lifebuoy heaved into the water nearby; the crew simply watched. Naturally the wretched fellow drowned, and when questioned later by the authorities all they had to say was that it would have been wrong to interfere. Interfere with what? they were asked. With the rights of the gods of the sea, they answered, meaning that a sacrifice was necessary from time to time in order to placate the spirits of the deep (see Launching a Ship, above, for additional comment on this point).

Knowlson cites the following passage from Sir Walter Scott's novel *The Pirate* (1821). Bryce the peddler is replying to someone who had remonstrated with him for not trying to save a shipwrecked sailor from drowning:

> *"Are you mad?" said the pedlar, "you that have lived sae lang in Zetland [Shetland] to risk the saving of a drowning man? Wot [know] ye not, if you bring him to life again he will be sure to do you some capital injury?"*

Knowlson adds, "The same superstition can be found among the St. Kilda [Scotland] islanders, the boatmen of the Danube, French and English sailors, and even out of Europe, and among less civilised races."

Raban gives an extract from the journal of Herman Melville (1819–1891) in which Melville tries to save a man who has fallen over the ship's side but others are reluctant to help:

> *I shouted "Man overboard!" & turned to go aft . . . I dropped overboard the tackle-fall of the quarter-boat, & swung it towards the man, who was now drifting close to the ship . . . By this time, a crowd of people—sailors and others—were clustering about the bulwarks; but none seemed very anxious to save him.*

In *Hamlet*, a surprisingly detailed description of Ophelia's drowning is given by Queen Gertrude, surprising because it seems that the queen must have witnessed the girl's death to report it so graphically; and if she was there, why didn't she get help? The answer would seem to be that Shakespeare was well aware of the "conventions" that attended the death by drowning of a fellow human being.

DAVY JONES'S LOCKER

"If you were born at sea, you will die on it."

JAPANESE PROVERB

Davy Jones is the eighteenth-century sailor's name for the maleficent wraith of the sea. As Tobias Smollett (1721–1771) wrote in *Peregrine Pickle* (1751), "This same Davy Jones, according to the mythology of sailors, is the fiend that presides over all the evil spirits of the deep" (of which there would seem to be no lack, considering the range and variety of beliefs and superstitions entertained by sailors throughout the history of seafaring).

Davy Jones himself lives at the bottom of the sea, a place known to all sailors as Davy Jones's Locker, the "sea chest," as it were, where Master Jones keeps all those goods and chattels which might come his way, such as sunken ships, all other manner of articles lost or thrown overboard, and men who had perished at sea (of whom their shipmates would say the deceased had "slipped their moorings"). "Davy Jones's

Locker" is thus the seaman's phrase for death itself; when a man has been buried at sea he is said to have "gone to Davy Jones's Locker."

There are a number of suggestions as to where the expression comes from, but the most plausible is that *Davy* is a corruption of *duppy* or *duffy*, a ghost/devil in West Indies lore, probably deriving from a West African word brought to the Caribbean by the slave trade. *Jones* is certainly a form of Jonah, that unhappy prophet of cetaceous acquaintance (see Jonah and the Whale, chapter 17), and Jonas being an alternative to Jonah, it was then transmuted to Jones, a common enough name among God-fearing seafarers. And among those very same folk ghost, devil, and harbinger of bad luck mix very well together; hence Davy Jones is the incarnation of all that is evil and ill omened in the sea.

FIDDLER'S GREEN

"Come lasses and lads, get leave of your dads,
And away to the Maypole hie,
For every he has got him a she,
And the fiddler's standing by."

ANONYMOUS, "COME LASSES AND LADS"

All classes of people have their notions of what heaven must be like, and sailors are no exception. Their concept of perpetual bliss is Fiddler's Green, a place of endless dancing and merriment to the music of jolly fiddlers, where grog, tobacco, and amiable women are available in a never-ending supply. In short, it is a seaman's paradise, a pleasure-girt celestial Elysium that happily resembled the more prosaic pleasures indelibly associated with a seafaring life: that is, the bars and bordellos of seaports such as Shanghai, Saigon, Portsmouth (England, not New Hampshire), San Francisco, and so on.

The essence of this pleasant dream of all seafarers is captured in John Conolly's poem "Fiddler's Green":

As I roved by the dock-side one evening so rare,
To view the still waters and take the salt air,
I heard an old fisherman singin' this song,
Oh—take me away boys, me time is not long.

Chorus
Dress me up in me oil-skin and jumper,
No more on the docks I'll be seen,
Just tell me old ship-mates I'm takin' a trip, mates,
And I'll see you some day in Fiddler's Green.

Now Fiddler's Green is a place I've heard tell
Where fishermen go if they don't go to hell

Where the weather is fair and the dolphins do play
And the cold coast of Greenland is far far away.

The sky's always clear and there's never a gale
And the fish jump on board with the flip of their tail
You can lie at your leisure, there's no work to do
And the skipper's below makin' tea for the crew.

And when you're in dock and the long trip is through
There's pubs and there's clubs and there's lassies there too
Now the girls are all pretty and the beer is all free
And there's bottles of rum hangin' from every tree.

I don't want a harp nor a halo, not me
Just give me a breeze and a good rolling sea
And I'll play me old squeeze-box as we sail along
When the wind's in the riggin' to sing me this song.

❈ SOURCES AND NOTES ❈

Section sources immediately follow each section title; full information for section sources is in the bibliography.

INTRODUCTION

2   **he devours them.**" Time-Life Books, *Explorers*, 1980, p. 21.

2   ***even under provocation.*** Brewer 1981, pp. 1,007–8, quoting from J. G. Lockhart, *Mysteries of the Sea: The Great Sea-Serpent.*

6   **must we do?** Gordon 1993, introduction.

9   ***They All Discovered America.*** Boland 1963.

9   ***pick him up).*** See Kennedy 1982.

9   **with imminent death.** See Leslie 1988.

10   **West Australian coast.** See Edwards 1979, Jacob and Vellios 1987, and Dash 2002.

10   **lost to history.** See Jacob and Vellios 1987 and, in particular, Gerritsen 1994.

10   **truly remarkable.** See *Icebound by North*, chapter 13.

11   ***we live or die.*** John Laing, 1860. Message washed ashore in a bottle on the sands of South Shields, England; quoted in Mason et al. 1980.

1. IN THE BEGINNING

GREAT FLOODS

Brewer 1981, Gordon 1993, Mercatante 1988, *Encyclopædia Britannica* 1961.

14   **fowls of the air.**" Genesis 6:5–7, about 700 B.C.

15   **and the earth.**") Genesis 10:13.

15   **replenish the earth.**" Genesis 9:1.

16   **of a talent.**" Revelations 16:21.

17   **of ancient Persia** The commentary, *Zend*, on the sacred writings, *Avesta*, of Zoroastrianism, the religion of Persia, sixth century B.C. to A.D. seventh century.

17   **led various researchers** For example, Immanuel Velikovsky, cited in Gordon, *Encyclopedia of Myths and Legends*, p. 170, also pp. 480–81.

MOSES AND THE RED SEA

Mercatante 1988, *Encyclopædia Britannica* 1961.

18   ***waters were divided").*** Exodus 21:14.

18   **Fabled Atlantis** In the extreme southwest of the Korea Peninsula there occurs each year a famous *tamasha*, a "parting of the waters" regarded by all South Koreans as nothing short of a miracle. In March it appears that the combined gravitational attraction of the sun and the moon causes the sea between the island of Chindo and the small neighboring island of Modo

to recede completely, leaving behind for a few hours a dry stretch of seabed to confound this Confucian nation. It may be not be coincidental that Irish missionaries in the south have over the years achieved what might be called modest success in claiming converts to Christianity. Simon Winchester, *Korea—A Walk Through the Land of Miracles* (Paladin-Grafton Books, London, 1988)

THE RAINBOW
19   **in the cloud."** Genesis 9:8–17.
19   ***damp runs away.*** Gordon 1993, Mercatante 1988.

MAUI, CREATOR OF NEW ZEALAND
Jordan 1993, Mercatante 1988, Robinson and Wilson 1962.

OCEANUS
Cotterell 1989, Hamilton 1942, Murray 1994, Seyffert 1995.

KING NEPTUNE
Mercatante 1988, Murray 1994, Robinson and Wilson 1962, Seyffert 1995.

POSEIDON
Gordon 1993, Grimal 1990, Hamilton 1942, Mercatante 1988, Murray 1994, Seyffert 1995.
23   **the Lectisternium)** See Seyffert 1995, p. 345.

AMPHITRITE
Mercatante 1988, Murray 1994, Seyffert 1995.
24   **in her keeping."** Seyffert 1995, p. 29.

APHRODITE
Gordon 1993, Murray 1994, Seyffert 1995.

PORTUNUS
Robinson and Wilson 1962, Seyffert 1995.

CASTOR AND POLLUX
Brewer 1981, Kemp 1976.

NEREUS
Grimal 1991, Hamilton 1942, Murray 1994, Robinson and Wilson 1962, Seyffert 1995.

HERO AND LEANDER
Hamilton 1942, Mercatante 1988, Seyffert 1995.

SCYLLA AND CHARYBDIS
Brewer 1981, Gordon 1993, Kemp 1976, Mercatante 1988, Murray 1994, Seyffert 1995.

MANANNAN, CELTIC SEA GOD
Cotterell 1989, Dixon-Kennedy 1996, Jordan 1993, Mercatante 1988.

2. FABLED LANDS

PILLARS OF HERCULES
Freuchen 1958, Hamilton 1942, Murray 1994, Seyffert 1995.

COLOSSUS OF RHODES

Brewer 1981, Kemp 1976, Seyffert 1995.

32   **spoils of war.** Seyffert 1995, p. 128, specifies the date as 278 B.C. and, at odds with other sources, the height as 280 feet.

32   **in 224 B.C.** Seyffert 1995, p. 128, has 222 B.C.

ULTIMA THULE

Ashe 1990, Brewer 1981, Palmer 1975.

32   **end of the earth,"** Palmer, 1975, p. 10.

33   **be put down.** Ashe 1990, p. 119.

33   **from the Orcades"** Quoted in Brewer 1981, p. 1,114.

33   **of the north;** Ashe, p. 119, seems to offer Iceland as the likely candidate.

33   **notion of America.** Ashe, p. 120.

33   **Gulf of St. Lawrence,"** Ashe.

33   **North American Continent).** Boland, p. 33.

THE HESPERIDES

Bellingham et al. 1992, Hamilton 1942, Murray 1994, Palmer 1975, Seyffert 1995.

TARSHISH

Palmer 1975, *Encyclopædia Britannica* 1961.

35   **in thy fairs").** Ezekiel 27:12.

TAPROBANE

Brewer 1981, Palmer 1975.

DISTANT OPHIR

Palmer 1975, *Encyclopædia Britannica* 1961.

37   **some three years,** See 1 Kings 10:22.

37   **to Ophir (India)."** Boland 1963, p. 26.

38   *gold moidores.* Moidores, from the Portuguese *moeda de ouro* (coin of gold), were gold coins of Portugal and Brazil from about 1640 to 1732.

MAGNETIC ISLANDS

Brewer 1981, Palmer 1975.

38   **geographer Ptolemy.** The dates of Ptolemy's birth and death are unknown, although it is clear that he flourished in the second century and that his principal work is dated A.D. 127–51.

HY BRASIL

Burman 1989, Kemp 1976, Palmer 1975, *Encyclopædia Britannica* 1961.

39   **this one circular,** See also Laputa in *Gulliver's Travels.*

ISLAND OF OGYGIA

Palmer 1975, Seyffert 1995.

ISLAND OF DELOS

Murray 1994, Palmer 1975, Seyffert 1995, Time-Life, *Ancient Mariners* 1980, *Encyclopædia Britannica* 1961.

LEMURIA, LOST CONTINENT

Gordon 1993, Palmer 1975.

LOST LAND OF LYONESSE

Ashe 1990, Dixon-Kennedy 1996, Palmer 1975.

42   **at low tide.** See also the long endnote to the Fabled Atlantis entry on p. 343.

3. LEGENDARY VOYAGES

44   **Hakluyt (1552–1616),** Hakluyt 1958.

SINDBAD THE SAILOR

Alderson 1992, Drabble 1995, Mercatante 1988.

44   **Garnerer of graveyards."** Alderson 1995, p. 182.

GULLIVER'S TRAVELS

Drabble 1995, Palmer 1975.

50   **word of it."** *The Oxford Book of Literary Anecdotes,* 1977, p. 71.

HANNO THE NAVIGATOR

Burman 1989, Freuchen 1958, Seyffert 1995, Time-Life, *Ancient Mariners* and *Explorers* 1980, *Encyclopædia Britannica* 1961.

51   **mists of time."** Time-Life, *Explorers* 1980, p. 22.

51   **the western coast."** Boland 1963, p. 27.

51   **available to us.** Seyffert 1995, p. 269.

52   **their right hand."** Burman 1989, p. 4.

52   **that of Columbus."** Burman 1989, p. 4.

PRINCE MADOC OF WALES

Boland 1963, Burman 1989, Kemp 1976.

53   **the West Indies.** Boland 1963, pp. 317–18.

54   **of derring-do."** Boland 1963, p. 316.

54   **of travel narratives."** Boland 1989, p. 198.

54   **who spoke Welsh.** Kemp 1976 p. 509.

VOYAGES OF SAINT BRENDAN

Ashe 1990, Boland 1961, Brewer 1981, Newby 1988, Severin 1978, *Encyclopædia Britannica* 1961.

55   **by the beacon."** Mercatante 1988.

55   **Brendan the Abbot).** Still published under the Latin title; see, for example, *Navigatio Sancti Brendani Abbatis: From Early Latin Manuscripts,* edited by Carl Selmer (Blackrock, Co. Dublin: Four Courts Press, 1989).

55   **900 and 920."** Ashe 1990, p. 265.

55   **Irish pagan sagas."** Mercatante 1988, p. 142.

55   **exhausting years."** Boland 1963, p. 110.

56   **their companions.)** Boland 1963, pp. 111–12.

56   **its authenticity.** Ashe 1990, p. 266.

VOYAGES OF GIL EANNES

Kemp 1976, Time-Life, *Explorers* 1980.

57   **pass Cape Bojador."** Time-Life, *Explorers* 1980

POLYNESIAN SEAFARERS

Lewis 1972, Morton 1980, Time-Life, *Pacific Navigators* 1980.

THE *KON-TIKI* EXPEDITION

Boland 1963, Freuchen 1958, Heyerdahl 1963, Jordan 1993, Robinson and Wilson 1962, *Encyclopædia Britannica* 1961.

60   **eastward to America.** *Encyclopædia Britannica* 1961, vol. 2, p. 259Q.
60   **the different islands."** Heyerdahl 1963, p. 15.
62   **coast of Ecuador.** Boland 1963, pp. 297–313.
62   **Kon-Tiki is safe."** Boland 1963, p. 309.
62   *traditions of* **pae-paes.** Heyerdahl 1963, p. 208.
62   **done long ago.** See Willis 1955, 1967.

4. SEA QUESTS OF OLD

THE ARGOSY

Kemp 1976, *Encyclopædia Britannica* 1961.

THE ARGONAUTS

Grimal 1990, Hamilton 1942, Mercatante 1988, Murray 1994, Seyffert 1995.

THE *ODYSSEY*

Hamilton 1942, Mercatante 1988, Murray 1994, Homer 1946, Seyffert 1995.

70   **shores and reef."** Hamilton 1942, p. 203.

VINLAND USA

Boland 1963, Brewer 1981, Burman 1989, Kemp 1976, Mowat 1965, Time-Life, *Vikings* 1980.

75   **in 1000,** Mowat 1965, p. 475, gives 995 as the year of Leif's departure.
75   **Baffin Island).** Boland 1963, p. 197, however, says it was Labrador.
75   **near Cape Porcupine;** According to Time-Life, *Vikings* 1980, p. 150.
75   **in Nova Scotia.")** Boland 1963, p. 198.
75   **of Newfoundland),** Time-Life, *Vikings* 1980, p. 150.
75   **Sacred Bay.** Time-Life, *Vikings* 1980, p. 151.
75   **Helge Instad.** Burman 1989, p. 192.
75   **Trinity Bay.** Mowat 1965, chapter 11.
76   **Newfoundland site.)** Boland 1963, chapter 10.
76   **Norse dwellings.** Time-Life, *Vikings* 1980, p. 151.
76   **loosely for "berry";** Time-Life, *Vikings* 1980, p. 151.
76   **feasted on "grapes."** Time-Life, *Vikings* 1980, p. 151.
76   **as authentic.** Mowat 1965, p. 371.
76   **1431 to 1449."** *Webster's Guide to American History* 1971, p. 639.

THE NORTHWEST PASSAGE

Freuchen 1958, Cook 1969, Kemp 1976, Time-Life, *Northwest Passage* 1980, Villiers 1967.

THE GREAT SOUTH LAND

Abranson 1977, Cook 1969, Kemp 1976.

82   **a Southern Continent."** Quoted in Cook 1969, p. 178.

MOBY DICK

Drabble 1995, Freuchen 1958, Philbrick 2000, Robertson 1958, Simmons 1993, Time-Life, *Whalers* 1980.

82   **Harold W. Ross,** Quoted in Thurber, *The Years with Ross.*

83   ***whaling mendacity.***"Robertson 1958, preface.

83   **January 23, 1874.)** Time-Life, *Whalers* 1980, p. 126.

5. MARITIME HISTORY

THE BRITISH ROYAL NAVY

Abranson 1976, Kemp 1976, Lind 1979, Rodger 1986, Time-Life, *Fighting Sail* 1980.

NAVAL SALUTES

Admiralty vol. 1 1972, Kemp 1976, Masefield 1984. For more on salutes exchanged between men-of-war, see *Admiralty* vol. 2 1972, pp. 459–60.

88   **to a cruiser,** Masefield 1984, p. 150.

PLIMSOLL LINE

Admiralty vol. 1 1972, Freuchen 1958, Kemp 1976, Time-Life, *Windjammers* 1980.

LLOYD'S OF LONDON

Freuchen 1958, Jeans, *Ship to Shore*, 1993, Kemp 1976.

89   **dates from 1688,** Kemp gives 1601 as the beginning of marine underwriting.

P&O SHIPPING LINE

Kemp 1976.

BEAUFORT WIND SCALE

Coles 1980, Freuchen 1958, Hiscock 1965, Kemp 1976, Meteorological Office 1967.

94   **for their excitement.** Newby 1988, p. 151, from Lyall Watson, *Heaven's Breath*, 1984.

6. NAUTICAL CUSTOM

THE *BUCENTAUR*

Abranson 1977, Kemp 1976, Time-Life, *Venetians* 1980.

97   **one bottom trusted")** Shakespeare, The Merchant of Venice, 1:i.

CROSSING THE LINE

Admiralty vol. 1 1972, Hampshire 1979, Kemp 1976, Morton 1980, Rogers 1929, Time-Life, *Windjammers* 1980.

98–99 ***a deep-water sailor.*** Rogers 1929, pp. 119–20.

99   ***at the yardarm.*** Hampshire 1979, p. 200, quoting Parson Teonge.

99   **Tropic of Cancer.** Kemp 1976, p. 214.

99   **over their heads.** Auguste Jal, *Glossaire nautique* 1848, in Kemp 1976, p. 214.

TO FLOG A DEAD HORSE

Jeans, *Ship to Shore*, 1993, Kemp 1976, Lind 1982, Rogers 1929.

THE GETTING OF GROG

Hampshire 1979, Kemp 1976, Masefield 1984, Rodger 1986, Time-Life, *Fighting Sail* 1980.

101–2   ***Port Royal Harbour.*** Quoted in Hampshire 1979, pp. 40–41.

TRAVELING POSH

Brewer 1981, Jeans, *Ship to Shore*, 1993, Kemp 1976, Rees 1987.

102   **the Suez Canal** Brewer, epigraph; see also Lind 1982.

102   **on the fare.** For an example of acceptance of this myth, see Kemp 1976, p. 664.

7. LIFE AT SEA

OCEAN WAVES

Coles 1980, Freuchen 1958, Hiscock 1965, Meteorological Office 1967, Moitessier 1977, Moitessier 1973, Morton 1980, Raban 1992, *Encyclopædia Britannica* 1961.

106   **two such waves.** See, for example, SS *Waratah*, chapter 11.

106–7   **6,000 miles).** See Freuchen 1958, p. 117.

107   *112 feet.* Raban 1992, p. 432; *The Sea Around Us* was published in 1951.

107   **long wave indeed.** Morton 1980, p. 186.

107   **considered exceptional.** But Draper in Coles 1980, p. 310, maintains that the highest waves in the northern parts of the North Sea are likely to reach 70 feet, and in the Atlantic 80 feet.

107   **there was one.** Morton 1980, p. 186.

108   *considerable distance.* Moitessier 1973, p. 220.

108   **apparent height."** Coles 1980, p. 25.

108   **some 1,000 miles** Coles p. 297.

108   **the average.** Coles 1980, p. 305.

108   **point of bending.** Coles, p. 309.

109   **can generate.** Moitessier 1977, p. 177.

TRADE WINDS

Freuchen 1958, Hiscock 1959, Jeans, *Ship to Shore*, 1993, Kemp 1976, Meteorological Office 1967.

THE SARGASSO SEA

Freuchen 1958, Kemp 1976, Rogers 1929, Time-Life, *Explorers* 1980.

112   **miles in area.** Time-Life, *Explorers* 1980, p. 62.

THE SEVEN SEAS

Brewer 1981, Freuchen 1958, *Encyclopædia Britannica* 1961.

113   **just one?** One sea, as Freuchen 1958, p. 33, points out, makes sense if we remember that the known world is really a series of large and small lumps of earth poking up through the vast sheet of water that covers much of the globe.

114   **seven ewe lambs.** See Genesis 21:28.

114   **years of work.** Exodus 23:10–11.

114   **years of famine.** Exodus 7:25; Genesis 41:25–27.

114   **with seven loaves;** Matthew 25:34–38.

115   *highest mountain.* Alan Villiers (1903–1982), Australian writer and sea captain, in Mason, et al., 1980, unpaginated; see bibliography.

CAPE HORN

Freuchen 1958, Jacob and Vellios 1987, Kemp 1976, Morton 1980.

116   **(1598–1600)** See Hakluyt 1958 in the bibliography.

117   *as sheet iron.* Richard Henry Dana, *Two Years Before the Mast,* 1840, chapter 31; see bibliography.

117   *man in it.* William Willis, *The Hundred Lives of an Ancient Mariner* 1967, chapter 4; see bibliography.

THE CAPE HORNERS
Kemp 1976, Morton 1980.

ON THE SPANISH MAIN
Kemp 1976, Time-Life, *Spanish Main* 1980.
119 **bordering coasts.** Kemp 1976, p. 820.

PRIZE MONEY
Kemp 1976, Morton 1980, *Encyclopædia Britannica* 1961.

FIRST RATE
Abranson 1977, Blackburn 1978, Kemp 1976, Lloyd 1968, Masefield 1984, Time-Life, *Fighting Sail* 1980.
122 **and fight her).** Masefield 1984, p. 15; Blackburn 1978, p. 365.

OF KNOTS AND LOGS
Kemp 1976, *Encyclopædia Britannica* 1961.

SCURVY
Hakluyt 1958, Kemp 1976, Morton 1980, Rodger 1986, Time-Life, *Explorers* 1980.
125 **until 1928).** Morton 1980 p. 270.
126 **and die thereby.** Hakluyt 1958, p. 233.
126 **of their feet.** Time-Life, *Explorers* 1980, p. 102.
126 **and lemon juice,** See Morton 1980, p. 275.
127 **as scurvy grass).** Morton 1980 p. 282.

DEEP-SEA DIVING
Kemp 1976, *Encyclopædia Britannica* 1961.

SEA CHANTIES
Time-Life, *Clipper Ships* 1980, Kemp 1976, Rogers 1929.
133 **through the fleet.** Time-Life, *Clipper Ships* 1980, p. 161.

8. THE CAPTAIN AND HIS SHIP

SHIP TYPES
Freuchen 1958, Jeans, *Ship to Shore*, 1993, Kemp 1976, Masefield 1984.

THE AGE OF SAIL
Blackburn 1978, Kemp 1976, Landström 1969, Tryckare 1975, Rogers 1929, *Encyclopædia Britannica* 1961.
139 **about in boats.** Kenneth Grahame, *The Wind in the Willows*, 1908.

THE CLIPPER SHIPS
Abranson 1977, Freuchen 1958, Kemp 1976, Morris 1987, Morton 1980, Time-Life, *Clipper Ships* 1980.
140 **one at that.** Time-Life, *Clipper Ships* 1980, p. 6.
140 **of his vessel."** Time-Life, *Clipper Ships* 1980, p. 6.

THE WINDJAMMERS
Abranson 1977, Tryckare 1975, Morton 1980, Newby 1972, Rogers 1929, Time-Life, *Windjammers* 1980, Willis 1955.

144 **the *Moshulu*,** See Newby 1972.

144 ***flax canvas again.*** Newby 1972, p. 120.

CHRISTOPHER COLUMBUS

Boland 1963, Burman 1989, Freuchen 1958, Kemp 1976, Time-Life, *Explorers* 1980

145 **it was there").** Boland 1963, p. 394.

146 **had been sighted.** The crew were exceedingly concerned about the sharks that persisted in following their ships, believing them to be an omen of disaster; also, during a great storm Columbus himself hurled a pack of playing cards into the ocean so as to calm the tempest. Haining, *Superstitions* 1979, p. 11.

149 **at their hands.** Time-Life, *Explorers* 1980, p. 77, reports seven months, not eighteen months.

149 **of the world."** Time-Life, *Explorers* 1980, p. 79.

149 **external world."** Burman 1989, p. 201.

149 **from Columbus."** Anyone interested in the who-first-discovered-America debate might care to read Boland's book, wherein he argues for the Phoenicians in the period 480–146 B.C., the Romans in A.D. 64, the Chinese Buddhist monk Hoei-Shin in 499, Brendan the Bold in 551 (see Voyages of Saint Brendan, chapter 3), Irish monks in the 900s, Bjarni Herjulfsson in 986, Leif Ericsson in 1003 (see Vinland USA, chapter 4), and some nine others, including the supposed Welsh prince Madoc (see Prince Madoc of Wales, chapter 3). Columbus then arrives in the region in 1492, although Boland and others have expressed doubt about whether Columbus actually set foot on what we might call American soil.

That his thesis has met with firm and sometimes unduly passionate resistance from the history and archeology establishments in America, Boland ascribes to the NEBC Principle—"No Europeans Before Columbus." His argument raises many interesting questions that demand objective answers; it seems increasingly doubtful—at least to this writer—that Columbus was the first to "discover" North America. That particular continent has been there for some time, and mankind has been messing about in boats for ages.

LORD ANSON

Kemp 1976, Morris 1987, Morton 1980, Rodger 1986, Time-Life, *Frigates* 1980.

CAPTAIN JAMES COOK

Freuchen 1958, Cook 1969, Jacob and Vellios 1987, Kemp 1976, Morris 1987, Morton 1980, Simmons 1993, Time-Life, *Pacific Navigators* 1980, Villiers 1967.

151 **June 11–12, 1770,** See Cook's log in Cook 1969; curiously, Kemp 1976 has July 11–12.

153 **July 13, 1771.** Cook 1969, from Cook's log; Kemp 1976 has July 12.

154 **July 29, 1775,** Kemp 1976, Cook 1969; Villiers 1967 has July 30.

155 **"stupid, polluted").** See Cook 1969, p. 253.

156 **a miracle."** Villiers 1967, p. 274.

JOHN PAUL JONES

Freuchen 1958, Kemp 1976, Time-Life, *Fighting Sail* 1980.

LORD NELSON

Freuchen 1958, Hampshire 1979, Kemp 1976, Time-Life, *Fighting Sail* 1980.

159 **maritime legend.** From Kemp 1976, under Pasco.

160 **as a whole"** Kemp 1976, p. 916.

9. A MURMURING OF MEN

162 **do it for!"** Dana 1973, p. 104.

THE *BATAVIA* WRECK AND MUTINY

Edwards 1979, Jacob and Vellios 1987, Dash 2002, private communication from KS of York, Western Australia.

163 **behind with him.** Edwards has *Weibbe*, Jacob and Vellios have *Wiebbe.*

164 **established in 1788.** See Gerritson 1994 for an interesting discussion of this possibility.

HMS *BOUNTY* MUTINY

Freuchen 1958, Kemp 1976, Masefield 1984, Morris 1987, Morton 1980, Nordoff and Hall 1954, *Encyclopædia Britannica* 1961.

165 **baked chestnut").** Quoted in Morton 1980, p. 304.

166 **all the Voyage."** Kennedy 1982, p. 141.

HMS *HERMIONE* MUTINY

Kemp 1976, Masefield 1984, Morton 1980, Pope 1998.

168 **recorded history."** Pope 1998, pp. 9 and 146.

168 **his whole nation."** Pope 1998, p. 147.

169 **lubbers overboard!"** Pope 1998, p. 142.

SPITHEAD AND THE NORE MUTINY

Dana 1973, Hampshire 1979, Kemp 1976, Masefield 1984, Time-Life, *Fighting Sail* 1980.

171 ***Margaret Hunter*** Quoted in Mason et al., *The British Seafarer* 1980.

172 ***to Davy Jones."*** Dana 1973, p. 284.

173 ***upon the air.*** Oscar Wilde, "The Ballad of Reading Gaol" (1898).

THE PRESS GANG

Kemp 1976, Masefield 1984, Rodger 1986, Time-Life, *Fighting Sail* and *Frigates* 1980.

10. BIG SHIPS AND BATTLES

RMS *TITANIC*

Bridges 1934, Kemp 1976, Kennedy 1982, Time-Life, *Great Liners* 1980, *Encyclopædia Britannica* 1961.

177 **tragedies to rest."** Robert D. Ballard, senior scientist, Woods Hole Oceanographic Institution, Massachusetts; from *Simpson's Contemporary Quotes* (Houghton Mifflin, Boston, 1988), p. 137.

HMS *ARK ROYAL*

Kemp 1976, Time-Life, *Men-of-War* 1980.

RMS *QUEEN MARY*

Abranson 1977, Kemp 1976, Kennedy 1982, Time-Life, *Great Liners* 1980.

179 **by the company."** Terry Coleman, quoted in Kennedy 1982, p. 310.

HMS *DREADNOUGHT*

Blackburn 1978, Kemp 1976, Macksey and Woodhouse 1991, Time-Life, *Dreadnoughts* and *Fighting Sail* 1980, *Encyclopædia Britannica* 1961.

180 **chapter 7).** See also Time-Life, *Fighting Sail* 1980, pp. 13–14.

180 **in 1859.** Kemp 1976 has 1858.

180 **USS *Monitor*** Macksey and Woodhouse 1991; Kemp gives the date of building as "early 1862."

182 **63,720 tons,** Kemp; *Encyclopædia Britannica* has 72,000 tons.

182 **sink this ship.**" Time-Life, *Dreadnoughts* 1980, p. 169.

THE SPANISH ARMADA

Freuchen 1958, Hakluyt 1958, Kemp 1976, Newby 1988, Time-Life, *Armada* 1980.

183 **Low Countreys.**" Meteran, in Hakluyt 1958, p. 358.

183 **Catholique Religion.**" Meteran, in Hakluyt 1958, p. 358.

184 **a month earlier.** See Newby 1988 for details of the Spanish experiences on the Irish coast.

184 ***the authours thereof.*** Meteran, in Hakluyt 1958, p. 397.

THE BATTLE OF COPENHAGEN

Kemp 1976, Time Life, *Fighting Sail* 1980, *Encyclopædia Britannica* 1961.

185 **"TIME, OFF O' COP'NHAÏGN"** Blicher was a resident of Copenhagen at the time of the bombardment. His quote was translated from the Danish by R. P. Keigwin and rendered in the dialect of Essex. *Skittles* are bowling pins. From *The Puffin Book of Salt-Sea Verse*, compiled and introduced by Charles Causley (Harmondsworth: Puffin, 1978).

185 **1793 to 1815,** Dates for the French Revolutionary Wars and the Napoleonic Wars vary according to the authority consulted.

THE BATTLE OF JUTLAND

Freuchen 1958, Kemp 1976, Macksey and Woodhouse 1991, Time-Life, *Dreadnoughts* 1980, *Encyclopædia Britannica* 1961.

188 **by its results.**" Time-Life, *Dreadnoughts* 1980, p. 125.

189 **still in jail.**" Time-Life, *Dreadnoughts* 1980, p. 157.

THE SINKING OF HMAS *SYDNEY*

191 ***men was saved.*** *Reader's Digest Illustrated Story of World War II*, 1970, pp. 120–21; Odgers 1994.

11. DEATH AND DISASTER

192 **dead shipmates.**" Philbrick p. 164.

193 ***Mignonette* in 1884;** Hanson 1999.

USS *SCORPION*

Clark 1990.

194 **what was happening.** Clark 1990, p. 132.

HMS *ROYAL GEORGE*

Kemp 1976, Rodger 1986, *Encyclopædia Britannica* 1961.

195 **Admiral Kempenfelt.** *Encyclopædia Britannica*; about 900, according to Kemp 1976.

THE *GILT DRAGON*

Beatty 1960, Gerritsen 1994, Jacob and Vellios 1987.

195 **in her hold.** Beatty 1960, p. 86, has this as "80,000 gold guilders and a great quantity of silver ingots"; Jacob and Vellios 1987, p. 71, report "eight cases of coins."

196 **state the following:** Beatty 1960 says they arrived on June 7, 1656.

196 ***still left there.*** Jacob and Vellios 1987, p. 71

196 **in the Southland.**" Jacob and Vellios 1987, p. 71.
196 **latitude 31°19'S.** Information from Ross Shardlow of Victoria Park, Perth, Western Australia.
196 **for lost sheep.**" Beatty 1960, p. 88.
196 **is buried.**" Beatty 1960, p. 88.
197 **local Aboriginal groups.** Gerritsen 1994.

HMS BIRKENHEAD
Kemp 1976.

RMS LUSITANIA
Kemp 1976, Time-Life, *Great Liners* and *U-Boats* 1980.
198 **(Captain Walther Schwieger).** Kemp 1976 has Schwieger firing two torpedoes, while Time-Life, *Great Liners* 1980, p. 137, reports only one torpedo.
198 **to be lowered.**" Reported in Lewis 1995, p. 90.
198 **cargo of munitions).** See *Webster's Guide to American History*, 1971, p. 381.
199 *so firmly contended.* *Webster's Guide to American History*, 1971, p. 381.
199 **Barbary pirate apologize.**" Time-Life, *Great Liners* 1980, p. 137.

SS WARATAH
Beatty 1960, Clark 1990, Garrett 1987, Hardwick 1967, Kemp 1976.
199 **mistakenly claims).** Clark 1990, p. 120.
200 **into wakefulness.**" Hardwick 1967, p. 49.
201 *for the liner.* Beatty 1960, pp. 92–93. See The Flying Dutchman, chapter 16.
201 **to the shore.** Hardwick 1967, p. 52.
201 **East African coast.)** *The West Australian*, July 16, 1999, p. 2.

THE WHALER ESSEX
Freuchen 1958, Hanson 1999, Jeans, *Ship to Shore*, 1993, Leslie 1988, Philbrick 2000, Simmons 1993.
202 **case in point).** See Hanson 1999.
202 **as any other.' "** Pollard quoted in Leslie 1988, p. 254.
202 **chapter 4).** See also Philbrick 2000 for a detailed examination of the *Essex* story.

THE WILLIAM BROWN
Leslie 1988.

WRECKER'S COAST
Bridges 1934.
204 **CORNISH WRECKERS**" From *The Puffin Book of Salt-Sea Verse*, compiled and introduced by Charles Causley (Harmondsworth: Puffin, 1978).

12. NAVIGABLE WATERS

THE AMAZON RIVER
Grimal 1991, Mercatante 1988, Murray 1994, Seyffert 1995, *Encyclopædia Britannica* 1961.
207 **feat of endurance,** Anyone interested in emulating Orellana's epic journey might, before setting off, care to peruse *The Incredible Voyage* (1984), the account by sailor-author Tristan Jones of his extraordinary adventures on a different route. He took his yacht *Sea Dart* up to Lake Titicaca, thence down the eastern slopes of the Andes, across the Mato

Grosso in Brazil, and down to Buenos Aires via the Paraguay and Paraná Rivers.

THE PANAMA CANAL

Freuchen 1958, Kemp 1976, Morton 1980, *Encyclopædia Britannica* 1961.

210 **the United States,"** *Encyclopædia Britannica* 1961, p. 172C.

210 **any Isthmian canal."** *Encyclopædia Britannica* 1961, p. 172C.

THE SUEZ CANAL

Freuchen 1958, Kemp 1976, Time-Life, *Windjammers* 1980, *Encyclopædia Britannica* 1961.

13. CASTAWAYS AND SURVIVORS

214 **our literary heritage."** Simmons 1993, p. xi.

ROBINSON CRUSOE

Freuchen 1958, Kemp 1976, Morton 1980, Simmons 1993, Time-Life, *Pirates* 1980.

215 **unpopular leader"),** Simmons 1993, p. 6.

216 **Owners of them."** Morton 1980, p. 350.

ICEBOUND BY NORTH

Horder 1988.

POON LIM

Kennedy 1982.

219 **become well known.** Robertson 1974.

219 **"grace under pressure."** Interview by Dorothy Parker, *New Yorker*, November 30, 1929.

220 **he said later).** Kennedy 1982, p. 342.

220 **he said).** Kennedy p. 342.

221 **soundly every night."** Kennedy p. 343.

HERBERT KABAT

Leslie, 1988.

JOHN CALDWELL

Caldwell 1957.

223 **ever undertaken."** Caldwell 1957.

TROPIC ISLAND HELL

Kemp 1976, Simmons 1993.

225 **points out,** Simmons 1993; see pp. 148–54.

226 **resourceful, confident."** Irvine quoted in Simmons 1993, p. 154.

226 **basis of a film.** *Castaway* (1987) was directed by Nic Roeg and starred Oliver Reed as Kingsland and Amanda Donohoe as Irvine.

14. AT ODDS WITH THE LAW

PIRATES

Freuchen 1958, Jeans, *Ship to Shore*, 1993, Kemp 1976, Morris 1987, Time-Life, *Ancient Mariners* and *Pirates* 1980.

229 **Indian Ocean).** Kemp 1976, p. 433; Time-Life, *Pirates* 1980, pp. 48–49.

230　**given to bulls;** See Francis Grose's *Dictionary of the Vulgar Tongue*, 1811.

BUCCANEERS

Kemp 1976, Le Golif 1954, Time-Life, *Spanish Main* 1980.

234　**and other flesh."** From Cotgrave's *French-English Dictionary*, 1611.

EARRINGS FOR CUTTHROATS

234　**of complaints).** Private communication with D. M., Bunbury, Western Australia, 1997.

HENRY EVERY

Kemp 1976, Time-Life, *Pirates* 1980.

WILLIAM KIDD

Freuchen 1958, Kemp 1976, Time-Life, *Pirates* 1980.

EDWARD TEACH ("BLACKBEARD")

Freuchen 1958, Kemp 1976, Time-Life, *Pirates* 1980.

240　**was Drummond.)** Daniel Defoe, *A General History of the Robberies and Murders of the Most Notorious Pyrates*, 1724.

241　***Queen Anne's Revenge.*** Kemp 1979, p. 860, has 1717 rather than 1716.

243　**were wounded.** Kemp p. 860 has fifteen, twelve of whom he says were hanged on the spot; Time-Life, *Pirates* 1980, offers no information on this point.

ANNE BONNY

Freuchen 1958, Kemp 1976, Time-Life, *Pirates* 1980.

MARY READ

Freuchen 1958, Kemp 1976, Time-Life, *Pirates* 1980.

15. SEA FANCIES

MERMAIDS

Freuchen 1958, Gordon 1993, Kemp 1976, Mercatante 1988.

247　**the female pudenda."**) Gordon 1993, p. 309.

247　**unalluring mermaids).** Kemp 1976, p. 542; German, vol. 46, no. 1, 1994, pp. 30–31.

248　**admire her beauty.** Although the image of Atargartis in German, vol. 46, no. 1, 1994a, p. 30, is remarkably unprepossessing.

248　**the weak spirit"** Gordon 1993, p. 310.

248　**heavenly harmony"** Gordon, p. 310.

248　**human appearance."** Kemp, p. 543.

248　**so occasioned.** Kemp, p. 542.

SIRENS

Brewer 1981, Gordon 1993, Murray 1994, Seyffert 1995.

THE LORELEI

Gordon 1993, Robinson and Wilson 1962.

SELKIES

Gordon 1993.

HALCYON DAYS
Brewer 1981, Hamilton 1942, Robinson and Wilson 1962.
252 *Halcyon days.* Hamilton 1942, p. 108.

KING CANUTE
Drabble 1995, *Encyclopædia Britannica* 1961.

16. MYTH AND MYSTERY

FABLED ATLANTIS
Ashley 1984, Berlitz 1976, Brewer 1981, Burman 1989, Drabble 1995, Hardwick and Hardwick
    1967, Kemp 1976, *Encyclopædia Britannica* 1961.
255 *and vanished.* Burman 1989, p. 133.
258 **"laser power sources."** Berlitz 1976, pp. 203–6.
258 **we call Atlantis."** Berlitz 1976, p. 210.
258 *through the centuries.* Burman 1989, p. 139.
258 **elusively—in Tibet.** Near the end of 1997, press reports from London (in *The West Australian,*
    December 31, 1997, p. 9) indicated that the search for Atlantis was far from over: a Russian team
    was convinced that Little Sole Bank, a subterranean hill in the Atlantic about 95 miles west of
    Land's End, England, would yield remains of the mythical lost city; on the other hand, a British
    team was confident that Lake Poopó, 12,000 feet above sea level in the mountains of Bolivia in
    South America, would prove to be the site of Plato's fabled continent. The Russians, led by
    classics scholar Professor Viatcheslav Koudriatsev, believed that Little Sole Bank was the former
    capital of Atlantis and that the area farther west of the hill—where the seafloor is claimed by these
    press reports to drop many thousands of feet—contains the ruins of this lost empire. (Present-day
    charts, however, indicate that the seafloor does not reach a depth of 10,00 feet until about 300
    miles west of Britain.)
      The British searchers, under the leadership of Colonel John Blashford-Snell, the well-known
    explorer and adventurer, pinned their hopes not on abyssal plains and mounts in the Atlantic but
    rather on the floor of a lake (Lago Poopó) more than 2 miles above sea level, in the Cordillera Real
    of western Bolivia. The colonel had, he said, by means of satellite technology identified a canal
    that corresponds with the dimensions given by Plato (a remarkable achievement, given the pre-
    sumably unknown units of measurement that existed in Plato's Atlantis of eleven or twelve thou-
    sand years ago). Blashford-Snell's canal was thought (by him) to be one of those that graced this
    ancient city.
      To date, ardent believers have sought high and low for Atlantis in America, Sweden, Palestine,
    central Asia, Carthage in North Africa, the Caribbean, Mexico, Spain, and Nigeria (it has even
    surfaced, so to speak, on Venus). Happily, there are still many countries available that might bear
    a profitable ransacking for this mythical empire. No doubt the good residents of Alice Springs in
    the red and very arid heart of Australia are confident that one day their bone-dry vistas of sandy
    desert and barren heat-cracked hills will be declared the original site of Lost Atlantis.

THE BERMUDA TRIANGLE
Berlitz 1977, Clark 1990, Gordon 1993, Shakespeare 1989, *Encyclopædia Britannica* 1961.
259 **of the Bermudas.** Shakespeare 1989, vol. 3, p. 48.
259 **chapter 7).** Berlitz 1977, p. ix.

260 **Training Flight 19).** According to Gordon 1993, p. 57.

260 **every description.** See Berlitz 1977, pp. 21–33.

260 **as it should."** Clark 1990, p. 79; Gordon 1993, p. 57.

260 **hear the base."** Gordon 1993, p. 57; Berlitz 1977, p. 2.

261 **about 8:00 P.M."** Clark 1990, p. 80.

261 **from outer space"** Clark 1990, p. 81.

262 **from Flight 19.** Clark 1990, p. 84.

262 **tore them apart."** Gordon 1993, p. 57.

263 ***extraterrestrial spacecraft.*** Berlitz 1997, p. 7.

263 **and inner space").** Berlitz 1977, p. 175.

263 **thousands of years."** Berlitz 1977 pp. 91, 89.

263 **the Bermuda Triangle."** *The West Australian*, September 1998.

The Flannan Isles
Clark 1990.

The *Flying Dutchman*
Cornelius Vanderdecken: Bridges 1934, Freuchen 1958, Hardwick and Hardwick 1967, Kemp 1976, Rogers 1929. Bernard Fokke: Bridges 1934, Freuchen 1958.

266 **have it posted."** Rogers 1929, p. 124.

267 ***the sea calm."]*** Hardwick and Hardwick 1967, comment p. 40.

267 ***strange red light.*** Bridges 1934, p. 183.

267 **became fatally ill** Hardwick and Hardwick 1967, p. 40.

267 **she drifted away."** Hardwick and Hardwick 1967, p. 40.

268 ***of the ocean.*** Bridges 1934, p. 184.

The *Mary Celeste*
Brewer 1981, Bridges 1934, Freuchen 1958, Hardwick and Hardwick 1967, Kemp 1976.

269 ***Marie Celeste.*** Bridges 1934, p 198; Brewer 1981, p. 711.

269 **to the confusion.** Bridges 1934, p. 198.

269 **and no other.** Hardwick and Hardwick 1967, p. 63.

269 **280 tons.** Hardwick and Hardwick 1967, p. 60; Kemp 1976, p. 531.

269 **Captain David Morehouse,** The Hardwicks gave this as "Moorhouse": Hardwick and Hardwick 1967, p. 60.

269 **bound for Genoa.** Kemp; the Hardwicks have November 7.

270 **from its davits";** Kemp, p. 531; Hardwick and Hardwick, p. 61.

270 **left half consumed."** Bridges, p. 98.

270 **like the tea."** Hardwick and Hardwick, p. 61.

271 **in the Caribbean,** Kemp says Haiti, the Hardwicks say Cuba.

272 **nothing but seawater.** Hardwick and Hardwick, p. 70.

The Schooner *Jenny*
Beatty 1960.

USS *Cyclops*
Clark 1990.

274 **the following year";** Clark 1990, p. 124.

274 **chapter 11).** For example, see Clark 1990, pp. 122–23.

274 **arrive at Norfolk,** Clark, pp. 124–25, has the *Cyclops* leaving Bahia, Brazil, for Baltimore, Maryland, but with an estimated time of arrival logged at the naval base in Norfolk, Virginia.

17. SEA MONSTERS

MONSTER CADDIE
White 1983; private communication, with thanks to H.T. of Victoria, British Columbia.

277 **are related species.)** See Victoria *Times Colonist,* July 7, 1998, p. 3.

CAPTAIN M'QUHAE'S MONSTER
Brewer 1981, Freuchen 1958, German 1992, 1994b.

278 **called the sea-serpent."** German 1992, p. 74.

278 *our lee quarter* A woodcut of the incident, published in the *Illustrated London News* on October 28, 1848, based on a letter from M'Quhae in the London *Times* on October 13, shows the creature to be about 100 yards downwind of the ship—see German 1992, p. 74.

279 *about its neck.* German 1992, p. 74.

HAIPHONG MONSTER
Bridges 1934.

280 *the same—creature.* Quoted in Bridges 1934, p. 240.

MONSTER KRAKEN
Brewer 1981, Freuchen 1958, German 1994b, Gordon 1993, Kemp 1976, Mercatante 1988, Rogers 1929.

280 **at the time).** Brewer 1981, p. 639.

280 **and a half wide."** Mercatante 1988, p. 389.

281 **(1686–1758)** Richard Ellis in German 1994b, p. 34, says Egede was Danish.

281 **surface and die.** Kemp 1976, p. 456.

281 **the creature's back** *Encyclopedia of World Mythology* 1975, p. 217.

282 *brilliant flaming eyes.* Richard Ellis in German 1990, p. 34.

282 **is an island;** Mercatante 1988, p. 389; Kemp 1976, p. 456.

282 **of its tentacles.** Kemp 1976, p. 457.

282 **off two tentacles.** Rogers 1929, p. 127.

282 **such an account).** Rogers, pp. 139–40.

283 **and terrible appearance."** German 1994b, p. 35.

283 **colorfully puts it),** Richard Ellis in German 1994b, p. 36.

LOCH NESS MONSTER
Ashe 1990, Brewer 1981, Gordon 1993, Kemp 1976, Mercatante 1988, Witchell 1976.

284 **name Loch Ness.** Ashe 1990, p. 269.

284 **the Billiabongs, below.)** Gordon 1993, p. 278.

RATTRAY HEAD MONSTER
Bridges 1934.

285 *see it again.* Bridges 1934, p. 244.

CAPE COD MONSTER
Bridges 1934, Freuchen 1958.

286 **an auxiliary stomach.** Bridges, p. 238.

CAPE SÃO ROQUE MONSTER
Bridges 1934.
287 **seen no more."** Bridges, p. 239.

HALIFAX MONSTER
Bridges 1934; see also Freuchen 1958.
287 **I ever see!"** Bridges, p. 241.
288 **the Yankee skipper."** Bridges, p. 241.

WHALER *DAPHNE'S* MONSTER
Bridges 1934.
288 **knots an hour."** Bridges, p. 242.

NAHANT BEACH MONSTER
Bridges 1934.

JONAH AND THE WHALE
Cotterell 1989, Freuchen 1958, Hardwick and Hardwick 1967, Mercatante 1988, Rogers 1929.
290 **valuable commodities.** See, for example, 1 Kings 10:22.
290 **by sperm whales."** Rogers 1929, pp. 139–40.
290 **such an incident.** Hardwick and Hardwick 1967, pp. 233–36.
292 ***lost all consciousness.*** Hardwick and Hardwick, pp. 235–36.

ORCS, WHALES, AND LEVIATHAN
Brewer 1981, Freuchen 1958, Gordon 1993, Mercatante 1988, *Encyclopædia Britannica* 1961.
292 **may include humans.** *Encyclopædia Britannica* 1961, p. 620G.
292 **literature, is male.** See Job 40:15–24.

THE BUNYIP OF THE BILLABONGS
Dixon et al. 1990, Wannan 1970, Gordon 1993.
293 **"with some satisfaction").** Wannan 1970, p. 102.
294 **two large tusks."** Dixon et al. 1990, p. 109.
294 **in a lagoon."** Wannan 1970, p. 102.
294 ***their way home.*** "Wannan, p. 103. See also The Getting of Grog, chapter 6.

18. WRAITHS OF THE SEA
295 **on being resolved.** Quoted in Garrett 1987, pp. 1, 2.
296 **to be genuine.** Garrett 1987, p. 9.

CAPES OF VIRGINIA PHANTOM
Bridges 1934, Freuchen 1958, Hayter 1959.
296 **cast the lead.** Bridges 1934, pp. 187–88.

GULF OF SAINT LAWRENCE GHOST SHIP
Bridges 1934.
297 ***the gloomy depths.*** Bridges, p. 187.

Long Island Sound Ghost Ship
Bridges 1934, Hardwick 1967.
298 **board were terrible:** Hardwick and Hardwick 1967, p. 41.

New Haven Ghost Ship
Bridges 1934.
299 *sea-mist in the sun.* Quoted in Bridges 1934, p. 187.

Ghosts of Dead Men
Bridges 1934, Freuchen 1958.
299 **out of time.** Bridges, p. 188.
299 **the port side.''** Bridges, p. 188.

The Vikings of Solway Firth
Bridges 1934.

Phantom Pilots
Hardwick 1967, Slocum 1956.
302 *whence it comes.* Slocum 1956, pp. 39–41.
302 **account for it.** Hardwick 1967, pp. 44–45.

19. SUPERSTITION AND BELIEF

Launching a Ship
Admiralty vol. 1 1972, Hampshire 1979, Kemp 1976.

Coin Under the Mast
Brewer 1981, Seyffert 1995.

Ships' Names
Hampshire 1979, private communication, with thanks to Ross Shardlow of Victoria Park, Western Australia.

Ships' Figureheads
Kemp 1976, Masefield 1984, Morton 1980; private communication, with thanks to Ross Shardlow of Victoria Park, Western Australia.

Departures
Kemp 1976, German 1993.

The Eyes of Her
Kemp 1976.
309 **Captain Bromley).** Quoted in Mason et al. 1980, unpaginated.
309 *as she is able.* Quoted in Mason et al. 1980, unpaginated.

Guiding Star
Private communication, with thanks to Ross Shardlow of Victoria Park, Western Australia.

The Lodestone
Brewer 1981, Kemp 1976.

310 **cut off his head."** Kemp 1976, p. 491.

UNLUCKY SHIPS
Morton 1980.
311 **to her timbers.** Morton, p. 198.
312 **"changed the wind."** Morton, p. 198.
312 **memento, it did).** Morton, p. 199.

WOMEN ABOARD SHIP
Hampshire 1979, Kemp 1976, Masefield 1984, Rodger 1986.
313 **to their vessel.** Kemp 1976, p. 847.

WHISTLING ABOARD SHIP
Hampshire 1979, German 1994b, Kemp 1976, Rogers 1929.
314 *a fair wind.* German 1994b, p. 63.

RINGING GLASS ABOARD SHIP
Jeans, *Ship to Shore*, 1993, Kemp 1976.

SHARKS ASTERN
Freuchen 1958, Knowlson 1930.
315 *as they get him."* Knowlson 1930, p. 182.

SHIP'S CAT
German 1994b.

COFFINS ABOARD SHIP
Hampshire 1979, private communication, with thanks to Ross Shardlow of Victoria Park, Western
    Australia.
316 *on a nearby beach.* I am grateful to Ross Shardlow of Victoria Park, Western Australia, for sup-
    plying this account.
317 **practically all seamen.** Hampshire 1979, p. 119.

FLOWERS ABOARD SHIP
Kemp 1976.

FLAGS, BAGS, BELLS, AND RAGS
Hampshire 1979, Kemp 1976, Morton 1980, private communication with Ross Shardlow of Victo-
    ria Park, Western Australia.
318 **portent of death,** Kemp 1979, p. 847.

UMBRELLAS ABOARD SHIP
Rogers 1929.

THE ALBATROSS
Brewer 1981, Haining 1979, Kemp 1976, Rogers 1929.
319 *to extend them.* Newby 1972, p. 120.
320 **did the deed.** Brewer 1981, p. 35; Kemp 1976, p. 23.
320 **dead albatross.** Haining 1979, p. 152.

Our Flat Earth

Jacob and Vellios 1987, Time-Life, *Explorers* 1980.

322 **330 to 320 B.C.** See Boland, *They All Discovered America*, 1963.

Saint Elmo's Fire

Kemp 1976, Raban 1992, Rogers 1929.

323 *be a storm.* Richard Henry Dana, *Two Years Before the Mast* 1840, chapter 24.

323 *stars in the sky.* Quoted in Raban 1992, p. 243.

323 **on which to build."** Rogers 1929, p. 126.

Priests Aboard Ship

Kemp 1976.

Ebb Tide

Kemp 1976.

Wren's Feather

Kemp 1976.

Death by Drowning

Knowlson 1930, Raban 1992.

326 *some capital injury?"* Knowlson 1930, p. 231.

326 *to save him.* Raban 1992, p. 242.

Davy Jones's Locker

Brewer 1981, Kemp 1976.

Fiddler's Green

Kemp 1976.

328 *me this song.* John Conolly, "Fiddler's Green," in Charles Causley, ed., *Salt-Sea Verse* (London: Penguin Books, 1978).

✳ SELECT BIBLIOGRAPHY ✳

This bibliography does not pretend to include all the works that deal with the lore and legend of the sea. Rather, it consists of the central books consulted for the particular topics covered in this work. A reader interested in pursuing particular themes should consult the sources shown after each entry title in sources and notes preceding this bibliography. (Note that not all books identified in the sources and notes section appear in this bibliography.)

Abranson, Erik. *Ships of the High Seas.* London: Peter Lowe, 1976. A large-format book showing many of the ships and ship types that have figured in history from early times to the present; informative text-essays for the general reader, excellentillustrations: paintings, b&w drawings, photographs. Glossary, index.

Admiralty Manual of Seamanship, volumes 1, 2, 3. London: Her Majesty's Stationery Office, 1972. Consolidated edition incorporating change 1. These three volumes introduce the naval entrant to the language, practices, and customs of professional seamanship in the Royal Navy; the manual focuses on modern warships, but much of the material derives from the days of the wooden navy; many excellent b&w drawings and tables. Appendices, index.

Alderson, Brian. *The Arabian Nights, Or, Tales Told by Sheherezade During a Thousand Nights and One Night.* New York: Morrow Junior Books, 1995. A delightful translation of selected tales brought to life from the original collection, avoiding the sometimes turgid prose of many other English translations; excellent color illustrations by Foreman.

Ashe, Geoffrey. *Mythology of the British Isles.* London: Methuen, 1990. An interesting and detailed discussion of the forces that have shaped mythology in this region; illustrated in color. Index.

Ashley, Leonard R. N. *The Wonderful World of Superstition, Prophecy, and Luck.* New York: Norton, 1984. A lively and readable account of a representative sample of superstitious beliefs concerning people, animals, plants, medicine, health, places, events, with a large section on astrology, luck, dreams, and so on. Useful index.

Bateman, Graham, and Victoria Egan, eds. *The Encyclopedia of World Geography.* Oxford: Roundhouse, 1993; U.S. edition edited by Peter Haggett, 2nd ed., New York: Marshall Cavendish, 2002.

Beatty, Bill. *A Treasury of Australian Folk Tales and Traditions.* Sydney: Ure Smith, 1960. An interesting roundup of stories and traditions pertinent to the Australian experience. (Not always accurate: Beatty has the whaler *Essex* "off the coast of Tasmania" when attacked by a whale in 1820, the incident that led to the cannibalism long famous in seafaring lore; in fact, the *Essex* was 1,200 miles northeast of the Marquesas, some 7,000 miles from Tasmania.) b&w illustrations. Good index.

Bellingham, David, Clio Whittaker, and John Grant. *Myths and Legends: Viking, Oriental, and Greek.* London: New Burlington Books, 1992. A very readable account of selected myths from Viking, Greek, and Oriental (Chinese, Indian, Japanese) sources; magnificently illustrated. Index.

Berlitz, Charles. *The Mystery of Atlantis.* London: Souvenir Press, 1976; U.S. edition 1976, New York: Avon. Tackles this age-old conundrum with missionary zeal; many b&w photographs presented under the coy rubric "could this be a temple?" etc.; interesting but not scientifically compelling.

Berlitz, Charles, with the collaboration of J. Manson Valentine. *Without a Trace.* London: Souvenir Press, 1977; U.S. edition 1977, Garden City, New York: Doubleday. Discusses a number of curious disappearances, all underlined with hints of possible extraterrestrial powers at work; b&w photographs, many suggesting major revelations imminent.

Blackburn, Graham. *The Illustrated Encyclopedia of Ships, Boats, Vessels, and Other Water-Borne Craft: Comprising an Alphabetical Directory of All Types of Craft Past and Present . . .* Woodstock, New York: Overlook Press, 1978. A large-format, magnificently illustrated encyclopedia of almost every kind of watercraft ever known, ranging from 4000 B.C. to modern times, highly recommended to students of the Age of Sail; over 600 b&w line drawings, many cross-referenced. Extensive nautical glossary, useful bibliography, index of named vessels.

Boland, Charles Michael. *They All Discovered America.* New York: Pocket Books, 1963. The well-known and controversial account of voyages to America said to have occurred many hundreds of years before Columbus; interesting but not decisive discussion supported by photographs and line illustrations. Index; selected reading list for each chapter.

Brewer, Ebenezer Cobham. *Dictionary of Phrase and Fable.* Also published as *Brewer's Dictionary of Phrase and Fable.* Rev. ed., revised by Ivor H. Evans, London: Cassell, 1981. U.S. edition revised by Adrian Room, 16th ed. rev., New York: HarperResource, 1999. Excellent compact guide, famous for its sound scholarship; useful as a secondary source.

Bridges, Thomas Charles. *The Book of the Sea.* London: G. G. Harrap & Co., 1927; rev. ed., 1934. A somewhat old-fashioned account of matters maritime, interesting for all that. Some photographs and color plates, many line drawings. No index.

Burman, Edward. *The World Before Columbus, 1100–1492.* London: W. H. Allen, 1989. A scholarly and well-written discussion that argues that all geographical discovery is really rediscovery; useful to readers who wish to pursue this topic. Extensive bibliography, good index.

Caldwell, John. *Desperate Voyage.* London: Transworld Publishers, 1957. Originally published 1950, London: Gollancz; U.S. edition 1991, Dobbs Ferry, New York: Sheridan House. A stirring account of a remarkable voyage from Panama to Australia by a man who had never before set foot on a sailboat. In 1946 Caldwell, an American merchant marine seaman anxious to get back to Mary, his Australian wife in Sydney, bought the 29-foot cutter *Pagan* in Panama and set out, ending up wrecked in the Fijis; the incredible story ends at Sydney airport, in the arms of his wife.

Clark, David. *Vanished! Mysterious Disappearances.* London: Michael O'Mara Books, 1990; published in the U.S. as *Vanished! True Tales of Mysterious Disappearances*, Chicago: Contemporary Books, 1991. A generally well-researched survey of some famous disappearances of persons, ships, and airplanes, written mostly for the popular market. Photographs, with suggested further reading for each topic. No index.

Coles, K. Adlard. *Heavy Weather Sailing,* 3rd ed. London: Granada Publishing, 1967, 1980. Published in the U.S. as *Adlard Coles' Heavy Weather Sailing,* edited by Peter Bruce, 30th ann. ed., International Marine, Camden, Maine, 1999. A classic, essential text for all deepwater sailors by a man who sailed for more than fifty years, in all kinds of weather; describes and analyzes the experiences of sailors who have survived storms and severe gales; b&w photographs and diagrams. Appendices, good index.

Cook, James. *The Explorations of Captain James Cook in the Pacific: As Told By Selections of His Own Journals, 1768–1779.* Edited by A. Grenfell Price. Sydney: Angus & Robertson, 1969. Originally published 1958, Melbourne: Georgian House; U.S. edition 1988, Norwalk, Connecticut: Easton Press. A biography of a man widely regarded as the greatest sailing ship seaman ever; covers Cook's three voyages, with commentary and notes, happily retaining Cook's wonderful spelling; excellent b&w line drawings. No index.

Cooper, Russell. *Shark Bay Legends.* Geraldton, Western Australia: L. J. Cogan, 1997. A history of the early days in the Shark Bay (central west) region of Western Australia; this general area is where the light cruiser HMAS *Sydney* was sunk by the German raider *Kormoran* on November 19, 1941, with the loss of all hands.

Cotterell, Arthur. *The Illustrated Encyclopedia of Myths and Legends.* Sydney: Collins Australia, 1989; published in the U.S. as *The Macmillan Illustrated Encyclopedia of Myths and Legends,* New York: Macmillan, 1989. A scholarly survey of myths and legends of some eighteen different cultures, each story presented in a compact and readable form. Well illustrated; includes a Micropedia listing more than a thousand short entries on mythological subjects; further reading suggested for each cultural area. Extensive index.

Dana, Richard Henry. *Two Years Before the Mast.* London: Arrow Books, 1973. Originally published anonymously, 1840; published in the U.S. as *Two Years Before the Mast: A Personal Narrative of Life at Sea,* New York: Modern Library, 2001. The famous account of life at sea as it really was in the early nineteenth century. Dana shipped aboard an American vessel as a common sailor for a voyage around the Horn; his experience of brutality and injustice afloat led him to write what almost immediately became a classic of the sea, which it remains to this day.

Dash, Mike. *"Batavia"'s Graveyard.* London: Weidenfeld & Nicolson, 2002; U.S. edition 2002, New York: Crown Publishers. Perhaps the best and certainly to date the most thoroughly researched account of the wreck of the Dutch East Indies ship *Batavia,* which in 1629 piled up on the reefs and sandy cays off the central Western Australian coast. A mutiny then turned into wholesale bloody murder; of the 322 people on board, at least 110 were slaughtered; copious notes. Good index.

Davey, Gwenda Beed, and Graham Seal, eds. *The Oxford Companion to Australian Folklore.* New York and Melbourne: Oxford University Press, 1993. A thorough if somewhat sober discussion of Australian folklore, written in a scholarly fashion; arranged alphabetically and cross-indexed; many contemporary photographs.

Dixon, R. M. W., W. S. Ramson, and Mandy Thomas. *Australian Aboriginal Words in English: Their Origin and Meaning.* New York and Melbourne: Oxford University Press, 1990. Deals with most (about 400) of the Aboriginal words assimilated into Australian English from the 250 or so languages spoken in Australia before white men arrived in 1788; written by recognized scholars; some b&w illustrations. Good index.

Dixon-Kennedy, Mike. *Celtic Myth and Legend: An A–Z of People and Places.* London: Blandford, 1996. An A–Z of people and places arranged in dictionary format; persons and sites associated with Celtic lore are explained in brief but compact detail; appendices list Celtic genealogies and non-Celtic deities and heroes (though, curiously, Jason of Argonaut fame is missing); very useful first reference. Excellent bibliography.

Drabble, Margaret, ed. *The Oxford Companion to English Literature*, rev. ed. New York and Oxford: Oxford University Press, 1995.

Edwards, Hugh. *Islands of Angry Ghosts.* Sydney: Angus & Robertson, 1969. Originally published 1966, London: Hodder & Stoughton. Arkon paperback ed., 1979. A detailed and well-researched account of the wreck of the Dutch vessel *Batavia* on the Western Australian coast in 1629 and the mayhem, mutiny, and bloody slaughter that followed; also describes the discovery of the wreck site in the 1960s. Index.

Encyclopædia Britannica. 24 volumes. Harry S. Ashmore, editor in chief. London: Encyclopædia Britannica, 1961 edition.

Encyclopedia of World Mythology. London: Octopus Books, 1975; U.S. edition 1975, New York: Galahad Books. Selected myths from Egypt, the Middle East, Ancient Greece, Ancient Rome, Northern and Central Europe, and the Celts, with the mythology of animals and plants; profusely illustrated in color. Extensive index.

Freuchen, Peter. *Peter Freuchen's Book of the Seven Seas.* London: Jonathan Cape, 1958; U.S. edition 2003, Guilford, Connecticut: Lyon's Press. This very readable, famous sea-lover's broad-ranging history of the significance to man of the world's oceans covers exploration and discovery, trade and empire, and the inevitable wars fought to gain control of it all; b&w photographs, line drawings, tables, maps. Good index.

Garrett, Richard. *Voyage Into Mystery: Reports from Sinister Side of the Sea.* London: Weidenfeld & Nicolson, 1987. A discussion of various mysteries to do with the sea: sea monsters, phantom ships, floating man-made islands, and other imponderables; some b&w photographs. No index.

German, A. W., ed. *The Log of Mystic Seaport.* Mystic, Connecticut: Mystic Seaport Museum, vol. 41, no. 2, 1989; vol. 42, 1990; vol. 44, no. 3, 1992; vol. 45, no. 2, 1993; vol. 46, no. 1, 1994a; vol. 46, no. 2, 1994b; vol. 48, no. 2, 1996. A quarterly bulletin on a wide variety of seafaring topics, well written, good illustrations.

Gerritsen, Rupert. *And Their Ghosts May be Heard.* South Fremantle, Western Australia: Fremantle Arts Centre Press, 1994. An extensively researched and compelling examination of the possibility (leading to a distinct likelihood) that many sailors shipwrecked on the coast of Western Australia in the sixteenth, seventeenth, and eighteenth centuries found refuge with various groups of Aborigines. Gerritsen argues his case with particular reference to Dutch seamen cast ashore along the central coast, between Perth and Shark Bay; maps, b&w line drawings, some photographs; copious notes. No index.

Gordon, Stuart. *The Encyclopedia of Myths and Legends.* London: Headline, 1993. A comprehensive and useful introduction to world mythology; arranged alphabetically, extensive cross-references; includes a concordance of themes discussed. Large bibliography.

Grimal, Pierre. *The Penguin Dictionary of Classical Mythology*, abridged ed. Edited by Stephen Kershaw, translated by A. R. Maxwell-Hyslop. New York and London: Penguin Books, 1991. Excellent introduction to the mythology of Ancient Greece and Rome (the English translation reads well); arranged alphabetically, with genealogical tables to help the reader navigate the complexities of family life on Mount Olympus.

Haining, Peter. *Superstitions.* London: Sidgwick & Jackson, 1979. Interesting and well-researched information on the myriad superstitions entertained by all manner of people;

written for the popular market; many b&w photographs and line illustrations. Index.

Hakluyt, Richard. *Voyages and Documents.* Edited by Janet Hampden. London: Oxford University Press, 1958. Issued by Oxford in *The World's Classics,* a selection from Richard Hakluyt's remarkable work of 1598–1600 *(The Principal Navigations, Voiages, Traffiqves and Discoueries of the English Nation)*; indispensable for the researcher seeking the flavor of original accounts. Excellent introduction by the editor; chronology of important maritime events, glossary of terms in common use four hundred years ago. Extensive index.

Hamilton, Edith. *Mythology.* Boston: Little, Brown, 1942. One of those rarities: an extremely accessible account of "timeless tales of gods and heroes" written by a world-renowned classicist; selected stories from Greek, Roman, Norse mythology; b&w line drawings, genealogical tables. Good index.

Hampshire, A. Cecil. *Just an Old Navy Custom.* London: W. Kimber, 1979. A fascinating account of the background of many of the naval expressions still used today, written by a man who spent a lifetime in the Royal Navy; many b&w photographs. Useful bibliography, good index.

Hanson, Neil. *The Custom of the Sea.* London: Doubleday, 1999; U.S. edition 1999, New York: Wiley. This is the true and well-written story of the British yacht *Mignonette,* wrecked in 1884 by a terrible storm during a voyage from Southampton to Sydney. When the survivors were finally rescued it was clear that they had resorted to cannibalism, Hanson's "custom of the sea." The trial of these survivors kept Britain awake at night. Select bibliography.

Hardwick, John Michael Drinkrow, and Mollie Hardwick. *The World's Greatest Sea Mysteries.* London: Odhams Books, 1967. An entertaining and informative summary of maritime mysteries, written for the general public but well researched; many line drawings. Bibliography, good index.

Hayter, Adrian. *"Sheila" in the Wind: A Story of a Lone Voyage.* London: Hodder & Stoughton, 1959. Soon after the end of World War II, Hayter, demobilized from the British army, set out to return home to New Zealand by way of the Suez Canal. The story of his voyage— which lasted six years (1950–56)—is a fascinating account of how a man, if he so wishes, can become entirely at one with the elements. (Nevertheless, he was washed ashore on the Western Australian coast in 1951; as a result, the author of this book, still a boy, met the man himself.)

Heyerdahl, Thor. *The "Kon-Tiki" Expedition: By Raft Across the South Seas.* Harmondsworth, England: Penguin Books, 1963. English translation by F. H. Lyon first published 1950 by Allen & Unwin, London. The famous voyage made by the Norwegian anthropologist Thor Heyerdahl and five companions: in 1947 they sailed a balsa raft from South America across the South Pacific to show that the Polynesians could have descended from seagoing Incas of Peru; the raft was eventually wrecked east of Tahiti; b&w photographs. Index.

Hiscock, Eric C. *Cruising Under Sail,* 2nd ed. New York and London: Oxford University Press, 1965; first published 1950 by Oxford University Press. Published in the U.S. as *Cruising Under Sail: Incorporating Voyaging Under Sail* in 1981, now in its 3rd ed., Camden, Maine: International Marine, 1985. Regarded by many as the bible for cruising sailors, written by a man who knew through long and varied experience what he was talking about; covers every facet of maintaining a sailboat and handling it in all kinds of weather; exceptionally well illustrated: b&w photographs and diagrams. Three appendices (including a bibliography), glossary, excellent index. Highly recommended.

————. *Voyaging Under Sail.* New York and London: Oxford University Press, 1959. A superb text on deep-sea voyaging by a man who was not only a consummate seaman himself but also a gifted writer and photographer. Hiscock discusses all aspects of preparing for sea and how to manage it when you get there; many b&w photographs; diagrams, tables. Appendices, excellent index. Highly recommended.

Homer. *The Odyssey,* translated by E. V. Rieu. New York and Middlesex, England: Penguin Books, 1945; reissued 1967. Revised translation by D. C. H. Rieu, 2003. The original is still one of the best and more readable accounts of the adventures of Odysseus, translated by a recognized scholar.

Horder, Mervyn. *On Their Own: Shipwrecks and Survivals.* London: Duckworth, 1988. A well-researched account of shipwrecked people who by various means and aided by not a little good luck have managed to survive the experience despite very adverse circumstances.

Irvine, Lucy. *Castaway.* London: V. Gollancz, 1983.

Jacob, Trevor K., and Jim Vellios. *Southland, The Maritime Exploration of Australia.* Perth, Western Australia: Ministry of Education, 1987. Excellent large-format volume produced for use in Western Australian schools; discusses the history of maritime contact with the Australian continent; abundant color illustrations. Reading list, good index.

Jeans, Peter. *My Word: Digressions on Language, Literature, and Life.* Perth, Western Australia: St. George Books, 1993. A collection of articles on language written for the *West Australian* newspaper. Index.

————. *Ship to Shore: A Dictionary of Everyday Words and Phrases Derived from the Sea.* Camden, Maine: International Marine, 2004. First published 1993 by ABC-CLIO, Santa Barbara, California. Surveys the extent to which seafaring language has for many hundreds of years been adopted into everyday English; dictionary format; illustrated with excellent b&w line drawings by marine artist Ross Shardlow; four appendices.

Jordan, Michael. *Myths of the World: A Thematic Encyclopedia.* London: K. Cathie, 1993. An interesting and well-written account of worldwide myths (Myths of Childhood, Myths of Immortality, etc.), arranged as chapters; not illustrated, but a useful appendix showing myths by culture. Index is neither extensive enough nor arranged satisfactorily.

Kemp, Peter, ed. *The Oxford Companion to Ships and the Sea.* London: Paladin, 1979; U.S. edition 1976, New York: Oxford University Press, reprinted 1988 with corrections. An excellent compendium of maritime lore, focusing mostly on sail, written by experts and edited by a distinguished naval historian (but occasionally at variance with other sources in the matter of dates; note, too, that the entry for Fremantle, the principal port of Western Australia, identifies that city as the state's capital, which no doubt will very much surprise the citizens of Perth while delighting those of Fremantle); dictionary format; well illustrated with many photographs and drawings.

Kennedy, Ludovic. *A Book of Sea Journeys.* London: Fontana, 1982. An anthology of some of the best writing by, and about, people at sea, from journals, letters, verbatim reports, fiction; ranges from 1500 to present times, covering a satisfying variety of seafaring experiences; illustrated.

Knowlson, T. Sharper. *The Origins of Popular Superstitions and Customs.* London: T. Werner Laurie, 1930; reissued 1994, London: Senate. Discusses the background to a wide range of popular superstitions (though including only a few nautical beliefs); useful only as a secondary source. Adequate index.

Landström, Björn. *The Ship: A Survey of the History of the Ship from the Primitive Raft to the*

Nuclear-Powered Submarine. Translated by Michael Phillips. London: Allen & Unwin, 1961. This is the famous and probably very best general survey of ship types available today; examines the history of mankind's association with the sea from prehistoric times to the present; magnificently illustrated in color and b&w. Highly recommended.

Le Golif, Louis Adhémar Timothée. *The Memoirs of a Buccaneer: Being a Wondrous and Unrepentant Account of the Prodigious Adventures and Amours of King Louis XIV's Loyal Servant, Louis Adhemar Timothee Le Golif, Known for his Singular Wound as Borgnefesse, Captain of the Buccaneers*. Translated by Malcolm Barnes. Edited by G. Alaux and A. t'Serstevens. London: Allen & Unwin, 1954. Originally published in French as *Cahiers de Louis Adhémar Timothée Le Golif dit Borgnefesse, Capitaine de la Flibuste*, 1952, Paris: Bernard Grasset. U.S. edition 1954, New York: Simon & Schuster. The plain, unvarnished, and always diverting account of a young man who, having studied for the Church and there found wanting, took passage to the West Indies, fell in with a band of buccaneers and filibusters, and entered on a heady life of roistering adventure.

Leslie, Edward E. *Desperate Journeys, Abandoned Souls: True Stories of Castaways and Other Survivors*. Boston: Houghton Mifflin, 1988. This is a particularly well-written account of survivors of maritime disasters, all of them true stories painstakingly researched and told in a clear and compelling fashion; highly recommended to students of the literature of the sea; extensive notes on each chapter. Excellent bibliography.

Lewis, David. *We, the Navigators: The Ancient Art of Landfinding in the Pacific*. Canberra: Australian National University Press, 1972; U.S. 2nd edition edited by Sir Derek Oulton, Honolulu: University of Hawaii Press, 1994. Dr. David Lewis is well known among yachtsmen not only for his wide experience and skill in world voyaging but also for his abiding interest in the traditions of long-distance oceanic navigation practiced by the Polynesian peoples for thousands of years; highly recommended to all mariners who use a GPS, the batteries of which will one day certainly expire, far out at sea.

Lewis, Jon, ed. *Giant Book of the 20th Century*. Sydney: The Book Company International, 1995. A collection of reports, letters, and extracts from longer pieces, all dealing with a wide variety of events, beginning with Kipling's account of a skirmish in the Boer War, 1900, ending with Nelson Mandela voting in South Africa, 1994; many of the accounts are eyewitness reports, all are engaging.

Lind, Lew. *Sea Jargon: A Dictionary of the Unwritten Language of the Sea*. Kenthurst, New South Wales: Kangaroo Press, 1982. An extensive collection of naval jargon used in the messes, wardrooms, and fo'c'sles of the English-speaking navies and merchant services of the world.

Lloyd, Christopher. *The British Seaman 1200–1860: A Social Survey*. London: Collins, 1968. U.S. edition 1968, Rutherford, New Jersey: Fairleigh Dickinson University Press; reprinted 1970. A detailed study of the life of the British sailor, 1200–1860, which examines the problems involved in manning the king's ships; an essential reference for the student of naval warfare; tables. Bibliography, index.

Macksey, Kenneth, and William Woodhouse. *The Penguin Encyclopedia of Modern Warfare: 1850 to the Present Day*. New York and London: Viking, 1991. Beginning in 1850 and ending in 1982 with the Falklands War, chronicles man's eternal preoccupation with fighting his fellow man; it describes, in a style that is always clear and concise, some fifty serious clashes, campaigns, and full-blown wars, as well as the rapidly evolving strategies and technologies that enable us to visit death and destruction on each other. Fully cross-referenced, dozens of maps and diagrams; chronology. Bibliography, excellent index.

Masefield, John. *Sea Life in Nelson's Time*, 4th ed. London: Conway Maritime Press, 1984; first published 1905; U.S. edition 2002, Annapolis, Maryland: Naval Institute Press. A nuts-and-bolts account of the kind of life that seamen led in the time of Nelson (1758–1805), written by a man who joined the training ship HMS *Conway* as a boy in 1891 and who went to sea at age fifteen, spending some years in windjammers rounding the Horn before leaving the sea to take up journalism; profusely illustrated, b&w drawings, woodcuts, and photographs. Bibliography, index.

Mason, Michael, Basil Greenhill, and Robin Craig. *The British Seafarer.* London: Hutchinson/BBC in association with the National Maritime Museum, 1980; unpaginated. The book from BBC Radio 4's serial history, *The British Seafarer* (1980); a wonderful collection of b&w photographs and drawings to illustrate the text, entirely extracts from the writings of those who went to sea and those who waited for them to return.

Mercatante, Anthony S. *The Facts on File Encyclopedia of World Mythology and Legend.* New York: Facts on File, 1988. One of the very best works available on world mythology; a large-format scholarly account of more than 3,000 myths, with many b&w line drawings; entries arranged alphabetically, with serial numbers for cross-referencing; a very extensive annotated bibliography divided into geographical, cultural, ethnic groupings; key to variant spellings. Cultural and ethnic index cross-referenced to the entries, and a massive general index. Highly recommended.

Meteorological Office. *Meteorology for Mariners, with a Section on Oceanography*, 2nd ed. London: Her Majesty's Stationery Office, 1967. The official handbook on all matters to do with weather, climate, oceanography as they affect those who insist on going down to the sea in ships; Columbus and Cook and all those hardy souls in the intervening three hundred years would have given much for this tome; many b&w drawings, tables, inserted charts. Good index.

Moitessier, Bernard. *Cape Horn, The Logical Route: 14,216 Miles without Port of Call.* Translated by Inge Moore. London: Hart-Davis MacGibbon, 1977. First published in English 1969, London: Adlard Coles. Published in the U.S. as *Cape Horn: The Logical Route*, Ferry, New York: Sheridan House, 2003. Originally published in French as *Cap Horn à la voile: 14.000 milles sans escale* in 1967, Paris: Les Éditions Arthaud/Flammarion. An account by the doyen of modern long-distance yachtsmen of a voyage with his wife from Tahiti to France by way of Cape Horn, told by a man who understands the power and the beauty of the world's oceans; b&w photographs, maps, diagrams.

————. *The Long Way.* Translated by William Rodarmor. London: Granada, 1973, reprinted 1983. U.S. edition 1973, Garden City, New York: Doubleday. Originally published as *La longue route* in 1971, Paris: Les Éditions Arthaud/Flammarion. In 1968 Moitessier set out in the Singlehanded Round the World Race, but after passing the three capes (Good Hope, Leeuwin, Horn) and while still in the lead, he withdrew and carried on into the Pacific once more, to be with friends; an interesting account of one man's relationship with the sea; color photographs, b&w diagrams, drawings.

Morris, Roger. *Pacific Sail: Four Centuries of Western Ships in the Pacific.* Southampton: Ashford, 1987; U.S. edition 1987, Camden, Maine: International Marine. This is a sumptuous visual feast of the ships that have voyaged across the Pacific in the past four centuries as they pursued exploration, warfare, and trade; accompanying the magnificent watercolors and b&w drawings are extended notes about details of rigging, sails, early navigation, and so on, as well as commentaries on the principal characters involved. Essential for students of sail; glossary. References, copious index. Highly recommended.

Morton, Harry. *The Wind Commands: Sailors and Sailing Ships in the Pacific.* St. Lucia, Australia: University of Queensland Press, 1975, reprinted 1980. A scholarly and very readable treatise on seafarers and their ships in the Pacific, spanning some four centuries of maritime affairs. Well illustrated with photographs, line drawings; glossary of nautical terms used. Extensive bibliography, excellent index. Highly recommended.

Mowat, Farley. *Westviking: The Ancient Norse in Greenland and North America.* Toronto: McClelland & Stewart, 1965; U.S. edition 1965, Boston: Little, Brown. A detailed, scholarly discussion of the voyages made by the Norsemen to the North American continent, beginning with their settlement in Iceland in A.D. 870; eminently readable, with meticulous reference to the sagas of the Norsemen; excellent appendices explaining chronology and sources; b&w maps. Detailed index. Highly recommended.

Murray, Alexander S. *Who's Who in Mythology: Classic Guide to the Ancient World,* 2nd ed, rev. and enl. London: Bracken, 1994; a reprint of the earlier enlarged *Manual of Mythology,* 2nd ed. A popular exposition, by a famous scholar, of the gods, heroes, villains in Greek and Roman mythology; somewhat more discursive than Seyffert (see below) but perhaps not as inclusive; sections on Norse, Indian, Egyptian mythology; b&w woodcuts. Good index.

Newby, Eric. *The Last Grain Race.* London: Pan Books, 1972; first published 1956, London: Secker & Warburg. U.S. edition 1984, New York: Penguin Books, reprinted 1986. The famous story of the last grain race between a number of square-riggers in 1938–39; nineteen-year-old Newby shipped aboard the four-masted bark *Moshulu* as Ordinary Seaman and completed the voyage, Belfast to Port Lincoln (South Australia) and return to Queenstown (Ireland); Newby relates the adventure of a lifetime in a clear and compelling style; b&w photographs.

———. *Round Ireland in Low Gear.* London: Picador, 1987, reprinted 1988. U.S. edition 1987, New York: Penguin Books, reprinted 1989. An entertaining account of a bicycle tour of Ireland in the 1980s. Newby is well known for his travel writing; as a young man he sailed in the last square-rigger grain race (see above); maps, line drawings. Good index.

Newton, Michael. *Monsters, Mysteries, and Man.* Reading, Massachusetts: Addison-Wesley, 1979. Useful for background to sea monsters, but somewhat breathless in its "discussion" of UFOs; some b&w photographs, line drawings. Modest index.

Nordhoff, Charles, and James Norman Hall. *Pitcairn's Island.* New York: Pocket Books, 1954; originally published 1934, Boston: Little, Brown. The final book in the *Bounty* trilogy (the first two are *Mutiny on the "Bounty"* and *Men Against the Sea*). All three give a fictionalized account of the famous mutiny and its aftermath, later romanticized out of all recognition (and belief) by Hollywood. Nordhoff and Hall diligently researched all available sources in writing these historical novels.

Odgers, George. *Diggers: The Australian Army, Navy and Air Force in Eleven Wars.* Sydney: Lansdowne, 1994. A large-format, richly illustrated survey of the involvement of Australian defense personnel in conflicts ranging from the Land Wars against the Maoris in 1860 to the (first) Gulf War in 1990, with two World Wars and other bitter conflicts in between and the inevitable peacekeeping missions that follow. Excellent index.

Palmer, Robin. *A Dictionary of Mythical Places.* New York: H. Z. Walck, 1975. Readable accounts of legendary settings such as the many mythical islands that feature in man's yearnings; b&w drawings.

Philbrick, Nathaniel. *In the Heart of the Sea: The Epic True Story that Inspired Moby Dick.*

London: HarperCollins, 2000; published in the U.S. as *In the Heart of the Sea: The Tragedy of the Whaleship "Essex,"* New York: Viking, 2000. Probably the best account available of the sinking, by an enraged whale, of the Nantucket whaleship *Essex* in 1820, an event that set in train not only one of the classic stories of cannibalism at sea but also became the source for Herman Melville's famous novel *Moby-Dick*. Extensive select bibliography, index.

Pope, Dudley. *The Black Ship*. New York: Henry Holt, 1998; first published 1963, London: Weidenfeld & Nicholson. In 1797, while cruising in the Caribbean, a group of seamen on board HMS *Hermione* waged the bloodiest mutiny ever to occur in the British navy: the captain and nine of his officers were summarily dispatched by cutlass, hatchet, and knife. Pope has masterfully told the story of this incident, together with details of how the navy, over a period of years, brought most of the mutineers to account.

Raban, Jonathan, ed. *The Oxford Book of the Sea*. New York and Oxford: Oxford University Press, 1992. An intelligent and evocative selection of writing that focuses on the meaning of the sea in literature; ranges from A.D. 900 to present times; excellent introduction.

Reader's Digest editors. *Reader's Digest Illustrated Story of World War II*. Sydney: Reader's Digest, 1970. A large-format account of the Second World War, told graphically in the form of essays, maps, dozens of excellent b&w photographs; chronology of outstanding events. Detailed index.

Rees, Nigel. *Why Do We Say—?: Words and Sayings and Where They Come From*. New York and London: Blandford, 1987. A survey of some popular phrases in current usage by a well-respected researcher in the field.

Robertson, Dougal. *Survive the Savage Sea*. Harmondsworth: Penguin Books, 1975; U.S. edition 1994, Dobbs Ferry, New York: Sheridan House. In 1972 the schooner *Lucette* was rammed and sunk in the central Pacific, west of the Galápagos Islands, by killer whales, with four adults and two children on board. Their vessel sank immediately. The family took to their rubber dinghy, and with food and water for only three days the Robertsons drifted for over five weeks before being rescued by a Japanese fishing vessel. A modern classic of survival at sea; b&w drawings and one photograph. No index.

Robertson, Robert Blackwood. *Of Whales and Men*. London: Macmillan, 1956; reprinted 1958, London: The Reprint Society, London. U.S. edition 1966, New York: Knopf. An intelligent and warm-hearted account of whaling in the Southern Ocean; b&w photographs.

Robinson, Herbert Spencer, and Knox Wilson. *The Encyclopædia of Myths and Legends of All Nations*, rev. ed. Edited by Barbara Leonie Picard. London: Edmund Ward, 1962. A modest but exceptionally well-organized and readable survey of myth worldwide; chapters devoted to individual cultures. Topical index and extensive general index. Recommended.

Rodger, N. A. M. *The Wooden World: An Anatomy of the Georgian Navy*. London: Collins, 1986; U.S. edition 1986, Annapolis, Maryland: Naval Institute Press. This is a scholarly and very readable investigation in considerable detail of life in the British navy of the eighteenth century; b&w photographs of ships and personalities of the period; glossary of sailing terms of the period. Index. Recommended.

Rogers, Stanley. *Sea-Lore*. London: G. G. Harrap & Co, 1929. A lively account of various aspects of life at sea, written in nontechnical language, with competent b&w illustrations by the author. Index.

Seligman, Adrian. *The Voyage of the "Cap Pilar,"* 3rd ed. London: Hodder & Stoughton, 1947; first published 1939; U.S. edition 1947, New York: E. P. Dutton. An account of one of the very last square-riggers to put to sea. In 1936 Seligman, his new wife, and a changing group of young men sailed this three-masted bark around the world, returning to London two years later at the end of 1938; an interesting and well-told tale.

Severin, Tim. *The Brendan Voyage*. London: Hutchinson, 1978; U.S. edition 2000, New York: Modern Library. Follows in the wake of the *Kon-Tiki* as one of the great sea voyages of modern times. Severin and his companions set out in 1976 to explore the possibility that the sixth-century Irish monk Saint Brendan could have sailed from Ireland to America; thirteen months later Severin's leather boat, the *Brendan*, made landfall at Newfoundland. A stirring account, with color photographs.

Seyffert, Oskar. *The Dictionary of Classical Mythology, Religion, Literature, and Art*, rev. ed. Edited by Henry Nettleship and J. E. Sandys. New York: Gramercy Books, 1995. Originally published in English in 1891 as *Dictionary of Classical Antiquities* (translated from the German), contains a wealth of information on various classical themes like myth, geography, marriage, gladiators, architecture, the Trojan War, and so on, profusely illustrated with hundreds of b&w line drawings and cuts. General index, illustrations index. Highly recommended.

Shakespeare, William. *The Complete Illustrated Shakespeare*. Edited by Howard Staunton. Bombay: Lalvani Publishing House, 1989. U.S. edition 1989, New York: Gallery Books. First published 1858, 1859, 1866, 3 vols., London & New York: George Routledge & Sons. A superb example of Victorian editing by one of the foremost Shakespearean scholars of his time; extensively illustrated, b&w line drawings; copious notes and glossary; consulted here for its contemporary comments on maritime matters in, for example, *The Tempest*.

Simmons, James C. *Castaway in Paradise: The Incredible Adventures of True-Life Robinson Crusoes*. Dobbs Ferry, New York: Sheridan House, 1993. This is a highly readable account of a number of castaways ranging from Alexander Selkirk on Màs a Tierra island (the original of Defoe's *Robinson Crusoe*) through the terrible *Essex* incident in 1820 involving cannibalism at sea to more modern episodes such as the famous Minerva Reef story in the west central Pacific, 1962; well researched and highly recommended. Further reading, extensive bibliography, index.

Slocum, Joshua. *Sailing Alone Around the World*. New York: Dover Publications, 1956. The account of the first single-handed circumnavigation of the world (1895–98), told with wit and charm by the man who became famous for doing it; Slocum is one of the few to have accomplished this feat without a motor of any kind (Harry Pidgeon is another, in 1921–25); many b&w line drawings.

Time-Life Books. *The Seafarers*. Alexandria, Virginia: Time-Life Books, 1980 and other dates, various authors. The famous series comprising these volumes: *Ancient Mariners, Armada, Atlantic Crossing, Clipper Ships, Dreadnoughts, East Indiamen, Explorers, Fighting Sail, Frigates, Great Liners, Luxury Yachts, Men-of-War, Northwest Passage, Pacific Navigators, Pirates, Racing Yachts, Spanish Main, U-Boats, Venetians, Vikings, Whalers, Windjammers*. All richly illustrated. Each includes bibliography and index. Highly recommended.

Tryckare, Tre. *The Lore of Ships*. New York: Crescent Books, 1975. A large-format survey of shipping from the early days of sail to the modern warship, very attractively illustrated with exquisitely executed detailed and informative drawings in color and b&w. Excellent index. Highly recommended.

Unsworth, Barry, ed. and intro. *Classic Sea Stories*. London: Bracken, 1994. A selection of nautical literature from ancient times to the present, embracing fiction and nonfiction sources from (in order of presentation) Ancient Greece, Ancient Rome, the Bible, Arabia, Persia, the Celts, Great Britain, the United States of America, France, Modern Greece, Holland, Germany, Poland, Finland, Iceland, Norway, Sweden, Denmark, Japan. Useful as supplementary source material.

Vare, Ethlie Ann, and Greg Ptacek. *Mothers of Invention: From the Bra to the Bomb: Forgotten Women and Their Unforgettable Ideas.* New York: Morrow, 1988. An interesting and challenging investigation of some important inventions commonly ascribed to men but which, the author shows, really owe their genesis to the earlier work of women; topics treated include Liquid Paper, automatic flight controls, calculus, computer languages, penicillin, smallpox inoculation, DNA molecule, X and Y chromosomes, and maritime signal flares.

Villiers, Alan. *Captain James Cook.* New York: Scribner, 1967. A biography of a great seaman—perhaps the greatest—by a man who himself was a master mariner and a writer of considerable note. Villiers recounts the three voyages of Cook in a simple, clear, and thoroughly compelling style; maps, b&w illustrations. Bibliography, index. Highly recommended.

Wannan, Bill. *A Dictionary of Australian Folklore: Lore, Legends, and Popular Allusions.* Sydney: Lansdowne Press, 1970. Reprinted with another subtitle 1987, Ringwood, Victoria: Viking O'Neil. The best compendium available on this subject, compiled by the acknowledged expert on Australian folklore; extensive articles arranged alphabetically; b&w photographs, line drawings.

White, Howard. "The Cadborosaurus Meets Hubert Evans," in Pat Norris, *Time and Tide: A History of Telegraph Cove.* Raincoast Chronicles, 16. Madeira Park, British Columbia: Harbour Publishing, 1995. Local stories and reports of matters maritime in British Columbia.

Williams, Gwyn A. *Excalibur: The Search for Arthur.* London: BBC Books, 1994. A well-written and scholarly account of the Arthurian legend; extensively illustrated with color and b&w photographs and paintings. Good bibliography and index.

Willis, William. *The Epic Voyage of the Seven Little Sisters: A 6,700 Mile Voyage Alone Across the Pacific.* London: Hutchinson, 1956. Published in the U.S. 1955 as *The Gods Were Kind: An Epic 6,700 Mile Voyage Alone Across the Pacific,* New York: Dutton. In 1954 Willis (a German-born American) sailed a balsa raft from Callao, Peru, to Pago Pago in American Samoa, taking some four months to cover 6,700 miles, a much greater distance than the *Kon-Tiki* seven years earlier (see Heyerdahl 1963); a classic tale. Maps, b&w photographs, appendix.

———. *The Hundred Lives of an Ancient Mariner: An Autobiography.* London: Hutchinson, 1967. The fascinating autobiography of an indefatigable adventurer, born in Germany and raised in America; in 1963, at age seventy, Willis built *Age Unlimited,* a steel raft, and—as with *Seven Little Sisters* (see above)—sailed it from Callao across the South Pacific, this time to the Queensland coast of eastern Australia, a voyage of over 11,000 miles in 204 days (recounted in full in *An Angel On Each Shoulder*).

Witchell, Nicholas, *The Loch Ness Story,* 2nd rev. ed. Lavenham, England: Dalton, 1976. A thorough but not entirely disinterested review of the Loch Ness tale; the author seems anxious to convince the reader of Nessie's existence; supporting b&w photographs are less than compelling. Bibliography and index.

❋ INDEX ❋